KNOCKOUT

KNOCKOUT

The Boxer and Boxing
in American Cinema

Leger Grindon

University Press of Mississippi / Jackson

www.upress.state.ms.us

The University Press of Mississippi is a member
of the Association of American University Presses.

Copyright © 2011 by University Press of Mississippi
All rights reserved
Manufactured in the United States of America

First printing 2011

∞

Library of Congress Cataloging-in-Publication Data

Grindon, Leger, 1949–
  Knockout : the boxer and boxing in American cinema /
Leger Grindon.
      p. cm.
  Includes bibliographical references and index.
  ISBN 978-1-60473-988-6 (cloth : alk. paper) —
ISBN 978-1-60473-989-3 (ebook) 1. Boxing films—
United States—History and criticism. I. Title.
  PN1995.9.B69G75 2011
  791.43'658—dc22   2010041348

British Library Cataloging-in-Publication Data available

To my wife, Sharon

CONTENTS

viii   Contents

ACKNOWLEDGMENTS

Throughout this project I have sought recommendations for improvements. My friends and colleagues have responded with generosity. Their assistance has contributed grace and reason to the manuscript and rendered the shortcomings that remain much less conspicuous.

Parts of this book have appeared as essays in journals, including *Cinema Journal* ["Body and Soul: The Structure of Meaning in the Boxing Film Genre," *Cinema Journal* 35:4, pp. 54–69, Copyright 1996 by University of Texas Press]; *Journal of Sport and Social Issues, Cineaste* [review of *Unforgivable Blackness, Cineaste* 30:22, Spring 2005, pp. 50–52]; and *Quarterly Review of Film and Video*, and in books including *Routledge Encyclopedia of Narrative Theory*, edited by David Herman, Manfred Jahn, and Marie-Laure Ryan (London: Routledge, 2005); *Encyclopedia of the Documentary*, edited by Ian Aitken (New York: Routledge, 2005); *Martin Scorsese's Raging Bull*, edited by Kevin J. Hayes (New York: Cambridge University Press, 2005); and *Clint Eastwood, Actor and Director: New Perspectives*, edited by Leonard Engel (Salt Lake City: University of Utah Press, 2007). Thanks to each of these publications for encouraging my work and extending rights to include materials from these essays in my book.

Many others have offered valuable help as this manuscript took shape. Middlebury College provided financial assistance through the Ada Howe Kent summer research fellowship and the Faculty Professional Development Fund. I learned from students at Middlebury College, including Molly Boyle and Maura Whang, who read and helped me with my manuscript. My faculty colleagues at Middlebury College have listened to my ideas, offered constructive advice, loaned videos, and read passages of various parts of my manuscript.

These individuals include Doug Sprigg, Holly Allen, Ed Smith, Ann Morey, Jeffrey Ruoff, Jim Ralph, Ted Perry, Don Mitchell, Chris Keathley, Jason Mittell, John Bertolini, and Tim Spears.

Cinema colleagues from far and wide have helped with their advice, letters of support, and intellectual encouragement. These colleagues include William Rothman, Charles Ramirez Berg, Susan Ryan, Aaron Baker, Charles Maland, Charles Musser, Toby Miller, David Herman, Ed Buscombe, Peter Lehman, Frank Tomasulo, Leonard Engel, Robert Sklar, Wheeler W. Dixon, and Kevin J. Hayes. Richard Porton and Cindy Lucia, editors at *Cineaste*, have been helpful friends and advisors. My friend, journalist George Bellerose, has offered me a perspective from outside the academy that provided common sense and gracious assistance. Sarah Kozloff has encouraged my work throughout the years with her unstinting good will and outstanding scholarly example. And finally I am grateful to the steadfast support and affection of my wife, Sharon. I thank all these as well as the wider community of friends and associates who contributed to this work.

KNOCKOUT

1

WHY THE BOXING FILM?
The Meaningful Structure of the Boxing Film Genre

Poetics must begin with genre.
—MEDVEDEV/BAKHTIN, [1978, 175]

The boxer stands alongside the cowboy, the gangster, and the detective as a figure that has shaped America's idea of manhood. Beyond the sport itself, the boxer's significance was developed through the fiction of Jack London and Ernest Hemingway, the painting of Thomas Eakins and George Bellows, and the drama of Clifford Odets. But no art has shaped our perception of the boxer as much as motion pictures. The pugilist arose as a popular figure in Hollywood cinema with the advent of sound and appeared in over one hundred feature films released between 1930 and 1960 (see appendix II for a listing of the most prominent titles). During the decade 1975–85, the screen boxer experienced a comeback in numerous films, including the enormously commercially successful *Rocky* series (1976–2006) and the critically esteemed *Raging Bull* (1980). More recently, *Million Dollar Baby* (2004), *Unforgivable Blackness: The Rise and Fall of Jack Johnson* (2004), and *Cinderella Man* (2005) testify to the boxer's continuing influence. However, aside from a few essays and a history of boxing in early cinema before 1912, there has been no significant study of the screen boxer (Sayre 1977, Sarris 1980, Baker 2003, Streible 2008). This book analyzes the boxing film in American cinema as a genre shaped by evolving conventions and engaged in a discourse vital to our culture.

The screen boxer embodies the physical: a strong man striving for power in a metropolis dominated by money, position, and cunning. His body becomes

3

a commodity that is consumed in his struggle for dominance. As a result, the boxer's body dramatizes an implicit discourse on the conditions of oppression. As Pam Cook explains, "The boxing pic has often been used as a vehicle for left-wing ideas, and the virile working-class hero is a prevailing image in the iconography of socialist politics" (Cook 1982, 42). Like Robert Warshow's gangster, the boxer is a tragic figure; he personifies a division between body and spirit, and since time dictates the deterioration of the flesh, he is destined for a fall (Warshow 1975). The reason for, and purpose of, suffering arise as questions central to the genre. The boxer's agony sparks a search for values beyond the body, raising questions about American materialism. Thus, the boxing film addresses the limitations of the physical and implies a quest for a worthy alternative.

Hollywood movies have been described as a cinema of stars and genres. A film genre is a flexible story formula based upon a body of conventions intuitively shared by the audience and filmmakers. Hollywood genres, such as the science fiction film, the Western, and the musical, have produced many of America's most popular and celebrated films. In the cinema, contemporary genre analysis has focused on evolving narrative conventions as dramatizations of pervasive social conflicts. As Thomas Schatz explains, genre criticism addresses familiar stories that "involve dramatic conflicts, which are themselves based upon ongoing cultural conflicts" (Schatz 1981, viii). Guided by the practice of Schatz, among others, I will define the boxing film genre and describe its conventions, including animating conflicts, model plot, major characters and settings, boxing's mise-en-scène, and the viewer's typical emotional response, followed by a consideration of genre history. This chapter concludes with a consideration of the goals of genre criticism and an outline of this book.

But first, a brief explanation of genre study is in order. Following anthropologist Claude Lévi-Strauss and his study of myths, commentators argue that the repetition characterizing film genres is similar to the practice of retelling myths in the oral tradition. Each genre portrays persistent social problems as dramatic conflicts, and each retelling presents an opportunity for an imaginative resolution of these problems from a fresh perspective. Though the resolution may offer only temporary relief from the anxiety provoked by these problems, the persistence and depth of the conflicts guarantee that more films will offer additional solutions, and the subject will continue to attract an audience because it portrays a compelling and widely shared problem. As a result, the dramatic conflicts manifesting these social problems establish the boundaries of its discourse. These dramatic conflicts also serve as the chief avenue connecting external social influences on these movies to changes in the form of the films. Resolution of these conflicts, or their decline in the social consciousness, will likely contribute to fading a genre's popularity. For example, the conflict between freedom in nature and the constraints of settlement in the Western is not as pressing for the contemporary audience as the conflict between invasive technology and personal identity found in the science fiction film.

Two perspectives on the myth model have arisen: the ritual and the ideological. The ritual approach emphasizes the experience of confronting conflicts and successfully bringing them to a resolution as a means of allaying anxiety (Schatz 1981; Cawelti 1976). This approach explains the popularity of genres in terms of the audience satisfaction that arises from the viewer's desire to resolve the social conflicts motivating these fictions. On the other hand, the ideological approach finds in the designs of the film industry, or other powerful social agents, an attempt to subdue the audience by distorting the nature and causes of prevailing social conflicts, deceiving or seducing the audience into believing in a simplistic and ineffective resolution. From this perspective film genres function as a means of social control. Genres may enjoy extended popularity when the audience's desire for ritual satisfaction intersects with an ideological drive for social control (Altman 1995, 36).

Rick Altman's concept of the generic crossroads illustrates how both perspectives may operate simultaneously (Altman 1999, 145–52). The generic crossroads arise in the plot when the protagonist must choose between a culturally sanctioned option and the alternative that produces generic pleasure. The protagonist continues to choose the subversive option, guaranteeing generic pleasure until the conclusion, when prevailing values are reinforced and the audience is eased back into familiar social behavior. The gangster chooses crime, the spy espionage, the lovers passion, the angry youth boxing—and the genre fan vicariously embraces these choices. However, the generic pleasure offered by the film rarely represents a viable solution for viewers, instead offering a thrill that distracts the audience from thinking the conflict through in a more effective manner. Genres thereby offer subversive pleasures regulated by the cultural institution constituted in and through the generic discourse.

The counter-cultural elements underlying the crossroads present genre as a more dynamic social force than either the ritual celebration or the ideological entrapment models would suggest. The process of generic engagement allows audiences to enjoy cultural resistance and may even leave them disappointed when they return to safety. As a result, genres are not so much a means of social containment as a vehicle for spectator exploration of ambiguous terrain. The polarity between ritual and ideology, or the subversive and the orthodox, is too limiting, as these concepts are colored by a belief that genre films exploit their audience. Rather than being anchored to a fixed constellation of values, genre conventions function more like a vocabulary for addressing the genre's fundamental dramatic conflicts. Robust genres offer a flexible range of options for exploring the underlying social problems that sustain the form. Consider the range of form and value in *Fat City* (1972), *Rocky* (1976), and *Raging Bull* (1980), all noteworthy boxing films from the same era. Without flexibility and variety, genres would fail to sustain an audience or attract filmmakers. Significant films are capable of presenting a fresh understanding of the dramatic conflicts posed by genre. Genre films can provide insight as well as reassure, excite, or deceive. Though routine work may be limited to ritual repetition, subversive thrills, or ideological manipulation, genre films at their best can produce emotional intensity, formal innovation, and thematic complexity to rival any narrative art. Classics of the American cinema, such as *The Searchers* (1956), *Vertigo* (1958), or *2001: A Space Odyssey* (1968), testify to the achievement of genre films.

So what defines the boxing film as a distinct genre? Two elements distinguish these films. First, the protagonist is a boxer, or part of a boxer's entourage, such as the manager, trainer, or publicist, or a former boxer. Second, boxing is an important element in the plot and key to the motivation of the protagonist. In an obvious case, such as *Cinderella Man*, the hero, Jim Braddock (Russell Crowe), is a prizefighter on a quest for the title. Almost as often, a boxer's manager serves as a central character, such as Frankie Dunn (Clint Eastwood) did in *Million Dollar Baby*. The figure of an ex-boxer haunted by his career in the ring is also common in films, such as *Requiem for a Heavyweight* (1962). In cases outside the genre proper, such as *Kiss Me Deadly* (1955), the boxer or boxing may make an appearance, but the instance is relegated to a minor episode. However, there are also films, for example *Pulp Fiction* (1994), that participate in the genre and have proved influential, even though on first impression they may seem distinct from the boxing genre. Furthermore, this study also addresses feature length nonfiction films, such as *When We Were Kings* (1996), that portray the boxer and boxing as central elements. With these boundaries in mind, let us follow Rick Altman's principle that "[t]he first step in understanding the functional role of Hollywood genre is to isolate the problems for which the genre provides a symbolic solution," and turn to the conflicts that set the Hollywood boxing film in motion (Altman 1987, 334).

CONFLICTS

The boxing film is founded on a series of dramatic conflicts that represent widespread social problems. Though not every conflict is evident in every film, these related conflicts give the boxing film unity and flexibility over time.

Six key conflicts distinguish the boxing film. They are: (1) the conflict between body and soul or material versus spiritual values; (2) the critique of the success ethic expressed as the conflict between individual competition fostered by market forces versus human cooperation and self-sacrifice; (3) a conflict between the opportunity success offers the boxer for integration into mainstream society versus loyalty to the marginalized community from which he arose; and (4) a masculinity crisis, traditionally associated with romance, arising from the conflict between the manly ethos of the ring and a woman's influence. Finally, a male emotional problem can arise from two related conflicts: when anger at injustice clashes with powerlessness to eliminate oppression, or when stoic discipline in the face of life's cruelty conflicts with sensitivity toward others. All these conflicts pose problems, vital to the experience of the audience, that have received a variety of treatments throughout the genre's history. For example, *Fat City*, with its critique of masculinity, poses many of the same gender conflicts found in *Hard Times* (1975), which valorizes masculinity. The dramatic conflicts central to the genre allow for a range of resolutions and attitudes, a flexibility that assures the evolution of the form.

A fundamental issue in the boxing film is the conflict between body and soul established by the tension between the material and the spiritual. Whereas Western philosophers emphasize consciousness in their ruminations on the body/mind division, the boxing film foregrounds the male body. This issue is readily acknowledged in that two boxing films (from 1947 and 1981) take *Body and Soul* as their title. A conflict arises when the gratification the boxer gains from his physical power is undermined by his recognition of its deteriorating force. As Joyce Carol Oates explains, boxing "is the most tragic of all sports because more than any human activity it consumes the very excellence it displays—its drama is this very consumption" (Oates 1987, 16). This confrontation with physical decline implies a grappling with mortality as well. The concluding line from *Body and Soul* (1947) makes this implication explicit. As the boxer Charlie Davis (John Garfield) leaves the ring forever, he mocks the gangster's threats, declaring, "What are ya gonna do, kill me? Everybody dies." A dominant theme of the boxing genre is how the fighter deals with his waning physical powers. Can he overcome the deterioration of his body by cultivating his soul? An additional question is frequently posed: What spiritual alternative to material rewards does the culture offer? The identification of the boxer with his body results in related problems that I have addressed in terms of the critique of the success ethic and the conflict between individual competition and human cooperation.

In accordance with the American ideal, social position and wealth are to be determined by individual competition rather than by heritage and class.

"The ceremonial weigh-in, the impersonal referee, and the bare ring represent equality, a rule-bound competition emblematic of the success ethic." *Iron Man* (1931). Courtesy of the Academy of Motion Picture Arts and Sciences.

American institutions have labored to foster fair competition that rewards talent, energy, and ambition in fulfillment of the proverbial "American Dream." The boxer, like Midge Kelly (Kirk Douglas) in *Champion* (1949), is typically motivated by poverty, and he is driven not merely to become a champion, but to become rich. In the boxing genre the ceremonial weigh-in, the impersonal referee, and the bare ring represent equality, a rule-bound competition emblematic of the success ethic. But these films constantly unmask the pretense of fairness and express the outsider's vulnerability. Everywhere the fix is on, the fighter is cornered, and the game is rigged. As a result the boxer, in a close relationship to Robert Warshow's gangster, embodies the Horatio Alger myth, but at the same time offers a critique of the success ethic (Warshow 1975). In the boxing genre the struggle of the lower-class man in the ring provides an analogue for the physical, psychological, and moral toll imposed by the drive for success. The boxing film often asks whether money is the only standard by which success can be recognized.

Contrary to the competition that characterizes the marketplace, American culture also prizes cooperation and self-sacrifice. This conflict rehearses the long-standing tension in American culture between the individual and the community. The boxer alone in the ring embodies an individual stripped to his essential skills. He is posed in contest not simply with his opponent, but against the collective values associated with the family, religion, and the community. Generally, as in *The Life of Jimmy Dolan* (1933), material success fails to overcome loneliness and spiritual alienation. A disquieting ambivalence emerges between the social need for cooperation and personal sacrifice and the ruthless drive to get ahead, to win at all costs. The critique of the success ethic first asks whether the competition is fair, and then asks whether the contest of one against all is the most humane way to organize society.

A nation of immigrants, America ideally embraces diversity and strives to promote opportunity regardless of an individual's origins. Nonetheless, a tension arises between the dominant culture and various subordinate ethnic and racial communities. As the boxer pursues success in the fight game, ethnicity and race identify him as an outsider. Even during the classical studio period the pugilist often came from an ethnic minority: for instance, the Italian-American Joe Bonaparte (William Holden) in *Golden Boy* (1939), the Jew Charlie Davis in *Body and Soul* (1947), or the Hispanic Johnny Monterez (Ricardo Montalban) from *Right Cross* (1950). By the 1970s the African American boxer achieved prominence in *The Great White Hope* (1970), *Hammer* (1972), and *Mandingo* (1975). Ethnic or racial identification intersected with class, with the boxer portrayed as a poor worker selling physical labor in an industrialized economy that found little value in his skills. As a result, the boxer generally represents an oppressed underclass struggling to rise. This tradition is long and can be traced back at least as far as Jack London's story, "The Mexican" (1911). However, success frequently presents an opportunity for the boxer to enter the dominant culture and perhaps compromise his loyalty to his native community. For example, in *The Ring* (1952) Tomas Cantanios (Lalo Rios) turns to prizefighting to gain self-respect and takes on the ring name of Tommy Kansas, evoking the American heartland and putting aside his Hispanic heritage. But the prospect of assimilation generally proves painful or is a delusion. When taking on the conflict between assimilation and loyalty to the ethnic community, the boxing film portrays both the tensions surrounding the melting pot ethos and the painful alternative of remaining an outsider.

The problem of masculinity is a manifestation of the gender conflict that pervades the boxing film (Cook 1982; Wood 1986). For example, *The Champ* (1931) portrays the boxer Andy (Wallace Beery) as an immature father whose childish behavior estranges him from his wife and places him under the care of his young son. The boxer's career unfolds in an exclusively male world, an eventuality that retards the fighter's emotional development and intensifies his divergence from women. Romance in the boxing film associates the female lead with mainstream culture and the family, whereas the boxer's society is defined not simply as male, but also as underdeveloped and apart. This exclusively male society often carries an implicit homoerotic edge, whereas romance provides the prospect of negotiating gender difference through marriage. Occasionally a comedy, such as *The Main Event* (1979), will move a woman into the boxing world, using gender incongruity for humor. At the other extreme, the boxer may be a brute who attacks defenseless women, as Mike Tyson does in *The Fallen Champ* (1993). Only recently have women boxers in *Girlfight* (2000) and *Million Dollar Baby* seriously attempted to bridge the gender divide by entering the ring rather than luring boxers away from the gym.

The conflict between anger and powerlessness also contributes to the masculinity crisis. Poverty, social marginalization, and sexual isolation produce anger. "Boxing is fundamentally about anger," suggests Joyce Carol Oates, "boxers fight one another because the legitimate objects of their anger are not accessible to them. There is no political system in which the spectacle of two men fighting each other is not a striking, if unintended, image of the political impotence of most men (and women)" (Oates 1987, 63). The anger, frustrated in the face of injustice, generates violence that becomes distilled, redirected, and displayed in the spectacle of boxing. The boxer is consumed by anger but unable to strike at the antagonist who torments him, whether it is the heartless vamp in *Iron Man* (1931), the double-crossing manager of *The Set-Up* (1949), or the consumer culture that belittles Jack (Edward Norton) in *Fight Club* (1999). The genre becomes a stage for the man of action to be disarmed by confusion and powerless in the face of domineering forces. These problems express the condition of modernity in which the anonymous forces of the metropolis disorient and overwhelm the individual. The boxer experiences the pain of victimization while being blocked from directly confronting his tormentors. The genre poses this question: Can rage finally address its cause, or will violence strike the innocent and destroy the boxer himself?

A second emotional difficulty arises from the restraint instilled by the discipline of boxing versus the development of sensitivity toward others that is necessary to cultivate human understanding. Often the boxer fulfills a stoic ideal by enduring pain, only to suffer emotionally because his reserve prevents him from responding to those he loves. Jake La Motta (Robert De Niro) in *Raging Bull* bases his boxing style on his ability to take a punch in order to land a blow. However, his talent for enduring punishment only blocks his response outside the ring to his family—and even to himself. In *Million Dollar Baby*, Frankie Dunn is estranged from his wife and daughter for reasons barely suggested to the audience, but he must overcome his masculine reserve in order to reach out to Maggie Fitzgerald (Hilary Swank). Ironically, the ability to endure pain and violence often only foments further suffering.

Though few members of the audience ever step into the ring, the dramatic conflicts that characterize the boxing film depict vital problems experienced throughout the culture. The genre thereby addresses issues of fundamental concern and maintains an audience. Through its engagement with these films the audience grapples, often subconsciously, with important social issues. Equally importantly, the films' conflicts establish the discourse upon which the conventions of plot, character, and setting are constructed. The conventions in turn elaborate a framework through which conflicts are experienced.

MASTER PLOT

The central narrative concept in film genre studies is the master plot, a series of typical events linked into a causal progression that establishes the conventions of a particular genre's story by dramatizing the conflicts that are the foundation of the genre. The master plot will be larger than most fictions in the genre, and although individual films will select from, vary, or add to the routine formula, the master plot incorporates the spectator's general expectations, often supplying background information assumed by any particular film. The master plot is similar to Schatz's genre myth or the folklorist Vladimir Propp's collection of "moves" constituting a tale (Schatz 1981, 264; Propp 1958). Frequently, a genre will encompass a few prominent master-plot patterns. For example, Rick Altman identifies the "fairy tale" the "show" and the "folk" as three plot variations in the musical film. Noël Carroll posits the discovery, the complex discovery, and the overreacher plots as horror genre master plots. Others have identified the rise-and-fall pattern in the gangster tale (Altman 1987, 127; Carroll 1990, 97–128). Following Propp, analysts frequently break a genre's master plot into a series of moves detailing narrative development. For example, Susan Sontag breaks down the 1950s science fiction film into five basic steps (Sontag 1969, 212–13). As Pam Cook has noted, the plot of the boxing film is usually organized around the rise and fall of the fighter's career (Cook 1982, 42). Of course, filmmakers themselves are well aware of prevailing conventions, and, as a result, parodies develop further evidence of the master plot. Stanley Donen's *Movie, Movie* (1978) includes a parody of the boxing film entitled "Dynamite Hands." I will use it, along with other standard works, as points of reference in outlining the master plot of the boxing film, which can be broken down into ten moves.

Move 1, The Discovery: The protagonist is found to have a remarkable talent for fist fights highlighting the physical excellence of his body. In "Dynamite Hands," Joey Popchik (Harry Hamlin) delivers sandwiches to the local gym. When a contender refuses to pay for his lunch, Joey lays him out with one blow, an event that immediately brings him to the attention of Gloves Malloy (George C. Scott), the boxing manager. However, the protagonist is reluctant to enter the ring. He knows better than to take on a dangerous and disreputable line of work. Joey intends to go to law school, and so he heads back to the deli. In *Hard Times*, Chaney (Charles Bronson) is discovered when he expeditiously knocks out the first "hitter," to the surprise and delight of the manager Speed (James Coburn). But the street fighter keeps his distance from Speed, who tempts him with a guarantee of lavish winnings. *Million Dollar Baby* offers a variation on the pattern in which the boxer Maggie Fitzgerald must pursue the reluctant manager Frankie Dunn before he finally agrees to train her.

Move 2, The Crisis: The values embodied in the protagonist's family and his sanctioned ambitions are endangered, resulting in a crisis that drives the reluctant, angry hero into the ring. In *Body and Soul*, Charlie's father, an innocent bystander, is killed during a gangland raid. Masculine pride provoked by poverty leads Charlie to forsake his education and accept the manager's offer to become a professional fighter. In *City for Conquest* (1940) Danny Kenny (James Cagney) resists a boxing career until his brother needs money to continue his studies and his sweetheart criticizes Kenny's lack of ambition.

Move 3, The Promise: The boxer trains diligently and confirms his potential with his first victory in the ring. Success beckons. For example, in *Kid Galahad* (1937) Ward (Wayne Morris) knocks out the champ's brother and assures Donati (Edward G. Robinson), the manager, of his talent. In *Gentleman Jim* (1942), Corbett (Errol Flynn), in his first regulation bout at the Olympic Club, downs Burke, the former champion.

Move 4, The Rise: In the gym the manager develops the boxer's craft, which is soon displayed in a series of victories during a provincial tour. A classic instance is the tour montage of speeding locomotives, falling fighters, cheering crowds, and sports headlines chronicling Bonaparte's rise in *Golden Boy*. For an earlier example of the rise, see *Iron Man* (1931). The boxer returns to New York as a contender, ready for the big time.

Move 5, The Deal: The boxer, blocked by brokers of the fight game, signs with a gangster-promoter against the advice of his manager, sweetheart, or other trusted confidant. The sensitive youth has become a ruthless competitor. The promoter, like Fuseli (Joseph Calleia) in *Golden Boy*, or Harris (Luis Van Rooten) in *Champion*, or Sidney (Charles Lampkin) in *Hammer*, guarantees the boxer a fight at the Garden, a title shot, success.

Move 6, Debauchery: The boxer abandons his previous regimen of training for parties and the fast life. The sweetheart from the old neighborhood, disturbed by this transformation, is pushed aside by the vamp. Sycophants replace true friends; the gangster takes over for the trusted manager. In "Dynamite Hands" Joey, now a contender, is seduced by the dancer, Troubles Moran (Ann Reinking), and in response his fiancée, Betsy (Trish Van Devere), retreats to her lonely life as a librarian. In *The Spirit of Youth* (1937), Joe (Joe Louis) deserts Mary (Edna Mae Harris), his hometown sweetheart, for Flora (Mae Turner), a cabaret singer, and soon the contender is spending his evenings at nightclubs.

Move 7, Big Fight 1: The protagonist gains the title or wins the fight that assures him celebrity status. The body triumphs, and society hails the boxer. Midge Kelly defeats Johnny Dunne (John Daheim) and gains the middleweight title in *Champion*. Jack Jefferson (James Earl Jones) defeats Brady (Larry Pennell), the white former champ, in *The Great White Hope*.

Move 8, The Dive: Rendered vulnerable by high living, isolated from his true friends and in need of cash, the boxer yields to pressure from the gangster-promoter and agrees to take a dive for some dubious reward. In *Body and Soul*, Charlie, now the veteran champ, accepts Roberts's (Lloyd Gough) proposition to throw his title defense and retire with a big pay-off. In *Raging Bull*, La Motta yields to Tommy (Nicholas Colasanto), the gang lord, and takes a dive to gain a title shot.

Move 9, Big Fight 2: In an extended bout, the boxer suffers terrible punishment, but in a late round he regains his will and defeats his opponent. Nevertheless, his career is over. Tommy McCoy (Robert Taylor) in *The Crowd Roars* (1938) endures a beating because a gangster betting against him has kidnapped his girlfriend, but once he learns of her escape, McCoy rallies to win the title and then announces his retirement. *Million Dollar Baby* presents a variation on this pattern. After appearing to dominate the champ, Maggie endures a blow struck after the bell that paralyzes the fighter, ending her career. The suffering she later endures becomes part of her spiritual victory.

Move 10, Resolution/Epilogue: The end of the boxing career signifies the decline of the body. Is there a resurrection or is the boxer finished? In the classic format, the protagonist is saved by leaving the fight game and returning to his sweetheart, as in Rocky Balboa's (Sylvester Stallone) closing embrace with Adrian (Talia Shire) after "going the distance," or Mountain's (Jack Palance) return home to train youngsters at the end of the teleplay "Requiem for a Heavyweight" (1956).

The four opening moves, along with "Big Fight 1," pose the premises setting up the basic conflicts that characterize the boxing genre. That is, the ascendancy of the body, manliness, anger and stoicism, the prospect of success in competition, and the opportunity for integration with mainstream culture are established. Later moves, particularly five, six and eight, challenge these values by compromising the success of the boxer. Now the vulnerability of the body is emphasized, romantic problems undermine masculinity, competition leads to isolation and places the boxer in jeopardy, the values of the ethnic community become apparent, a sense of powerlessness emerges, and insensitivity separates the fighter from his true friends. Big Fight 2 brings these conflicts to a climax and the epilogue confirms resolution.

"Though no single film can present the entire myth," Rick Altman explains, "the system of generic variations creates a myth, a single coherent narrative mediating cultural conflicts" (Altman 1987, 331). So a work may portray only a part of this narrative pattern while still operating within the conventions of the genre. Films such as *The Champ* or *Requiem for a Heavyweight* dramatize the final move, while others, such as *Raging Bull*, skip the opening, merely suggesting the initial episodes of the conventional plot. A "comeback" variation is conspicuous in films like *Somebody Up There Likes Me* (1956), *Rocky*, or *Cinderella Man* that begin with the boxer as loser and reverse the common trajectory by ending with a victory. Works that seem tangential to the genre, such as *The Quiet Man* (1952) or *On the Waterfront* (1954) assume the conventional plot as a starting point for their fiction.

David Bordwell has emphasized a linear structure in the classical Hollywood narrative featuring a tight causal linkage motivating the action from one scene to the next at an accelerating pace; this structure is dominant in the boxing film (Bordwell 1986). Rick Altman, in contrast, argues for multifocalization of the genre narrative, focusing on multiple romantic couples, parallel plot lines, or pauses for spectacle events, qualities that are evident in the musical. The widespread parallel between the chief genre quest (the pursuit of the championship) and a romance (the boxer courting the beloved) is found in the boxing film as in most Hollywood productions. (The romance will be described in more detail when I characterize the female lead.) Occasionally, boxing films incorporate a more conspicuous parallel structure, as with the boxer Danny and the dancer Peggy (Ann Sheridan) in *City for Conquest*, the two soldiers Prewitt (Montgomery Clift) and Warden (Burt Lancaster) in *From Here to Eternity* (1953), or the veteran fighter Tully (Stacy Keach) and the novice Munger (Jeff Bridges) in *Fat City*. Furthermore, major bouts serve as spectacles, though they often develop the plot rather than pausing the narrative. So while linear narrative dominates the boxing master plot, elements of multifocalization are also evident.

CHARACTERS

The male protagonist can be either the boxer or his manager. Though most boxing films foreground the prizefighter, some films, such as *Kid Galahad*, highlight the manager. In many films, such as *Iron Man, Hard Times*, and *Million Dollar Baby*, boxer and manager receive comparable treatment. The distinctions between these figures emphasize the body/mind split and express key conflicts. The manager is the technician and strategist, a rationalist. He is frequently compromised because he represents business, as opposed to the family. The divergence between boxer and manager recalls Robert Ray's observation that American cinema cultivates an opposition between the outlaw hero and the official hero (Ray 1985, 58–63). While the boxer or outlaw hero embodies the natural and intuitive individualist who resists social rules, the manager or official hero represents institutional wisdom and community values.

Satellite figures circling near the protagonist further develop this character. The trainer usually assumes a role as the caretaker of the body, though he may, like Poe (Strother Martin) in *Hard Times*, also minister to the soul. The punch-drunk ex-fighter frequently appears as a harbinger of the boxer's fate. In films such as *The Crowd Roars*, as he reluctantly embarks on a ring career the protagonist acknowledges the mindless pug. In later works, characters such as Ben (Canada Lee) in *Body and Soul* and Bruiser (John de Carlos) in *Hammer* develop the figure. In films, such as *Right Cross* or *The Harder They Fall* (1956), the sportswriter appears as a knowing individual; as an expression of intellect he is related to the manager, but he is more detached. Occasionally he assumes the role of first-person narrator, a confidant of the audience and cool observer of the boxer's fate.

The boxer embodies the physical ideal of old-fashioned, self-reliant masculinity. He is a strong man of action who finds himself disarmed by guile, finance, technology, changing times—in short, the forces shaping the modern city. Like the gangster, he strives to rise above the crowd and grasp the success warranted by his physical power. Unlike the gangster, whose work is done in private and whose mode is conspiratorial, the boxer is a public figure, one whose body is fully exposed to be applauded or sometimes reviled. However, he is seldom idealized. Instead, his rage, simplicity, or a misguided consciousness highlights his common nature. Emphasis on the male body, its power, beauty, and deterioration, ties the boxer to sexuality and to the female as portrayed in mainstream cinema. In this regard he becomes analogous to a prostitute who also uses her body as a commodity and whose body, as a result, suffers abuse. Whereas the prostitute trades upon a false association with romantic love, the

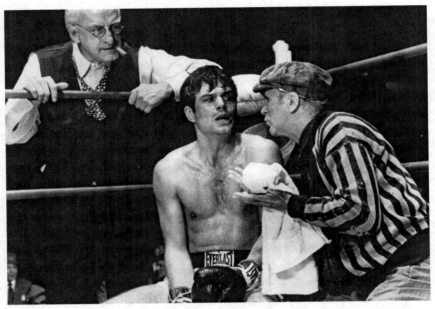

The manager, the boxer, and the trainer: "Dynamite Hands," *Movie, Movie* (1978). Courtesy of the Academy of Motion Picture Arts and Sciences.

boxer redirects his anger for commercial advantage. Like the prostitute, the boxer is vulnerable because he is anchored to the flesh. Competition in the ring must finally allow the boxer to understand himself as a man, or else he is doomed to suffer a grim fate, trapped by the limitations of his body.

Two literary sources exercise an important influence on the boxer: the biblical story of Samson [Judges 8: 14–16] and Jack London's short story "The Mexican." *City for Conquest* acknowledges the biblical influence by calling its protagonist, middleweight Danny Kenny, "Samson." The biblical Samson, like the boxer, is physically overpowering. In the first demonstration of his might, Samson "tore the lion asunder" with his bare hands; his bestial attributes cast doubt upon the spiritual aspects of his humanity. Central to the tale is the problem of difference: difference between Jew and Philistine, oppressed and oppressor, men and women. Samson, to the consternation of his parents, marries a Philistine, only to be betrayed by his wife and her people. Again and again women set up Samson (Delilah being the last and most successful) and, as a result, he must fight his way out of captivity. His story is a cautionary tale about assimilation.

Though a leader of the Hebrews, Samson's dual nature is firmly anchored to his body, where physical strength finds a counterpoint in sexual weakness. More important, his intense physicality suggests a spiritual flaw. In spite of his ties to the Lord, Samson is spiritually crippled, blind to the conspiracies of his enemies, and finally, literally blinded by them. Though the Lord allows Samson a final vengeance upon the Philistines, as a result of his weakness he perishes with his tormentors. The link between Samson and the boxer is grounded in the body, where extraordinary strength carries with it a counter balancing weakness, a trope that is central to the genre's discourse. The dual nature of the physical is hidden from the hero by his blindness to the spiritual, which carries the protagonist to his doom.

The portrait of the boxer as oppressed, resistant, and motivated by racial identity finds another classic expression in Jack London's "The Mexican." The protagonist, Felipe Rivera, a young man of eighteen, is "the Revolution incarnate." After the murder of his parents by soldiers of Porfirio Diaz in a strike crackdown, the young man offers his service to the political resistance. At first the resistance leaders suspect the sullen stranger and assign him only menial chores. Felipe supplements his political work by donating to the cause money he secretly raises as a sparring partner, even though he despises prize fighting, "the hated game of the hated Gringo." When his comrades find the success of their struggle to be in financial jeopardy, Felipe declares that he will raise the needed $5,000. North of the border he lands a fight with a popular champion and rather than accept a percentage of the purse insists on a "winner-take-all" payment. Faced with a veteran "Gringo" opponent, an unfair referee, and a crowd hurling racial slurs, Felipe participates in a fight that incarnates the revolutionary struggle. Battered and half dead, the Mexican triumphs.

In the London story, prizefighting embodies both the oppression of the dominant culture and the resistance of those battling for justice. The tale offers a revision of the biblical David and Goliath story. Here David's skill with his sling and his musical ability are replaced by Felipe's reliance on nothing more than his body, a replacement emblematic of the boxer's poverty and the elemental quality of his struggle. The body serves both as a tangible canvas for suffering and as a weapon, a means of retribution. Felipe's political education is assumed as a natural consequence of his suffering. The story portrays class struggle, reinforced through racial and national difference, as the seedbed of political upheaval.

"The Mexican" model finds its basis in action: Boxing is an analogue for the political struggle itself. The Samson model finds its basis in consciousness: boxing expresses social forces that engulf the fighter, whose awareness is too limited—or comes too late—to save him. These competing narratives serve different discursive functions. "The Mexican" portrays an overt, simplified heroics based on a direct link between individual determination and the achievement of social justice. The story assures audience members that righteousness is evident and that they can triumph, no matter how imposing their adversaries. Self-confidence, will, and a righteous alliance with communal values are the ingredients of heroism in this tradition.

The Samson model is anti-heroic. Here boxing is analogous to exploitation; the sport represents an oppressive system that consumes the boxer. The personal courage and good intentions of the fighter are futile until he recognizes that the game itself is corrupt. As a result, knowledge becomes central to the tale, because one's adversary is often unclear or intangible. Limited understanding prevents the Samsonesque boxer from contesting the oppressor with the full force of his character. The protagonist must experience an elevation in consciousness in order to see clearly and to escape from boxing. Furthermore, the individual cannot function apart from his community, which serves as the base of his strength. This tradition offers cautionary tales of flawed fighters whose victories are shadowed by defeats.

The antagonist in the boxing film, like the protagonist, often comprises multiple figures: the gangster-promoter and the hero's chief rival in the ring. For example, in *Champion*, Harris, the gangster-promoter, replaces the manager, leading to Kelly's fall, while Harris's ally is Johnny Dunne, Kelly's ring opponent. The gangster-promoter, an evil transformation of the manager, is associated with monetary corruption and the moral compromises necessary to business prosperity. In the economic analogue underlying the genre, the boxer represents physical labor, the manager, technical expertise, and the promoter, capital. Sometimes the manager betrays his loyalty to the boxer by helping the gangster-promoter, as in *Body and Soul* and *The Set-Up*. As a gambler, the promoter is a shadow investor who uses capital to make money from the physical toil of others. For him, value lies not in labor and craft, emblematic of the work ethic, but in wealth itself. As a result, success is divorced from work, and the Puritan connection between salvation and prosperity is corrupted. The promoter also violates the code of fair competition, for as a gangster he uses force outside the boundaries of the ring and employs others to execute his violence. A personification of degradation, the promoter is solely interested in financial gain. Like market forces, he is impervious to human feeling.

The hero's ring opponent embodies the moral assault undertaken by the gangster-promoter. Whereas the gangster-promoter signifies exterior social forces pressuring the boxer, the ring opponent often becomes a phantom or psychological antagonist representing a weakness residing in the boxer himself. As Joyce Carol Oates observes, "The boxer faces an opponent who is a dream-distortion of himself" (Oates 1987, 12). For example, in *Right Cross*, Heldon (Eddie Lou Simms), the inconsequential opponent of champion Johnny Monterez, recognizes that Monterez drops his left hand as he throws a right punch. The champ's weakness allows Heldon to score an upset. More to the point, the flaw in Johnny's defense represents a character flaw, his exaggerated feeling of being victimized by prejudice. This motif invites, and frequently receives, a racial treatment, with African Americans assuming a symbolic function as the black phantom that personifies psychic turmoil. For example, in *Golden Boy*, Joe kills Chocolate Drop in the ring and as a result comes to terms with the violence in himself. Jimmy Reeves and Ray Robinson embody La Motta's troubled psyche, inflicting defeat and retribution upon Jake in *Raging Bull*. Gerald Early has noted there is "a very simple and very old idea here, namely, that the black male is metaphorically the white man's unconscious personified" (Early 1988, 50). So the antagonist in the boxing film takes on the body/soul division, splitting into exterior social forces portrayed by the gangster-promoter and interior psychic turmoil embodied by the ring opponent.

The opposition between body and soul and the critique of the success ethic shape the romance as the boxer's affections move from the neighborhood sweetheart to the vamp. Whether she is the librarian of "Dynamite Hands," the painter of *Body and Soul*, or the manager's convent educated younger sister in *Kid Galahad*, the sweetheart is associated with spiritual uplift under the rubric of family, religion, or culture. In contrast, the vamp, like Grace (Marilyn Maxwell) in *Champion*, offers the pleasures of the flesh; she preys upon the hero's body even as she drains away his money.

Romance also poses gender conflict. How can a man retain his masculinity and at the same time achieve a fruitful union with a woman? The heroine of the boxing film does not simply represent romantic fulfillment, but challenges the exclusive male world of the ring. Marriage, domesticity and family mean giving up the diversions of fighting and the male coterie of the gym. In order to cultivate his soul, the boxer must take on attributes associated with the feminine; otherwise he will perish with his body. As noted above, *The Champ* (1931) portrays the fighter as an overgrown boy, and similar childlike qualities mark Kid Mason (Lew Ayres) in *Iron Man*, Joe Bonaparte and Kid Galahad. Heroines such as Lorna Moon (Barbara Stanwyck) in *Golden Boy*, Fluff (Bette Davis) in *Kid Galahad* and Oma (Susan Tyrrell) in *Fat City*, are experienced, knowing women who have been drawn into a male milieu, thereby compromising the spiritual advantage associated with their femininity. They become figures that are doomed unless they marry and reestablish their position within a family. Like the schoolteacher in the Western, the heroine of the boxing film acts in opposition to a male ethos that the hero must reject in order to mature.

The opposition between the crowd and the family moves characterization toward collective figures that further amplify the conflicts between career and home, business and parenthood, individual and community. While *Golden Boy* vividly idealizes the family as a foundation for the spirit, the boxing film usually presents the family in crisis. Divorce in *The Champ*, the abusive father in *Somebody Up There Likes Me*, the estrangement of Frankie and Maggie from their families in *Million Dollar Baby* all present the family as a ruptured institution. While the boxing racket is associated with the tumult of urban life, the family harks back to rural and small town values—think Donati's mother on the farm in *Kid Galahad* or the family shop in *Golden Boy*. Even though the fighter frequently undertakes his career for his or her family, the drive for success strains or destroys kinship bonds. Usually the parent, as in *Golden Boy*, *Body and Soul*, and *The Ring*, opposes the fight game. Opposition between business and family, widely recognized in the gangster film, is shared by the boxing genre and points to the broader conflict between the individual and the community at the core of American culture.

The crowd, on the other hand, expresses the heartless detachment of the urban throng. As Robert Warshow notes about the gangster, "One must emerge from the crowd or one is nothing" (Warshow 1975, 132). So the boxer, because of his conspicuous stand in the ring, holds himself above the crowd. The audience for the bout is made up of two types: individuals who are particular characters from fiction, and figures constituting—individually or collectively—the crowd. Their chief spokesmen are the radio announcer, the press corps, and the referee. The crowd is forcefully sketched in *Golden Boy* and fully developed in *The Set-Up*. These raucous spectators invest passion in the boxer's struggle, but they remain unmoved by the humanity of the combatants. For the general public, the fighter is a vehicle for entertainment, strictly a commodity. The crowd consists of a mass of consumers emblematic of the callousness of the market system. The crowd can take pleasure in an event that would be criminal outside the ring, buying off their conscience for the price of a ticket. The kinship bonding of the family finds its opposite in the predatory character of the crowd.

SETTING

The boxing film establishes a meaningful division between those settings that are independent of the fight game and those that are specific to boxing, e.g., the ring, the gym, and the training camp. These settings foster oppositions that further express the conflicts at the heart of the genre.

The hotel—transient, public, and commercial—serves as a counterpart to the stability, intimacy, and humanity of the home. The touring boxer moves from hotel room to hotel room, but sometimes even the hometown fighter, like Tully in *Fat City*, seems condemned to live in hotels. The demands of the boxer's vocation, unlike those of respectable professions, threaten domesticity. So Frankie Dunn urges Maggie Fitzgerald to save her money and buy a home in *Million Dollar Baby*. This division is amplified in the opposition between the metropolis and a rural setting. For example, in *Kid Galahad* the boxer's goal to earn enough money to buy a farm and leave the city is reinforced when he falls in love with his manager's sister, whom he meets at her country home. The hotel and the city come to represent the heartless forces of modernity, whereas the home and the country express the more natural comforts of a preindustrial age.

Objects and locales also express a dichotomy between work and leisure. Prominent among the non-boxing settings are urban entertainment sites: the nightclub, pool hall, restaurant, or bar. Here a contrast is between excess and balance, debauchery and culture. Wild parties contrast with the strict regimen of training. Recreation represents not refreshment before a return to work, but rather the boxer's compensation for ascetic denial. In the frenzied metropolis a balanced, integrated life is abandoned for the vicious cycle of rigorous work discipline, followed by diversion carried to excess. In the urban milieu, the pleasures of the flesh take the place of artistic solace: Joe Bonaparte gives up his violin for a fast car; in the middle of a drunken party, Charlie Davis is reminded of his decline by Peg's portrait. Physical titillation rather than spiritual cultivation signals the boxer's debauchery. In addition, a troubling reversal occurs when the boxer enters the ring and finds himself at work, even as the crowd takes pleasure in the assault on his body.

The locales distinctive to boxing stand apart from normal life; they constitute a professional realm that gradually confines the boxer until he faces his opponent alone. These sites move from conventionally socialized spaces, such as the manager's office, to exclusively male enclaves such as the gym, the training camp, and the dressing room, finally reaching the ring, where the boxer stands exposed, isolated, and embattled. The manager's office and the dressing room are often locales for secretive scheming and deal making, sites for the set-up. The progress from the periphery to the ring is a process of unveiling, a movement toward a fundamental truth. As a result, this passage is frequently highlighted, particularly in the boxer's walk to the ring for a crucial bout, as in *Champion* or *Raging Bull*. In the ring, however, the boxer stands alone and must come to terms with himself. On the one hand, the ring stands for the boundaries of the self, and the bout represents an enclosed, internal struggle. On the other hand, the ring serves as a stage for a commercial spectacle, and the public violence enacted there contrasts with the gangster's secret transgressions. The spectacle of the fight provides an iconography that links the private and the public conflicts driving the boxer. The boxing film is not simply about rise and fall, but about exposing the body in order to reveal the fundamental struggles of the soul.

Within the ring two questions are posed: Can the boxer master his body? Can the boxer embrace his soul? The first is resolved when the protagonist gains the championship, when he wins "Big Fight #1." At this point the fighter achieves an idealized command over his physical self. The culmination of the boxing film, however, comes with "Big Fight #2," in which the boxer must come to terms with his aging body and can only overcome physical decline through spiritual understanding. Typically this moment comes as in *Body and Soul*, with the realization that the boxer must not throw the fight after all. The existence and nature of a spiritual alternative to physical being thus becomes a vital concern for these films.

The ring is the site of sanctioned violence and becomes the key setting for exploring the consequences of anger and the meaning of suffering. Can the aggression characteristic of the boxer be understood and redirected? In Fight #2 the boxer endures a severe beating in the ring, and even if he emerges victorious, as in *Golden Boy*, he retires after the bout. How is the boxer's suffering to be understood? As a proof of self worth (*Rocky* for example)? As punishment (*Champion*)? As a source of purification in preparation for renewal (*Body and Soul*)? Or perhaps the boxer's ordeal is meaningless, as one could argue is the case in *Fat City*. The climactic bout explores the boxer's inner self and asks whether violence bred by anger will destroy or liberate the spirit. These bouts present a struggle in which the boxer must finally learn from loss, that is, learn from the decline of his physical prowess or be trapped within a decaying body. The theme of resurrection commonly attributed to *Raging Bull* seems upon reflection to be endemic to the boxing genre as a whole.

Violence in the boxing film responds to broader trends, as outlined by John Cawelti in "The Myths of Violence in American Popular Culture" (Cawelti 1975, 521–44). The myth of equality achieved through violence is dramatized in the boxer's rise and debunked in his fall. The boxing film reexamines the myth of the honorable code of violence that Cawelti associates with the Westerner and the hard-boiled detective. This code depends upon ritual and discipline, so the exercise of violence serves justice. The boxing film emphasizes the rituals and discipline of ring violence, but it also regularly shows that the rules attempting to contain violence are corrupted and that the violence of the ring inevitably spills outside its boundaries. In the boxing film the honorable code of violence is seldom tenable.

The myth of regeneration through violence presents a more complex and provocative point of comparison. Cawelti, referring to the work of Richard

Slotkin, reviews the myth of the white captive who eventually turns on the Indians who have abducted him and destroys them. He writes:

> The violence in this myth, Slotkin feels, was related to the settler's imaginative tendency to project onto the Indians his own latent desires for freedom, sensuality, and escape from the spiritual rigors of the Christian community. Thus, in the myth of the captive, the ultimate rescue and destruction of the Indians are also symbolically a destruction of the captive's own feared desires for lawlessness and the lascivious freedom of the wilderness (Cawelti 1975, 538).

In the boxing genre, the pugilist can be viewed as a captive of the dominant, urban culture. He must finally turn on the wealth and assimilation which it represents and destroy the gangster promoter and his alter ego, the ring opponent, in order to return, cleansed, to the traditions of the native community from which he arose. But in the boxing genre the captive's regeneration is seldom realized, for violence in the boxing genre often combines righteous anger and blind self-destruction in an explosive mix that, like Samson, brings down the Philistines and the strong man together.

BOXING'S MISE-EN-SCÈNE

The boxing film designs its featured bouts according to a principle of intensified realism. In addition, these films integrate the development of the fight with the dramatic conflicts propelling the plot. The boxing sequences serve as the genre's distinctive spectacle, physical action that punctuates the plot at key intervals like song and dance numbers in a musical. The typical Hollywood boxing film moves steadily toward an extended bout that brings the movie to its climax, "Big Fight 2" of the master plot. As a result, we anticipate the final boxing match, like the concluding chase in a crime film or the confrontation with the monster in horror, as the culmination of the fiction.

The visual realism of the boxing genre generally strives to replicate the experience of the fan at ringside. As a result, the camera records the action from just above the ropes, through the ropes, or at a low angle under the ropes, placing the viewer in a ringside seat. The composition shows both fighters from head to toe, capturing their full movement like the choreography of two dancers. This perspective, which can be amplified by multiple cameras surrounding the ring, establishes the foundation for the visual action. Variations on this composition may include longer shots within the arena, aerial shots from above the ring, overlapping images of fighters and the crowd, or shots of the boxers punching projected over a number indicating the round. Historical development of this aspect of the boxing film brought the camera inside the ring to record closer shots of the boxers. Variations also include headshots of a fighter taking a blow or hurling his punch, or shots of a gloved fist pounding the opponent's body, or close-ups of the fighter's eyes as he looks for an opening. During the thirties close-up inserts of the action were included in boxing films, though such shots often seem awkwardly posed. After World War II, most famously in *Body and Soul*, the operators with lightweight cameras sometimes maneuver inside the ring to portray the boxers in motion. But these variations are exceptions to the standard ringside position that even in innovative work still orients the majority of the shots. Throughout the genre films maintain a visual design based upon the boxing fan's ideal perspective. *Raging Bull* is a striking exception to this principle, because its visual concept is based on the subjective experience of the boxer rather than an ideal spectator position. As a result, this film appeals to an expressionist rather than the dominant realist aesthetic.

The realistic perspective is confirmed by a comparison of nonfiction to fiction. The camera position in newsreel records of famous bouts is similar in perspective to the standard position used in fiction films. For example, the recording of the second Joe Louis-Max Schmeling bout of 1937, as seen in *Joe Louis, For All Time* (1984), uses a ringside camera to film the entire bout. Two years later the closing fight in *Golden Boy* uses almost identical camera positions. The realistic aspiration of boxing sequences leads many filmmakers to incorporate nonfiction footage of a crowded arena like Madison Square Garden, images of anonymous fans responding to a fight, and sequences from actual boxing matches. Films such as *Iron Man* (1931), *Golden Boy*, *The Joe Louis Story*, and *Somebody Up There Likes Me* mix nonfiction footage with staged shots to underline the authenticity of their boxing sequences. However, fiction films portray boxing with greater intensity by using a wide variety of camera positions and other formal devices to amplify the sensation of watching the fight.

In fiction films editing arguably provides the chief formal means of intensifying the sensation of boxing. Barry Salt explains that the mean average shot length (asl) in his extensive sample of Hollywood films from 1934 to 1939 is nine seconds (Salt 1992, 214). By comparison the asl in the big fight sequences in *Kid Galahad* (1937) is 4.5 seconds and in *Golden Boy* 4.35 seconds. The editing pace of the actual boxing images is even faster. In the newsreel of the Louis-Schmeling bout the asl is 14 seconds. So fiction films use the dynamic editing pacing typical of action sequences to increase the sensation of being at ringside. Furthermore, a variety of formal devices, including shifts in perspective and composition, contrasts in light and color, soundtrack segments of the roar of the crowd, as well as camera movement all work to intensify the realistic representation of boxing. While the formal design of boxing is based upon an intensified realism, it is also forcefully integrated with the narrative action.

The boxing film brings together the principle characters for the climactic boxing match. The dramatic space of the bout is organized into three principle zones: first, the ring where the bout unfolds; second, the corners where the boxers consult with their managers, trainers, and other members of their entourages before the bout and between rounds; and third, the space occupied by spectators, whether in the arena or listening at a distance in dressing rooms or sitting beside radios or in front of televisions. The camera position places the viewer among the characters who are witnessing the fight. A basic visual principle of the boxing mise-en-scène is crosscutting between the fight itself and witnesses to the bout. As a result, the viewer, positioned at ringside with the camera, is incorporated into the montage with the fictive spectators. The reactions and commentary of these witnesses becomes a dramatic filter through which the viewer experiences the fight.

The climactic bout organizes its dramatic time into stages. First, suspense rises with presentation of prefight ceremonies such as the entrance of the boxers to the ring, their introduction, the meeting with the referee, and so on. The next stage consists of the fight itself. Finally the postbout celebration—which may include the victor's embrace of his manager, the reunion of the boxer and his beloved, or the boxer thumbing his nose at the gangster promoter—concludes the scene. The fights themselves are usually condensed into a few key rounds. Sometimes, as in *Golden Boy*, the entire bout only lasts two rounds. More commonly, the film will present the first round or two in some detail, then condense the intervening rounds with a montage, finally focusing on the closing round or two. The corner exchanges between the fighter and his manager are central to explaining the development of the bout. A turning point or moment of epiphany frequently marks the dramatic action as the match takes a decisive turn because of the boxer's key realization or some change in his plan. As a result of the physical battle and the boxer's suffering, he gains insight or completes his personal development. Hence the bleeding and battered body of the boxer is an important aspect of the iconography of the bout. For example, after being knocked down the champ decides the dive is off, and he decides he will fight to win. Usually "Big Fight #2" brings the conflicts propelling the drama to a conclusion, and these conflicts shape the visual organization of the fight.

Intensification of sensation with exaggerated staging elaborates on these formal devices. Reactions of the spectators are vital, but most important is the fight itself. Cinematic boxing designs the bouts without the ebb and flow of a typical prizefight. Whereas most ring competition develops with maneuvering for position, jabbing and clinches, screen bouts are filled with haymaker punches and knockdowns. It's as if a baseball game were all strikeouts and home runs. For example, in *Rocky*, Balboa knocks down Apollo Creed (Carl Weathers) when he scores his first punch, even though the veteran champion has never before been knocked down in his career. Then, in contrast to this demonstration of Rocky's prodigious power, the bout goes the full 15 rounds to a decision, though the film includes only the opening and closing rounds. So screen boxing presents hyperbolic content, as well as using form to intensify the realistic elements of being at the fights.

For detailed treatment of boxing sequences see the analysis of *Kid Galahad*, *Somebody Up There Likes Me*, *Body and Soul* and *Raging Bull* later in this book.

EMOTIONAL RESPONSE

Genres trade on the expectations of the viewer familiar with the conventions of plot, character, and setting. In addition, genres promise a standard emotional response, such as laughter in comedy or fear in the horror film. The typical emotions elicited by the boxing film are nostalgia and pathos.

Bittersweet longing for the past finds expression in the boxing film in multiple ways. Boxing itself is a simple sport with minimal rules and trappings. The boxer, stripped bare facing his opponent, harks back to man's primitive origins, before even his skill as a toolmaker distinguished him. The boxer, enclosed by the metropolis, yearns for the farm or the village, or expresses ambivalence about assimilation or a desire to return to his ethnic or racial community. Devices evoking the past, such as the flashback in *Body and Soul* or the retrospective narration in *Million Dollar Baby*, fit comfortably into boxing films. Other films, such as *The Set-Up* or *Requiem for a Heavyweight*, portray the close of the fighter's career and constantly allude to past success or failure. At least as early as *Gentleman Jim* the genre embraced period settings, which become more prevalent in the 1970s with features such as *The Great White Hope*, *Hard Times*, and *Mandingo*. The biography film offers another opportunity for a fond usage of the past in films like *Raging Bull*, *Ali* (2001), and *Cinderella Man*. Even Rocky Balboa's evocation of Rocky Marciano, the last white American heavyweight champion, who retired undefeated in 1956, colors *Rocky* with longing for an earlier time. By the 1970s the genre conventions themselves carry an antiquated simplicity that evokes the classical studio period.

The use of nostalgia varies widely, from the sentimental (*Rocky*) to the self-conscious (*Raging Bull*), but the genre regularly elicits a distinctive feeling of lost time, inviting reflection on the relationship between past and present. Nostalgia finds its etymological root in the Greek words for home and pain; pathos bears a close relationship, as its Greek etymology is rooted in the word for suffering. Witnessing suffering is central to spectatorship in the boxing genre. "Boxing is about being hit rather more than it is about hitting," Oates explains, "just as it is about feeling pain, if not devastating psychological paralysis, more than it is about winning" (Oates 1987, 25). The literal and figurative imprisonment of the boxer in *The Champ* (1931) and *Raging Bull* crystallizes the wrenching agony cultivated by the genre. In *The Champ* Andy has been thrown into jail once again for brawling. Coming to his senses the next day, he realizes that his behavior harms his son, and he reluctantly decides to send the beloved Dink (Jackie Cooper) off to Linda, Dink's mother and Andy's estranged wife. But when the boy visits Andy he pleads from the other side of the cell bars to remain with his father. Andy turns to insult and anger, finally striking the boy to drive him away. In tears, Dink departs broken hearted. Tormented at hitting the child and grieving at the loss of his son, the prisoner relentlessly pounds the cell wall with his fists until they are bloody and broken. In a similar fashion near the end of *Raging Bull*, Jake La Motta finds himself thrown into solitary confinement after resisting the police. Having alienated his family and friends, Jake is utterly alone, and he bemoans his bestial stupidity, finally pounding his head and his fists relentlessly against the concrete wall in despair. The boxer's agony, like the gangster's death, is a fundamental element of the genre.

The reason for and purpose of suffering arise as questions central to the genre. Ideally, strong emotions spark a recognition that links the conflicts animating the work to the viewer's experience. Furthermore, the narrative resolution may release the viewer from the trauma elicited by the conflict. Such a release can prove enormously satisfying, even if it does nothing to remedy problems in the lives of the audience. Longing for a lost time, pondering the relationship between past and present, and experiencing the boxer's suffering characterize the emotional discourse common to the boxing film.

HISTORY

This genre model is not a stable formula; rather, this model has evolved in response to changing conditions within the film industry, boxing culture, and society at large. Chapter two presents a detailed history of the boxing film and develops the cycle as an important unit of analysis. (Principle cycles of production are listed in appendix 1.) The social conflicts animating a given genre are a fundamental cause for its rise and development. Those conflicts may intensify, diminish, or change in the experience of the audience, and over time significant shifts in the social experience of these conflicts will be manifested in film. On the other hand, other genres or forms of cultural expression may prove more compatible to the expression of these problems, so a film genre may decline even if the social conflicts contributing to its development still exist. As a result, the deep, underlying sources of a genre may be difficult to track from one movie to the next. Nevertheless, over the long term the changes in a genre are evident, and one can inquire into the details of its evolution and their immediate causes.

Film genre scholars generally analyze a genre's evolution in two parts: shifting internal elements evident within a genre's component films, and external factors that arise from the surrounding culture. Internal changes can be found in the play between dominant and subordinate traits within a genre. At any particular moment a film genre has a dominant trait: for example, battles between cowboys and Indians in the Western. But repetition and predictability weary the audience, so a subordinate trait—for example, a cattle drive or the building of the railroad—becomes dominant. The reshuffling dominant and subordinate positions among the elements of a genre becomes key to tracing its evolution. Of course, it may be difficult to specify a single dominant trait, but a number of elements may characterize a genre for a period, only to recede as the form evolves (Neale 1995, 172–75).

The movement of traits from dominant to subordinate is revealing in the boxing film. The rise and fall of the gangster-promoter figure and his related plot move, the set-up or dive, are central elements in the genre, but during the Depression cycle this character was absent. However, the Popular Front period brought the gangster-promoter to the fore as the principle antagonist in numerous films, such as *Kid Galahad*, *The Crowd Roars*, and *Golden Boy*. The dive also appears, but it has yet to become central. However, in the noir cycle both traits come together and dominate. In *Body and Soul*, the gangster-promoter develops into a seemingly respectable businessman instead of a thug, and the dive takes center stage. In another noir film, *The Set-Up*, the mechanics of the dive constitute most of the plot. However, with the end of the noir cycle the gangster-promoter and the dive both lose importance. They remain in the back-story of *On the Waterfront*, and they are a peripheral issue in *Somebody Up There Likes Me*. Only in rare cases, such as *The Harder They Fall*, do they shift back to the dominant position they held during the noir cycle. However, the gangster-promoter and the dive continue to function as vital subordinate elements in later films, such as *Raging Bull* and *Pulp Fiction*. Characters like Jergens (Thayer David) in *Rocky* exhibit the shady influence of the gangster-promoter figure, while shedding the prototype's most corrupt behavior. An understanding of the play between dominant and subordinate traits in a genre informs our understanding of how the form evolves.

The linguistic approach offers a more complex perspective on the play between internal elements. This method applies linguistic terms to genre traits—dividing films into semantic elements, such as characters, settings, costumes, etc.—and syntactic elements, such as the master plot or conflicts between characters, that place these figures in relationship to one other, (Altman 1995). For example, musicals include singing and dancing numbers as an important semantic element, and the manner of their syntactic integration into the film is crucial. Over the history of the genre they may appear in an unrelated series of vaudeville numbers all clustered at the conclusion of the plot, as in *Footlight Parade* (1933), or they may be more fluently integrated with the narrative, as in *Top Hat* (1935). Rick Altman argues that a genre reaches maturity when a relatively stable relationship between semantic and syntactic elements takes hold. (Altman 1987, 98–99).

Semantic-syntactic relations in the boxing film stabilized during the Popular Front cycle. The rise-and-fall plot central to the boxing film was evident at least as early as *Iron Man* (1931), and it stabilized the genre by the late 1930s, binding semantic elements like characters to a familiar master plot. The noir cycle embellished the master plot with a retrospective flashback structure. Films like *Gentleman Jim, Somebody Up There Likes Me*, and *Rocky* shift the syntax by imposing a positive attitude, ending the drama with the boxer's triumph and eliminating the decline, whereas the "after the ring" cycle focuses its plot on how the boxer comes to terms with his fall. *Million Dollar Baby* employs a classic rise-and-fall story and marries it to a retrospective voice-over narration to develop a complex syntactic structure. However, at the foundation of the boxing film a series of dramatic conflicts integrate the genre's semantic markers, most conspicuously its typical characters, with relatively stable syntactic relations of the master plot.

A film genre is not an independent formula straining toward self-realization; rather, a genre's evolution is regularly motivated by external influences both from the film industry and the culture at large. Genres themselves feed off one another and thereby constantly incorporate new elements (Neale 1995, 170–72; Altman 1999, 123–44). Filmmakers mix and match qualities from successful films, trying to produce the next hit. *Alien* (1979) incorporates *Jaws* (1975) and *Star Wars* (1977). *Red River* (1948) sets the *Mutiny on the Bounty* (1935) sea saga amidst a Western cattle drive. As a result, genre mixing has come to be understood as a key catalyst for genre development. The experimental stage of a genre often arises as a spin-off from an established form. The boxing film arose from the urban crime drama, particularly the gangster film. So the relationship of a film genre to the constellation of genres popular at any particular time is vital to genre evolution, particularly with regard to the introduction of fresh elements. (Neale 1995, 167–70).

While numerous approaches have been deployed to analyze the internal evolution of film genres, external influences need further attention. World events and social trends shape popular filmmaking, though this influence is filtered through, or mediated by, existing institutions and aesthetic forms (Neale 2000, 213). The influence of Al Capone on Tony Camote in *Scarface* (1932), or Muhammad Ali on Apollo Creed in *Rocky* verges on the explicit or weakly mediated. On the other hand, in *The Great White Hope* the contemporary struggle for racial justice is viewed from the perspective of the Jim Crow era, and the experience of Jack Jefferson evokes the recent legal action against Muhammad Ali for refusing to serve in the Vietnam War. In that case the mediation is stronger. External social influences constantly shape film content, and they range in degree from the weakly to strongly mediated. (See chapter two for a detailed analysis of external influences on the history of the boxing film genre.)

An effective genre history takes into account both internal changes and external influences. Understanding the relationship between them is essential. Genre history should contribute to our understanding of both the best work in the field and the shifting cultural attitudes expressed by the genre as a whole.

GOALS

The goals of genre criticism operate at the specific level of the individual film and at the general level of the genre as a whole. Genre criticism seeks to illuminate the distinctive experience of particular works by placing them in the context of a tradition of conventions, effects, and themes. At the same time, genre criticism must analyze a significant body of films from the genre as a unified field that expands the boundary of the individual film and undergoes development as new work appears. Such an investigation seeks to articulate common patterns that unify the works in a genre, patterns that the audience and filmmakers may only sense in broad outline. Beyond simply identifying these conventions, the analyst should strive to understand how they function in the narrative process to excite emotion and communicate meaning. Furthermore, the genre student must be sensitive to innovations that may distinguish particular works and/or mark a shift in the historical evolution of the form. In studying the historical play between repetition and innovation, genre criticism should attempt to coordinate the formal and aesthetic history of its subject with the commercial life of the film industry. From a larger perspective, the genre critic seeks to illuminate the social significance underlying entertainment. Audiences are attracted to movies because they portray stories that engage their emotions, provoke their curiosity, and stimulate their thought in a situation that releases them from the responsibility to act, but invites their contemplation. Finally, genre criticism aims to give viewers deeper engagement or appreciation, as the analyst strives to uncover the complexities and pleasures of the form.

This study of the boxing film addresses both the specific level—individual films—and the general level of the genre as a whole. The goal is to offer an understanding of the design and meaning of the boxing film genre as well as to provide illuminating analyses of individual films in the context of genre. The book is organized into eight chapters and an epilogue. This first chapter outlines the principle conventions operating in the genre. Chapter two offers a detailed history of the American boxing film from the coming of sound to the end of the twentieth century. Each of chapters three through seven features one of the dramatic conflicts shaping the genre and analyzes films from different cycles of production that portray these conflicts. These chapters emphasize the continuity of the dramatic conflicts unifying the genre as well as the shifting nature of each conflict. Chapter eight analyzes a single film, *Raging Bull*, as an ambitious production embracing aspects of the "art" cinema, but one constructed upon the foundation of genre conventions, thereby creating the outstanding achievement in the field. Finally, the epilogue considers three boxing films that attracted a large audience in 2005—*Unforgivable Blackness: The Rise and Fall of Jack Johnson*, *Million Dollar Baby*, and *Cinderella Man*—and take stock of the genre at the twenty-first century mark.

The boxer animates a powerful social discourse that extends beyond the boundaries of sport, through the cinema, and into the consciousness of our culture. The boxing film portrays the evolution of this archetypal American character, and in doing so it presents more than the rise and fall of a champion; it exposes the body in order to reveal the spirit. More than a brute, the screen boxer dramatizes conflicts and aspirations central to American experience.

2

GANGSTERS, CHAMPIONS, AND THE HISTORY OF THE BOXING FILM

Composing a history of the genre's development is an indispensable task in film genre study. The American boxing film is a series of productions whose form and meaning change in response to conditions in the film industry, boxing culture, and society at large. Since the coming of sound, well over 150 feature length boxing films have been released. Three periods of intense activity mark the development of the genre: 1930–42, 1946–56, and 1975–80, with a minor revival in the 1990s that continues today. The boxing film genre may be further divided into six cycles and three clusters of films. These include: the Depression cycle, 1931–33; the Popular Front cycle, 1937–42; the noir cycle, 1946–51; the "after the ring" cycle, 1950–56; the racial and ethnic prejudice cycle, 1950–54; the failed hybrids cluster, 1956–57; the "comeback" cycle, 1975–80; the African American documentary cluster, 1993–2005; and the masculinity crisis-postmodern cluster, 1993–2005. (See appendix 1 for more details.) Attention to the cycle as a sub-unit of a film genre is an important means of isolating and investigating the factors propelling change. Furthermore, a focus on cycles responds to the critical imperative to emphasize the breaks and discontinuities in genre history, rather than tracing a smooth evolution (Neale 2000, 213–14).

Cycles are a series of similar films produced during a limited period of time, often sparked by a benchmark hit that sets the standard for the series.

Historical analysis of film genres benefits from a sharp focus on cycles of productions. Cycles are often associated with a particular film studio, like Universal's horror films in the 1930s, or Arthur Freed's musicals at M.G.M. in the 1940s and 1950s. In the poststudio era, cycles more frequently are associated with a series, like the James Bond films, or sequels, such as the *Star Wars* productions, or the work of a particular filmmaker, such as Sergio Leone's spaghetti Westerns. However, a cycle becomes generic when it extends beyond a particular company, character, or filmmaker, and its formula is replicated with variations across the film industry or the entertainment world. A generic cycle is limited in duration, taking place for example, over a decade, like the espionage film cycle consisting of, among others, *The Ipcress File* (1965), *The Spy Who Came in From the Cold* (1965), and the Matt Helm series (1966–69) that followed in the wake of the James Bond films in the 1960s. Cycles represent important phases in the development of genres, as seen in the series of slasher films that followed the success of *Halloween* (1978) in the horror genre. The rise and fall of distinct cycles provide a useful tool through which to better understand the concept of genre itself.

Sometimes genre films fail to generate a coherent model or common motifs among productions dating from the same period. I distinguish such groups as clusters rather than cycles. The 1955–57 "failed hybrids" group of boxing films presented two hits, *Somebody Up There Likes Me* (1956) and *The Harder They Fall* (1956), however, instead of sparking further production, these hits marked a dead end in the boxing genre, which remained dormant for over a decade. More recently, the 1990s produced a covey of boxing films, including two clear-cut commercial successes, *Pulp Fiction* (1994) and *When We Were Kings* (1996), but the cluster offers no coherent direction, and the links between the films are weak. The genre cycle or cluster offers an important unit for analysis where various concepts of historical change can be tested.

Thomas Schatz's *Hollywood Genres* (1981) provided an influential treatment of genre evolution. Schatz presents a four-stage pattern that he finds prevalent in film genres dating from the studio era. A first, experimental stage, during which conventions are tested and shared among a series of fictions, is followed by a second, a classic stage characterized by harmony and balance in which a stable set of conventions allows the genre to present its social message with clarity and force. Third comes a period of refinement as variations are added to the pattern. Fourth, a self-conscious, baroque stage brings development to a close. In this final phase, formal embellishments on the genre are accented to such an extent that they become the substance of the work. In many respects Schatz's development model follows an organic pattern of birth, flowering, and decline (Schatz 1981, 36–41).

Schatz's descriptive categories of development can be useful in character-izing a generic cycle, but they should be used flexibly along with other descrip-tions. For example, I find that the boxing genre went through experimental, classical and refinement stages during the studio era, but other cycles might be described as encompassing a culmination stage, a revival, and an amplifica-tion phase. A self-conscious baroque cycle is absent from the studio era, but this cycles does appear near the end of the twentieth century. Furthermore, competing cycles can manifest distinct traits during the same period. My study of the boxing film finds that cycles of production present a variable historical trajectory that does not fall into a fixed pattern or linear progression.

Three external factors work together to generate the rise and fall of genre cycles: commercial success, industrial compatibility, and supporting cultural phenomena. Most immediately, genres grow out of a hit film that other pro-ducers rush to emulate, combining the successful pattern with engaging varia-tions. Film industry factors, such as censorship, developing technologies, or shifts in industrial organization can influence generic development. Audience desires must be linked to Hollywood priorities if a genre is going to sustain the formal stability and social meaning necessary to flourish (Altman 1995, 36). For example, censorship directed against the gangster genre in the 1930s rebounded to promote the boxing film as an alternative format for violent urban action, capable of incorporating elements of the gangster film without exciting the censors. Finally, and maybe most importantly, the genre needs to draw upon related cultural phenomena: a best-selling novel, a popular athlete, political trends, shifting audience demographics, or the values and problems of society at large. When World War II carried the bulk of the male audience into the armed forces, leaving women as the principle patrons of the local movie theater, the boxing genre, with its pronounced male orientation, was curtailed. On the other hand, after the war, government investigations of racketeering in professional boxing helped to revive the genre.

My survey of the history of the boxing film characterizes the chief cycles of film production in order to explain the cinematic influences, film industry practices, and social trends that shaped the evolution of the genre.

EXPERIMENTAL PHASE: THE BOXING FILM TO 1935

In the early years of cinema, between 1894 and 1915, celebrated boxing matches were a profitable and common subject for filmmaking. The spectacle of gambling and mayhem, coupled with a moral revulsion against the sport, resulted in banning, so that by 1896 prizefighting was a crime in all but a few states. However, films could avoid legal restrictions and bring the sport to its urban fans (Streible 1989). Then the controversy surrounding the rise of the African American champion Jack Johnson extended the restrictions on boxing to the movies themselves.

Jack Johnson defied the color caste system of the Progressive era. With a self-confident smile and tremendous athletic prowess, he embodied the fears whites harbored against "uppity" blacks—as well as the hopes of African Americans for freedom from oppression. The first African American to win the heavyweight championship, Johnson held the title from 1908 until 1915. The central event of his career was the 1910 bout against Jim Jeffries, then the unde- feated former champ, who came out of retirement as "the Great White Hope" to challenge Johnson for the title. The nationally publicized fight in Reno, Nevada, was hyped as a racial confrontation, attracting thousands of fans and coast-to- coast media attention. Johnson's easy victory sparked violence against blacks and riots across the nation that left eight dead. In response, calls to ban boxing and boxing films circulated, and eventually the federal government passed the Sims Act of 1912, prohibiting the importation and interstate transportation of filmed prizefights. Though not entirely effective, the law restricted the record- ing and presentation of actual boxing matches in motion pictures until it was rescinded in 1940. As a result of the Sims Act, commercial resources and public attention shifted to fictitious portrayals of the boxer in film.

Ranging from the brute in D.W. Griffith's *Broken Blossoms* (1919) to the comic fop in Buster Keaton's *Battling Butler* (1926), the boxer became a com- mon screen presence appearing in over twenty productions in the 1920s. Spurred by the spread of commercial prizefighting to eastern cities, New York State legalized boxing in 1920, and with the rise of popular champions, particu- larly Jack Demsey and Gene Tunney, the boxer developed into an archetype within popular culture. Between 1930 and World War II, over seventy boxing features were produced in Hollywood. The proliferation of films, along with the increasing standardization of the Hollywood studio system, accelerated the process whereby a type, in this case the boxer, developed in concert with a series of narrative conventions which could be identified as a genre. As a result, the boxing genre moved from an experimental stage in the early 1930s into a classic phase by the decade's close. That is, a series of diffuse motifs developing in a cycle of popular films coalesced into a more unified body of traits readily identified by the public and film producers as a distinct genre.

Two boxing films, *The Champ*, starring Wallace Beery in an Oscar winning performance, and *Iron Man*, adapted from a novel by W. R. Burnett, were com- mercial hits in 1931 and brought new prominence to the boxing film. Together they set the pattern for a cycle of films that appeared during the first half of the decade. Both pictures feature male bonding: father to son in *The Champ*, the boxer to his manager in *Iron Man*. In each case a woman (the mother in *The Champ* and the wife in *Iron Man*) appears on the scene, destroying the comradeship between the men and causing the boxer's fall.

In both films the boxer is a boyish figure incapable of dealing with women or assuming adult responsibilities. His success in the ring serves as a counterpoint to his failure in life. The boxer thus expresses a critique of the pre-industrial warrior figure: The modern man dependent upon physical power as a source of worth is an anachronism. The strong man devoid of intelligence and emotional maturity is destined for a fall. Rather than a heroic model, the boxer, like the gangster, is a doomed protagonist, and his fate excites pathos in the audience.

The crisis the boxer faces is closely linked to the working class and physical labor; his peril is like that faced by men dependent on manual skills in an industrial economy. This quality makes the boxer an evocative figure capable of embodying the helplessness and fear of men confronting the major economic crisis of the twentieth century, the Great Depression. The threat to men's ability to generate wealth and exercise power is readily projected onto gender relations in *The Champ* and *Iron Man*.

A lynchpin of masculine value is a man's success with women, and the two films highlight primary arenas for male-female relations: parenting in *The Champ* and erotic experience in *Iron Man*. Widespread male anxieties aroused by the Depression find expression in Andy's failure as a father and Kid Mason's failure as a husband. In both cases the protagonist is not only defeated in his profession, but also abandoned, even betrayed, by his wife (for a detailed commentary on *Iron Man*, see Grindon, 2006).

The success in 1931 of *The Champ* and *Iron Man* was followed by a cycle of boxing films that held an audience through 1932 and 1933. Prominent among the cycle were *Winner Take All* (1932), *The Life of Jimmy Dolan* (1933), and *The Prizefighter and the Lady* (1933). These films respond to masculine failure by reasserting the boxer's power over women. By 1935 the trend had waned. Classic conflicts characterizing the genre, differences of gender and class and the need for spiritual sustenance in the face of the body's decline, were already taking shape, but only in the closing years of the decade did the range of conventions fully develop into their classic form.

CLASSIC CONVENTIONS TAKE SHAPE, 1937–40

The second cycle of boxing films in the 1930s was initiated by *Kid Galahad* in 1937 and included such popular films as *The Crowd Roars* (1938), *Golden*

Boy (1939) and *City for Conquest* (1940), as well as "race" films such as *Spirit of Youth* (1937) and *Keep Punching* (1939) aimed at African Americans. In these films the character of the gangster, ethnicity, and art gave shape to developing generic conventions. These conventions carried New Deal values that invested the genre with a fresh political attitude.

In 1937 the boxing film became associated with urban crime by developing the gangster and racketeering into significant conventions. Two factors behind this development are the intensification of censorship within the Hollywood industry and the corruption of professional boxing.

Increasing rigor in the enforcement of the American film industry's Production Code of 1930 is widely reported in film histories (Sklar 1994, 173–74; Maltby, 1993). July 1934, is a key point in Hollywood production practices, as that month marked the establishment of the Production Code Administration under the leadership of Joseph Breen, whose job it was to enforce restrictions on sexuality and violence. Public outcry against the valorization of crime in gangster films such as *Little Caesar* (1931), *The Public Enemy* (1932) and *Scarface* (1932) was a major factor behind the more rigorous censorship. Nonetheless, the gangster quickly resurfaced, if slightly muted, in readily marketable form. In 1935 the "G-Men" cycle refashioned screen criminals like James Cagney into federal officers. Later, in 1938–39, the "boy's gang" cycle featured Humphrey Bogart and Cagney as criminals in such films as *Dead End* and *Angels With Dirty Faces*. The boxing genre also provided fictions into which the gangster, off center yet conspicuous, could be easily and fruitfully integrated. In addition, the legal violence of prizefighting could replace the gangland mayhem held in check by the Breen Office. As a result, combat in the ring served both to highlight and veil otherwise objectionable criminal violence, satisfying the audience while still keeping the censors at bay.

Kid Galahad established the model for the integration of the gangster into the boxing movie. The film follows Nick Donati (Edward G. Robinson), the fight manager, as he discovers and develops a young prospect, dubbed Kid Galahad (Wayne Morris) by Fluff (Bette Davis), Donati's mistress. Donati's chief rival in the fight game is Turkey Morgan (Humphrey Bogart), a mobster whose rackets include boxing and whose fighters have regularly held the championship. Galahad rises through the ranks of boxers and is preparing for a title bout when Donati discovers the fighter romancing his young sister. Enraged, Donati plots with Morgan to sabotage Galahad in the ring and make a score gambling on the bout. Donati misdirects his boxer during the early rounds, and Galahad takes a terrible beating. But finally Nick's sister and Fluff, who secretly loves Galahad, prevail upon Donati to win the fight. Nick sets Galahad straight, and the fighter revives and triumphs. After the fight, Morgan has a shoot-out with Donati for backing out on their deal. Morgan and Donati are both killed, and Galahad retires from the ring with his sweetheart.

Kid Galahad places boxing at center stage, but criminal schemes constitute an essential subplot. Fists fly both in the ring and outside it, settling quarrels among the rivals. The climactic bout finds its counterpoint in the gun battle between Robinson and Bogart. The boxing tale provides a framework for perpetuating screen violence while moving gangland bloodshed to the margins.

Scandals associated with professional prizefighting contributed to the plausible integration of the gangster and the boxer into motion pictures after 1935. From the time of champion Gene Tunney's retirement in 1928, until Joe Louis came to national attention in June 1935, heavyweight boxing was marred by disputed decisions, suspicious characters, and a widespread belief that the fix was on. On June 12, 1930, Jack Sharky floored Max Schmeling in the fourth round of a heavyweight title fight, but the referee disqualified Sharky for striking a low blow. For the first and only time, the title was awarded to the boxer sprawled on the canvas. In the 1932 rematch, the American Sharkey won a fifteenth round decision over the German Schmeling, after which the judges were accused of national favoritism in what has been described as the "worst decision in championship boxing history" (Sammons 1988, 88). At the same time, the Italian circus strong man Primo Carnera pursued his career as a boxer with frontmen ineffectually masking his sponsors, the gangsters "Dutch" Schultz and "Owney" Madden. Carnera rose through the heavyweight division owing to a series of fraudulent match-ups and dives that eventually led to his boxing license being revoked in California and New York. In spite of Carnera's suspicious record and infamous associations, he secured a title match and defeated Jack Sharkey in June 1933 in a sporting event fraught with mobsters. The heavyweight championship continued to change hands quickly, with Max Baer defeating Carnera in 1934, and then James Braddock downing Baer the following year only to delay a title defense for two years. By mid-decade it was widely believed that the most prestigious title in boxing was severely compromised, and that the sport was controlled by gamblers and unscrupulous promoters.

In light of these events, one might expect the gangster to have established himself in the boxing film early in the decade. But the racketeer, while present, assumes no significant role in the films of this cycle. In neither *The Champ* nor *Iron Man* does the underworld play a part. Though James Cagney plays a boxer in *Winner Take All*, shortly after playing a mobster in *The Public Enemy* (the film in which Cagney rose to stardom), gangsters are absent from *Winner Take All*. The gangster is most conspicuous in *The Prizefighter and the Lady*, in which the gambler Willie Ryan proves a sophisticated romantic rival to the boxer. Though Ryan indulges in threats after the fighter steals his mistress, *The*

Prizefighter and the Lady features none of the violence that one expects from a crime film.

By contrast, *Kid Galahad* clearly reveals the criminal lineage of its villain, Turkey Morgan. We see Morgan fixing fights, directing thugs, and threatening his enemies. In the popular photo book *The Classics of the Gangster Film*, Robert Bookbinder calls *Kid Galahad* "a textbook example of how a gangster film should look and feel" (Bookbinder 1985, 49). After *Kid Galahad*, the gangster and his double-dealing become fixtures of the genre. *The Crowd Roars* (1938) features Pug Walsh who, to fix a fight, kidnaps the boxer's beloved; the gangster Fuseli tempts Joe Bonaparte with a title shot in *Golden Boy*; and in *City for Conquest*, Googi matches the protagonist's rise in the fight game with his rise as a mobster. By 1940 the conventions of the boxing film include crime as a key element.

Crime gives the boxing film a political accent evocative of the New Deal. The gangster-promoter serves as an analogue for the corrupt capitalist, becoming a pivotal figure in the economic critique underlying the boxing film. He is also the force behind key moves in the typical plot, "the deal" and "the dive." The gangster-promoter arises out of the New Deal ethos suspicious of capital and wary of the market opportunities offered to the boxer, an archetypal laborer. The gangster-promoter embodies the critique of the success ethic and contributes a timely symbol to the political meaning of the boxing film.

In the boxing films of the late 1930s, the protagonist is identified as an ethnic American; as a result, he introduces the conflict between assimilation and loyalty to the immigrant community. During the early 1930s the working class origins of the boxer were clear, but his ethnicity was not highlighted. Even when the Irish-American James Cagney played the boxer, or Max Baer, a Jew, these characters' ethnic identities were never acknowledged. During the late 1930s, however, ethnicity moves to center stage. Nick Donati in *Kid Galahad* and Joe Bonaparte in *Golden Boy* are identified with their Italian-American background, just as Tommy McCoy in *The Crowd Roars* and Danny Kenny in *City for Conquest* are explicitly Irish-American. The problem of assimilation emphasizes the lower-class status of these ring figures, producing the animating conflicts in the film. Ethnic distinctions haunting these characters echo the appearance of Joe Louis at the forefront of American popular culture.

The rise of Joe Louis in 1935 stimulated both the box office popularity of the boxing film and the genre's political undercurrents. Louis's first nationally publicized fight against Primo Carnera on June 25, 1935, filled Yankee Stadium, drawing the biggest fight crowd to New York since 1930. The press hailed Louis for reviving interest in boxing, describing him as the greatest gate attraction since Jack Dempsey. These expectations were confirmed in September 1935, when Louis knocked out another former champion, Max Baer, in the fourth round, drawing a gate which exceeded a million dollars, the largest since the Dempsey-Tunney title fight of 1927. Until 1935, no African American since Jack Johnson lost the title in 1915 had fought an important heavyweight bout. Declining interest in heavyweight boxing, owing to public suspicion and mediocre athletes, was among the many factors that gave Louis his opening. Louis remedied boxing's woes with his physical ability and respectful demeanor. Furthermore, he embodied opportunity, the rags-to-riches ethos of America, even as the racial tensions he sparked were carefully managed so as to attract friend and foe to his ring exploits. Louis proved an antidote to falling revenues, and the boxing business embraced him. By the fall of 1935, the sports press believed him to be the dominant heavyweight, even though the champion, James Braddock, delayed meeting the young contender until 1937.

The public notoriety and commercial success Joe Louis brought to prizefighting sparked the revival of the boxing film. Warner Brothers released *Kid Galahad* in the final week of May 1937, exploiting the publicity surrounding the Louis-Braddock championship bout scheduled for June 22. In the *New York Times* Frank Nugent described the picture as the "Louis-Braddock preliminary" (Nugent, 1937). Warner Brothers dared not make an African American the protagonist; nevertheless, the picture evokes the Louis phenomenon. Nick Donati, the Italian American boxing manager, provides a link. Donati displaces the boxer as the chief protagonist and, more conspicuously, his status as an ethnic outsider is emphasized. Donati supports his Italian mother on a bucolic farm outside the city, and he sends his kid sister, the embodiment of assimilation, to a convent school where she is shielded from the underworld of boxing. In spite of Donati's protection, Kid Galahad, a wholesome Anglo-Saxon farm boy, meets and falls for the sister. Boxing provides an avenue for the ethnic outsider to move into mainstream culture. The ring serves as an emblem for opportunity and transition, but Donati can see only the moral decay and ruthless competition of the boxing world. Blinded by jealousy for the dominant culture's male ideal, embodied in Galahad, and desire to control the integrity of his ethnic family, he opposes the romance and is killed as a consequence. Donati embodies the tormenting conflict between assimilation and loyalty to the native community. Resolution of this conflict is projected onto his sister, who marries the representative of the American heartland, Galahad, and leaves for life on the farm.

The conflict between assimilation and the native community regularly evokes pathos owing to the suffering of the ethnic protagonist. Tommy McCoy endures the deaths of his parents, Danny Kenny is blinded, Joe Bonaparte is tormented by guilt at killing his ring opponent; in each case the route to assimilation is painful or unrealized. The desire for integration itself is frequently depicted as ambivalent. Joe Louis served as an example of ambition and determination in the public's eye during the late 1930s, but he also represented a threat, the integration of African Americans into the mainstream culture. By foregrounding ethnicity the boxing film dramatizes the widespread public anxiety about assimilation Joe Louis raised.

Louis's success was not simply the result of his athletic prowess, but was also associated with a contemporary political movement, the Popular Front, a post-1935 anti-Fascist alliance of liberals and Communists. In the decade following 1935, Joe Louis was a leading symbol of racial equality in the United States, helping to set the stage for the politics of integration in professional sports and in the culture at large. A hero for African Americans, Louis, was also embraced as a representative of mainstream white America. Mike Jacobs, Louis's business manager, was a savvy Jew who, like Louis, had risen from the ghetto. Jacobs helped to turn the liability of Louis's race to astonishing commercial advantage. In publicity for the Carnera fight in June of 1935, Louis was associated with beleaguered Ethiopia, then under assault from Mussolini's Italy. A more intensive campaign of political association surrounded Louis's second bout with the German Max Schmeling, scheduled for June 1938. Before Louis became champion, the two men had met, and Schmeling had upset the younger contender with a twelfth round knockout. Before the rematch, the press, encouraged by Jacobs, touted Louis as an example of American determination and opportunity to rise versus the Nazi Schmeling. Even President Franklin Roosevelt obliged by inviting Louis to the White House in the spring of 1938. The newspapers quoted the President telling the champ, "Joe, we need muscles like yours to beat Germany" (Mead 1986, 134). When Louis overpowered Schmeling in a first round knockout, the victory became his most celebrated triumph for, among other reasons, its political resonance. As Chris Mead wrote in his biography of Louis, "There was no question that the American public attached a strong symbolic importance to the second Louis-Schmeling fight and accepted Louis—a black man—as the representative of American strength and virtue. That was revolutionary" (Mead 1986, 142). A few years later in *The Negro Soldier* (1943), the War Department rallied African Americans behind the struggle against Fascism with footage from the Schmeling fight, followed by shots of Joe Louis himself in training for combat. By the end of the 1930s, Joe Louis was closely allied with the politics of racial equality promoted by the Popular Front as a hallmark of anti-Fascism. Because of the latent politics associated with boxing, it came as little surprise when Clifford Odets, the playwright most conspicuously associated with the Left during the Popular Front era, employed the boxing genre as a basis for drama.

Odets's *Golden Boy* opened in November 1937, only months after Louis won the heavyweight title. The production went on to become the most popular and profitable play staged by the Group Theater. The influence of the Hollywood boxing film and the rise of Joe Louis shape Odets's hit play. The play itself makes an important contribution to the Popular Front politics associated with the boxing film and the transformation of the art motif in the genre.

Golden Boy portrays the rise of young Joe Bonaparte, a promising violinist, who gives up his music for boxing. For his Italian American father, Joe's abandonment of the violin for fighting turns an ideal aspiration to crass ambition. But Tom Moody (Adolphe Menjou), the fight manager, sees Joe's promise and enlists his mistress, Lorna, to ensure the fighter's dedication by making clear to him the benefits of success in the ring. Conflicts proliferate as Joe's victories make him a contender. Lorna loses her heart to the young boxer, as Fuseli, the gangster, muscles in on Moody's claim to Bonaparte. The crisis prompted by the gangster reaches its climax in the big bout when Joe's knockout punch kills his opponent in the ring. Tormented, Bonaparte leaves the fight game and, with Lorna, returns home to his father.

Golden Boy was conceived while Odets was working in Hollywood on the screenplay for *The General Died at Dawn* (1936). After the play opened many critics pointed to Odets's recent return from Hollywood and the influence of the movies on the drama. Charles E. Dexter, writing in the *Daily Worker*, noted the similarities between *Kid Galahad* and Bette Davis's "sensitive, but hard boiled good-bad woman" and *Golden Boy* (Dexter, 1937). Indeed, numerous parallels between the film and the play are readily apparent. These similarities include not only the rise of a fighter, but also the ethnic theme and the morally compromised heroine divided in her affection between the older manager and the young boxer. Odets embraced these connections, invoking Walt Whitman in an article for the *New York Times* and adding, "The movies are now the folk theatre of America." Though he faulted films as "puerile" Odets argued, "[I]t is about time that the talented American playwright began to take the gallery of American types, the assortment of fine vital themes away from the movies. This was attempted in 'Golden Boy'" (Odets 1937, 1–2).

A connection with Joe Louis is suggested, but not made explicit. Louis was the most celebrated prizefighter of the era, and the play was written during the months of his fabulous rise. And the closing bout between Bonaparte and the African American boxer Chocolate Drop serves as an allusion to Louis. After killing Chocolate Drop in the ring, Bonaparte is filled with remorse, which awakens the boxer's social conscience. The 1939 film adaptation elaborates Bonaparte's final confrontation with his dead opponent's entourage. Joe senses his fellowship with his rival and his own political jeopardy. He recognizes

Art becomes associated with romance, the family, and religion as part of an ensemble of values representing an alternative to the ring. Joe Bonaparte (William Holden) plays his violin in *Golden Boy* (1939). Courtesy of the Academy of Motion Picture Arts and Sciences.

boxing as a blinding competition that promises fame and fortune, but only results in senseless battles and defeat for all. His epiphany drives him from the ring, and back to music, his family, and Lorna. This confrontation with an African American, and the guilt it instills, thus become catalysts for transformation. Such a change reflected the hope of leftists like Odets that, because of Joe Louis, society's awakened consciousness of African Americans would result in better treatment of African Americans. Finally, when a musical version of *Golden Boy* opened in 1964, Joe was African American, a change suggesting that the original inspiration for the character was Louis.

Then there's the violin. As a young man Joe Louis's mother gave him money to take violin lessons. However, Joe used the cash to pay dues at the Brewster Recreation Center where he took up boxing. For a while the ruse continued, with Louis heading for the gym instead of his music lessons. When his mother discovered that boxing fired Joe's enthusiasm, she encouraged and supported his training. Playing hooky from violin lessons became an integral part of the Louis legend, repeated in the press and retold in films such as *The Joe Louis Story* (1953) and the documentary *Joe Louis, For All Time* (1984). More to the point, violin references in boxing films served as allusions to Louis. For example, in *Kid Galahad*, when Donati exclaims, "Boxing is no place for feeling. A fighter is a machine not a violin player," his words evoke Joe Louis. And *Golden Boy*'s Joe Bonapart is an accomplished violinist who gives up his music for fighting. This unlikely character transformation not only serves as a connection between the two Joes, but also develops the art motif by moving it to the center of the story, then turning it on its head.

During the early 1930s the boxing film associated art with upper class elitism and two-timing villains. In *Iron Man* the promoter who betrays the boxer is not a gangster but a theatrical producer. Effete and refined, the impresario seduces the champ's wife and saps his strength with the accoutrements of culture—flowers, a piano, the wardrobe of a dandy. In *Winner Take All* the signs of high culture mark the society vamp, who displays the boxer as a sexual trophy picked up during her "slumming" among the lower classes. With *Golden Boy* the function of art is reversed: Art becomes a manifestation of truth and beauty instead of a sign of decadence. "Playing music," Joe Bonaparte declares, "I'm a man . . . nothing is closed to me." In the conflict between body and soul, *Golden Boy* moves art from the realm of the material to that of the spiritual. The humanity of working people inspires their artistic talent and appreciation. In the film production of *Golden Boy*, art becomes even more prominently associated with romantic love, the family, and religion, all part of an ensemble of values representing an alternative to the brutish competition of the ring. In 1940, the year after the film release of *Golden Boy*, the motif becomes central to *City for Conquest*. Here Danny Kenny, a child of the ghetto, goes into the ring to satisfy his beloved's ambitions to be a dancer and to support his brother's musical education. In the end, although he has become blinded by boxing and estranged from the woman he desires, Danny finds solace in his brother's success in Carnegie Hall. Under the influence of the Popular Front, art becomes, not an indicator of class conflict, but an alternative to the cruelty of the market and a manifestation of spiritual renewal. It represents the just society. And the art motif continues to function in the boxing film. For example, Rocky's spirit soars as he jogs up the steps of the Philadelphia Art Museum. With greater complexity, *Raging Bull* shows the retired Jake La Motta pondering his past as he recites Shakespearean texts used in his tawdry stage act.

In summary, the Hollywood boxing films from the late 1930s absorbed conventions from the gangster film in response to censorship codes and rode the wave of the Joe Louis phenomenon, absorbing the political values associated with the champion. Beginning with *Kid Galahad* in 1937, these films reshaped conventions into an ensemble of traits that would mark the genre for the next fifty years. These early films appropriated the ethnic outsider from the gangster film and refashioned a critique of the success ethic. In addition, they reinforced the body and soul opposition central to the genre by appropriating the art motif as a manifestation of spirit. Many artists associated with the original *Golden Boy* production at the Group Theater, such as Elia Kazan (*City for Conquest, On the Waterfront*), John Garfield (*They Made Me a Criminal, Body and Soul*), and Martin Ritt (*The Great White Hope*) would later use the boxing film as vehicles for political expression. Other Hollywood filmmakers recognized the boxing film as a means of linking politics with popular entertainment. In this regard *Golden Boy* represents a key influence in the development of the classical genre model.

WAR TIME VARIATION: FROM PATHOS TO COMEDY IN THE BOXING FILM, 1941–42

As the boxing genre began the new decade, a variation of the classical conventions arose. *Here Comes Mr. Jordan* (1941) and *Gentleman Jim* (1942) were both acclaimed and popular motion pictures firmly grounded in the conventions of the boxing film. Nevertheless, they display marked distinctions in motif, theme, and emotional address from the films of the preceding decade. Now a Popular Front perspective meant going to war. The critique of boxing was abandoned for a celebration of warrior virtues; pathos and loss gave way to comic fantasies and historical romance. While elements of the classical model are evident in the fresh generic mix, social values are changed.

America's preparation for, and entry into, World War II established the social foundation for this change. In the spring of 1940, France had fallen and British forces were trapped at Dunkirk. In September 1940, Roosevelt's Lend-Lease policy was funneling arms to Britain. In April of 1941 Roosevelt and Churchill jointly issued the Atlantic Charter calling for "the final destruction of Nazi tyranny." In June 1941, the Nazis turned on their Russian ally and invaded the Soviet Union. The Popular Front was revived in an attempt to halt the Fascist advance. By the time Columbia Pictures opened *Here Comes Mr. Jordan* in New York on August 8, 1941, the nation was participating in the war in all but name. In June 1942, Japanese expansion was halted at the Battle of Midway; in October, the British counteroffensive at El Alamein sent the German forces into retreat; and in November, the Allies invaded North Africa. When Warner Brothers premiered *Gentleman Jim* on November 26, 1942, the same day *Casablanca* opened, American soldiers were fighting and dying in the Pacific and North Africa. At a time when millions of Americans were training for combat, or actually under fire, the screen boxer in *Here Comes Mr. Jordan* and *Gentleman Jim* became emblematic of the American fighting man.

Here Comes Mr. Jordan and *Gentleman Jim* were hits. *Mr. Jordan* ended the season with seven Academy Award nominations including "Best Picture," ultimately winning two Oscars for "Best Screenplay" and "Best Original Story." Just over a year later the success of *Gentleman Jim* testified to the continuing appeal of the boxing tale. The *Hollywood Reporter* called the movie "the best prize fight film offering ever to reach the screen" (*Hollywood Reporter* 1942). *Variety* and the *New York Times* extolled its commercial prospects (Scho, 1942, 8; Crowther 1942, 40).

Here Comes Mr. Jordan fashions a hybrid of a Frank Capra-like political comedy and a boxing film. The pairing of screenwriters Sidney Buchman (*Mr. Smith Goes to Washington*, 1939) and Seton I. Miller (*Kid Galahad*) suggests this link. Joe Pendelton (Robert Montgomery) is in training for a championship bout when he is killed in a plane crash. Joe immediately finds himself at heaven's gate under the care of Mr. Jordan (Claude Rains), a divine agent who discovers that the boxer has been called to his death fifty years too soon. With Joe's body destroyed, Mr. Jordan leads his spirit on a search for another in which Joe can realize his earthly destiny. In the course of this quest, Joe thwarts the schemes of an unscrupulous financier and falls in love before finally being resurrected as a boxer who wins the title. The movie provides heavenly reassurance that divine agents will shelter the common man faced with death, just as government bureaucrats provide assistance to soldiers at the front.

In *Gentleman Jim*, historical romance and the biography film, rather than comic fantasy, serves as bases for a genre hybrid. *Gentleman Jim* portrays the rise of Jim Corbett from San Francisco bank clerk to heavyweight boxing champion. Corbett defeated the legendary John L. Sullivan for the title on September 7, 1892, but more importantly, he was the first to win with gloved fists under the modern Marquis of Queensberry rules. Corbett marked the transition from illegal bare-knuckled brawls to respectable rule bound competitions. The athlete earned a reputation as a "scientific" boxer who depended on speed, training, and strategy to overcome bigger opponents. He defeated Sullivan even though the champion bested Corbett by twenty-five pounds. Moreover, he knocked out his opponent while hardly enduring any blows himself.

The costume film starring Errol Flynn cultivated attitudes which, on the one hand, reinforced the war effort, and, on the other, distinguished it from the established conventions of the boxing genre. *Gentleman Jim* is about "scientific progress" in the fight game. The protagonist represents new techniques that allow a fighter to triumph while remaining unscathed. Such developments served to reassure the public that the American soldier would be protected by the modern methods adopted by the armed forces. Furthermore, the picture looks back to the nineteenth century to remind the audience of fundamental

American values that are worth fighting for: family, upward mobility, progress, and fair play. In this respect, the film's nostalgia for an idyllic lost time promises a transition toward a new and better era. The ethos of historical progress ties the film to the prospect of a better world after the Allies prevail.

The resolutions of both pictures distinguish them from the conventions of the 1930s boxing film. In films such as *Golden Boy*, *They Made Me a Criminal* (1939), or *The Crowd Roars*, the conclusion shows the boxer turning his back on the tainted glory of prizefighting. The boxing films of the preceding decade nudged viewers away from traditional warrior virtues and a masculine dependence upon physical strength. However, *Here Comes Mr. Jordan* and *Gentleman Jim* end with the boxer gaining the championship and his beloved. This reversal is typical of the ideological flexibility of film genres. Both of these last pictures defuse the social critique embodied in earlier boxing films and celebrate the warrior virtues they wish to promote in the American soldier. Though *Here Comes Mr. Jordan* and *Gentleman Jim* appear to have little connection with the expanding conflict, attention to their transformation of the conventions of the 1930s boxing genre suggests the influence of World War II. Such a reversal was difficult to sustain: With men at the front and the domestic audience predominantly made up of women, the boxing film faded from the screen during the war years. Yet in the decade 1946 to 1956 a major resurgence of the boxing genre occurred, with the conventions established in the 1930s again serving as the foundation for the next cycle of films.

POSTWAR REFINEMENT: BOXING'S NOIR CYCLE, 1946–51

In the decade from 1946 to 1956 the boxer appeared in over fifty Hollywood features from Academy Awarding winning hits such as *Body and Soul* (1947) and *Somebody Up There Likes Me* (1956), to routine programmers, such as the Joe Palooka series from Monogram Pictures (eight films dating from 1946 to 1951). Popular films from the 1930s, such as *Iron Man* and *The Crowd Roars*, were remade. *Body and Soul* is the seminal work of this postwar cycle, which featured three other influential films: *The Killers* (1946), *Champion* (1949), and *The Set-Up* (1949). Together these movies establish the distinctive genre refinements that characterize boxing noir. In this cycle the boxing world is pictured as a competitive marketplace where money talks, duplicity reigns, and human values are degraded. The struggle for success in the ring has transformed the talented young man into a corrupt cynic marked by anxiety and regret. He asks himself if it is too late to escape from the materialist jungle and recover the values he once held dear.

By 1946 the common ingredients of the boxing film genre were widely acknowledged by film critics, filmmakers, and presumably the general audience. Writing on *Body and Soul* producer John Houseman dubbed it "'Golden Boy' without his fiddle," observing that it "conforms almost exactly to the stereotype of prize-fight pictures." He went on to review the conventions distinguishing the boxing film that ally *Body and Soul* to the genre cycle of 1937–40 (Houseman 1947). However, in the years after the war new influences, social and cinematic, refined the genre. These influences included criminal investigations into the corruption of prizefighting; the difficulties of the returning World War II veterans; a cycle of social problem films; Ernest Hemingway's stories about boxers; and the film noir style. The intersection of these influences produced the most celebrated boxing films of the studio era.

In December 1946, District Attorney Frank S. Hogan of New York began a decade-long crusade to clean up professional boxing that received widespread press attention. The story exploded in January 1947, when Hogan questioned middleweight contender and soon to be champion Rocky Graziano. Hogan called Graziano and Sugar Ray Robinson, the welterweight champion, before a grand jury, and the boxers testified to being offered payoffs and pressured to throw fights, although they refused to identify the racketeers who had approached them. The New York State Athletic Commission revoked Graziano's boxing license; Robinson was fined $500 and suspended for thirty days. Neither penalty remedied the criminal infiltration of boxing, but stories of corruption in boxing continued to fill the newspapers, and politicians seized the opportunity to call for reform. Even more troubling, investigations and press reports revealed a nationwide racket controlling professional prizefighting.

At the top of the criminal hierarchy stood the mobster Frankie Carbo (Sammons 1988, 141–46). Known as the boss of boxing, Frankie Carbo exercised control over the sport, evading criminal conviction for over two decades before he was finally imprisoned. His police record of seventeen arrests dates from the second decade of the century, but sending Carbo to prison proved more difficult than indicting him for crimes. In September 1947, Carbo acknowledged before the New York State Boxing Commission that he controlled boxing at Madison Square Garden. The Commission imposed a modest fine of $2,500. District Attorney Hogan pursued the racketeer for over a decade before sending him to prison in December 1959. Though Carbo eluded the law for years, in 1947 his activities came to public attention, influencing a cycle of boxing films that portrayed with renewed force the influence of organized crime over prizefighting.

Though in 1947 law enforcement had little success prosecuting racketeers involved with boxing, owing to motion pictures the crusade garnered public support. Boxing historian Jeffrey Sammons explains: "Hogan's best ally was Hollywood. . . . The release of *Body and Soul*, a fictional yet representative account of prizefighting . . . stirred anger and fear among the game's functionaries. . . . Indeed, if the film deserved criticism it was for understating rather than exaggerating boxing's ills" (Sammons 1988, 145). As *Variety* observed, *Body and Soul* is "[a] topical yarn obviously designed to take advantage of the recent New York inquiry into sport 'fixing.' . . Garfield's name, coupled to a potential exploitation hinging on a widely ballyhooed N.Y. State Boxing Commission probe of bribery last winter, gives 'Body' a strong box office chance" (Kahn 1947, 15). The publicity provoked by the corruption of professional boxing allowed the boxing film to gain new popularity and reanimated its link to the social problem film established during the rise of Joe Louis. Furthermore, as noted in chapter one, the noir cycle saw the rise of the gangster-promoter and the dive as dominant genre elements.

During and immediately after World War II, the social problem film enjoyed extraordinary critical acclaim and box office success. This trend arose out of Hollywood's support for the war effort. Motion pictures were no longer simply entertainment, and newsreels, documentaries, and fiction films were designed to promote social goals—particularly military victory. The spread of this tendency beyond the war effort is apparent in 1945 in *The Lost Weekend*, a movie about alcoholism that won Academy Awards for "Best Picture," "Best Director," "Best Actor," and "Best Screenplay." The following year, *The Best Years of Our Lives*, dramatizing the problems of returning war veterans in adjusting to civilian life, swept the major Academy Awards and went on to become the box office leader of the decade. In 1947, *Gentleman's Agreement*, a critique of anti-Semitism, won Oscars for "Best Picture" and "Best Director." In highlighting the need for reform in professional boxing, *Body and Soul* linked the genre to the trend towards social problem films. *Time* acknowledged the film's "stout 'socially conscious' sentiments," and in the *Nation* James Agee called the movie "discreetly leftist" (*Time* 1947, 101; Agee 1947, 511).

The defeat of the Axis powers and the shocking revelation of the Holocaust presented a receptive context in which to press for increased racial justice in the United States. *Body and Soul* reached out to include African Americans. The ethnic motif personified by the Jew Charlie Davis expanded with the noteworthy addition of the African American Ben Chaplin as the champ dethroned and then befriended by Charlie. Allusions to Joe Louis in the films of the late thirties or marginal black men, such as Chocolate Drop and his entourage in *Golden Boy*, developed into a forceful, dignified character, who is both a victim of the boxing racket and the voice of Charlie's conscience. As Thomas Cripps writes in *Making Movies Black*, "More than any other movie of its time it (*Body and Soul*) played a political angle with a minimum of compromise and, at least for one big scene, with a black figure at its center" (Cripps 1993, 210). The connection between the social problem film and the boxing genre had already been established in the late 1930s, but *Body and Soul* developed this connection so as to address social issues both explicitly and implicitly. While explicitly portraying the corruption of professional boxing and racial injustice, implicitly *Body and Soul* develops the conflict between market forces and personal integrity. From a broader perspective, the boxing film can be said to have portrayed the problems of post–World War II masculinity, with the prizefighter often standing in for the returning veteran. As Richard Maltby notes, "The central male protagonist of films noir of 1946–48 is almost invariably marked as a veteran by one means or another" (Maltby 1993, 46). This collocation is particularly evident in *The Killers*, in which the boxer, Hemingway's Ole Anderson, retires after an injury in the ring and drifts into the underworld, where he meets his death.

Ernest Hemingway's stories of prizefighters, dating from the 1920s, influenced boxing noir just as Dashiell Hammett's and Raymond Chandler's "hardboiled" fiction provided a foundation for the noir detective. Not only was Hemingway a famous fiction writer and wartime journalist, his stories translated into big box office in forties Hollywood. In 1943 the film adaptation of Hemingway's *For Whom the Bell Tolls* brought in over $7 million, making it the second biggest commercial hit of the year. Two years later *To Have and Have Not*, another box office leader, earned over $3.5 million (Schatz 1997, 466–67). In 1946 advertising for *The Killers* touted its Hemingway source in the absence of any recognized stars, and the film became a hit with over $2.5 million in domestic rentals. (Schatz 1997, 388). "Fifty Grand" was an acknowledged influence on *Body and Soul*, and "The Battler" was the source for a 1955 television production starring Paul Newman that anticipated *Somebody Up There Likes Me*. Even when *Champion* and *The Set-Up* turned to other literary sources, these screen adaptations were marked by Hemingway's sensibility.

For Hemingway the boxer embodied a disillusioned masculinity, a warrior virtue beset by problems that elude understanding. His prizefighters appear in three short stories, "The Battler" (1925), "Fifty Grand" (1927), and "The Killers" (1927). All three of Hemingway's boxers are alienated by the modern world; each is a doomed loner whose physical prowess is undermined by the complexity of social relations. "The Battler" portrays the boxer as a sociopath victimized by his unbridled aggression. In "Fifty Grand" money corrupts a valiant fighter. Ole Anderson in "The Killers" awaits his appointment with death. These stories cultivate paradoxical qualities: Ad Francis in "The Battler" is friendly and then hostile; Jack Brennan in "Fifty Grand" is a champion and a cheat;

Ole Anderson is a gentle prizefighter, a man of action passively accepting his doom. All three stories question the viability of simplistic masculinity, which is thrown into doubt by experience. Hemingway simultaneously valorized, debunked, and complicated the warrior ethic associated with the prizefighter in the cultural imagination.

Hemingway's boxers provide a link between the disillusionment following World War I and the problem of the returning veteran after World War II. Since Hemingway was an ambulance driver as well as a casualty in the First World War, his fiction from the 1920s has long been associated with the malaise following that conflict. The disenchantment that became widespread and even fashionable following the warfare of 1914–18 was not so conspicuous after the victory of 1945. Nonetheless, the experience of modern warfare leaves scars, whether physical or psychic, that makes the transition back to civilian life difficult, and even impossible for some. Whereas the hopes of the returning war veteran found expression in the popular and celebrated *The Best Years of Our Lives*, the more covert feelings of cynicism, confusion, or helplessness were often portrayed in a less obvious fashion. To express these misgivings, the boxer could stand in for the soldier. Rather than acting as a haven for a primal masculinity, prizefighting in Hemingway's work serves to corrupt physical virtue through commercial means. In some respects, this disarming of warrior values parallels the effects of modern warfare, in which the industrialization of combat has undermined physical prowess. Hemingway's boxers serve as an eloquent touchstone for the war veteran as he was portrayed in motion pictures during the postwar years. These disillusioned fighters replaced Clifford Odets's Golden Boy as the central literary influence on portrayals of the boxer in post–World War II film noir.

Meanwhile, the style and values of film noir reinvigorated the conventions of the thirties boxing tale. By 1946, the noir movement had already established its success with hit films like *The Maltese Falcon* (1941), *Double Indemnity* (1944), and *Mildred Pierce* (1945), and its practices were incorporated into other urban crime films. The noir style features darkness as its signature element; its shadowy black and white photography expresses at once the loss of ideals, moral ambivalence, and the corruption at the foundation of a nightmarish world. An example of noir influence appears at the beginning of *Body and Soul*, when the silhouette of a swaying body bag awakens Charlie Davis from his anxious sleep. Flashbacks create a complex temporal scheme in the noir style, as the past controls the present and constrains the protagonist. Many of the boxing films in the noir cycle use the flashback, which appears most frequently in *The Killers*, with its eleven flashbacks revealing the cause of Ole's death. This self-conscious style employs unstable compositions, startling editing shifts, and

Boxing noir in *The Set-Up* (1949). Courtesy of the Academy of Motion Picture Arts and Sciences.

voiceover narration to emphasize a tormented psychology attracted to doom. Lust is often favored over romance, as with Midge Kelly's predatory sexuality in *Champion*, and violence takes on a brutal, even sadistic edge in the numerous beatings the noir boxer suffers in and out of the ring. Realism is often combined with the bizarre, as with the perverse spectators watching the bout in *The Set-Up*. The dim, deserted boxing arena into which the fighter flees from mobsters in *Champion* and *The Set-Up* establishes a characteristic setting for boxing noir. The empty ring haunts the boxer; he runs but cannot escape the corrupt thugs who have robbed his craft of dignity. The serious fight takes place outside of public view, after the lights go out, in the darkness, and with the odds stacked against the lonely boxer. Between 1946 and 1951, screen boxing became a racket. Hoods were no longer confined to the margins; instead, the corrupt underworld controlled the boxer. Whether battered and dispirited, or equal to the mobster in his ruthlessness, the fighter teetered on the verge of breakdown. The boxer's embattled psyche suggests the scarred veteran struggling to adjust in peacetime. The guilt ridden, nightmare realism of film noir portrayed the conflicts of the screen boxer in a fresh and compelling fashion.

CULMINATION, AMPLIFICATION, DECLINE: POSTNOIR CYCLES, 1950–56

Intensification of the Cold War prompted the noir cycle's fade-out. In February 1950, Senator Joseph McCarthy initiated his campaign against Communists in the State Department, fueling the growing conflagration of suspicion, accusation, and dread that came to be known as "McCarthyism." In June 1950, the war against Communism became deadly when the North Koreans invaded South Korea and American forces under the banner of the United Nations intervened to halt the Communist advance. In March 1951, the House Un-American Activities Committee (HUAC) resumed the investigation of subversives in the film industry that it had begun in 1947. This time, the hearings went on for two years rather than two weeks. Under pressure from HUAC and other "patriotic" organizations, the Hollywood blacklist gained renewed force (Cogley 1976, 410–31). Social criticism was often accused of offering support to the nation's enemies. Business in the motion picture industry continued to slump from its peak in 1946, with studio profits falling from $33.6 million in 1949 to $30.8 million in 1950, $31.1 million in 1951, and $23.9 million in 1952, their lowest level since 1940 (Finler 1988, 287). Dorothy B. Jones has documented the decline of the social problem film in Hollywood from its height in 1947, through a downturn in 1948–49, to its low point between 1950 and 1952. While the social problem film did not completely disappear, "The years 1950–52 can be described as a period when the industry radically reduced the number of social theme movies, and devoted itself to escapist fare of various kinds" (Jones 1972, 220). Nonetheless, the boxing film genre continued to feature social problems, albeit in muted form.

Though the classic traits of the boxing noir cycle declined, its residual influence was apparent. Hemingway's melancholy tough guys remained a staple, and "The Battler" became a teleplay in 1955. A shift toward the psychological rather than the political arose in social problems films. Noir stylistics were evident in crime films such as *99 River Street* (1953), social problems pictures like *On the Waterfront* (1954), and also appear in unexpected places, such as the flashback to the boxing ring in a romantic comedy, *The Quiet Man* (1952). Three distinct trends shape the postnoir era: culmination of the classic dramatic conflicts that come "after leaving the ring"; amplification of the ethnic-racial prejudice theme by foregrounding Hispanics and African Americans; and generation of new genre hybrids that failed to take hold.

Between 1952 and 1954 three popular and Oscar winning motion pictures featured a retired boxer as the protagonist: *The Quiet Man, From Here to Eternity* (1953), and *On the Waterfront.* Like *The Killers*, each of these films portrays the boxer after he departs from competition, although his experience as a fighter is central to the drama. A similar plot device appears in modest productions from the same period, including *99 River Street* and two television productions, "The Battler" (1955) and "Requiem for a Heavyweight" (1956). The model plot of the boxing genre provides a crucial foundation or "back story" for these films. In response, they develop an illuminating extension of the genre tradition. This cycle of films about the retired boxer testifies to development of the internal structure of the boxing film genre. In many respects, *The Quiet Man, 99 River Street, From Here to Eternity, On the Waterfront*, and "Requiem for a Heavyweight" bring the conflicts distinguishing the boxing film to a resolution and mark the culmination of the genre as Hollywood's classical studio period (1920–60) comes to a close. Furthermore, these productions anticipate the eclipse of the boxing film, for after a final flurry of releases in 1955–56, the boxing film remained nearly dormant for twenty years.

Taken together these films employ the conventions of the boxing film genre in a variety of ways. Nonetheless, common patterns emerge. In each case boxing constitutes a tormenting past with which the protagonist must be reconciled. In the tradition of film noir, boxing in the "after the ring" cycle evokes a forceful, dark psychological experience. Not simply a memory, the ring career has become a disturbing state of mind lodged in the subconscious and crying out for rectification. In boxing noir the flashback was widely used, but in the "after the ring" cycle a variety of modes are employed to portray past trauma and set the stage for its reconciliation. In these films the boxer must recall and acknowledge his fall and in a symbolic manner return to the ring—often literally resorting to fisticuffs—in order to initiate rebirth. Typically, the ex-prizefighter is a loner, an individual struggling not so much against a rival as to overcome inner torment, thereby putting an end to his isolation by establishing a bond with others and reformulating his social position.

In each case the agony of the ring animates the psychic conflicts motivating the drama. Two historical examples animate the crisis of masculinity embodied by the screen boxer: the ethnic commoner threatened by the Depression featured in the Popular Front cycle, and the returning World War II veteran struggling to find his place in peacetime society, a thematic undercurrent in the noir cycle. Boxing can reference both competition without human fellowship and the warrior experience of combat violence. These two widely shared social phenomena continue to characterize the boxer during the "after the ring" cycle. However, these films assume a more introspective, thoughtful attitude. The torment generated by ring memories provokes reflections about the ethics of violence and the meaning of suffering. The former boxer of *The Quiet Man, 99 River Street, From Here to Eternity, On the Waterfront*, and "Requiem for a

Heavyweight" uses his physical experience to reconcile a spiritual crisis. The animating conflicts of the genre serve as themes for these dramas, and each film works toward a distinctive resolution (for a detailed commentary on *The Quiet Man*, see Grindon, 2007).

A subordinate cycle that appeared during the postnoir era featured ethnic and racial prejudice, such as that in films like *Right Cross* (1950), *The Fighter* (1952), *The Ring* (1952), and *The Joe Louis Story*. These films are noteworthy for developing the Hispanic or African American boxer as a protagonist who suffers from discrimination and expresses his social anger in ring battles. However, displacement of his rage prevents him from coming to terms with the causes of his oppression and creates neurosis. Despite his success in the ring, racial prejudice continues to plague the boxer. He must find a better way to fight back and realize social justice. The political heritage of Joe Louis was a conspicuous influence on these films. Nonetheless, they divided their focus between calling attention to injustice and diffusing concern by attributing problems to maladjusted individuals or to foreign influences. The most ambivalent of these films was the initial release, *Right Cross*, a well-appointed M.G.M. feature starring June Allyson, Dick Powell, and Ricardo Montalban. Three others were low budget independent productions, but their position at the margins of the industry allowed a more daring approach, particularly in the most successful film of the group, *The Ring*. Together these films testify to the muted heritage of the social problem film.

The most noteworthy formal change initiated by this cycle was the demise of the corrupt gangster and the self-conscious style of noir, and their replacement by the journalist serving as a major character. Before *Right Cross*, the sports writer was a minor figure frequently lumped together with his peers during press conferences, or seen sitting with his typewriter at ringside as a representative of the crowd. In *Right Cross*, the sportswriter Rick Garvey (Dick Powell) functions as a rational counterpoint to the hotheaded boxer, and the sportswriter is also a melancholy loser in a romantic rivalry with the prizefighter. The journalist as protagonist of the boxing film follows in *Iron Man* (1951), *The Joe Louis Story*, and most conspicuously, *The Harder They Fall* (1956).

From 1955 to 1956, the boxer and boxing remained prominent in film and television. In 1955, the boxer plays a subsidiary role in *It's Always Fair Weather* (1955), *Kiss Me Deadly* (1955), and *The Big Combo* (1955), moving to center stage in *Killer's Kiss* (1955) and the teleplay "The Battler." The following year two boxing films and a teleplay enjoyed significant commercial and critical success: *The Harder They Fall*, *Somebody Up There Likes Me*, and the award-winning television production, "Requiem for a Heavyweight." These pictures sought fresh energy through cross fertilization with other genres: *It's Always Fair Weather* borrows from the musical; *Killer's Kiss* from the documentary; *The Harder They Fall* from the newspaper exposé movie; and *Somebody Up There Likes Me* from the biography film and the juvenile delinquency picture. Nevertheless, these films constitute the last glimmer of a fading genre. After numerous productions in the decade following World War II, the boxing film suddenly, and almost completely disappears from the screen.

The major boxing films dating from 1955 and 1956 strike a retrospective pose, evoking the melancholy typical of the noir boxer. *It's Always Fair Weather* portrays the disillusionment of World War II veterans estranged from their Army buddies ten years after their victory and embittered by the course of their civilian lives. *The Harder They Fall* adapts Budd Schulberg's 1947 best-selling novel. His exposé of boxing was itself based upon the fixes and corruption that characterized the fight racket in the early 1930s. The writer Rod Serling, acknowledged that "Requiem . . . " was inspired by the humiliation of the great champion Joe Louis in the course of his retirement. *Somebody Up There Likes Me* was a biography film of Rocky Graziano, middleweight champion from 1947 to 1948, whose public testimony before Frank Hogan's investigating committee was a highlight of the boxing scandals that anticipated *Body and Soul*. Each of these films harked back to the initiation of boxing noir in the years immediately following World War II, and this perspective signaled the close of an era. 1962 saw remakes of two boxing hits: *Kid Galahad* was fashioned into a musical for Elvis Presley, and a film version of *Requiem for a Heavyweight* appeared. But these pictures did not revive the genre. Rather, the forced premise of Presley as boxer and the tired tone of the recast teleplay only confirmed the sense that the boxer was spent and no longer served as a vibrant figure who spoke to the culture at large. At that point, few would have anticipated the powerful reemergence of the boxing film genre during the period 1975 to 1980.

WHY DID THE BOXING GENRE FADE?

Starting in 1931, a steady ebb and flow saw the boxing film through a series of cycles: *The Champ* and *Iron Man* had initiated a cycle that lasted from 1931 to 1933; *Kid Galahad* began the cycle that lasted from 1937 to 1942; *Body and Soul* was central to the wave of boxing films that appeared in the decade after World War II. Since 1956 produced moderate success for boxing films, why did this long running genre disappear?

The changing economy of the film industry was one factor in the genre's disappearance. By the late 1950s, the old studio system of large scale in-house mass production had shifted to the package unit system, which split the field into lavish high budget films produced by the old major studios, lower cost independent films, and releases put out by minor production houses, such as American International Pictures. The last category of producers often directed their product to a niche audience, like the beach party or motorcycle films aimed at teens. In the shifting production practices of the late 1950s, the boxing film was unable to find sponsors despite a strong earlier record for attracting independent producers.

Competition from television also played a large role in the decline of the boxing film. In an effort to compete with the new medium, Hollywood concentrated on lavish productions that could exploit factors such as Cinemascope or color, displaying their technological advantage over the small home screen. Successful Broadway musicals and historical epics, such as *The King and I* (1956) or *The Ten Commandments* (1956), became trend-setting hits of the mid-1950s. Like noir crime films, the boxing genre was associated with low budget, black and white production that could be easily matched by television dramas. Furthermore, live boxing broadcast on TV was able to satisfy a craving for ring action. In 1952, boxing on television reached five million homes and claimed 31 percent of the available audience. By 1955, the audience had increased to eight and a half million. Television could siphon off the audience for boxing fiction, and it could also quickly gauge a decline in public interest. By 1958, lower ratings for boxing led to a cutback in network telecasts; by 1959 boxing was drawing only about 10 percent of the available audience (Sammons 1988, 133, 174).

Television ratings reveal a declining public interest in boxing. In the late 1950s, sport fans appeared to be shifting their attention to other sports, such as professional football. The NCAA dropped boxing as an intercollegiate sport in 1960. Interracial bouts sparked audience interest; however, when Rocky Marciano retired as heavyweight champion in 1956, the major contenders in the stellar division were almost all African American. Though Ingemar Johansson, a Swede, interrupted black domination of the division for one bout, the leading boxers in the heavyweight division, African Americans Floyd Patterson, Sonny Liston, and Muhammad Ali failed to generate broad based interest. It was only after Ali became a hero of the counterculture in the late 1960s that this trend was reversed. As general interest in boxing declined, the audience for the boxing film also diminished.

The flexibility of the boxing story had allowed for ready hybridization with other genres, such as crime films, the social problem film, the biopic, and so on. But rather than gaining momentum from addition of provocative elements from other genres, the boxing film could lose the momentum from a hit to competing genres. After the success of *Somebody Up There Likes Me*, the juvenile delinquency drama (from which the film drew) sustained itself, while the boxing film faded. Other sports, like pool in *The Hustler* (1961) or poker in *The Cincinnati Kid* (1965), assumed the prominent place previously held by boxing. In spite of its upbeat treatment in *Somebody*, the boxing film featured suffering, and the milieu of the prizefighter generally presented the bleak atmosphere found in *The Harder They Fall*, "Requiem for a Heavyweight," and the long standing noir tradition. This grim heritage was apparent in *Monkey on My Back* (1957). The production followed the biopic form in portraying the life of Barney Ross, a boxing champion and war hero. But most of the film treats a sensationalized social problem by focusing on Ross's struggle with drug addiction, exploiting the recent success of *The Man with the Golden Arm* (1955). Ross's torment highlights the boxer's suffering, as he loses his job, friends, and family to his self-destructive addiction. The film limps toward a positive resolution when the protagonist finally enrolls in an army rehabilitation clinic. Hollywood's preference for happy endings always faced a challenge in the boxing drama, a challenge that most producers preferred to avoid.

I have argued that the conventions of genres generate characteristic dramatic conflicts, and that a concern for these conflicts attracts viewers. As a result, one may suppose that when a genre declines its distinctive conflicts lose their hold on the public's attention, or else the audience migrates to other, more attractive forms of expression. The decline in the boxing film between 1956 and 1970 suggests a diminished engagement with the principle conflicts driving the genre. I have summarized these conflicts as the critique of the success ethic, problematic gender relations, assimilation versus loyalty to the native community, suffering and the problem of male emotion, and body versus soul.

The economic crisis of the Depression intensified conflict between the market system and the people it was to serve; however, with post–World War II prosperity during the Eisenhower Administration, this tension relaxed. It seems that with liberal New Deal reforms such as Social Security and unemployment insurance, and with the more sophisticated government management of the economy (not to mention enormous federal expenditures on defense, highway construction, and other projects), the market once more served the people. The conservative Republican administration accepted the innovations of the mixed economy as appropriate to sustaining national prosperity. Furthermore, the international struggle against communism prompted Americans to value their market system as superior to that of their Soviet adversaries, rather than to see it as a source of anxiety. The conflict between market forces and Judeo-Christian values evident in the critique of the success ethic no longer offered a compelling subject.

The gender conflict and the conflict between assimilation and the native community were also waning. Class and gender tensions exacerbated by the Depression and the intensification of gender conflict in the years following World War II were replaced by a broader social harmony. With the movement westward and into the suburbs, ethnic neighborhoods in older cities were losing their influence as well as their numbers. Spread of technologies, like the television and the automobile, also promoted a more mobile and homogeneous culture. The educational and housing benefits of the post–World War II GI Bill supported these developments with massive funding. A decade after World War II ended their impact was widespread. The baby boom that followed the war reinforced traditional parenting roles as the defining gender models. Only in the next decade, with the rise of a new feminism, would gender roles experience a fresh challenge.

One development, however, disrupted the harmony. The plight of African Americans gained new attention with the Supreme Court's 1954 order in *Brown v. The Board of Education* for an end to segregation in the nation's public schools. The changes initiated by the Court sparked renewed struggles for racial justice. However, this change failed to find expression in the boxing film. Such an absence may seem surprising after the influence of Joe Louis and the conspicuous achievements of African Americans in the ring. However, the political appeal of Joe Louis depended, among other things, on opposition to the doctrines of racial superiority propagated by the Nazis. Louis represented a broad coalition of racial and ethnic groups that opposed Fascism. By contrast, Soviet Communism trumpeted racial equality, often featuring the injustices of American racism as examples of political failure. So the civil rights struggles of African Americans in the late fifties and the sixties did not find fertile ground for expression in the boxing film. Instead, the ineffectual Floyd Patterson, the thuggish Sonny Liston, and the loud-mouthed Cassius Clay—soon to be Muhammad Ali—failed to match the exemplary sportsmanship of Joe Louis and Jackie Robinson. In sum, social change reduced the ethnic assimilation conflict in some respects; with regard to injustices suffered by African Americans, the boxing film no longer offered an attractive avenue for expression.

In contrast, the problem of male frustration found new forms of expression during this period. Juvenile delinquency films expressed the distress of angry young men, occasioned not so much at social injustices as by psychological anxieties growing out of the family, sexuality, and a search for direction. The innovations of Method acting and new stars such as Marlon Brando, Montgomery Clift, James Dean, and Paul Newman cultivated performance styles in which sensitivity triumphed over traditional masculine restraint. In 1956, with the rise of Elvis Presley to national attention, rock and roll became a fresh and pervasive means of expressing the thwarted emotions of young men and women. During the early fifties, the boxer continued to serve as an influential embodiment of masculine struggles. But after the middle of the decade the prizefighter lost his grip on the popular imagination. Joe Louis was no longer exceptional, and title bouts between two African Americans became common. Rather than being representative of opportunity, the boxer was becoming emblematic of the ghetto and failed to attract the sympathy of the broader public. The pugilist's social presence was being constricted to that of an oppressed racial minority, and as a result, his influence declined.

Maybe the most compelling conflict expressed by the boxing film is between body and soul, material versus spiritual values. The boxer represents the physical, and the body's inevitable decline demands a shift toward more intangible values. The economic crisis of the Depression and the sacrifices called for by global warfare also drew the culture's attention to spiritual values in the face of scarcity and violence. The "after the ring" cycle of the early fifties portrayed this conflict vividly and met with critical and commercial success. However, the economic prosperity and growing social harmony that took hold by the mid-fifties under the political leadership of President Dwight Eisenhower seemed to allow for an alliance between material comforts and spiritual renewal. Between 1940 and 1960 the nation experienced a boom in religion, with church membership growing from 50 to 63 percent of the population. This rise was often linked to increased prosperity. In a speech in Atlantic City, President Eisenhower's pastor, the Rev. Edward Elson, declared, "The fruits of material progress have provided the leisure, the energy, and the means for a level of human and spiritual values never before reached" (O'Neill 1986, 212). The most telling evidence of the pervasiveness of this blend of material success and spiritual values could be found in the work of the era's most popular religious writer, the Protestant minister Norman Vincent Peale. Peale's best-selling books included *The Power of Positive Thinking* (1952), in which God's message, according to Peale, was to get ahead. The minister offered numerous tips about social success for those lagging behind. The cultural shift from self-sacrifice to consumption diminished the conflict between body and soul, thereby reducing a compelling theme central to the boxing film.

With the close of the era of studio production, the fading genre appeared to be a vestige of the Depression and the post–World War II noir movement. The numerous screen pugilists who once seemed ubiquitous now seemed products of the mass production practices of the bygone classical studio era and the radio days that preceded televised boxing. In short, the boxing film seemed to be an entertainment relic whose popularity was restricted to a particular time and place. No doubt that time and place fostered elements which generated artistry and an audience for the genre, but the future would see a revival of the boxing film out of fresh circumstances, a revival which built upon traditions established during the studio era.

COMEBACK: *ROCKY* (1976) AND THE REVIVAL OF THE SCREEN BOXER IN THE 1970S

From *Hard Times* and *Mandingo* in 1975 through *Raging Bull* and *Any Which Way You Can* in 1980, the boxing film experienced an astonishing resurgence during the 1970s. Martin Scorsese observed, "There were so many boxing pictures being made in the seventies that I dreaded the moment in the future when I wouldn't be able to sleep and the only thing on TV would be the poorest of them" (Thompson and Christie 1989, 80). Seventies boxing films included literary adaptations (*Fat City*, 1972), stage hits (*The Great White Hope*, 1970], "blaxploitation" films (*Hammer*, 1972), parodies (*Movie, Movie*, 1978), biography films (*Raging Bull*, 1980), remakes (*The Champ*, 1979), and romantic comedies (*The Main Event*, 1979). *Rocky*'s enormous commercial and critical success stood at the center of the cycle. The Sylvester Stallone film spawned a six film series; each of the first four ranked among the top three box office hits in the year of its release. The 1970s generated the most important cycle of boxing films since the close of the studio era. The causes for the revival of the boxing film included film industry trends as well as broader social influences, but they can be summarized around two phenomena: the film industry revival that came to be known as the "New Hollywood" and the comeback of heavyweight champion Muhammad Ali.

The "New Hollywood" arose in the wake of the near collapse of the old studio system. The motion picture business began the 1970s in crisis and roared back to prosperity at the decade's close, the revised industry dubbed "New Hollywood." The industry recession of 1969–71 was the most severe slump in Hollywood since the Great Depression. The year 1969 alone produced $200 million in losses, only to be followed by another $300–400 million loss before the end of 1971. Among the many failures were two boxing films directed by Hollywood stalwarts Martin Ritt and John Huston: *The Great White Hope*, a lavish production based upon the Pulitzer Prize–winning Broadway play, which nonetheless lost over $7 million, and *Fat City*, a critically acclaimed literary adaptation that died at the box office. As a result of the crisis in Hollywood, management changed in the film industry and new filmmakers got unprecedented opportunities.

The uncertainties of the 1970s gave rise to the practice of targeting films to specialized audiences rather than the general public. These films could make a profit as long as costs were contained. One example was "blaxploitation" films. Although movies portraying race relations and starring African Americans, particularly Sidney Poitier, had risen to prominence in Hollywood during the 1960s, 1970 brought the appearance of low budget crime thrillers featuring largely African American casts and intended to reach an urban black audience *Cotton Comes to Harlem* (1970) was the first all-black film to become a cross-over box office hit. The independent *Sweet Sweetback's Baad Asssss Song* (1971) followed. Produced on a budget of less than $500,000, the film had an aggressive tone and pilloried white authorities as part of a pronounced racial appeal to African American viewers. Even though its X rating made it difficult to book into many theaters, the picture earned over $4 million. M.G.M. soon released *Shaft* (1971), a film about a tough African American private eye fighting white mobsters. The movie, whose audience was 80 percent black, was one of the most profitable of the year. Soon Warner Brothers picked up the independent *Superfly* (1972), about a Harlem drug dealer attempting to go straight, and it proved nearly as successful. Between 1972 and 1975 a plethora of African American low budget action pictures was churned out. Among these was the boxing film *Hammer. Mandingo*, which portrayed white slavers in the antebellum South staging fights between their black chattels, was even more successful. These low budget independent productions addressed their audience in a manner soon adopted by the mainstream boxing film. They appealed to an oppressed community by presenting an action hero battling predatory outsiders.

An upswing in the film industry became apparent in 1972 with the enormous success of *The Godfather*. For the remainder of the decade, particularly after 1975, business continued to improve. By 1980, Hollywood was once again prosperous. Benchmark works for the Hollywood comeback of the late 1970s were *Jaws* (1975), *Star Wars* (1977), and *Halloween* (1979). Steven Spielberg and George Lucas assumed leadership of the industry. Rather than pursuing a critical reevaluation of the Hollywood tradition, a self-conscious indulgence in the cinematic past guided their success. Optimism borrowed from Walt Disney (*E.T.*, 1982) and affectionate play with old forms (*Raiders of the Lost Ark*, 1981) combined to produce an adolescent sensibility based on allusion, wisecracks, fast action, and sentiment. In 1982 Noël Carroll lamented that the "ferment, uncertainty and experimentation" of the late 1960s and early 1970s had settled into a "loving evocation through imitation and exaggeration of the way genres were" (Carroll 1998, 257, 248). The boxing film played a role in the turnaround. Walter Hill's *Hard Times* was a harbinger. Its mythic treatment of the boxer (Charles Bronson) combines a nostalgic 1930s setting with tough action. Its masculine ideal embodied old-fashioned individualism in response to the counter culture. Furthermore, the relaxed ratings code in the "New Hollywood" allowed for a more intense portrayal of ring violence. By the close of the decade, three leading male action stars, Charles Bronson, Sylvester Stallone, and Clint Eastwood, had all portrayed a boxer in hit films. Even Barbara Streisand used the fight film as the basis for a comedy. Two boxing films, *Rocky* and *Every Which Way But Loose* (1978), registered blockbuster profits, and sequels followed that continued to sell tickets at a torrid pace.

Rocky became the most popular boxing film in screen history. Produced on a modest budget of one million dollars, the brainchild of Sylvester Stallone earned over $100 million in the US and Canada in its initial run. Though the press initially registered a mixed evaluation, there was widespread reporting of the film's emotional impact, the "tears" and "cheers" of audiences (Leab 1988). *Rocky* won three Academy Awards for 1976, including "Best Picture" and "Best Director." In his history of American cinema in the 1970s David A. Cook described *Rocky* as "the sleeper of the decade" (Cook 2000, 291). As Andrew Sarris noted, "*Rocky* is now regarded by the bottom-line boys as the fight movie to end all fight movies" (Sarris, 1977). Near the close of the century, *Rocky* was voted among the "100 greatest American movies" in a poll conducted by the American Film Institute.

The screen boxer of the late 1970s addressed issues widely felt in the culture. He responded to the challenge to manliness occasioned by the military defeat in Vietnam; to the challenge to masculinity posed by the women's movement; to the economic threat to the middle class as the U.S. economy stagnated; and to the pressure originating with other, subordinate groups—particularly African Americans—felt by the white ethnic working class. Whereas the boxer expressed a liberal ethos critical of dominant values and sympathetic to minority groups during the Depression and after World War II, the cycle of films from the late 1970s shifted this political sensibility. In many respects the contrast between Joe Louis and Muhammad Ali suggests this change. Louis was associated with racial justice and garnered almost universal admiration, especially during and after World War II. Ali was a more complex celebrity, one who simultaneously excited hostility and devotion and embodied the tumultuous changes of his time.

Muhammad Ali's comeback was the boxing highlight of the 1970s. During Ali's first reign as heavyweight champion, from 1964 to 1967, he dominated all contenders. Nonetheless, he excited controversy and hatred because of his embrace of the militant politics of the Black Muslims. In 1967, Ali was stripped of his crown for refusing to be drafted during the Vietnam War; his trial resulted in a fine of $10,000 and a five-year prison sentence. During the next four years of legal appeals, Ali became a spokesman for the politics of social change, denouncing racism and the Vietnam War. In October 1970, Ali's boxing license was reinstated, and a title fight with the champion, Joe Frazier, was scheduled. The social conflicts then dividing America became associated with the fight. Despite being an African American, Frazier was pegged as a representative of tradition, the white man's champ by Ali and by the press. For his part, Ali, a black separatist and a war resister who proclaimed his opposition to prevailing values, spoke for the counterculture. On March 8, 1971, Ali lost a fifteen-round decision to Joe Frazier in one of the most socially resonant championship bouts in boxing history (Sammons 1988, 212–14). Later that year, the U.S. Supreme Court ruled unanimously to overturn Ali's conviction for draft evasion. Many came to admire Ali for making economic sacrifices for his political beliefs. Furthermore, the public was disenchanted with the Vietnam War, and the Muslims now seemed tame compared to the growing militancy of groups such as the Black Panthers. By the time of Ali's 1974 bout with George Foreman, in which he regained the title, he was a popular favorite. Ali was invited by President Gerald Ford to the White House and was named *Sports Illustrated*'s "Sportsman of the Year." Just as Joe Louis influenced the boxing film of the classical era, Muhammad Ali became a catalyst for the comeback of the screen boxer in the 1970s. His personification of black pride resonated with the ethos of the blaxploitation films. A poster of Ali was conspicuously displayed in *Hammer*. One of Ali's boxing alter egos, Ken Norton, played the boxer in *Mandingo*. The cinema had to produce the greatest "white hope" to combat Ali. And Rocky Balboa, who fought champion Apollo Creed, a thinly veiled surrogate Ali, embodied that hope in *Rocky*. As Sylvester Stallone explained, "*Rocky* came out of that fight between Wepner and Ali....And of course Apollo Creed was a thinly disguised impersonation of Ali. If Ali didn't exist, I don't think people would have bought the premise of *Rocky*. But the fact that Ali did exist gave the film validity ..." (Hauser 1991, 301).

In the films of the 70s cycle, boxing is typically associated with the values of a racial, ethnic, or class community. A veteran fighter finds his identity challenged in a decisive ring battle with an outsider, and he must make a comeback to assert his self-worth. *Rocky*'s commercial success prompted the pathos of *The Champ* (1979) and the four *Rocky* sequels. Though genres typically are united around similar dramatic conflicts, the expression and resolution of those conflicts varies across the field. A group of boxing comedies that mocked the ring sport and its primitive masculinity arose in opposition to the sentiment found in *Rocky* and *The Champ*. *The Main Event* was the most conspicuous of these productions, while the "Dynamite Hands" segment of *Movie, Movie* supplied a well-observed parody. Whereas *Rocky* and *The Champ* express a conservative ethos, the boxing comedies display a more liberal sensibility. Clint Eastwood combines pathos and humor in *Every Which Way But Loose* and *Any Which Way You Can*. These contrasting attitudes also contribute to the complexity of Martin Scorsese's *Raging Bull*. This biography film of middleweight champion Jake La Motta mixes genre conventions with the aesthetics of the art cinema and is, for many, the stellar achievement of the Hollywood boxing film genre.

The boxing film of the 1970s arose from the conventions of the classic fight film, but it developed distinctive traits. As Noël Carroll explains, "[T]he reworking evokes a historical genre and its associated myths, commonplaces, and meanings in order to generate expression through the friction between the old and the new" (Carroll, 1998, 245). Though the plot features the various elements of the standard rise and fall pattern, a "comeback" variation, which follows the fighter's attempt to revive his career, was conspicuous during this cycle. The genre, like the boxer himself, sought to compete once again. Classic films, such as *The Champ* (1931) and *The Set-Up*, used an understated comeback motif, but *Fat City*, *Rocky*, *The Champ* (1979), and *The Main Event* gave the comeback fresh prominence. The motif recalls Muhammad Ali, who regained the heavyweight championship twice in the 1970s. The comeback also had social implications. Rivalry with resurgent and competing racial and ethnic groups replaces the villainous gangster promoter, who represented harsh forces of the market in the 1930s and 1940s. Rocky Balboa's beleaguered Italian-American loses his gym locker to an African American, faces a black television interviewer's onslaught of questions, and is threatened with humiliation in the ring by Apollo Creed. Resistance of outsider threats to the native community replaces the problem of assimilation. Rather than exhibiting the progressive ethos of the Popular Front era, the 1970s boxer displayed a backward look, often longing to return to values that prevailed before the movement for racial justice and the Vietnam War. New literary influences, so formative during the classic era, lacked force. Celebrated works, such as *The Great White Hope* and *Fat City*, failed to retain an audience when they were made into movies. Classic movies, from *The Champ* through *Somebody Up There Likes Me*, served as bases for the most successful productions. As a result, the boxing films of the 1970s exhibited a nostalgic, old-fashioned, even retrograde quality.

Gender problems also helped create an audience for these films. Anxiety over changing gender roles and the demands of the women's movement is conspicuous in the 1970s boxing film. The economic threat posed by the Depression and the scars of World War II had prompted the boxer's torment during the classic era, when female characters often embodied these fears. However, during the 1970s cycle, women themselves were the problem. Opposition between the neighborhood sweetheart and the scheming vamp no longer presented women along a moral divide. Some women, like the TV newswoman in *Rocky*, abandoned traditional female roles. Sympathetic companions, such as Lucy (Jill Ireland) in *Hard Times*, became too demanding despite the modesty of their requests. Seducers like Lynn (Sondra Locke) in *Every Which Way But Loose* were puzzling to the point of mystery. The boxer no longer attracted a forceful, dynamic companion like Lorna in *Golden Boy* or Peg (Lilli Palmer) in *Body and Soul*. Instead, *Rocky* features the timid Adrian, and *Every Which Way But Loose* picks up the compliant Echo (Beverly D'Angelo). The boxer frequently retreats into self-sufficiency or anchors himself in the male world rather than pursuing romance. This movement points to the new character of the ring protagonist.

The 1970s boxer continues to be a working-class laborer, but one with a more primal, unreflective character. There are no more wise guys like Joe Bonaparte in *Golden Boy*, Charlie Davis in *Body and Soul*, or Midge Kelly in *Champion*. Neither does the boxer move toward an epiphany, like Terry Malloy (Marlon Brando) in *On the Waterfront*. Instead, an intensified innocence, reminiscent of Frank Capra's Mr. Smith or Joe Pendleton from *Here Comes Mr. Jordan*, becomes the standard affect. The psychic struggle that Robert Wise uses to deepen character in *The Set-Up* and *Somebody Up There Likes Me* is exchanged for an emphasis on the body. Charles Bronson, Sylvester Stallone, and Clint Eastwood give the boxer's physical presence new stature. Training often features body building and jogging to build up the physique, rather than sparring. Instead of recognizing the ephemeral nature of the body and turning to spiritual values, the boxer allies himself with horses, cats, or orangutans. Such alliances associate the boxer with the strength, loyalty, grace, and simplicity of animals. In casting aside sophistication, the boxer becomes more than a brute. He aspires to an almost Franciscan sense of physical innocence without a calculating intelligence or psychic complexity. The trend develops into a retrograde longing for childhood, for a time before confusing adult problems take hold. The body versus soul conflict fades, as the physical becomes an avenue to an elevating simplicity.

Ali's comeback influenced the boxing film revival of the 1970s, but it wasn't consonant with it. These films wrestle with social issues and cinematic tradition that arose from a backward look. On the whole, the boxing films of that era tried to stare down the disillusionment resulting from the social turmoil of the 1960s and fight back social change. The result was an unusual mixture of pathos and humor, a concern for innocence and for the body, and a puzzling look at the growing cultural divide between men and women. These social and aesthetic forces established the context for one of the most complex and celebrated films of the "New Hollywood," *Raging Bull*.

THE BOXER IN THE 1990S: DOCUMENTARY AND POSTMODERN CLUSTERS

No hit boxing movie released since the 1970s has influenced a cycle of films like *The Champ* (1931), *Kid Galahad* (1937), *Body and Soul*, and *Rocky* influenced the boxing films of their respective eras. However, the 1990s did produce two notable, almost contrary, developments in the boxing film: first, a series of award-winning documentaries—*The Fallen Champ: The Untold Story of Mike Tyson* (1993), *When We Were Kings* (1996), and *On the Ropes* (1999)—looked for fresh stories in the lives of actual boxers, and second, baroque, postmodern treatments of the boxer in *Pulp Fiction* (1994) and *Fight Club* (1999) self-consciously played with the formulas of an established tradition.

The boxing documentaries developed dramatic narratives around compelling personalities whose experience intersected with the conventions of the boxing fiction film. *The Fallen Champ* functions like a noir biography of Mike Tyson, in which the stellar athlete rises from the ghetto only to be brought down by vamps, crooked promoters, and his own undisciplined aggression. *When We Were Kings* portrays the Muhammad Ali–George Foreman championship bout of 1974 as a rousing underdog comeback worthy of *Rocky*. *On the Ropes* presents a trainer at a Brooklyn gym and three of his fighters, including a woman, as they each use boxing to build their self-esteem and struggle to escape from poverty. Unlike the champions Tyson and Ali, the heartbreaking failures of these fighters overshadow their modest success. Each documentary was motivated by distinct circumstances: *The Fallen Champ* was made quickly for a television network that sought a timely response to controversy; *When We Were Kings* evolved slowly from a concert film into an homage to a boxing legend; and *On the Ropes* arose from everyday experience, and its intimate perspective on common people was far from the cult of champions celebrated in the other two films. No common cause links these productions.

The controversy surrounding former heavyweight champion Mike Tyson's trial for rape generated *The Fallen Champ*. Tri-star TV executive Diane Sokolow invited the distinguished documentary filmmaker Barbara Kopple to provide a woman's perspective on the champion and a convicted felon in a feature planned for NBC television. Kopple established her reputation with Academy Award winning documentaries about labor struggles, *Harlan County, USA* (1976) and *American Dream* (1990). Investigation of a celebrity athlete seemed foreign to the class struggle, leftist politics, and "direct cinema" style that distinguished Kopple's earlier work, but the volatile mix of race and feminism, and politics and sport must have tantalized the director. Tri-star imposed a tight deadline on the Tyson project, and Kopple needed to complete the film before the controversy surrounding the boxer faded from public memory. A collection of fight films, press conferences, TV news broadcasts, and other found footage of Tyson provided the foundation for the film. As a result, *The Fallen Champ* is largely a compilation of footage supplemented by interviews and evocative location imagery (Feaster 1992, 45). The documentary was first broadcast on February 12, 1993, about a year after Tyson went to jail. The work presents various, often contrary, opinions that the filmmaker holds in a delicate balance. The film enjoyed multiple broadcasts on both network and cable television, and the strong critical reception culminated in Barbara Kopple being honored with the 1994 Director's Guild of America award for "Outstanding Achievement in Documentary."

When We Were Kings had a much more extended and convoluted history. Leon Gast, a New York filmmaker and still photographer, was commissioned to shot the three-day music festival that was to precede the 1974 heavyweight championship bout between George Foreman and Muhammad Ali. The plan was to produce a concert film conceived as an African American Woodstock shot in the "direct cinema" style. However, four days before the title fight, George Foreman received a cut over his eye while training, an event that required the bout to be delayed for six weeks. The concert went ahead as scheduled, but the tie-in with the fight was aborted and the audience small. Nonetheless, Gast and his crew remained in Zaire for two months, filming both the music festival and extensive footage of the boxers and their entourages as everyone lingered owing to the delay. Over 300,000 feet of film was shot, but financing for the concert movie dried up. Gast gradually paid off the lab bills for his footage and for twenty-two years nursed plans to finance the completion of the project. In 1989, David Sonenberg, a successful talent manager in the music business, raised money for the production, and over the next six years he and Gast put together eight different versions. Finally, they decided to shift the focus onto Muhammad Ali and acquired additional fight footage and archival material to frame the story around the boxing champion. Sonenberg also added two new songs at the close of the film, "When We Were Kings" and "Rumble in the Jungle." Then in 1995 Taylor Hackford joined the team and convinced members to stage additional contemporary interviews. The final ingredient, a screening at the Sundance Film Festival, drew seventeen offers to distribute the motion picture. Its successful theatrical run culminated in an Academy Award for Best Documentary Feature" in 1997 (*When We Were Kings* 1996, 14–19).

Nanette Burstein and Brett Morgen were film students at New York University's Tisch School when they began *On The Ropes*. Burstein met her subjects at the Bedford-Stuyvesant gym, where she was training as a boxer in the same neighborhood that produced Mike Tyson. The filmmakers used a school camera to shoot their subjects over two years, during which George Walton initiated his career as a professional boxer, Tyrene Manson competed for a Golden Gloves title until her conviction on a drug crime, and Noel Santiago sought the discipline necessary for success in the ring. Working in the "direct cinema" style, the two filmmakers recorded a wealth of intimate dramatic footage. The engaging material gained the novice filmmakers the support of veteran documentary editor Nancy Baker (*Harlan County USA, Streetwise*), financing to complete their feature documentary, and theatrical distribution. Upon release the film won the award for "Best Documentary Feature" from the Directors Guild of America, an award from the International Documentary Association, and an Academy Award nomination.

These films bear witness to the conjunction between the documentary and the boxing fiction film. Numerous boxing films had already incorporated documentary footage of boxing to lend their fiction veracity, as in *Iron Man* (1931), *Golden Boy*, and most conspicuously, *The Joe Louis Story*, in which newsreels of Louis's fights constitute a substantial part of the film. Furthermore, the boxing biography film tradition represented by *Gentleman Jim*, *Somebody Up There Likes Me*, and *Raging Bull* presents a ready link between nonfiction and the fiction tradition upon which productions such as *The Fallen Champ* drew. In the 1990s filmmakers turned to actual boxers in search of fresh stories from the ring to help generate an experimental stage in the development of the genre. As a result, in the following years these successful documentaries would influence the shape of boxing fiction films. The next decade saw a big budget biography film, *Ali* (2001) that drew on *When We Were Kings*. *Undisputed* (2002) modeled its antagonist on Mike Tyson's prison term. And *Girlfight* (2000) parallels aspects of Tyrene Manson's career taken from *On the Ropes*.

As a group these documentaries present a mixed view of boxing's relationship to the oppressed poor, particularly African Americans. *When We Were Kings* shows Ali as a soulful leader of the African American community seeking his roots in Africa. In *On the Ropes* boxing is portrayed, in part, as a search for self-esteem and identity—even if the sport's economic rewards are negligible. *On the Ropes* presents redemptive stories in which the transformation of characters is left unresolved or stillborn. By contrast, *The Fallen Champ* portrays boxing as another form of victimization that prevents the fighter from understanding social oppression or coming to terms with his inner demons.

The common features of the boxing drama foster a variable understanding of the sport's social significance. In addition, each film draws upon established conventions and conflicts familiar from the boxing film, both of which lend these documentaries an impact similar to that associated with fiction films.

✦ ✦ ✦

While documentaries returned the boxing genre to an exploratory stage, searching for fresh material in the lives of boxers, a parallel trend emphasized self-conscious play with the conventions of the genre. The baroque strategies of these films pointed to a genre that had exhausted its subject and was merely spinning out formal pirouettes. Here the sensibility was cynical rather than earnest, knowing rather than innocent, decadently complex rather than straightforward and honest. The genre was moving in opposite directions simultaneously. It was difficult to recognize that *Pulp Fiction* and *Fight Club* arose from the same tradition as *When We Were Kings*.

Many wonder at a claim that *Pulp Fiction* and *Fight Club* are boxing films. Both movies seem far removed from our expectations of the genre, yet each plays with elements central to the tradition. *Pulp Fiction* offers the clearer case. The underworld vengeance plot arises from a double cross in a fixed fight. Butch (Bruce Willis), a ring veteran, is paid off by the mobster Marcellus (Ving Rhames) to throw a bout. Instead, the boxer knocks out his opponent, makes a big gambling score, and prepares to skip town. Marcellus sends Vincent (John Travolta) to murder Butch; instead, the boxer kills the enforcer. However, circumstances soon find Butch and Marcellus allied in captivity. After Butch rescues the mobster, Marcellus absolves the fighter of his earlier betrayal, and allows him to escape from the criminal underworld. A boxer and a bout are central to *Pulp Fiction*, and the film plays upon the familiar conventions of the genre, as when *Pulp Fiction*, though a showcase for violence, teases its audience by keeping its bout off screen, when most boxing films build up to their featured ring spectacle.

Fight Club uses amateur, bare-knuckle bouts, as featured in *Hard Times* and *Every Which Way But Loose*, as an incubator for manhood. More central is the forlorn narrator who regains his masculinity through the recklessness, aggression, and suffering of fistfights. The experience overcomes the alienation of consumer culture and returns men to primal bonding in an underground cult of boxing. In *Fight Club*, a masculinity crisis acts as a benchmark for a wider challenge to the culture, and boxing becomes the key step in a primitive cure. Allusions to the boxing film invoke an earlier, more innocent cinema unschooled in the sophisticated play of forms evident in *Pulp Fiction* and *Fight Club*.

Postmodernism's self-conscious mixing of elements develops a baroque style in these boxing films. The postmodernist sensibility emphasizes heterogeneity, rather than trying to smoothly integrate new hybrid elements with older conventions. So the gaps between disparate conventions are apparent, and the unity of the work gives way to an off-balance, at times startling, play with form. Quentin Tarantino explains, "The starting point is, you get these genre characters in these genre situations that you've seen before in other movies, but then all of a sudden out of nowhere they're plunged into real-life rules" (Tarantino/Smith 1994, 34). The postmodernist gesture to the boxing film is distinct from a parody like "Dynamite Hands," but it also displays a conspicuous historical understanding.

Another postmodern trait is the complexity, even disorderliness, of design that contributes to shifts in tone, self-conscious style, and an uncertain meaning. The complex narrative organization of *Pulp Fiction* plays with temporal sequence, so that it is difficult to understand the causal connection between events. Most jarringly, Vincent, a leading character, is killed halfway through, only to reappear and play a significant role later in the film—but earlier in the temporal sequence of events. These complications undermine our expectations and leave us off balance. A shifting tone complements the mix of time—playful jokes, adolescent humor, and trivial conversation blend with matters of life and death. Underworld thugs philosophically debate in detail issues of ethics, metaphysics, and existential values while illustrating their arguments with banal references to popular culture, such as the comparative worth of different brands of fast food burgers. Seemingly significant mysteries, such as the glowing contents of a briefcase that characters fight and die to protect, are never revealed; at the same time these enigmas allude to Hollywood crime films of another era, for example the briefcase is reminiscent of another such item in *Kiss Me Deadly*. In similar fashion, *Fight Club* transforms the status of leading characters from substantial to imaginary and the consequences of shootings from lethal to annoying. At the center of the film is an unreliable narrator whose mentor and partner turns out to be nothing more than a phantom alter ego. The landscape of consumer culture and psychotherapy babble becomes a dungeon imprisoning the protagonist in his own twisted stream of consciousness. In the end, the effects of narrative action seem arbitrary and confusing.

In spite of the disorderliness and uncertainty in *Pulp Fiction* and *Fight Club*, both films feature visual bravado and cinematic craft that testify to refined artistry. As a result, jarring, contrary elements cannot be dismissed as simply incoherent. This approach has produced an enormous range of reactions and interpretation, ranging from extravagant praise and detailed explication to condemnation for being utterly corrupt and cynical. While playing with the conventions and imagery of the boxing film, *Pulp Fiction* and *Fight Club* move beyond the boundaries of the genre and stake out new territory for expression. Both films invite repeated viewing and careful interpretation. For more detailed commentary, see chapters six and seven below.

The contest between documentary and postmodern influences in the boxing film brings the genre to a provocative intersection at the end of the twentieth century. The boxing film is an important player in the history of Hollywood cinema. The plots, characters, setting, emotional address, and dramatic conflicts at work in *Kid Galahad*, *Body and Soul*, and *Rocky* are part of our national film heritage. And that heritage continues to serve as the basis for films in the twenty-first century, which has already produced *Girlfight*, *Ali*, *Million Dollar Baby*, and *Cinderella Man*. There seems no reason to expect that the boxing film will fade from view. Rather, the vocabulary developed by these movies stands ready to spark future hits and fresh cycles of production.

3

"DOWN FOR THE COUNT"
Critique of the Success Ethic in the Boxing Film

The foundation of film genres rests upon social problems shaped into dramatic conflicts. Among the most long-standing conflicts in American culture is that between competitive individualism and self-sacrifice for the common good. Competitive individualism is closely linked to "the American Dream" that one can gain wealth, power, and social position through fair compensation for hard work and talent. The myth of Horatio Alger hinges on this "Dream," which famously employs market forces to provide an anonymous means for distributing rewards and enforcing punishment, like Adam Smith's "invisible hand." Self-sacrifice is usually associated with our Judeo-Christian heritage and family values. In the boxing film, the contest in the ring became an analogue for market competition and individual struggles for dominance. The rise of the boxing film in the 1930s coincided with the failure of the market system during the Depression. As a result, the boxing film presented an evolving critique of the American success ethic and often promoted contrasting values. However, the nature of that critique changed with the development of the genre and shifts in cultural attitudes

During the Depression cycle, *The Life of Jimmy Dolan* (1933) clearly presents the conflict between competitive individualism and self-sacrifice. The film portrays an alternative to the success ethic in a movement westward and a return to the land. A home for crippled children embodies self-sacrifice and serves as the inspiration for the boxer's renewal. After World War II, the noir *Champion*

(1949) intensifies the critique of the success ethic by turning the boxer into a ruthless anti-hero who cynically betrays friends, family, and lovers in his quest for success. Though the boxer is doomed, the film provides no viable alternative to a frenzied competition. *Every Which Way But Loose* (1978) uses comedy to undermine middle-class respectability and challenge common formulas for success. The Clint Eastwood film struggles to relax into a crude working-class highway culture, but only generates a discomforting anxiety. *The Fallen Champ: The Untold Story of Mike Tyson* (1993) views the success ethic from the perspective of the African American community, seeing it as a spectacle of dread that divides an embattled people. The boxing film genre uses changing historical perspectives to express the ongoing ambivalence in American culture toward market values and the success ethic.

THE LIFE OF JIMMY DOLAN (1933): ALTRUISTIC VALUES TRIUMPH OVER THE SUCCESS ETHIC

The Life of Jimmy Dolan portrays an early instance of the critique of the success ethnic in the boxing film. Here the boxer is a jaded materialist who undergoes a rebirth into a self-sacrificing communitarian. The film begins as the competitive individual triumphs. Jimmy (Douglas Fairbanks, Jr.) knocks out his opponent to win the light heavyweight title. After his victory, the Champ presents himself to the press as a model athlete devoted to his mother and promoting clean living. However, during a later private celebration, the boxer is exposed as a fast-living cynic with a bottle in hand and a blonde on his arm. Dolan trusts no one and endorses platitudes to exploit the gullible public. When a reporter sneaks into the Champ's quarters and threatens to blow his cover, the boxer strikes his adversary, and the journalist falls and hits his head, then dies. The Champ immediately dozes off, too drunk to recognize his jeopardy. Panic stricken, his manager, Doc Woods, and Goldie West, the boxer's woman, pack Jimmy into a car and drive him out of town to his training camp. There they scheme to depart together, rob the obnoxious pug, and leave him for the police, but in attempting a getaway their car crashes and explodes into flames. Inspecting the wreck, the police conclude that it was Dolan, not the manager, who died, and they close the murder case. Once the boxer awakens and discovers his predicament, he flees to his attorney for help. The attorney double crosses him, steals his remaining savings, and convinces him to change his name and go on the lam to avoid capture. Frightened and destitute, the boxer assumes the name Jack Dougherty and tramps west. The boxer's cynicism is realized in all the grim particulars of his fall.

The name change and return to nature both signal the boxer's rebirth. Broken and ill, Jack stumbles onto a western farm run as a home for crippled children by Peggy (Loretta Young) and her Auntie, Mrs. Moore (Aline MacMahon). The two women take Jack in and nurse him back to health. During his recovery, the boxer becomes one with the caring farm family, and when he discovers that the home is threatened with foreclosure, he decides to try to raise the money needed to save it by fighting a touring professional. But his plan is derailed when a police detective, Phlaxer (Guy Kibbee), arrives to investigate the whereabouts of the murder suspect, Jimmy Dolan. In order to avoid discovery Jack hides his boxing prowess, particularly his distinctive southpaw style, but the detective eventually sees through his disguise. Masking his championship skills in order to avoid arrest, Jimmy takes a terrible beating in the ring, but he manages to hang on for four rounds and win the two thousand dollars needed to save the farm. Nevertheless, the police detective apprehends Dolan and prepares to take him back to face charges. But once the detective witnesses Peggy's and Mrs. Moore's gratitude, he begins to reconsider his decision. Finally, Phlaxer recognizes that the cynical boxer has indeed become a new man, and he frees Jack to remain and marry Peggy.

The Life of Jimmy Dolan portrays values that would remain central to the boxing film for the next fifty years. The boxer's physical triumph is allied to a moral crisis that the narrative resolves, ending with a physical punishment in the ring that becomes part of a spiritual rebirth. In 1933 this modest production appeared fresh to the contemporary press. *Variety* called the film a "neat, sure-footed picture," noting that the boxer's "regeneration is rather different from that of the average picture pug" (Char. 1933, 11). Mordaunt Hall in the *New York Times* agrees, noting that the film follows "a different trend from the average chronicle concerned with a fighting Adonis" (Hall 1933, 22). Years later Roger Dooley concurred that *Jimmy Dolan* broke the formula set in this cycle of boxing films by *Iron Man* (Dooley 1981, 252). The freshness of the former arises from the film's critique of the success ethnic and its promotion of alternative values.

The Life of Jimmy Dolan first portrays the boxer as corrupted and then engineers a transformation made possible by his departure from the ring. The film mixes elements from boxing films dating from earlier in the 1930s cycle. As in *The Champ* and *Iron Man*, the boxer is plagued by limitations. But in *Jimmy Dolan*, weakness arises from a callous individualism in which money provides the only basis for cooperation, and in which even one's closest associates are poised for a betrayal whenever it is to their advantage. The earlier pictures portray the pug's demise and leave him a broken man. In contrast, *Jimmy Dolan* ends with a positive resolution after combining the downtrodden fighter with elements similar to those used in *Winner Take All*: the trip west from the city to a healing place close to nature, and the single woman with an ailing child, here multiplied into a brood of crippled waifs. The transformation of the cynical boxer into a loving companion willing to undertake a selfless endeavor seems appropriate in the months following Franklin Roosevelt's inauguration and the birth of the New Deal—particularly at Warner Brothers, a studio openly sympathetic to the new administration.

Significantly, the boxer does not simply find renewal in romance with Peggy, but in a larger communitarian endeavor, the home for crippled children. Peggy tutors the tramp in the ideals of the home and chides him for his talk of "rackets" and "suckers." In self-sacrifice Jack finds his redemption. *The Life of Jimmy Dolan* expresses an ethos typical of its historical moment, contrasting the cynical individualism of the boxer Dolan with the new communitarian ideals of Jack Dougherty. The cynicism associated with boxing, the city, and urban decadence finds its source in "the roaring twenties," the triumph of the individual "go-getter," the relaxation of personal morality during Prohibition, the sports culture that found its idol in Jack Dempsey. The fall from champion to fugitive parallels the boom-to-bust experienced by the American economy. Jack Dougherty is a figure of the Depression, a man who climbed to the top of his profession, who depended only upon himself, and then lost everything. His identity evaporates along with his possessions. Broke and humiliated, he becomes a tramp. His fall leaves him fearful and ashamed, feelings which cultural historian Warren Sussman argues characterized the American people during the Depression (Sussman 1984, 193–95).

As an image of the workingman victimized by the Great Depression, *Jimmy Dolan* is related to the protagonist from *I Am a Fugitive From a Chain Gang* (1932). Upon leaving his attorney's office with no choice but to lose himself on the road, Jimmy cowers in a building's shadow, lowers the brim of his fedora, and turns up the collar of his coat, becoming the humiliated everyman hiding in the crowd. However, in contrast to *I Am a Fugitive From a Chain Gang*, *Jimmy Dolan* gives its hero a mission and a benign father figure, Phlaxer, who finally recognizes and rewards the boxer's regeneration. The solution to the working man's crisis lies in the West, with a return to the farm, a farm which represents not the independent Jeffersonian model, but a social commitment to helping others crippled by circumstance. In its closing scene the film associates the communitarian ideal with an older, preindustrial tradition, even as the New Deal sought to ally its reforms to longstanding American values. As they are about to part at the train station, the detective Phlaxer accuses Dolan of being a "sucker" for helping orphans. He dismisses these acts as only fit for an 1894 melodrama, old fashioned "sob stuff." But when Dolan embraces the charge, claiming that in spite of his capture he would "do it all again," the detective, convinced that Dolan is a new man, admits, "[M]aybe I got the wrong guy." The policeman catches the train alone, waving goodbye to "Dougherty." *The Life of Jimmy Dolan* responds to the pathetic failures of the boxer in *The Champ* and *Iron Man* by criticizing the cynical individualism of the "success ethic" and offering a communitarian ideal in its place. In this respect it becomes a harbinger of later developments; the film itself would be remade in 1939 as *They Made Me a Criminal*.

CHAMPION (1949): IRONY AND THE ANTI-HERO

The critique of the success ethic arose in the boxing film as a response to the economic crisis of the Great Depression. A heartless competition linked market forces to an analogue in the boxing ring, and then to the ruthless gangster promoter. The refinements of the film noir cycle darkened and intensified this theme. The gangster promoter was transformed from a thug into a powerful businessman who, though apparently respectable, uses intimidation, stealth, and violence to assert his dominance. The figure suggests an intersection between big business and crime. During the noir cycle, a complicated psychology contributes to the fighter's moral ambivalence, especially his attraction to evil. The complexity of the noir style adds to the labyrinth that traps the boxer.

Champion was among the most successful films in the boxing noir cycle. The Stanley Kramer production grossed $3 million in the domestic market after a cost of $450,000, becoming a substantial hit and a very profitable film in a year of broad declines in revenues throughout the film industry (Eder 1992). *Champion* garnered Academy Award nominations for best actor (Kirk Douglas), best supporting actor (Arthur Kennedy), best screenplay (Carl Foreman), best black and white cinematography (Frank Planer), and best musical scoring (Dimitri Tiomkin), and it won the award for best film editing (Harry Gerstad). The commercial and critical success almost duplicated the record set by *Body and Soul* two years earlier.

In *Champion*, the noir critique of the success ethic develops from its source in Ring Lardner's famous short story, "Champion" (1916). The Lardner tale is a satiric comment on the Horatio Alger success story. In Lardner a brute becomes a champion boxer, but the public refuses to relinquish its heroic preconceptions about the success ethic. Lardner's Midge Kelly begins by beating his crippled brother and abusing his mother, and continues his villainy unabated. The writer employs humor in portraying the scoundrel's progress and closes ironically, as

The noir anti-hero in *Champion* (1949) darkens the success ethic. Courtesy of the Academy of Motion Picture Arts and Sciences.

the sports press praises the despicable champion. Carl Foreman, the screenwriter, explained that he needed a more complex and sympathetic protagonist to sustain a feature film (Lambert 1949, 132). The motion picture deploys psychological drama in place of Lardner's satire. However, the film maintains the story's ironical perspective in criticizing the success ethic—albeit in a tone distinct from that of the short story.

Irony involves a split in the meaning of the sign, for example, Lardner's champion, far from being a model for behavior, is demonic. The short story uses a humorous incongruity between what the success ethic imagines a champion should be and what he is. The author amplifies this split with comic detachment. The film develops a somber psychological tone, employing repetition and reversal to invest identical acts with fresh, and sometimes contrary, meanings. Here the lineage of Hemingway's "Fifty Grand" is evident. Though the Hemingway story avoids psychologizing, it deploys irony in its conclusion as Jack Brennan scores a victory by assuring his own defeat. Hemingway's boxer also suggests the anti-heroic, though the tension between glorification and critique is handled with greater subtlety than in *Champion*. Nonetheless, the pattern of repetition and reversal in *Champion* is dense and meaningful. An evocative early example occurs during Emma's second rendezvous with Midge. She internalizes her father's accusation that she is "sneakin' around," telling Kelly that she feels "sneaky," and when her lover replies to her suggestion that they marry by answering that it would be "bad for both of them," she repeats "bad" giving it an introspective, moral inflection contrary to Midge's intent. This division functions in a manner distinct from that employed in Lardner's tale, but it invests the film with a dark irony. Through a shifting perspective arising from repetition and reversal, *Champion* portrays the conflict between competitive individualism and altruistic values.

Champion highlights the anti-hero in the boxing film. While adapting the typical story of the pug's rise to the title, the plot parallels the fighter's growing athletic prowess with his moral decline. Midge Kelly (Kirk Douglas) is a noir cousin of Charlie Davis from *Body and Soul*, but important distinctions arise between the two fighters. Charlie is a decent guy victimized by circumstances who finally breaks free from the forces corrupting him. Midge, in contrast, becomes inflamed with a desire to assault those who have exploited him, and he embraces the behavior of a scoundrel. The boxer fires his fatherly manager, deserts his wife, and betrays his brother. Eventually Midge uses everyone, whether ally or enemy, in his climb to the top. In *Champion*'s noir vision the boxer internalizes the gangster. The noir anti-hero offers a critique of the success ethic through negation.

The plot is neatly organized around the three acts or phases in the boxer's career. The first portrays the failure of the American Dream. In the second, the protagonist takes up boxing and rises to become champion. In the final act, he falls. Each act features a different "romance" for the boxer, and each pairing involves a paternal male authority that contrasts with Midge Kelly. Furthermore, Johnny Dunne (John Daheim), a middleweight contender and idealized male, appears to challenge Kelly's prowess in each of the three acts. The three romances emphasize the fighter's growing physical attraction in contrast to his deteriorating sensibility. The dominant formal device is a series of evocative repetitions and reversals that cultivate dramatic irony.

In act one, Midge and his brother, Connie (Arthur Kennedy) set out to achieve the dream of success only to be victimized. Tramping west to claim a share they purchased in a roadside diner, the brothers are assaulted and robbed in a boxcar. Destitute, Midge is lured into prizefighting by the promise of easy money in Kansas City, but an experienced pug thrashes the amateur, and then a crooked promoter cheats Midge out of his fee. Upon arriving in Los Angeles, the Kelly brothers discover that their business prospect is a fraud, and the two end up serving customers rather than running an eatery. Though ready with his fists, Midge loses fights on the train and in the ring. His romance, too, proves to be an alluring prospect transformed into a trap. At the diner, Midge flirts with the waitress Emma (Ruth Roman), the owner's daughter. Confessing to her during an evening rendezvous, Midge tells of being abandoned by his father; poor and helpless he dreamed of finding his old man and beating his head off. Now he knows that it is "every man for himself." Midge declares his determination to get somewhere, to make money, to be somebody. Emma's sympathy rises because she too was abandoned by her mother. Emma's father, Lew, bitter because of his wife's desertion, crushes the younger couple's budding passion by insisting on a shot-gun wedding. Cornered again, Midge runs off after the wedding in spite of his bride's devotion. The romance continues Midge's victimization and emphasizes the grim consequences of ruthless individualism. Mutual victimization draws the couple together, but they respond differently. Midge readies himself to become as harsh as the world he encounters and prepares to strike back. Emma blames herself, sinks into despair, and harbors an unrequited love for the fighter.

Act two begins with Midge and Connie finding a good father who guides their rising fortunes. Tommy Haley (Paul Stewart), the boxing manager, first spots Midge when the fighter takes a beating in Kansas City and offers to train the feisty youngster. After fleeing his marriage, Kelly heads for the gym. During their second encounter, Tommy discourages Midge: "The fight business stinks. Go home." But Kelly insists, and Tommy agrees to guide the novice. The manager shepherds his boxer's climb until Midge arrives in New York City, a contender. Tommy arranges a fight with Johnny Dunne, the leading challenger for the middleweight crown, who Midge first encountered as the headliner in Kansas City. However, in order to get the benefit of a premiere bout, Kelly must agree to lose so Dunne's title shot will be assured. Always at Dunne's side is an "expensive" blond, Grace Diamond (Marilyn Maxwell), who snubs Midge. The slight infuriates Midge, who violates his promise and knocks out Dunne.

This indiscretion blocks the fighter's progress: He is attacked by thugs and then banned from the ring by insiders. Nonetheless, Grace soon becomes the victor's prize. In order to smooth the route to the middleweight title, Grace engineers a switch in managers, prodding Midge to break with Tommy and sign with Jerry Harris (Luis Van Rooten), a businessman who controls the fight racket. Harris guarantees Kelly a title shot. After Tommy's dismissal, Connie, outraged at Midge's betrayal, leaves his brother. Soon Midge has the crown. His rise culminates in the good father being thrown over by the self-seeking vamp. No longer a victim, Midge ruthlessly dominates those around him. The pattern of act one has been reversed: A benign father and a heartless gold-digger are substituted for bad fathers and a good woman; the protagonist is a wiseguy instead of a sucker. In each case, virtue gives way to vice.

The third act includes the boxer's fall. Now a champion, wealthy, powerful, and admired, Midge is free to shape his destiny. He is attracted to Palmer (Lola Albright), the young wife of Jerry Harris. Palmer embodies the art motif, as she dances with the boxer, takes Midge to museums, and invites him to pose for her sculpture. She represents the aspirations of the spirit, but she is degraded by Harris's money. Soon Palmer and Midge are lovers, but the naïve woman is disillusioned when Kelly accepts a payoff from her husband to end the affair. Unlike the import of *Body and Soul*, here the spirit surrenders to the flesh. Again the film poses a counterpoint between the father and romance; now the suave, money manager Harris controls the young artist-wife. Midge turns from love a second time and submits to the father's ugly patrimony. Though Midge Kelly embodies the success ethic, he has become despicable.

The plot of *Champion* is based upon a flashback structure reminiscent of *Body and Soul*, beginning when the Champion goes into the ring for his final title fight and finally circling back to the bout. The plot is designed around a series of repetitions and reversals that expands the flashback into a resonant structure. After accepting Harris's payoff, Kelly must prepare for a title defense against Johnny Dunne, now on the comeback trail. In order to prepare for the challenging rematch, Midge enlists Tommy. The embittered manager agrees to train the fighter in exchange for a large percentage of the purse. Connie, too, experiences reconciliation, befriending Emma and planning to marry her once she secures a divorce from Midge. The cycle of repetition is completed with Midge's second seduction of Emma, followed by an assault on the crippled Connie when his brother protests. The middleweight champion enters the ring surrounded by those he has betrayed: Grace, Harris, Palmer, Connie, Tommy. Even the engaging Johnny Dunne was subjected to Kelly's turn around in their first bout. The punishment Kelly endures in the ring, absorbing a beating round after round, appears to be retribution for the boxer's crimes. But the battered champion comes back in spite of his villainy and knocks out the challenger. But the circle still remains to be closed. Kelly retires to his locker room and, driven out of his mind by the beating, he rants, evoking the past in his death throes. The Champ repeats his joyful locker room outburst from his first ring victory, combined with his anger upon being instructed to throw the first Dunne fight:

> Connie, Connie, we're on our way, Connie. I can tell from the crowd. I can tell every time I hit 'em. . . . Listen, I won the fight. Did you hear that crowd? For the first time in my life, people cheering for me. . . . Are you deaf? Didn't you hear them? We're not hitchhiking anymore. We're riding. Those fat bellies with the big cigars aren't going to make a monkey outa me. I can beat 'em. You know I can beat 'em.

Midge slams a locker with his fist, slows to stare at his broken hand, then reaches out, cries "Tommy" and collapses, dead. At the end, film returns to the sympathetic Midge, building pathos in the audience and reminding us of the suffering that motivated his cruelty. These conflicting emotions complement the repetition and reversal that culminates in the narrative circling back in its resolution to the earliest episodes. In order to revive sympathy for the anti-hero, the viewer needs to understand that the twisted values of the success ethic produced Midge's infamy.

The character split associated with irony is most conspicuous in the matching of the good and bad brothers, Midge the scoundrel and Connie the saint. In many respects this is a tired device, especially since Connie has no function apart from Midge. Their familiarity is emphasized by Arthur Kennedy's already having played the devoted brother to James Cagney's boxer in *City for Conquest*. Connie broadly functions as a constraining conscience for his uninhibited brother. He follows Midge and Emma to the beach and looks longingly on from high ground while the couple cavorts. He expresses reservations when Midge takes pleasure in fighting and later scolds the boxer's betrayals. His crippled leg accentuates the ineffectualness of his attempts to guide his brother. Connie is the boxer's feminine counterpart. After their father ran off, Midge was sent to an orphanage, but Connie stayed with his mother. His feminine name underscores the gendered contrast, and its formal equivalent, Constance, serves as an antithesis to his brother's disloyalty. Connie offers a nurturing, moral, self-conscious, and even passive alter ego to his self-indulgent, aggressive sibling.

Together the two portray a dual perspective on the crisis involving masculinity and the war veteran so widespread in boxing noir. Once Midge's aggressive instinct is rewarded in the ring, he indulges its pleasures and bullies others.

Soon he threatens women and attacks cripples just like he goes after middle-weights. He is reminiscent of the combat veteran so enflamed by violence that he cannot readjust to civil society. By contrast, Connie is the cripple who has become a staple of the genre in the noir period. The Swede has his broken hand in *The Killers*; Ben had his battered brain in *Body and Soul*; Rex inhabits a wheel chair in *Whiplash* (1948). These maimed fighters are a development of the punch-drunk pug and even more closely resemble the blinded Danny Kenny from *City for Conquest*. In a timely fashion, these cripples proliferate in the genre after the war and evoke pathos similar to that excited by veterans maimed in combat.

Midge gains complexity with his shadow brother that reinforces the cathar-sis of his call to Connie at his death. Connie responds in his closing statement, which mixes affirmation and negation: "He was a champion. He went out like a champion. He was a credit to the fight game to the very end." The statement implies that a scoundrel and a champion are one and the same, and that Kelly's behavior arises from the values of the success ethic. Nonetheless, unlike Lard-ner's story, the closing criticizes neither the sports press nor the public, instead affirming Connie's allegiance to his brother. It ends the film on a statement with dual import, underlining dramatic irony as a dominant device in the design of the work.

The reversals skillfully developed by the film serve to highlight character division. Kelly agrees under pressure to throw the first bout with Dunne, but upon experiencing Grace's condescension, he is enraged to the point that he demolishes her paramour in the ring. After Kelly tells Grace that he will be loyal to Tommy, an abrupt shot change finds him in Harris's office ready to sign with a new manager. The most obvious reversal in the film arises from its return to the initial moment of the flashback. The background story under-mines the glorified introduction of the champion, but now we know he is a scoundrel. However, other repetitions, such as Midge's death speech, evoke sympathy for the anti-hero. Again, this circling back establishes a multivalent perspective related to the humorous irony in the Lardner story, now employed for pathos, rather than humor. *Champion* does more than simply introduce the anti-hero to the boxing genre, it deepens character psychology and develops the flashback into a comprehensive pattern of repetition and reversal.

EVERY WHICH WAY BUT LOOSE (1978): MOCKING SUCCESS

The revival of the boxing film in the 1970s brought pronounced change to the genre. Among the most prominent differences was a redefinition of the

Phil Beddo (Clint Eastwood) is a boxer surrounded
by challengers, yet uncertain as to his mission.
Courtesy of the Academy of Motion Picture Arts
and Sciences.

success ethic. The presentation of boxing as an analogue for the competitive
marketplace faded, but the specter of success still haunts these comeback tales.
Rocky anticipated defeat, but wanted to "go the distance" in order to assert his
self-esteem. Though the sharp conflict between market forces and altruistic
values recedes, the boxer still grapples with the motive for, and significance of,
his quest. *Every Which Way But Loose* is remarkable for its overturning of mainstream, middle-class values and affirmation of working-class habits defined by
a post–Vietnam War highway culture. The title points to the uncomfortable
sensibility of a protagonist embattled by challengers, yet uncertain as to his

mission. The result is a film divided by two moods, humor and pathos, that turns from the traditional values of the success ethic.

In *Every Which Way But Loose*, Clint Eastwood, in his biggest box office success to date, plays Philo Beddo, a California trucker who earns extra cash hustling bare-fisted pickup fights, much like the bouts of Chaney in *Hard Times*. This loosely plotted, redneck comedy is organized around Philo's quest for the bare-fisted boxing title, his pursuit of the country-western singer Lynn Halsey-Taylor (Sondra Locke), and a friendship with his orangutan alter ego, Clyde. In addition, Philo fights with the clownish motorcycle gang, the Black Widows, and with a couple of LA cops he crosses in a barroom brawl. The comedy is filled out with his foul-mouthed geriatric ma (Ruth Gordon) and his sidekick brother, Orville (Geoffrey Lewis). Many of Eastwood's advisors at the Malpaso Film Company advised him against filming the screenplay, and Eastwood acknowledged that "Most sane men were skeptical" (Kapsis/Coblentz 1999, 77). In his biography of the star, Richard Schickel reports that when it was first screened for critics the film was considered "unspeakable" (Schickel 1996, 355). *Variety* described the picture as "third rate material," observing, "[T]his film is way off the mark. If people will line up for this one . . . they'll line up for any Clint Eastwood picture" (Hege 1978, 30). David Ansen in *Newsweek* described the film as a "plotless junkheap." Gene Shalit in the *Ladies Home Journal* called it an "unstructured shambles." Rex Reed in the *New York Daily News* labeled the film a "disgrace" (Zmijewsky and Pfeiffer 1988, 208). But Warner executives sensed a hit and backed the film with a strong promotional campaign. The cash rolled in. The modest $3.5 million production brought in $87 million in earnings in 1980. *Every Which Way* opened at Christmas time in 1978, and by the end of 1979 it ranked second in domestic box office for the year, outdistancing *Rocky II* in third place. The boxing film had its second blockbuster hit in three years.

Now that scholars scrutinize Clint Eastwood's career, the *Which Way* movies are treated with measured respect as well as amazement (Smith 1993, 173–80). Indeed, in spite of its vulgar comedy and casual storytelling, *Every Which Way But Loose* made a distinctive contribution to the boxing film. The uncertainty of its tone, with switches from raucous humor to romantic confusion, from burlesque to melancholy, give it a complexity that was initially taken to be incompetence. Now it appears to be much more provocative than the more unified, but predictable sequel *Any Which Way You Can* (1980). Eastwood's widely discussed cultivation of ambiguity in the motivation of his character, again more pronounced in the initial *Which Way* production, invites speculation, which is enriched by its consideration in the context of the actor-director's body of work. Even the film's offensive jokes and ragged continuity contribute to a sympathetic portrait of white working-class culture. Though *Variety* wrote that, "Clearly, this sort of thing exists on a plane either beyond or beneath criticism," careful analysis of the film highlights important underlying values (Cart. 1980, 16).

Every Which Way But Loose establishes a new landscape for working-class culture in the fight film. The Eastwood movie portrays a highway culture based upon the car that replaces the fight film's customary backdrop, a run-down inner city neighborhood. The film begins with Philo trucking along a San Fernando Valley freeway; it ends with him driving his pickup back to California. The yard around Philo's home is littered with vehicles in various states of disrepair. Philo and Orville are regularly found with their heads under the hood or on their backs beneath the engine. Beddo drives a truck; his brother runs a towing service; Ma is constantly trying, but failing, to get her driver's license renewed. More time is spent with characters in cars than in any home. Instead, trailer parks, motels, diners, bars, and even a car wash constitute the landscape of this picture. In discussing his films, Eastwood claims, "The location just has to correspond with the concept of the film, to the atmosphere created by the story" (Kapsis/Coblentz 1999, 63). Here the locale is built around a highway culture in which the trucker is the personification of masculine freedom.

Every Which Way But Loose portrays working-class life as a choice rather than a dead end for failures. By contrast, Joey Popchick of "Dynamite Hands" wants to escape from the ethnic ghetto to become a lawyer. Rocky Balboa hopes to rise from the impoverished surroundings of lower class Philadelphia. But Philo Beddo embraces country-western bars, endless traffic, and roadside commerce. Instead of seeing boxing as a means of improving his social position, he enjoys brawling. The aspiration to climb up from poverty, a motivation central to the classic boxing film, no longer drives the protagonist. Rather, the film's setting is expressive of the people who inhabit it. This vision of a working-class culture independent of demeaning social hierarchy is a fresh element in the boxing film.

In Elliott J. Gorn's study of nineteenth-century prizefighting, *The Manly Art*, he identifies boxing as part of a masculine working-class life exhibiting values distinct from, and resistant to, the respectable middle-class (Gorn 1986, 129–47). His description of prizefighting culture invites comparison with *Every Which Way But Loose*. Gorn finds the saloon at the center of the masculine subculture, where honor and physical prowess serve as keys to manliness. The Eastwood film opens with Philo returning to the work place with his truck, and then immediately departing for a local bar. Before finishing his beer, Beddo exchanges blows with another patron in a quarrel over peanuts and quickly decks the stranger. The fight is so weakly motivated that it lacks dramatic credibility; nonetheless it underlines the role of honor as a catalyst for physical rivalry, one that will soon spark other fights, particularly with the Black Widow motorcycle gang. Throughout the film Philo returns to bars where conviviality can quickly turn to brawling over a minor slight. The film begins by indulging these old-fashioned, lower-class male values.

Gorn emphasizes the contrast between working-class culture and the middle-class in terms of money, gender, and violence. The saloon world glorifies free spending and gambling as demonstrations of loyalty and courage, versus the middle-class emphasis on prosperity, investment, and ownership. The gambling engendered by Philo's pick-up fights and organized by Orville serves as one basis for their brotherhood. The working class elevates a rough conviviality often characterized by drinking, vulgar humor, and brawling, whereas the respectable value the intimacy of family and home, together with the business world, a sober, public domain. The cursing mother, beer drinking orangutan, and fist fighting brothers dismiss middle-class respectability. Finally, Gorn explains that the middle class strives to ban violence, or if necessary, control it. For the working class, violence is an accepted part of experience, cultivated and honored in sports like boxing. Indeed, these qualities distinguish boxing as a product of lower-class life, qualities underlined in the physical comedy of *Every Which Way But Loose*, which thumbs its nose at respectability.

The plot of the film moves between a heroic quest for romance and glory, and comic diversions involving the motorcycle gang, Ma, and the cops. Loose progression arises from the film's extended comic episodes, which undermine the dramatic momentum building around the heroic quests. The two plot lines coexist without being well integrated. Furthermore, these competing plot lines express contrasting moods: raucous humor and masculine pathos. They are paralleled by the Philo/Clyde relationship in which Beddo pursues the heroic while the orangutan serves the humorous. A weak rise and fall pattern emerges as Beddo ascends toward a conclusion which punctures his ambitions, but the comic episodes rescue the film, preventing it from closing on a bleak note.

In his admiring 1983 profile of Clint Eastwood, Norman Mailer highlights *Every Which Way But Loose* as among Eastwood's most important films and asks, "Is it out of measure to call him the most important small town artist in America?" (Mailer 1983, 7). The vulgarity of the film's humor may divert one from its significance, nonetheless social attitudes linked to small town America, or more precisely, the white working-class, resonate through *Every Which Way But Loose*. Philo is positioned between two comic adversaries, the Black Widow motorcycle gang and two L.A. cops. The aging bikers could easily be refugees from *The Wild One* (1954), with youthful delinquency transformed into middle-aged buffoonery. Their mixture of Nazi regalia and hippy long hair add to the caricature of renegade bohemians who bait Philo and bully other truckers.

The gang ethos pits Beddo as an individual against the conformity of these "rebels," who always move as a group and follow their leader. The L.A. cops inhabit the other end of the political spectrum as figures of established authority. They chase Philo after he defeats them in a bar brawl, wanting to restrain his rambunctious behavior. Finally, Ma curses the government bureaucracy that denies her the right to drive, and curses again when Philo and his ape refuse to acknowledge the bounds of family decency. The upshot of these shenanigans is that Philo can thumb his nose at government bureaucrats and enforcers, and alternately assail those who challenge the habits of common folk. Ma cannot pin down a rambling man, but then Ma's obscenities puncture any claim to family values. This freewheeling mix captures a working class sensibility that resists tangible politics, while at the same time portraying a network of social allegiances and class antagonisms. Hostility toward the relics of a counterculture, the representatives of government, and middle-class decorum suggest lower class conservatism in step with the values of the soon-to-be President Ronald Reagan. But the comic play undermines any coherent sensibility.

By contrast, Philo's heroic quest assumes a serious tone that probes the values of working-class manliness. Beddo is a bare-fisted fighter whose independence resists regulation. When Lynn asks why he didn't turn professional, he replies, "Too many rules." The fighter is closely associated with labor, as each of his three bouts is staged in a workplace: a trucker's parking lot, a meat packing plant and at a quarry or mining yard. The locales link boxing to physical labor but also to the screen heroes from earlier in the "comeback" cycle. This motif, as well as the fights themselves, are similar to the work sites turned boxing arenas in *Hard Times*. *Every Which Way* invokes Rocky at the meat packing plant. Amid the animal carcasses Philo's opponent even shouts, "I want you" in the manner of Apollo Creed as the contest is about to begin. Philo's drive to be champion does not arise from low self-esteem like Rocky's, or from a need for cash like Chaney's. Nonetheless, the independent Philo harbors a desire to be the best that prompts him to seek out the renowned Tank Murdock. That is, the boxer's motive here arises out of a competitive drive for dominance that suggests the traditional success ethic. Furthermore, the champion Murdock is associated with Lynn, hence success in fighting is equated with success in romance. Lynn lives in Denver, like Murdock, and she reports to Philo about his prowess. After Lynn suddenly departs from L.A., the trip to find her coincides with the journey to meet Tank. Philo's confrontations with both are closely linked. However, rather than affirming the prowess of the boxer, his quest ends by questioning the values he embodies.

Murdock presents a problem because no matter how many local guys Philo knocks out, the reputation of the distant champion reminds the trucker that he is not the best. Doubt festers. In a similar manner, Lynn Halsey-Taylor undermines the boxer's confidence. The film title alludes to the tense and confused feelings she excites in the boxer. As the picture opens, Beddo walks through the trucking company's office making familiar gestures toward a number of women, thereby establishing his self-confidence as a ladies' man. Later that night he puts down an attractive coed with intellectual airs at the country western bar. Though Lynn warms to his attentions, the singer eludes bedding down with him. Later, after receiving an expensive outfit and a fistful full of cash from Philo, Lynn suddenly disappears from the trailer park. Puzzled, the boxer takes the road east in pursuit and bumps into her almost by chance. She embraces him. Reassured by their lovemaking, Beddo arrives at their rendezvous the next day, only to be stood up again. Reminiscent of Marlene Dietrich's cabaret vamp in Josef Von Sternberg films, Lynn lures unwary men with her duplicitous tune, "What's a Girl To Do?" But she offers a provocative revision of the conventional sweetheart-vamp division. She reverses the gender roles to dominate the men in her life. Skylar, her traveling companion, fulfills the role of the stable, dependable man under the control of a woman, but he is physically ineffectual. By contrast, Lynn's array of bar conquests are powerfully sexual, but potentially threatening men. She takes them for their money and her pleasure, and leaves them by the roadside, departing with Skylar. She satisfies her need for both aspects of manly companionship by using an array of men. In contrast to Philo's frustrations with Lynn, Orville succeeds in picking up a woman selling fruit at a road stand. Her name, Echo (Beverly D'Angelo), suggests a male fantasy. But Echo serves the film largely as a contrast to Lynn and as a means of amplifying Philo's longing. Philo's most important confidant and soul mate is his orangutan Clyde.

The animal motif is well developed in the 1970s boxing film. Picking up on Terry Malloy's pigeons in On the Waterfront, Rocky stations its heroine at a pet shop and gives the fighter friendly turtles and a trusty dog, dubbing the protagonist "the Italian Stallion." In Hard Times, Chaney stares at a caged bear before his bout in Cajun country and expresses his tenderness with his cat. The thoroughbred in The Champ (1979) serves as a love token between father and son. While recognizing the bestial nature of the pugilist, these films also associate him with the gentleness, power, and devotion typical of animals. So the boxer's physicality is portrayed as an elevated innocence, a source of virtue as well as a limitation. Clyde becomes an alter ego for Philo Beddo in Every Which Way But Loose. The orangutan is introduced when the trucker enters a dim outbuilding upon returning home with peanuts he won at a bar brawl. In the darkness the boxer is attacked, and before he can pick himself up from the floor he begins scolding his pet for the assault. What was initially perceived as a sneak attack on the belligerent protagonist becomes a humorous send-up of the first fistfight. Right away the animal expresses the bestial and the brotherly in the hero, as well as a troubled, unacknowledged shadowy other self, with which the boxer must wrestle.

The alliance between Philo and Clyde also conveys humor and pathos. The Black Widows first provoke Beddo when they compare him to Clyde, riding at his side in the pickup. Of course, Clyde is regularly at the fights, screeching or cowering in reaction to the combat. Nowhere is Clyde's comradeship as well developed as in response to the boxer's longing for Lynn, especially after Orville meets Echo. Beddo leaves Orville and Echo at the motel while he and Clyde travel through a round of bars and strip clubs, the orangutan listening to his buddy's troubles. Later that night Philo returns to the room and insists that Orville help him immediately find a mate for Clyde. Philo's own sexual anxiety becomes projected onto his simian confidant. His companionship with the animal expresses the boxer's simplicity and underlines the mysterious complexity women pose for him. Of course, the implication that the fighter is little more than an animal is handled in a comic and sympathetic fashion. Animals are presented as blessed in their loyal, instinctive, and affectionate nature. This simplicity marks most of the film's comic action, which consists of little more than acrobatic brawls between Philo, the Black Widows, the cops, or Ma, all of which develop out of the initial bout between Philo and Clyde in the dark. Philo always emerges victorious from humorous combat, but his heroic quest meets a different end.

The heroic quest of Philo Beddo culminates with his arrival in Denver. On the same night he finds Lynn and fights Tank Murdock. The comic tone of the picture prepares one for a happy ending; instead, these disturbing encounters express the boxer's pathos. Philo discovers that Lynn is playing at the Zanza Bar and goes to the club. After the singer finishes her set, she leaves for a quiet spot behind the club with Harlan, a handsome guitar player from her band. Outside Lynn embraces Harlan, exhibiting the same allure she displayed toward Philo at the Palomino. At this point Beddo appears at a distance. Philo, wearing a large black cowboy hat and denim jacket, contrasts visually with Lynn, who is wearing the white speckled country western ensemble Philo brought for her in L.A. The opposing black and white costumes suggest those of rivals in a Western melodrama, and the mise-en-scène reinforces this association. The camera follows Lynn, looking up to the tall man in the black hat standing at a distance across the lot. The two exchange looks, and Philo begins his advance. Then the camera picks up the reverse angle from just behind Philo's head as he walks toward Lynn. The showdown is at hand. The couple is face to face in a single shot. After dismissing Harlan, Lynn gives Philo a tongue-lashing ("I've been trying to get rid of you practically since the first night we met." "How come you don't know when to disappear?" "You're just not too smart, are you?"). Taken aback, he stammers and finally concedes, "I'm just not too smart, that's all." From the shadows a man approaches: Lynn's mysterious "friend" Skylar, who is balding, of modest stature, and timid. Philo stares amazed at his inconsequential rival. "You hustle for him?" he asks. Enraged, Lynn repeatedly shouts, "I hate you," as she strikes the immobile boxer. Her blows knock off his cowboy hat and draw blood from his nose and mouth. Dazed, the man endures the assault without a response. Finally, with Lynn pausing in exhaustion and tears, Philo walks slowly from the scene without even retrieving his hat. The transparent conventions of the traditional Western are gone. The simple signs of virtue, the black hat and white dress, are now merely costumes. In a disturbing epiphany, the heartless woman humiliates the protagonist, who retreats powerless and confused. The tough guy is taken down by the vamp and shown to be an innocent.

Immediately after being vanquished from the romantic arena, Philo returns to more familiar contests between men. But here, too, his success is thwarted and his values overturned. The next shot finds Philo at the work yard, where Orville has set up a fight with Tank Murdock. The legendary brawler appears to be a middle-aged roughneck, whose beer belly girth now exceeds the breadth of his shoulders and strong arms. The younger Beddo easily dominates the aging champ. After a few knockdowns, Murdock appears to be spent, and the crowd, largely composed of his supporters, boos. Swinging wildly, Tank becomes a pathetic figure. Philo hears the crowd's shouts as he waits to see if his rival has anything left: "This is it for Tank"; "This guy is going to be the new Tank Murdock"; "Are we going to make money on this guy?" Philo confronts his future in his struggling opponent. The spectators murmur heartlessly in a manner suggestive of Lynn's tirade. Philo hesitates, lets down his guard, and Tank scores a knockdown blow. Lying in the dirt, Beddo gets a look at Orville, but he stays down even though he has been unhurt thus far. The fighter, faced with the legendary champion, loses his desire for the title after all. In a gesture that turns Rocky's desire to "go the distance" on its head, Philo privately accepts defeat and the bout ends. Eastwood explained in an interview, "The guy purposely loses the big fight at the end because he doesn't want to go around being the fastest gun in the West" (Kapsis/Coblentz 1999, 126). The long-standing convention of the boxing genre, the dive, receives a fresh treatment in *Every Which Way But Loose*. The young challenger is not bribed to take a fall. Rather, he surrenders his ambition for the championship and secretly resigns.

The self-confident tough guy, who Eastwood consciously relates to his Western hero, fails in his quest for romance and glory. But more importantly, he questions the success ethic that has guided him. Lynn faults his ability to recognize genuine affection, to distinguish between a lustful tryst and romantic devotion. His drive for physical dominance also suffers when he sees the legendary champion and, in a moment of recognition, turns away from "success". The rise and fall of the boxer becomes condensed in the image of Tank, an aging champion whose skills are nearly exhausted. The pathos of Tank's decline haunts Philo's sentimental education. The success ethic has led to a dead end.

Philo never offers a reaction to the failure of his quest. Instead, the film shifts to a comic episode mocking the aging theme, with Ma finally securing a driver's license from an elderly bureaucrat who takes a liking to the old lady. The film closes with Philo, Clyde, Orville, and Echo passing the bumbling cops and the Black Widows in crippled vehicles on the road back to L.A. They laugh together as the credits roll. This puzzling ending is typical of Eastwood. As he explains in an interview, "I like to leave them that way, still in the process of finding their way" (Kapsis/Coblentz 1999, 67).

Every Which Way But Loose represents a distinctive treatment of the success ethic. The traditional conflict between market forces and altruistic values is never entertained. Money is not an issue. Philo and Orville work, but they readily drop everything and depart on a trip with hardly a worry. The protagonist has no desire to rise socially; neither is Philo driven into the ring as a result of social injustice or anger. Philo embraces his working-class culture without reserve. The trucker fights for fun or honor, and his drive to be champion appears almost instinctual. The boxer displays a child-like innocence beneath his tough pose. The pathos of failure is all the more disarming because it is so unexpected.

Every Which Way But Loose insists on the physical. Common alternatives to the success ethic—family, learning, religion, art, or romantic love—are either mocked, as is the case with Ma and the family, or portrayed as duplicitous, as with Lynn, a musician. By contrast, the physical, most forcefully embodied in Clyde, is elevated with comic exaggeration. The film implies that if only Philo's needs could be as simple as Clyde's, he would elude suffering. Even the image of aging embodied by the failing Tank Murdock finds its response in the laughter in the episode featuring Ma's aging. The physical comedy dismisses ideals as a pretentious answer to the limitations of being. The serious aspirations of the boxing drama dissolve in favor of laughter as the proper response to the frailty of the body. The film's abiding physical comedy ultimately belittles the torment of the boxer as exaggerated male posturing. *Every Which Way But Loose* is more complex and coherent than the critics perceived it to be. It blends humor and pathos, the contrasting sensibilities of the late-seventies boxing cycle, and offers a fresh critique of the success ethic. Nevertheless, the film fails to portray any guiding values for the working-class culture it celebrates.

THE FALLEN CHAMP: THE UNTOLD STORY OF MIKE TYSON (1993): THE DREADED SPECTACLE OF SUCCESS

The 1990s saw the boxing film seek a fresh perspective with a turn to documentary and a focus on the African American fighter. Nonetheless, the new attention to race and nonfiction appropriated the themes and conventions of the boxing film genre as important elements. The resulting mix yielded a powerful variation on the critique of the success ethic.

In "The Black Intellectual and the Sport of Prizefighting," Gerald Early concludes with ambivalence. On the one hand, he acknowledges the impact of the legendary black champions Jack Johnson, Joe Louis and Muhammad Ali as embodiments of free men expressing themselves through their physical prowess and public celebrity, thereby asserting an uplifting influence upon the African American consciousness. On the other hand, Early recognizes that the black boxer is an essentially apolitical and self-destructive figure whose public persona poses a troubling model for the black community. He writes:

> The ambiguity here that I think is a crucial issue for the black intellectual and prevents him from celebrating boxing in the way the white intellectual can is that boxing, finally, for the black fighter is an apolitical, amoral experience of individual esteem, which the black fighter purchases at the expense of both his rival's health (and often his own) and his own dignity. The black fighter is a figure of intense and aching symbolic adverseness, of the American black's learned self-hatred. For the black intellectual, boxing becomes both a dreaded spectacle and a spectacle of dread. (Early 1994, 28)

The opening chapter in Ralph Ellison's *Invisible Man* (1952) offers a horrifying elaboration upon the dreaded spectacle in the "battle royale." The book begins with the invisible man, an African American, invited to give a commencement address to the town's leading white citizens. However, upon arriving at the hotel, the narrator is pushed into the battle royale. Here he finds himself with nine other young black men, all outfitted for boxing, blindfolded and placed in a ring. They are each to fight the others until two dominate. Then the masks are removed and the final pair face off until one wins by a knockout. As the boxers swing wildly at unseen opponents, drunken whites surrounding them laugh and urge them on. The narrator and Tatlock emerge from the melee to fight each other to the finish. In a clinch, the invisible man whispers an offer to his rival. He will give him the prize money, if he takes the fall. "I'll break your behind," Tatlock replies. The bout ends with Tatlock victorious and the narrator carried to his corner after a knockout. He awakens trying to remember his speech about humility as the guiding force for racial progress.

Ellison's fiction may strike one as simply allegorical, but battle royales were a common experience for black fighters in the early decades of the century. Jack Johnson, in particular, was an experienced practitioner, and Gerald Early suggests that Johnson served as a model for Tatlock. Here the exploitation of the boxer who competes and suffers, blinded and confused, for the amusement of his racial oppressor, is vividly portrayed. But there is no political epiphany, as there is in *Golden Boy*. Even the secret attempt of the black fighters to cooperate for their own benefit is thwarted by Tatlock's desire to win. For Gerald Early, *The Invisible Man*'s battle royale captures most successfully the terrifying significance of prizefighting for the African American. "For Ellison there are no real victories for the black fighter," Early writes, "for the prizefight into which the fighter is both coerced and seduced is itself an utter corruption and distortion of democratic values and American individualism" (Early 1994, 32).

Few champion boxers have embodied the fears of Gerald Early and Ralph Ellison as vividly as Mike Tyson. Barbara Kopple's award-winning documentary, *The Fallen Champ: The Untold Story of Mike Tyson*, portrays the boxer's rise and fall as a dreaded spectacle of success. The documentary features the classical conventions of the boxing film, and its authenticity invests them with fresh emotional force. In *The Fallen Champ* the boxer's success leads to his self-destruction and produces a dreaded spectacle in which a divided African American community fights among itself.

The Fallen Champ documents the rise of Mike Tyson from Brooklyn delinquent to heavyweight champion, and then his fall from the title and his trial for rape in 1992. The film introduces the budding fighter as a troubled youth serving time in a correctional institution. Tyson's prodigious physical talent is discovered by a savvy old trainer, Cus D'Amato. D'Amato adopts the twelve-year-old and infuses skill, confidence, and self-respect into the boy. Saved from a life on the streets, Tyson quickly comes to prominence, winning the Junior Olympics heavyweight title at fifteen. Turning professional at eighteen, Tyson rises through the ranks of fighters, guided by his managers D'Amato and Jim Jacobs. Just before Tyson's title shot, D'Amato dies. But Mike wins the championship, honoring the memory of his adopted father. He becomes the youngest man to wear the heavyweight crown. Then Jacobs dies abruptly. Without his benign mentors, the immature Tyson finds himself a national celebrity. Dizzy with fame and fortune, he falls into the clutches of a scheming vamp, the actress Robin Givens, and an unscrupulous promoter, Don King. Soon the invincible boxer is estranged from his gifted trainer, Kevin Rooney, and tormented, then divorced, by his ruthless wife. It is not long before he is knocked out by a second-rate journeyman boxer. While trying to reorient himself, Tyson judges a beauty contest, becomes attracted to a provocative contestant, lures her to his room, and wakes to face an indictment for rape. During his trial the film effectively balances the contending claims for guilt and innocence, and concludes with Tyson departing for prison, his promise tarnished, his future uncertain.

The Fallen Champ builds its narrative around a rise-and-fall pattern modeled on classical boxing fiction. In act one the young delinquent is turned into a boxing prodigy by sensitive tutors who guide and protect him. In act two, he triumphs in the ring, but his success only makes him vulnerable to predators who exploit his wealth, shatter his confidence, and undermine his strength as a fighter. The closing act portrays the fall as a sexual debacle that results in the boxer's trial, conviction, and imprisonment. Tyson returns to jail, circling back to the position from which he arose. Finally, the film asks why such a talented man should be lost. Mike Tyson embodies a victim torn asunder by a division between a powerful body and a naïve consciousness. His story presents a dreaded spectacle in which success carries the seeds of its own destruction.

The Fallen Champ fluently incorporates generic conventions from the boxing fiction into the documentary. A repertory of familiar types gains veracity from their authentic embodiments: Tyson, the boxer as social underdog on the rise; Cus D'Amato, the fatherly manager who guides his progress; Kevin Rooney, the astute trainer; Robin Givens, the vamp; Don King, the gangster promoter; Jack Newfield and other crusading reporters exposing the ring world; unscrupulous attorneys; and the anonymous, heartless crowd. All are there. The familiar tale hardly needs retelling, but it seems to arise from the culture without prompting. At times the specificity of these allusions is uncanny. The film opens with shots of pigeons flying from Brooklyn tenement rooftops. Tyson's boyhood friends explain that Mike used to fight, steal, and fly birds. The images evoke Terry the washed-up boxer in *On the Waterfront*, the desire for flight, and the sense of victimization associated with the colloquial sense of "a pigeon" to characterize Tyson, the slum child. Desiree Washington, the good-girl beauty queen, takes her cue from Peg in *Body and Soul*, whom the boxer Charlie Davis meets at a beauty contest. Rather than courting the heroine with respect, as Charlie does, Mike brutally forces himself upon her, and so a crime smothers the saving grace of romance. The conspicuous poster for *Rocky* in D'Amato's gym only seems the most obvious symbol in a documentary whose intersection with the conventions of the boxing film genre invests the film, and maybe even the events themselves, with a grim texture of inevitability.

In a more general, but equally revealing sense, the film testifies to the influence of the classical genre model and its noir refinement. Big-time boxing appears to be a tawdry arena of exploitation in which the relation of victim to victimizer can shift in an instant. Tyson changes from the enthusiastic prodigy to the cynical millionaire, but fails to gain the social consciousness necessary to protect himself from the forces that bring him down. The film's politics arise from a tale of opportunity lost, but that opportunity seems no more promising than the battle royale portrayed in Ralph Ellison's *Invisible Man*. The reviews of Tyson's fights present one black man after another beaten before a big spending crowd and a large, anonymous TV audience. Tyson and Washington each strive for a success that transcends, rather than acknowledges racial distinctions, but their tales confound the facile optimism of the Alger ethos. These African American youths devour one another's hopes.

Narrative patterns and conventional figures taken from fiction are integrated with documentary devices. The film's investigation collects testimony from a range of interviews that reveal contending opinions. The authorial voice is undecided, as Kopple relates warring views, only to move along to the next episode, raising doubts rather than arguing for a position. The facts do not speak for themselves; messages are mixed and contrary. The film opens with the trainer Rooney pleading: Why is the best boxer of his generation languishing in the pen? This speech is followed by Desiree Washington's assertion that she simply wants to help a troubled man. Cus D'Amato is portrayed as a fatherly helper until Teddy Atlas, the discharged trainer, argues that D'Amato's ambition for Tyson prevented him from exercising the discipline needed to instill respect for others in his adopted son. The trial unfolds with the case for the prosecution and that of the defense explained, and then others assert that another defense strategy may well have freed the accused. Opposing perspectives posit a quizzical viewer placed at an emotional distance from the protagonist. The fallen champ becomes a divided figure, a prodigy whose talent was crippled by social limitations, a victim and victimizer pursuing a success that only bred failure. The neutral narrative tone of *The Fallen Champ* seasons its ambiguity with an Aristotelian sense of fear and pity occasioned by the fall of the mighty.

Tyson himself is portrayed as a divided protagonist. In the opening credits, Kopple uses a vertically divided image of the boxer to express this break. She also presents the mismatch between Tyson's body and his speech to emphasize discord; "Iron Mike" has a colossal physique matched with a soft, "little boy" voice. A division arises between the world of boxing and normal life. Jim Jacobs explains that he tried to keep Tyson out of trouble by immersing him in a constant round of training and bouts. Earlier reports describe problems in the Catskill high school that Mike attended while living with Cus. Schoolmates nicknamed the imposing adolescent "Mighty Joe Young," and occasionally Mike intimidated teachers or erupted in emotional outbursts. The D'Amato gym was his refuge in a community where he often felt out of place. But Catskill pals and girlfriends also remember Tyson's sweet personality. Maybe the anxieties of adolescence, class differences, and an escape from the male boxing enclave could have been negotiated, but suddenly the kid lost his trusted mentors and became a national celebrity at twenty. Then fame and money gave Tyson freedom as well as making him a mark for predators. Soon even his boxing regimen broke down, and he lost the heavyweight title. In the end, Tyson appears to be a displaced person, a prodigy whose talent distinguishes him from others, but leaves him confused, suspicious, and self-destructive. Kopple uses a striking image of the boxer jogging alone at the beginning and end of the film to convey Tyson's isolation. A lonely, uncertain road stands in for the fighter's misguided quest for success.

The African American community is divided in *The Fallen Champ*. Tyson's African American social worker and his black high school girl friend voice affection and concern. But Don King and Robin Givens are like villains out of a B movie. The series of black men beating each other in the ring evokes Gerald Early's "dreaded spectacle," the racial community at war with itself. Tyson finds no refuge in being black. Even when Louis Farahkan and the black Baptist ministers come to Mike's defense during the trial, the film juxtaposes them with another black pastor affirming Washington's character and a group of African American women complaining that racial spokesmen defend a celebrity at their expense. The film's innumerable interviews relate contrary opinions from all sides, further promoting the image of an African American community divided, among other things, along the lines of class and gender.

Mike Tyson's relations with women highlight these divisions. The mismatch between the poised, educated and articulate middle-class women, Robin Givens and Desiree Washington, and the reform school pug presents a clash of cultures that is exacerbated by the boxer's orientation to an almost exclusively male world. On the one hand, *The Fallen Champ* portrays Robin Givens as a greedy tease who exploited the fighter. On the other hand, female fans pursue Mike in droves, offering themselves as sexual partners and short-circuiting Tyson's need to learn the manners of courtship, to cultivate the habits of intimacy, or to gain a female confidant who could have nurtured him. In short, money and celebrity protect Tyson from pressures that might have promoted maturity in the young man. Washington, in contrast to many of Tyson's other female followers, appears to be a star-struck innocent, whose small town upbringing does not prepare her for her encounter with a celebrity who uses her as if she were another groupie. This boxing film ends not with a climactic bout, but with the champ taking down Desiree Washington—and being knocked out in return in an evocation of Ellison's battle royale. The trial only underlines the division within the African American community. The question of whether Mike Tyson received justice fades, overwhelmed by scenes of black men and women preying upon each other.

Mike Tyson failed to become the legendary champion that appeared to be his destiny. Barbara Kopple draws upon the tradition of the boxing fiction film in shaping her documentary about the demise of a prodigy. The boxer's story echoes Gerald Early's claim that "the black fighter is a figure of intense and aching symbolic adverseness." In *The Fallen Champ*, Tyson's story becomes a dreaded spectacle of success.

◆ ◆ ◆

Genre criticism investigates the fundamental social problems that serve as the foundation for a series of works. The critique of the success ethic has been an important element in the boxing film for over seven decades. This element of the genre speaks to our culture's discomfort with market competition as the principal standard for achievement. The genre serves as testimony that throughout our history, anxiety over competitive individualism has remained intense. In spite of the Judeo-Christian ethic of self-sacrifice for the common good, competitive individualism often overrides the need for a community to work together. Popular culture expresses these concerns, and the boxing film has made a significant contribution to this critique. Examining four films via the genre method reveals a flexible treatment of a fundamental social value in changing historical circumstances. The films offer distinct interpretations— from the optimistic alternatives of the early New Deal, to the cynical negation of the noir cycle, to the raucous comic disillusionment of the 1970s, and finally to a racial perspective on the success ethic as a false ideal inciting exploitation instead of engendering fellowship. Genre films arise, like myths in the oral tradition, from fundamental social tensions that serve as a basis for dramatic conflicts. The longstanding conflict between competitive individualism and self-sacrifice will stimulate future filmmaking as our culture continues to wrestle with this problem.

4

"ON THE ROPES"

The Conflict between Assimilation and the Indigenous Community

Only the most desperate are able to overlook the brutality and hardship of boxing and pursue a career in the ring. The lower class origins of the screen pugilist was already an established convention in the early sound period, but by the late 1930s the boxer had become clearly marked as an ethnic outsider—and later a racial outsider—as well. Prizefighting became an avenue to acceptance by the dominant culture and a means of resisting oppression. However, the boxer frequently experiences a conflict between the opportunity success offers for integration into mainstream society, and loyalty to the marginalized ethnic or racial community from which he arose. Assimilation into the dominant culture means not only gaining wealth and respect, but also putting aside the heritage and fellowship that are part of minority ethnic origins. The melting pot ethos of American culture sees the immigrant shedding his native habits in order to take on an amalgamated national identity. However, the boxing film testifies to the pain of negotiating between the contending communities making up the nation.

The rise of Joe Louis was an important catalyst for the appearance of this conflict in the boxing film. African Americans, an enslaved rather than an immigrant population, experienced more severe oppression than other ethnic and racial groups, and their community was most despised. As a result, African Americans were excluded from integration into American culture, and miscegenation between blacks and whites was outlawed in many states. So the specter of integration evoked by Joe Louis was particularly threatening. In Hollywood films the black boxer only slowly emerges, with the ethnic outsider initially being Italian, Jewish, or Irish—or, later on, Hispanic. Though the African American fighter began to appear on screen in the years after World War II, it is only after 1970 that he moves to the forefront of the boxing film. Along with the move from the white ethnic outsider toward an African American protagonist, there is also a movement from an assimilation model toward valorization of the ethnic or racial community in a more pluralist nation. In the conflict between opportunity and loyalty the boxing film genre initially favored opportunity, but over the years loyalty became a clear option.

Evolution of the tension the ethnic-racial outsider experiences when caught between opportunity to enter the mainstream and loyalty to his indigenous community can be seen in the prominent cycles of the boxing film genre. In 1937, *Kid Galahad* portrays the agony of assimilation for an Italian-American. In the early 1950s, *Right Cross* and *The Ring* highlight prejudice as a social problem, and present a shift in the conflict between the dominant and minority communities. During the blaxploitation era, *Mandingo* offers African Americans a cautionary tale about befriending the master. In 1996, *When We Were Kings* valorizes the bond between African Americans and their forbearers in Zaire, elevating the heritage of a distinct black community. In each of these films, as well as in many other boxing films, the opportunity versus loyalty conflict functions as a pivot for the drama. Nonetheless, the perspective on the problem and its resolution changes markedly during the evolution of the boxing film.

KID GALAHAD (1937): THE PAIN OF ASSIMILATION

In "*Bordertown*, the Assimilation Narrative and the Chicano Social Problem Film," Charles Ramírez Berg addresses the ethnic struggle for assimilation in Hollywood movies (Berg 1992, 29–46). *Kid Galahad* shares many traits with Berg's alternate model, a story in which assimilation proves successful after the ethnic protagonist overcomes problems in his character. More important for the boxing film, Berg recognizes that the struggle toward assimilation in the movies often involves moral compromise, a loss of identity, and even death for the ethnic protagonist. Furthermore, American success itself is often portrayed as incompatible with human values and antithetical to the ethnic heritage of the immigrant. The assimilation narrative is a painful story fraught with ambivalence toward American society.

Kid Galahad presents assimilation as an arduous family quest in which American culture seems promising, but also decadent and dangerous. The film promotes the melting pot concept of American culture, which invites immigrants to integrate into mainstream society. The manager and his boxer represent, respectively, the ethnic and the Anglo-American; they are initially allied as a boxing team and later conflict when the boxer courts the manager's sister.

The Italian-American boxing manager Nick Donati (Edward G. Robinson) holds center screen. Donati's visit to his mother and sister in their country home emphasizes his ethnic character. Mom cooks minestrone while she and her son have a conversation in Italian. Their chat underlines Nick's foreign heritage and by contrast his growing assimilation, because the Italian vocal mannerisms that impede his mother's English are absent from Nick's speech. Their distance from one another is emphasized when Mrs. Donati scolds her son for never coming home. The new generation is leaving behind the ethnic family for mainstream urban life.

The association of boxing with the economic volatility and moral ambiguity of the market is a key to *Kid Galahad*'s treatment of assimilation. The openness of the boxing business provides an opportunity for the immigrant to rise. Here Nick Donati has found his chance as a deal maker, a wily craftsman who fashions the boxer into a fierce competitor. Donati insists that his fighter follow his instructions absolutely, firing his boxer in the opening scene because he fails to execute Donati's commands. After abandoning his investment in a fighter, the self-confident Donati blows everything on a big party, certain he will be in the money again soon. As a businessman, Donati is characterized as an adventurer always looking for the way to the top, a manipulator constantly flirting with the sinister. But in spite of his vicissitudes, Donati exemplifies success. He lives extravagantly, exercises power with confidence, and has a beautiful woman on his arm. Nick is thoroughly at ease in the world of the rackets, at the intersection of the underworld and respectable society. As a result, Donati is tainted by the illicit practices of the market and only partially assimilated.

In contrast to Donati, three Anglo-Americans represent the ideals and the corruption of American life. The boxer is from the American heartland. Ward Guisenberry (Wayne Morris) comes to the city to earn the money he needs to buy a farm. Nick spots the hulking rustic's powerhouse right and turns him into a champion. After his first bout, Fluff (Bette Davis), Nick's mistress, dubs Guisenberry "Kid Galahad" because of his purity. The gangster Turkey Morgan (Humphrey Bogart) represents the corrupt, established power opposing Donati's ethnic outsider. The racketeer's vulgar name, taken from a bird long associated with America's national heritage, and the Anglo-Saxon "Morgan" links the

Nick Donati (Edward G. Robinson), the ethnic manager, directs the contender from the heartland in *Kid Galahad* (1937). Courtesy of the Academy of Motion Picture Arts and Sciences.

rival boxing manager with the dominant culture. Nick's ambition to win the championship controlled by Morgan suggests his drive for success, as well as an attraction to evil. Fluff serves as the bridge between the corrupt and the ideal. As Nick's illicit lover and a woman of the demimonde, she represents urban decadence. But her unrequited love for Galahad, her artistry as a singer, her self-sacrifice in promoting the happiness of others all embody mainstream ideals. Through her alliance with Marie (Jane Bryan), Nick's sister, she facilitates the assimilation of the Donati family. The three principal Anglo-Americans present a variable society, ranging from the innocent to the criminal. In *Kid Galahad*, assimilation involves navigating between the culture's promise and its dangers.

Donati fails to assimilate because the conflict between the market and the family turns him away from marriage, and his flawed ethnic temper leads to his tragic death. However, his young sister Marie realizes a union with the best in American culture through her engagement to Galahad.

The corrupt practices of the boxing world cut off Donati from the virtues of family. When a dressing room bum makes a disparaging remark about Nick's mother, Donati angrily pins him to the wall declaring, "Nobody in this game mentions my family. I keep them out of it." The boxing racket serves as a dangerous half step toward integration into an ideal America. The business of prize fighting offers Donati the opportunity for wealth and power, and he uses those resources to support his mother and educate his sister. But the vital next step involves a return to the earth and the hearth. Here Donati falters. The urban market, which he acknowledges to be corrupt, has claimed his soul and, at the conclusion, claims his life. The conflict between the market and the family amplifies the contest between the opportunity to enter mainstream culture versus loyalty to the native community. For the Donatis this conflict exemplifies the painful process of assimilation.

The market is juxtaposed to the family, just as boxing is set off against the farm, and Donati is contrasted with Galahad. Unlike Donati, Galahad succeeds in mastering boxing and returning to the agrarian world. After Donati persuades Guisenberry to pursue his fortune in the ring, Fluff warns the farm boy of the dangers he will encounter, which she calls "a rotten life that'll knock those clear cut illusions of yours higher than a kite. [You will] Get mixed up with crowds . . . of fast-living spenders and punch drunk gunmen." After Morgan threatens Galahad, the boxer hides at the Donati farm, and there he meets Marie. In the country he enjoys barnyard chores, Mama Donati's cooking, and flirting with Marie. The American innocent shares in the joys of the ethnic family and becomes an instrument for assimilation. Ward's purity is closely associated with the ideals of the family and the land; his courtship of Marie leads to her assimilation into an American ideal. This ideal is not the Horatio Alger model of wealth and upward social mobility, but rather the Jeffersonian concept of the independent farmer living close to nature. Outside of town, the values of farm and family are closely integrated and presented in contrast to the urban market as represented by Donati and boxing.

The assimilation theme circulates around the issue of marriage. When the film opens, Nick and Fluff are a loving couple. But Nick ignores Fluff's suggestion of marriage, and he keeps her away from his mother and sister in the country. When Fluff tells him that a fighter is leaving the ring to wed, their exchange is telling:

N: Married? . . . That's the craziest . . .

F: People still believe in it. Nick, you don't notice a lot of things. You're so wrapped up in the game, that, well, you forget, people have feelings, and are human.

N: There isn't any room for feelings in this game. A fighter's a machine, not a violin player.

The world of the ring only respects aggressive tempers; tenderness and affection are beaten down. For Nick, boxing is a tarnished racket on the edge of the underworld, a place where the ideals of marriage and family play no part. Nick dismisses the prospect of marriage. As inhabitants of the urban demimonde, he and Fluff are ineligible for a sacred union. Nick's reluctance to wed his Anglo-American companion proves fatal.

A volatile, stereotypically ethnic temper is one of Nick Donati's defining flaws. In the opening scene, the manager fires his fighter even though the trainer reminds Nick he will lose "a million dollars." Fluff chides her companion for his outbursts and keeps her lover's self-destructive behavior in check:

> F: Someday that temper of yours is going to throw you for a loss.
> N: Not while you're around to flag it down.
> F: Just the trouble, I might not always be around.

In contrast, Fluff keeps her feelings under wraps, only hinting at her desire for marriage or her growing affection for Galahad. Donati fails to sense her mood and is surprised when Fluff leaves him because of her unrequited love for the boxer. Once the balance between Donati's temper and Fluff's restraint is lost, the ethnic flaw leads to the manager's downfall.

Initially, intuition links Donati's anger to justice. After firing his fighter, Donati discovers that the boxer did not simply ignore his instructions, but was paid off by Morgan to take a dive. As a result, a desire for vengeance fires the manager's competition with Morgan. Donati develops Galahad as a means to strike back at his rival. Galahad's Anglo-American purity associates the ethnic's vengeance with justice.

In contrast to Donati's justified anger at being cheated by Morgan, Donati manifests demonic anger linked to a passionate defense of the ethnic family and in contrast to the restraint of the Anglo-Americans. When Fluff leaves Nick because of her yearning for Galahad, Donati loses a check over his volatile temper. As a result, his anger takes a vicious turn upon discovering the courtship between Ward and Marie. Nick is furious that a mug from the rackets has soiled his family. Enraged, he strikes Marie, and in return Galahad punches his manager. From that moment, Donati begins to plan his fighter's destruction, and he strikes a bargain with Morgan to engineer a beating for Galahad in the ring. Ethnic emotion without Anglo-American moderation loses its moral bearing. Intuition no longer links temper to justice. In "Big Fight 2" the painful conflicts surrounding assimilation play themselves out and shape the design of the bout.

The heavyweight championship fight brings the film to its rousing conclusion. Running for over 14 minutes, this episode constitutes about 15 per cent of the ninety-four minute film. The scene establishes the classic design of a boxing sequence as used during the Hollywood studio era. *Variety* applauded the sequence as "superb" and unprecedented in its treatment of boxing (Land 1937). In his review for the *New Republic*, Otis Ferguson concurred: "*Kid Galahad* is the best prize-ring film I've seen—both for the explosive pace of its fight scenes and for the edge of its realism.... Michael Curtiz kept the direction clean, particularly in scenes about the locker rooms and ringside, where there was some of the most bloody realism and mauling ever made up for cameras" (Ferguson 1971, 181–82).

An intensified realism marks the visual design. The principle camera position is at ringside, presenting a spectator's ideal view of the bout. In addition to the standard ringside perspective, *Kid Galahad* offers an array of alternate views, including distant shots of the ring with the crowd visible, overhead images of the boxers, overlapping images of the boxers and the crowd or boxers and numbers indicating the round. In addition, the camera moves inside the ring for intermediate shots of the fighters shown from waist up, close-up blows to the body, and head shots of the boxers throwing or taking punches. There are even point-of-view shots of Galahad exchanging looks with Donati in his corner. However, these close-up insert shots lose continuity and lack the fluency the genre will achieve by the late 1940s. About half of the shots, approximately eighty-one out of 186, in the sequence are of boxing and they present a wide variety of perspectives, the vast majority of which are those of the spectator. The knockout blow is pictured in a distant shot of the ring (this possibly a nonfiction image, because at the decisive blow, the camera is so far away that the features of both boxers are indecipherable). The array of camera positions is notable, especially in contrast to those used in the celebrated bout in *Golden Boy* two years later, which restricts itself to the ringside perspective. Nonetheless, both *Kid Galahad* and *Golden Boy* succeed in staging convincing bouts as seen from an ideal spectator's position.

The competition in *Kid Galahad* is intensified with exaggerated staging. The first round is presented in full, with both boxers continuously throwing huge punches. The outsized attacks result in three knockdowns in the first round, with Galahad falling twice and McGraw once. The second round continues in the same manner, until condensation of the fight quickly takes the film through round seven. In the corner episode, Nick instructs Galahad to shift to defensive tactics for round eight, which is portrayed long enough for Morgan to recognize that Donati has broken their deal. Then the fight skips quickly to round eleven, in which Galahad is again knocked down by McGraw, only to come off the canvas to knock out the champion and win the title.

The dynamic editing quickly shifts among the variety of perspectives on the fight, as well as condensing the eleven- round bout into key highlights. The sequence as a whole has an average shot length (asl) of 4.5 seconds, twice the pace of the typical Hollywood film of the late thirties, and also faster than the asl in characteristic Michael Curtiz films from the period (Salt 1992, 214–15). Intensification through editing accelerates the pace of the bout, and crosscutting to the reactions of the spectators excites moviegoers by cueing responses to the dramatic action.

Editing places Donati at the center of the episode. In addition to the realistic representation of boxing, the bout portrays Nick's conflicting feelings, his anger at Galahad versus his love for Marie, his ethnic temper versus his desire for the title, his pain at being an outsider versus his longing for assimilation. As a result, an expressionist drama of interiority balances the realistic presentation of the fight. A classic example of crosscutting between the ring battle, the response of the manager, and the reaction of the spectators integrates the expressionist and the realist. The dramatic space is organized with Donati as its pivot, surrounded by Fluff and Marie in the crowd, Silver the trainer (Harry Carey) in Galahad's corner, the antagonists Morgan and Buzz in Chuck McGraw's corner, and the two boxers in the ring. The scene is given added realistic flavor with a nonfiction establishing shot of the crowded arena, followed by shots of the ringside announcer, the press corps, and anonymous spectators. However, the decisive events take place in Galahad's corner as Donati struggles with his conflicting emotions.

The drama progresses toward the turning point, when Donati decides to win the bout after all. Each developing stage occurs in Galahad's corner, and its consequences influence the fight. First, Donati instructs his boxer to aggressively attack McGraw, even though the manager knows this maneuver will be to the advantage of the champion. After Galahad is knocked down twice in round one, a conflict develops between Donati and Silver as the trainer urges a defensive strategy. In response, the manager angrily dismisses his assistant and pushes Galahad to continue the assault. As the fight progresses, Fluff realizes what is happening and during round seven marches down with Marie to confront Nick at ringside. Just before the women arrive, Nick and Galahad exchange glances. The manager sees his fighter fading; in close-up he looks down with a wrinkled brow. Regret begins to emerge within Donati. Then Fluff and Marie make their plea. The camera assumes Nick's point of view as the two women he loves look up toward him. Fluff scolds Donati for "[l]etting that rotten temper of yours throw you off the deep end." Marie begs, "Don't do this to him because he loves me." This is the turning point. Nick agrees to change, and introspection calms his manner. After the women depart the camera moves closer to Donati, emphasizing his transformation. Between rounds he tells Galahad, "We're changing. We're changing." A backlit close-up cut gives the manager a glow that expresses his righteousness. The manager calls back the trainer and sets Galahad on a course toward victory.

Donati's love and reason have prevailed over his ethnic temper. After the knockout has made Galahad champion, Nick's triumph is short lived. Though implicitly he has agreed to Marie's marriage to Ward, bringing the assimilation of the ethnic to its conclusion, this painful struggle kills Donati: after the bout Nick dies in a shootout with the vengeful Morgan. The boxing match sets the stage for Nick's transformation. Initially the manager is bent on revenge and plans to punish his boxer by engineering his defeat. However, Donati's epiphany results in a change of heart. Intensified realism produces an enthralling ring battle, but the underlying struggle that determines its outcome is the moral, psychological strife within the manager.

In the ebb and flow of Donati's feelings, *Kid Galahad* portrays a drama of ethnic emotion. On the positive side, ambition is moderated by an alliance with Anglo-Americans. In contrast, Donati's turn from marriage and his defense of the ethnic family blocks his progress. Furthermore, his overbearing, almost incestuous, restriction of his sister temporarily prevents her assimilation. After Nick's death, Marie marries Ward and leads him from boxing back to the farm.

Kid Galahad presents a painful tale of assimilation in which the flawed ethnic protagonist can only take the initial steps toward integration with mainstream American culture. Donati dies unsuccessfully negotiating the conflict between the opportunity offered by the business of boxing, versus loyalty to the ideals of the ethnic family. Resolution is passed to the protagonist's younger sister, who marries an idealized American.

RIGHT CROSS (1950) AND *THE RING* (1952): CONTRASTING TREATMENTS OF PREJUDICE

With the rise of the social problem film after World War II, considerations of ethnic and racial prejudice became conspicuous in the boxing film. The influence of Joe Louis, who remained heavyweight champion until 1949, grew increasingly evident. *Body and Soul* featured the African American Ben (Canada Lee) in a prominent role as the exploited champ defeated by Charlie Davis for the title. *The Set-Up*, adapted from a narrative poem about a victimized black boxer, was initially designed with the African American James

Edwards in the lead. Though the social problem film reached a low point between 1950 and 1952, in these years the boxing film highlighted ethnic and racial prejudice in a cycle of four films: *Right Cross*, *The Fighter* (based on the Jack London short story "The Mexican"), *The Joe Louis Story*, and *The Ring*. Though Nick Donati was identified as an ethnic American, the discrimination suffered by Italian Americans was implied rather than portrayed in *Kid Galahad*. In the films from 1950 to 1952, the boxer is plagued by prejudice, and the Hispanic or African American fighter became the protagonist for the first time in a Hollywood production. As a result, the conflict between the opportunity to enter the social mainstream versus loyalty to the native community developed in new directions. A comparison between *Right Cross* and *The Ring* illuminates the change.

The two films come from opposite ends of the Hollywood industry. *Right Cross* was a well-crafted production made by a major studio and designed to promote two of M.G.M.'s rising stars: June Allyson, fresh from the successful sports picture *The Stratton Story* (1949), and Ricardo Montalban, who affirmed the connection between the combat veteran and the boxer by entering the ring after appearing in the hit war drama *Battleground* (1949). Though the *New York Times* labeled *Right Cross* "lightweight" (T.M.P. 1950, 39), *Variety* called the motion picture "good entertainment" and predicted that it would "play well in most situations" (*Variety* 1950, 11). The film made enough of an impact to be followed shortly by two more boxing movies featuring Hispanic fighters as oppressed ethnics, *The Fighter* and *The Ring*.

The Ring lacks the production values of *Right Cross* or the literary pedigree of *The Fighter*, but is the most successful of the three in portraying social problems. The King Brothers poverty row production uses unknown actors, awkward technique, and location shooting allying the film with the documentary and the neorealist movement. Charles Ramirez Berg praises *The Ring* for its understanding of prejudice and its humane treatment of Chicanos (Berg 1992, 43). However, in the political climate of 1952, the film's perspective provoked criticism. The *Hollywood Reporter* attacked the film as "a depressing, rather pointless harangue on American discrimination . . . that does this country a disservice abroad" (Gevinson 1997, 849). Most other reviewers ignored the film. *The Ring* only reached a fraction of the audience for *Right Cross*. Nonetheless, the former's frank understanding of power relations and fresh reversal of genre conventions invest the picture with conviction.

Both films use prejudice against Mexican Americans as a basic motivation for the boxer. *Right Cross* features the temperamental boxing champ Johnny Monterez, whose exaggerated fear of discrimination undermines his romance with Pat O'Malley, his manager, and his friendship with sportswriter Rick

it's a new kind of thrill for June Allyson!
she's never been loved like this before!

M-G-M Presents
The Love Story That Pulls No Punches
JUNE ALLYSON · DICK POWELL
RICARDO MONTALBAN
in
'RIGHT CROSS'
LIONEL BARRYMORE

"The Stratton Story" girl and that "Battleground" star together!

Written by CHARLES SCHNEE   Directed by JOHN STURGES   Produced by ARMAND DEUTSCH   A METRO-GOLDWYN-MAYER PICTURE

The temperamental champion (Ricardo Montalban) fears that if he loses the title his lover will desert him, a lowly Mexican. Courtesy of the Academy of Motion Picture Arts and Sciences.

Garvey (Dick Powell). Johnny suspects that if he loses the title Pat will desert him, a lowly Mexican. He knows that, like all fighters, his dominance in the ring is only temporary. The crisis deepens when Johnny hurts his right hand in training, and the doctor tells him privately that the injury could become permanent if he continues to fight. Furthermore, Johnny is a hot-tempered Latin whose impulsive moods thwart those caring for him. This stereotypical ethnic trait turns the victim of discrimination into one who perpetuates it. Advertising for the film shows the embracing couple from *Right Cross*, with Pat declaring, "I love you Johnny, but you make it too tough."

By contrast, *The Ring* grounds its plot in the experience of social oppression. The film opens in Los Angeles on Olvera Street, a landmark honoring the founding of the city by Mexicans. Now, however, condescending tourists patronize Mexicans in stereotypical poses. The Cantanios family suffers from discrimination. Papa Cantanios reports to his wife and children that he has been laid off his job and has little prospect of finding other work. Tomas (Lalo Rios), his son, takes his girlfriend Lucy Gomez (Rita Moreno) to a skating rink, only to be turned away because Chicanos can skate only on designated nights.

While Lucy is walking into a nearby bar, Anglos harass her, and Tomas's frustrations explode into a fistfight. The Mexican American boxing manager, Pete Genusia (Gerald Mohr) sees the fight and recruits Tomas. In *The Ring*, rage at social oppression fuels the desire to fight.

Right Cross exhibits ambivalence toward discrimination. It gives credence to Johnny's fears through an association with Joe Louis, the nation's most famous example of talent overcoming prejudice. A boxing flaw links Johnny to Joe Louis. Max Schmeling's victory over Louis in their famous first fight in 1936 arose from Schmeling exploitation of Louis's tendency to drop his defending left hand when he threw a right. Schmeling counterpunched over Louis's drooping left and eventually knocked out his favored opponent. In *Right Cross*, Johnny exhibits the same tendency and, as a result, loses the concluding bout and his title. The tie to Louis and prejudice highlights the boxer's most celebrated weakness, which clouds Johnny's implied connection to righteousness. In addition, Monterez tells Rick about his cousin Luis, a hoodlum who lands in jail as a result of poverty, anger, and restricted opportunities. "Who is Luis? Me . . . me ten years ago," Johnny declares. However, all the ethnic hostility in the film comes from Johnny Monterez and his family. In friendship, Johnny calls Rick "Pedro," burying his suspicion of Anglos behind the Hispanic name. Johnny tyrannizes his sister by forbidding her courtship with an Anglo-American, and embraces fears inherited from his mother. "There's no gringo alive," Mama Monterez declares, "who don't think he's better than ten *mexicanos*." Pat, and especially Rick, scold the boxer for assuming that ethnic discrimination will undermine his friendships and his romance. "You go on hating what you call the gringo world," Rick warns, "You're going to destroy yourself." Like many Hollywood films, *Right Cross* wants to appeal to a wide spectrum of opinion, so it incorporates contrary attitudes even though this mixture leads to a confusing and unsatisfactory film. *Right Cross* affirms ethnic prejudice as a social problem, but portrays it as a neurotic response of the victim. As *Time* magazine observed, *Right Cross* "falls into the bad Hollywood habit of glimpsing truth only long enough to falsify it" (*Time* 1950, 100).

The Ring affirms the reality of prejudice, but it also portrays boxing as an ineffective response. Developing his skills in the gym, Tomas gains self-esteem and ready cash from success in his initial bouts. His buddies from the neighborhood applaud his courage. His younger brother idolizes Tomas, the boxer. Women are drawn to the athlete. However, the glory from his early victories is short-lived. The brutality of prizefighting disgusts Tomas's father, and the danger distresses his girlfriend. When Tomas moves up the ranks from preliminary contests to more competitive bouts, he loses repeatedly and prepares to quit. Then one evening he visits an upscale diner with his buddies, and a waitress snubs the Mexican-Americans. When a policeman arrives on the scene he recognizes the boxer Tommy Kansas (Tomas's ring name), and demands that the young men be treated with respect. Aroused again by the experience of discrimination, Tomas returns to the gym eager to intensify his training. Nonetheless, the athlete falls prey to his own delusions. Harry Jackson, a boxing promoter, panics when a fighter drops out of his headline bout at the last minute. In order to avoid refunding his gate, Jackson offers Tomas, scheduled to box a semifinal, a handsome payoff to face the veteran contender Art Aragon in the main event. Pete, Tomas's manager, agrees to the match only if a set-up is arranged to protect his boxer from serious injury. A deal is struck allowing the novice to look good for four rounds, and Aragon agrees to take it easy on the fresh kid. However, the self-confident Tomas, contrary to his manager's advice, goes all out against the imposing Aragon, believing he can win. Angry at the double-cross, Aragon gives Tomas a terrible beating, ending his ring career. For most, boxing offers no exit from the ghetto. Tomas finds himself humiliated. Nonetheless, the Mexican American manages to escape without long-term injury. Ironically, though Papa Cantanios opposed boxing, Tomas uses $450 earned from the set-up to help finance a small business for his father. Relieved that her beloved has escaped from boxing, Lucy experiences new hope for Tomas. She urges him to use his fighting spirit to combat injustice rather than waste himself in the ring.

In *Right Cross* the ethnic protagonist embraces the opportunity to move into the dominant society by curbing his loyalty to his native community. The avenue to the mainstream is presented to Champ Johnny Monterez in two ways: economic and personal. By signing with a new promoter Johnny can assure his financial security after he retires, but doing so risks alienating Pat, his manger, and girlfriend. On the other hand, Johnny can invest his confidence in Pat's devotion and Rick's friendship. The film portrays Johnny overcoming his fear of prejudice by turning from his suspicion of Anglos and embracing his friends. Johnny's reassurance only comes after his career ends and Pat affirms her commitment by accepting his marriage proposal. *Right Cross* portrays prejudice as irrational behavior, akin to the excessive emotions stereotypical of the Latin sensibility. Nonetheless, the ethnic boxer succeeds in assimilating owing to the patience and affection of his Anglo friends. Assimilation is allied to reason, and the writer Rick becomes its spokesman, as he reconciles the lovers after their quarrels. Though Johnny's ethnic loyalty is portrayed as misguided, the intensity of his feelings, as much as his physical power attracts Pat. Rick, the rational one, is thwarted in his unrequited longing for Pat. *Right Cross* poses a more balanced blend of the dominant and the ethnic cultures than that portrayed in *Kid Galahad*. Here the ethnic man brings the Anglo woman (actually an

Irish-American) into his culture with the fiesta at his home to celebrate their engagement. The ethnic outsider retains some distinctive traits while accepting his American identity.

In *The Ring*, the Mexican American realizes that the assimilation promised by boxing is an illusion. He must base his future on loyalty to the ethnic community. Pete, the boxing manager, holds out the promise of assimilation to Tomas. Though a Mexican American who addresses Tomas as "amigo," Pete has a car, fedora, business suit, and trench coat that make him look like a successful Anglo. He takes Tomas to a drive-in, where he flirts with the blonde carhop and leaves her a big tip. She encourages Tomas, explaining that becoming a boxer "is wonderful." Pete assures the young man, "I'm showing you the quickest way to get someplace, to be somebody. As good as any Anglo. Better than any Anglo you can lick." On the other hand, Papa Cantanios and Lucy warn Tomas against boxing. As he embarks on his first fight, Tomas receives a silk robe monogrammed "Tommy Kansas" from Pete. The Anglo name, with its allusion to the American heartland, emphasizes that boxing is assimilation. Indeed, it is "Tommy Kansas" who is recognized in the upscale, Anglo restaurant and treated with respect. However, boxing is finally characterized as a misguided, self-indulgent quest. Tomas brushes aside the guidance of his trainers, the advice of his father, and his girlfriend. Furthermore, his manager refuses to be frank after he realizes that Tomas lacks the talent to be a success in the ring.

The closing bout presents an evocative variation on the conventional "set-up." Here two Mexican American fighters face each other, and cooperation is juxtaposed with competition. Rather than a corrupt deal, the set-up shields a vulnerable protagonist. But the overconfident Tomas betrays those guarding his safety and provokes retribution. The set-up reveals the delusions the boxer entertains, and shows that the cooperation of Mexican Americans is preferable to brutal competition between them. In spite of the painful beating involved, the set-up saves Tomas by ending his ring career, earning him $450 for his father's business, and sending him on to a more productive life. The assimilation Pete promised turns out to hold a painful lesson. Tomas fails in the ring, but recognizes the illusions that boxing can foster. His loyalty to the ethnic community is demonstrated when he burns his "Tommy Kansas" robe, buys the retail stand for his father, and attends to Lucy's call to fight social injustice rather than waste his energy in the ring. *The Ring* follows the typical format of the boxing film but reduces its scale, keeping the film closer to the experience of the vast majority of boxers, whose careers end in disappointment. The plot incorporates the rise-and-fall pattern without its protagonist becoming a serious contender. The film explicitly portrays boxing as a means of redirecting the rage engendered by oppressive social forces, but it also affirms the truism that prizefighting will only lead to self-destruction in return for a paltry taste of success. In many respects, *The Ring* is a summary of the conventions of the social problem film as they are realized in the boxing genre.

Amidst the repressive social conditions of the early 1950s, the boxing film genre provided a convenient veil for social problem films. Both *Right Cross* and *The Ring* use discrimination against Mexican Americans to drive their plots. However, the major studio production discounts the Anglo-American responsibility for prejudice, blaming Hispanics for exaggerating its effect. On the other hand, the low budget film offers an earnest treatment of the injustice suffered by the ethnic minority. In response to the problem, *Right Cross* promotes assimilation with mainstream culture, while *The Ring* portrays assimilation as illusory and commends loyalty to the ethnic community. Both films testify to the connection between the boxing film and the social problem picture, however, the films' disparate resolutions of the conflict between assimilation and ethnic loyalty underline their differences.

MANDINGO (1975): THE BOXER AND THE MASTER

Near the close of the blaxploitation era, *Mandingo* offered a provocative treatment of the conflict between opportunity and loyalty by casting the African American boxer as a slave in the antebellum South. During the 1970s, Hollywood reached out to niche audiences, such as African Americans, so the interests of a particular community were highlighted rather than the values of the general population. One consequence of this marketing ploy was the promotion of racial loyalty as opposed to assimilation in the mainstream. Blaxploitation films celebrate the action hero who defends the black community against predatory outsiders. *Mandingo* offers a variation on this pattern. Here the action hero accepts an alliance with his white master that leads to his doom. With the replacement of the old Production Code by a new movie ratings system in 1968, censorship was relaxed. Sex and violence became more explicit on screen, and previously forbidden subjects, like miscegenation, could be openly portrayed. Furthermore, Muhammad Ali replaced Joe Louis as the champion who shaped the image of the boxer in popular culture. After becoming champ, Ali had proudly dropped his "slave name," Cassius Clay, and announced his membership in an African American separatist religion, the Black Muslims. So Ali transformed the ethos of integration associated with Joe Louis into a pose of resistance. Under these circumstances, the black boxer became the protagonist in films such as *The Great White Hope* (1970) and *Hammer* (1972). The most successful boxing film from the blaxploitation movement, *Mandingo*, reshapes the traditional conflicts surrounding assimilation to produce an indictment of white racism.

Mandingo's pulp sensationalism excited outrage and controversy. The film was adapted from Kyle Onstoot's 1958 best-selling potboiler (over nine million copies sold, the ads claimed), which had little chance of being brought to the screen until the old Production Code was scraped. The antebellum plantation film that was adapted from the novel featured male and female frontal nudity, rape, sadism, infanticide, incest, and imaginative executions—among other excesses of Southern slaving. The lenient "R" rating given the film prompted criticism from the U.S. Catholic Conference, which responded with its most severe "condemned" warning. But the movie was more than an exploitation film. The Dino De Laurentiis production engaged the veteran Hollywood crime and adventure film director Richard Fleischer (*20,000 Leagues Under the Sea, The Vikings, The Boston Strangler*) and screenwriter Norman Wexler (*Serpico, Joe*). The two film veterans revised the relatively benign treatment of antebellum slave culture promoted by such influential movies as *The Birth of a Nation* (1915) and *Gone With the Wind* (1939). The production was anchored by an experienced cast that included James Mason and Susan George, and it introduced the heavyweight boxer Ken Norton, whose stellar moment was his victory over Muhammad Ali in 1973. Despite its personnel, the movie was lambasted. *Variety* set the tone by dismissing the film as "ludicrous" and "crude" (Murf 1975, 48); the *New York Times* chimed in, declaring *Mandingo* "immoral" and "vicious" (Canby 1975, 19); and the *Wall Street Journal* called it pornographic and dishonest (Boyum 1975, 12). The only positive notice I found in the popular press appeared in *Andy Warhol's Interview*, which applauded *Mandingo* as a "good trashy melodrama" (*Andy Warhol's Interview* 1975). However, a more deliberate appreciation followed with Andrew Britton's detailed interpretation in *Movie*, which concluded, "*Mandingo* is a masterpiece of Hollywood cinema" (Britton 1976, 22). Later, the film received a screenplay award from the N.A.A.C.P., and more recent praise appeared in Ed Guerrero's *Framing Blackness* (Guerrero 1993, 31–35) and Robin Wood's essay, "*Mandingo:* The Vindication of an Abused Masterpiece" (Wood 1998, 265–82). The public was more responsive than the press. According to *Variety's* box office survey for 1975, *Mandingo* was a solid hit and ranked eighteenth among the year's releases, with over eight and a half million dollars in tallied domestic revenues out-grossing award-winning features such as *Nashville* and *Alice Doesn't Live Here Anymore*, action fare like *Rollerball*, and another successful boxing film, *Hard Times*.

Mandingo is a tale of succession. Hammond (Perry King) is the only son and heir to the Falconhurst estate. He limps as a result of a childhood injury, and his weakness engenders an insecure masculinity as well as an abnormal sensitivity to the welfare of his black slaves, weaknesses his father Maxwell (James Mason) tries to root out. Ham is dispatched by his father to engage a wife and purchase a Mandingo (a pure blooded West African) from the slave market. Ironically, both are intended for breeding: the wife to produce an heir, and the slave to expand the resources of the plantation. The son returns with three individuals, rather than two, in tow: Blanche (Susan George), his new wife; Mede (Ken Norton), the Mandingo; and another slave, Ellen (Brenda Sykes), whom Ham has taken as his mistress. All three serve to first alleviate, and later exacerbate, Ham's weakness. Ham trains Mede to fight other slaves for the amusement of the planter class and the glory of the plantation. Though Mede realizes Hammond's hopes as a fighter, and even befriends his master, complications arise. Blanche acts like a loving bride, but when her new husband discovers that she has been deflowered, he becomes estranged, preferring to satisfy his lust with his compliant slave mistress, Ellen. In revenge, Blanche blackmails the unwilling Mede into a liaison. When Blanche's long awaited first born testifies to her indiscretion, Hammond murders his wife and the fighter—but not before the rebellious and embittered slave Mem shoots the depraved plantation master, Maxwell. At the conclusion, Hammond's vengeance appears to have obliterated his humanity and prepared him for the brutal task of becoming the new master of Falconhurst.

The title character in *Mandingo*, the boxer Mede, functions as an alter ego, compensating for the weakness of his master—first with men, and then with women. For both Hammond and Blanche, the boxer Mede embodies an idealized male physicality that they appropriate heartlessly. Nevertheless, both white master and mistress develop a genuine affection for Mede, even though their culture punishes any fellowship that crosses racial lines. In *Mandingo*, boxing becomes a competition deprived of social consciousness in which the chattels are devoured enacting the aspirations of their masters. Mede goes to his doom with little resistance, but the rebellious slaves, Cicero and Mem, provide the political counterpoint in their call for black solidarity against their oppressors.

Typical of the blaxploitation era, *Mandingo* excites racial tensions with its call for allegiance to the black community. *Mandingo* evokes the iconography of *Gone With the Wind* ad copy, in which Rhett carries Scarlet in his arms. The *Mandingo* ad design employs a similar sketch style in which two half-clothed, mixed race couples embrace. Ken Norton and Susan George pose in a kiss on the left, while Perry King carries off Brenda Sykes, in the manner of Rhett and Scarlet, on the right. The poster reads: "Expect the savage. The sensual. The powerful. The shameful. Expect all that the motion picture screen has never dared to show before. Expect the truth. Now you are ready for 'Mandingo.'" *Mandingo* promises a revealing treatment of a taboo experience,

Mandingo evokes the iconography of *Gone With the Wind* ad copy, in which Rhett carries Scarlett in his arms. Courtesy of the Academy of Motion Picture Arts and Sciences.

miscegenation. As a result, integration is portrayed at its most provocative, and unlike the wholesome couple of *Guess Who's Coming to Dinner* (1967), the advertisement for *Mandingo* highlights interracial sex. The inflammatory poster contrasts with traditional assimilation values, which promote marriage between ethnic groups. *Mandingo* exults in historical revisionism with its play upon the imagery borrowed from its famous predecessor. Indeed, history is central to its address.

The film grounds racial identity in the American past, specifically the antebellum South, but revises the common understanding of history's relationship to the present. The appeal to history broadens the specter of racial oppression by exploring its sources. Rather than a nostalgic portrait of the "good old days," *Mandingo* asks the audience to remember the crimes incited by race. A lynchpin tying the past to the present is the boxer and his link to Muhammad Ali. *Mandingo* alludes to Ali indirectly through Ken Norton, whose principle claim to fame was his ring victory over Ali. Norton's Mede functions in *Mandingo* as an anti-Ali. Rather than acting as a resistance leader, like the Champ, this plantation boxer ties his fate to his master and ignores the agitation of his slave comrades. In spite of Mede's service to master and mistress, the contest between the whites destroys him. The racial divide is so entrenched in social relations that individual alliances across the color line cannot be sustained; neither do they ultimately change the balance of power between oppressors and oppressed. As a result, Mede falls scapegoat to the failures of his masters. The historical perspective offered by the film acts as a warning that recent gains for African Americans need to be pressed to counter longstanding injustice. *Mandingo* presents a cautionary tale to African Americans, one directed against the optimism of expanded civil rights and prospects for racial integration. The message of that history is to be wary of the master and remain loyal to your racial community.

Mandingo uses boxing to juxtapose interracial friendship with fellowship among blacks. The boxing motif is presented in three conventional stages: the discovery of Mede's fighting skills; Mede's training; and the contest with Topaze. Each episode underlines the growing bond between Hammond and Mede. In the first episode, Madame Caroline's slave orders Mede to leave the brothel courtyard, and he replies, "I'm Master Hammond's slave and I'm staying." He identifies himself as Hammond's property rather than with his own name. A fight ensues between Mede and the other slave, with Mede emerging victorious. At its conclusion, Hammond rushes to soothe Mede's bruises. When offered double the cost of his slave, Hammond refuses to sell, but he does accept the Marquis's challenge to match Mede against the Marquis's champion, Topaze. During the three training scenes Hammond supervises Mede's progress, and when they are ready to return to New Orleans for the bout, Mede assures his master with a smile that he will "whup anybody you want." The contest begins with Mede taking a brutal beating, and the tormented Hammond cries, "I yield the fight. Stop it." However, when Mede recognizes his master's distress, he is reinvigorated and takes command of the fray. After Mede's victory, Hammond turns down a $10,000 offer for the slave, even though he decides to relieve his charge from ever fighting again. Mede's progress as a fighter becomes the means for creating a special relationship with his master.

The ties to Hammond are contrasted with the antagonism that arises between Mede and the rebellious blacks Mem and Cicero. Mem accuses Mede of being a "white man's fightin' animal," and asks, "[W]hen you gonna learn the color of your skin?" Between the training sessions and the New Orleans fight,

Cicero flees the plantation, and Mede tackles the fugitive in the bush. Preparing to hang, Cicero glares at Mede, and accuses him of killing a black brother. The contrast between Mede's growing affection for Hammond and the antagonism among the blacks reaches a climax in the battle with Topaze. Here, two slaves fight each other to the death for the amusement of their masters. The biting, scratching, and wrenching that goes on during the fight underscores the equation between slaves and animals, but Topaze's eye gouging and Mede's bloodied face also suggests the blindness of slaves fighting each other rather than combating their enslavement. Master Hammond cries, "We won," as Mede watches the dead Topaze carried from the ring, anticipating his own demise. The boxing in *Mandingo* illustrates misplaced racial loyalties. Mede allows a personal rapport to obscure his oppression.

Mandingo highlights a culture reproducing itself, illustrating in particular how contradictions surrounding patriarchy, racism, and the family subjugate white and black alike. Romance degenerates into predatory sexuality. The breeding of blacks and the selling of children are the basis of Falconhurst, where slaves are the only crop raised for market. The plantation represents the antithesis of the family, while also being the focus of inheritance and familial continuity. Hammond's discovery that Blanche is not a virgin threatens the crippled masculinity she was intended to fortify. As a victim of her predatory brother, who abused her when she was fifteen, Blanche is already marked by familial corruption, yet any appeal for redress will only result in her further victimization. She initially views her engagement as an escape from a fallen family, but ignored by her husband at Falconhurst, she becomes a prisoner again. The barren mistress of a human breeding farm, the tormented Blanche embodies contradiction. The idealized Southern belle is here a victim of incest, shunted aside for a slave mistress, starved for affection, and imprisoned on the plantation. Frustrated and alone, Blanche blackmails Mede into an affair that suggests their similarity as individuals. The parallel couples, Ham and Ellen and Blanche and Mede, both conceive children. When Ellen confides in Hammond that they will have a child, she requests that the baby be freed. However, the conception only incites a jealous Blanche to attack Ellen, resulting in the child's miscarriage, and Blanche's own child is murdered when the newborn is discovered to be a mulatto. The idealized American melting pot of migrant peoples mingling together to produce a new nation is given a grotesque twist owing to the contending fear of racial pollution. The film ends with the death of progeny, rather with a fruitful succession.

Mandingo employs an ironic substitution, posing a relationship between boxing and romance. First, Mede fights Topaze as an antidote for his master's inadequacy. After his ring career has ended, the boxer becomes a tool for

Blanche's vengeance. Now his physical excellence mocks rather than elevates the crippled master. *Mandingo* invites a comparison between the slave fighters and the Blanche/Mede tryst. The slaves should be comrades battling their oppressors; similarly, Blanche, the victim of sexual abuse, should befriend Mede rather than exploit him. Both couples consist of victims who arouse our sympathy, yet they prey upon each other rather than cooperate in resisting their common foes. *Mandingo* suggests a grotesque similarity between boxing and romance arising from an ideology that turns allies into enemies. The quartet of Hammond, Mede, Blanche, and Ellen rotates in a round of substitutions that illustrates how race shapes relationships in spite of good intentions. *Mandingo*'s insight is grounded in racism's power.

In *Mandingo*, though white and black are marked as social groups, individuals, while exhibiting their own ethnic and psychological character, are pressed to comply with the prevailing ideology. The races separate into slavers and enslaved, the slaves into the compliant and the resistant, the slavers into the depraved and the sensitive. However, the fiction complicates the simplicity of these divisions. The compliant (Ellen and Mede) and the sensitive (Hammond and Blanche) strike alliances across racial lines, but they are led to mutual destruction by the grotesque social system that demeans them. The corruption of white culture extends its malignant influence beyond slavery into gender relations and sexuality. Mede accepts his slave status and the favors that his master offers. Before being hung, Cicero stares enraged at Mede and cries, "I'd rather die than be a slave." The conclusion of *Mandingo* affirms race as the frame for identity. Determined to punish Mede for his liaison with Blanche, Hammond ignores the pleas of his lover Ellen. He casts her aside, declaring, "Don't you think that if you get in my bed you're anything but a nigger." Faced with execution by his supposed friend, Mede petitions unsuccessfully and cries out after being shot, "I did 'n think you was somehow better than a white man, but you is just white." At the intersection of social conditions and individual experience, the film builds a web of relationships that smothers a common humanity, and rewards domination of men over women and whites over blacks. Black identity coalesces in response to racism. In *Mandingo*, fellowship among African Americans begins with resistance and must be sustained by resistance.

Mandingo suffers from weakness in the development of its African American characters. Though both Mede and Ellen have strong scenes, the psychological drama is dominated by Hammond and, in later episodes, Blanche. Even though "all of *Mandingo*'s scenes are shot from a point of view sympathetic to the African American perspective," as Ed Guerrero observes, the black characters lack the dimension of their white counterparts (Guerrero 1993, 33). Robin Wood notes the "film's weak spot" arises from being "unable to cross racial boundaries to the extent of developing a corresponding empathy with its black characters" (Wood 1998, 282). Ellen's attraction to Hammond is never satisfactorily explained, and Mede never achieves a depth of motivation. *Mandingo* suggests that the African American community emerges out of a history of slavery that cannot be simply overcome by personal effort, but the community of slaves in its fictive world is never well established.

Mandingo shares the anxiety felt by Richard Wright, Ralph Ellison, and Gerald Early when faced with the boxer who is supposedly an idealized hero for African Americans. In spite of their nobility, black fighters are debased by the brutality of their craft and controlled by white institutions. The enslaved boxer in *Mandingo* vividly expresses the reservations expressed by these black intellectuals, as well as the racial tensions in a popular culture liberated from traditional constraints in the post–civil rights era. Confronted by white racism, assimilation for the blaxploitation boxer was a deceptive lure or a foolhardy dream. Identity had to be established in loyalty to the racial community.

WHEN WE WERE KINGS [1996]: THE BOXER AS CHAMPION OF THE RACIAL COMMUNITY

When We Were Kings looks back to the blaxploitation era to acclaim the boxer as a champion of the racial community. Assimilation is no longer an option. Rather, African American culture functions independently within the nation and struggles to recognize its African heritage. The documentary portrays the 1974 title bout between heavyweight champion George Foreman and underdog Muhammad Ali, which promoter Don King staged in Zaire. From the beginning, the film highlights Ali's mix of championship boxing, black politics, and loquacious bravado. Don King touts "the Rumble in the Jungle" as reestablishing links between African Americans and their ancestral home. The dramatic conflict in the film arises from ideological tension between the apolitical Foreman, who fails to affirm his racial consciousness, and Ali's heroic quest to be a champion of the black community. A chronicle of press conferences, training, travel, and especially preparation for a black music festival precedes the fight, building the expectation that Foreman, a heavy favorite, will annihilate Ali and end his career. The audience is well prepared for the stirring upset, and the aftermath pays homage to Ali as a leader of the African American community.

When We Were Kings builds its narrative around a pattern of heroic recognition similar to the classic "David and Goliath" tale. Muhammad Ali, the underdog, must fight for his people against the imposing giant, heavyweight champion George Foreman. Like David, Ali is a trickster preparing his "rope a dope" to fight the Philistine behemoth, a yokel ready to bring down the conjurer with his overpowering blows. Stripped of his title by the American legal system, Muhammad Ali cultivates an association with Africa, the black homeland emerging from colonial exploitation. The first act of the film focuses on Ali's background as a fighter and the announcement of the forthcoming title bout in Zaire, now the Congo. Episodes from Ali's early career are associated with the civil rights struggle and further matched with images from the anticolonial rebellion in the Congo. The film portrays the young Ali promoting racial pride, and the older man who now serves as a missionary reuniting black America and black Africa. The film's second act follows the Americans to Africa, and as they prepare for the bout Ali meets his brethren in Zaire, serenaded by songs from the black music festival such as "Say It Loud, I'm Black and I'm Proud." The former champion ties himself so closely to the destiny of the black community that the Africans express surprise when George Foreman arrives and they discover that he is black too. Muhammad Ali assumes the mantle of righteousness in the tradition of Jack London's "The Mexican," but his opponent is neither Western imperialism nor white America. Rather, it is George Foreman, the sullen slugger, who more readily fits the mould of the boxer burdened by an underdeveloped political consciousness, an athlete who approaches the bout simply as a professional competition. Ali ties his quest to awakening black America from the apolitical detachment personified by Foreman. The third act of the film begins with the injury to Foreman that delays the fight, allowing Ali and the Africans time to cultivate their alliance. The act culminates with the bout and Ali's victory, which becomes a triumph for a renewed American-African brotherhood. The closing act meditates on the meaning of Ali as a historical hero and suggests a reunification of black and white America in their mutual admiration for the heroic boxer. The film embraces Ali as a crusader for the black community, one whose courage evokes a time "when we were kings," when heroism raised common men and women to majesty.

When We Were Kings attempted to revive African American solidarity in the 1990s through a quest for racial identity. The film highlights the connection between blacks in America and in Africa, but finally the quest focuses on the black boxer as a race hero. Sports achievement is thoroughly absorbed by the racial context. History and memory link the racial politics of 1974 to the need for revival in 1996. In the film Spike Lee explains, "Today's generation, they don't know anything. . . . They don't know who Malcolm X is, JFK, Jackie Robinson, Muhammad Ali. It's scary. These kids are missin' a whole lot if they don't know about the legacy of Muhammad Ali because no matter what era you live in you see very few true heroes." The crossing between continents becomes crossing back through time to embrace the heritage embodied in Muhammad Ali.

When We Were Kings promotes a renewed bond with African Americans' ancestral home and seeks a common humanity with African culture. Immediately after winning the heavyweight title in 1964, Muhammad Ali changed his name and identified himself first and foremost as a black man. Ali's long-standing cultivation of his racial identity, often at the expense of other black fighters, fed into the promotion of the 1974 title bout with Ali as a bridge between America and Africa. In the opening lines of *When We Were Kings* Ali declares, "Yeah, I'm in Africa. Africa's my home. Damn America . . . Africa's the home of the black man." The contrast between Ali and Foreman develops in part from Ali's continual reaching out to the African people. The documentary offers a repeated sequence of Ali running and shadow boxing on the highway. Africans surround the boxer and enjoy his mock punches at the camera. A man of the people, Ali plays to the crowd; his identity arises out of his solidarity with others. Here, the boxer is interactive rather than isolated, funny and engaging rather than distant and directionless. Foreman, by contrast, offers a professional greeting but fails to strike any rapport with the people of Zaire. Malik Bowens explains that Foreman arrived with his two German Shepherds, dogs the Belgian colonizers used to attack the Congolese. So the Africans associate Foreman with their oppressors. Foreman appears to be private and parochial in contrast to the racial internationalism that wins Ali the support of the Africans. *When We Were Kings* develops this theme further in footage of the music concert of black American artists, such as B.B. King and James Brown, which is intercut with African singers and drummers as a means of highlighting the ties between these communities. Songs such as "I'm Coming Home" underline the musical bond between black identity and the African homeland.

Though a documentary, *When We Were Kings* uses structures similar to those used in fiction films to portray its themes. For example, the film employs the conventions of melodrama to portray the triumph of the heroic boxer. As Peter Brooks has explained in *The Melodramatic Imagination*, melodrama involves a quest for value through feeling (Brooks 1976). An aesthetic of emotional intensity is cultivated through simplification, repetition, and intensification. By contrast, irony poses a split in the meaning of its signs. Melodrama strives to line up all its formal devices behind common themes and, particularly, behind its appeal to the emotions, in order to achieve maximum intensity. To this end it sacrifices complexity of character to a strong moral opposition acted out by primal types: Ali the crusader versus Foreman the slumbering giant. The melodramatic plot regularly employs a deception that hides the hero's true worth behind the machinations of the villain and the maladjustment of the social order. Finally a reversal, which defies realistic expectations, unmasks the villain and allows society to return the hero to his proper position. The surprising nature of the reversal propels the surge of emotion that greets the triumphant hero. Muhammad Ali, deposed by political enemies and boxing rivals, fills the role of the melodramatic hero. Winning against heavy odds and against expectations further enhances the mode. The simplicity of boxing and the historical authenticity of the event contribute to an effect often discredited in fiction as naïve.

When We Were Kings exploits the melodramatic potential of "the Rumble in the Jungle." The detachment of "direct cinema," the style originally intended for the concert film, is abandoned for a work that wholeheartedly valorizes Ali. Rather than being objective, When We Were Kings becomes a hymn to black solidarity. It finds a base in its clear focus on Ali and the development of the opposition between the fighters, already exaggerated during the promotion for the fight. Then the film builds two countervailing motifs: on the one hand, Foreman's prowess and the boxing world's conviction that Ali stands little chance; on the other hand, Ali's engaging personality and his moral stature as a spokesman for black people. The audience is caught up in its attraction to Ali and the likelihood that he will be humiliated. Furthermore, melodrama distrusts language and seeks alternate, extra-linguistic forms to convey emotions, what Brooks calls the "text of muteness." When We Were Kings combines three principle elements to serve this function: rhythmic editing of images, music and song from the prefight concert that was the original subject of the film; and the boxing action culminating in Ali's knockout of Foreman. All these elements contribute to a powerful melodramatic impact made even more intense by its unusual cultivation in a documentary.

As in boxing fiction films, the romance in When We Were Kings proves central to the boxer's self-realization. Almost all fiction films interweave two plot lines: a quest, such as seeking the boxing title, with a romantic subplot. Nonfiction films may include a quest, but, as Harry Cohn once observed, "[D]ocumentaries are films without women." There is no romance. However, this documentary employs romance as a key to its politics. When We Were Kings uses a rhetorical figure to portray Africa as Ali's secret romantic partner. Director Leon Gast bases this conceit around a story told by George Plimpton about Ali visiting Zaire President Mobutu shortly before the bout and consulting Mobutu's witch doctor. The witch doctor reassures the challenger that a succubus will take the strength from his opponent and bring Ali victory. The film uses the image and sound of the African singer Miriam Makeba to embody the succubus. Unlike the other participants in the prefight concert, Makeba is removed from the concert sequence. Instead, she is introduced in a close up headshot without identification at the opening of the film. Makeba is singing, but her vocal is limited to a breathing sound, and the image quickly disappears without explanation, followed by Ali declaring, "Yeah, I'm in Africa. Africa's my home . . . the home of the Black man." The same image of Makeba returns midway through the film at the time Foreman is injured during training, causing a postponement of the bout. Shortly before the fight, Plimpton relates the story of Ali and the witch doctor that informs the Makeba image. Then during the fight, as Ali's "rope a dope" strategy begins to take its toll on Foreman, Plimpton confides to Norman Mailer that the "succubus has got him." Again the Makeba image and sound reappear, as Ali strikes the knockout blow and her full significance becomes clear. She has served as Muhammad Ali's ally in upsetting the champion. She embodies Africa itself. She is the romantic figure whose union with the hero brings the villain to his knees. This "romance" is a poetic trope employed by the filmmaker to seal the union between Muhammad Ali and the Pan-African celebration. The symbolic and collective character of the romance elevates the boxer's movement beyond physical excellence to assume a community leadership that becomes essential to his heroism.

The spirit woman aiding Ali represents the union between two distant black populations who are reaching out for mutual support. Though Spike Lee claims that the last generation of black Americans has realized a new kinship with Africa, in general the years since the Zaire bout testify to the negligible impact of the event on intercontinental relations. Gerald Early argues that the "film simply obscures the tragedy of the political pretensions of this event" (Early 1997, 12). But the goal of Ali and *When We Were Kings* was to animate a feeling of union between these peoples and to invest that feeling with a moral dimension that could have political consequences. The lack of later, more concrete political benefits does not nullify that aim. The film portrays and promotes the emotional alliance between America and Africa.

Interviews dating from 1995 through 1996 with Norman Mailer, George Plimpton, Spike Lee, Thomas Hauser, and Malik Bowens constitute the closing stage in the production of *When We Were Kings*. These commentators cultivate an intimacy with the viewer. They join the audience in remembering 1974, and in the cases of Mailer, Plimpton, and Bowens, recall participation in the events. These witnesses become like fictional characters whose emotional stories establish a bond with the audience. Mailer and Plimpton had already published extensively on the fight, so their memories are well rehearsed stories underlined with a wistful sweetness. But even the younger man, Spike Lee, holds a distinct relation to Ali. In some respects Lee has achieved a position in the film industry comparable to the one Ali holds. Lee became a leader in the film industry, which was largely closed to African American directors. As such, he is a hero, here looking back on another who inspired him, and he reminds his listeners that great deeds can be achieved. These engaging characters contribute to the heartfelt tone of this documentary.

Norman Mailer and George Plimpton play important roles in the racial politics of *When We Were Kings*. Apart from these commentators, whites are marginal to the film. But Mailer and Plimpton have a distinctive function. Their treatment of black internationalism illustrates their role. The black spokesmen, Spike Lee and Malik Bowens, testify to the revival of ties between black people in America and in Africa. Norman Mailer, on the other hand, reports on the brutality of the Mobutu regime. He casts doubt upon the intercontinental ballyhoo, and instills a wary distance between the audience and African politics. These contrasting attitudes underscore the racial differences in *When We Were Kings*. More centrally, Mailer and Plimpton voice the most detailed, eloquent, and personal reports of any commentators who appear in the film. As a result, they convey an impression of white people commenting with benign detachment on the black world. Mailer characterizes Foreman as an embodiment of "negritude," and Plimpton marvels as Don King quotes from Shakespeare. In writing about the film, Gerald Early even complains that the choice of commentators displayed a lack of consideration for African response to the event (Early 1997, 12). The boundary between participant and commentator becomes the signpost of the racial divide in a world in which blacks act and whites reflect.

However, in its resolution *When We Were Kings* closes this racial division with two personal stories. First, Mailer tells of an encounter with Ali at an *Esquire* magazine party over a decade after the Zaire fight. The humorous anecdote relates how Ali praised Mailer's youthful appearance, only to tease his young wife, after Mailer departed, for staying with such an old man. The lighthearted story conveys Ali's playful chicanery even as it exposes Mailer's masculine inadequacy in the presence of the Champ. Plimpton remembers Ali giving a commencement address to the Harvard graduating class, urging the graduates to use their learning to promote social justice. At the end of the speech a member of the largely white audience cries out to Ali, "Give us a poem." After a pause, the boxer responds with what Plimpton claims is the shortest poem in the English language, "Me, We." So the documentary closes with a heartening attempt to cross the racial divide. Mailer, metaphorically, becomes a participant entering the ring with Ali at the party and is knocked out. Plimpton and the Harvard graduates receive advice from the Champ, who urges them to action.

With his poem Ali affirms the union of black and white, as well as the bond between the individual and the community. Racial identity is cultivated and affirmed in *When We Were Kings*, and finally that identity becomes the basis for mutual respect and common purpose in the uplifting resolution.

When We Were Kings employs a retrospective montage that sums up its portrait of the boxer. The sequence invokes the memory of the viewer by shifting from color to black and white and repeating images from earlier in the film. The montage crystallizes the filmmaker's thoughts and provides an opportunity for the viewer to reflect back upon the experience of the film.

The montage in *When We Were Kings* presents Ali's heroism as a manliness that extends beyond his feats as a boxer. The 3-minute sequence falls into seven distinct parts. Part one presents Ali's rise as a boxer from the celebration of his Olympic gold medal until he gains the heavyweight title in 1964. Part two presents him as a religious Muslim, seen in prayer together with Malcolm X and Elijah Muhammad and pointing accusingly at an American flag. The following part, "Justice on Trial," portrays the legal persecution Ali endured and the vindication he enjoyed. In part four Ali is an admired celebrity: surrounded by autograph seekers; advising children;, enjoying the company of other leaders, such as Jackie Robinson; clowning with singers, such as the Beatles and the Jackson Five; and in a portrait shot with boxing legends Joe Louis and Ray Robinson. Part five casts Ali as a racial leader speaking to crowds of black people. Part six returns to boxing, with Ali knocking out a series of opponents, beginning with George Foreman and ending with Sonny Liston. Part seven offers a closing reprise in images of Ali's many moods, clowning on a pile of money, sitting in his boxing corner, standing at a blackboard, and finally lost in thoughtful introspection. Only two of the montage's seven parts focus on boxing, and Ali is presented as a hero because of his leadership of the black community. Frequently—and most vividly in part five—Ali is portrayed as a towering presence among crowds of people, taking his fighting spirit from the ring into the social arena. All this cutting moves to the song "When We Were Kings," which establishes the tempo and informs the images with its lyrics. As the song proclaims, "When one man climbs, the rest are lifted up ... to a higher destiny." The song title emphasizes the notion that Ali's triumphs elevated more than the man alone; they raised the entire African American community. His achievement reached far beyond the boxing ring. The hero in *When We Were Kings* emerges as a crusader for social justice whose identity as a fighter is based in his racial community. The montage valorizes Ali's leadership and inspires the audience to acknowledge prospects for heroic action that combines physical excellence with social responsibility. *When We Were Kings* sends its audience to the door with a feeling that heroism is possible in everyday life.

✦ ✦ ✦

For decades the boxing film portrayed the fighter as an ethnic or racial out-sider who experiences a conflict between entering the mainstream culture and loyalty to his indigenous community. A historical investigation of the genre reveals a significant development of this theme. During the Hollywood studio era, the conflict usually concerned the difficulties for oppressed white ethnics of entering the dominant culture. These films promoted the melting pot con-cept of America, arising from successive waves of immigrants struggling to find their place in a unified national culture. Films like *Kid Galahad, Right Cross*, and *The Ring* portrayed the painful, at times unsuccessful, process of assimila-tion. Gradually the genre extended its view to include ever more embattled eth-nic groups, moving from Jews and Italian Americans to Hispanics and finally to African Americans. More recently, the boxing film has featured a pluralist image of America as a nation composed of multiple, independent communi-ties cooperating or in conflict. In this context, the African American screen boxer has struggled to maintain his loyalty to the black community while com-bating white racism. *Mandingo* presents a cautionary tale warning that loyalty to the racial community must take precedence over personal alliances across racial lines. *When We Were Kings* embraces uplift by celebrating heroic leader-ship with an aspiration to link black Americans to their African homeland. The conflict between mainstream culture and the indigenous community is by comparison a more volatile theme than the critique of the success ethic. The evolution of this conflict is central to a penetrating understanding of the boxing film, both fictional and documentary. However, an investigation of this theme reveals greater complexity when the theme is viewed as a genre trend rather than an aspect of a single film. Such a perspective surveying the history of the genre brings this issue into sharp, illuminating focus.

5

ROMANCE AND THE RING
Gender Conflict in the Boxing Film

Over 90 percent of Hollywood films include a romance. Genres usually distinguish themselves by their treatment of courtship and couples. In the Western, the saloon girl and the schoolmarm try to bring the cowboy in from the range. The singing couples of the musical often embody the conflict between work and entertainment. Violence twists romance in the gangster film, and a perverse sexuality thwarts the couple. In the boxing film, the masculine milieu of the prizefighter polarizes men and women. Though the vamp may parade through the boxing world to entice the pugilist, the sweetheart must draw him from the ring for marriage to be realized. Boxing constrains the mingling of masculine and feminine traits necessary to establish a fruitful relationship between a man and a woman. As a result, a crisis of masculinity is characteristic of the genre. The boxer must choose between remaining loyal to the manly ethos of the ring, or compromise his masculine bravado to successfully court a woman. How that crisis is posed and resolved creates a pivotal dramatic conflict in these films. The evolution of this problem allows us to chart the shifting gender relations in our culture.

Contrasting two versions of *The Champ* (1931 and 1979) illustrates the possible ideological variability within a genre. These films treat parenting and gender from two distinct perspectives. The first portrays masculine flaws, while the second blames the career woman for neglecting her child. In the post–World War II era, *The Set-Up* (1949) developed the analogy between the combat veteran and the boxer. In this film the pugilist must overcome traumatic violence

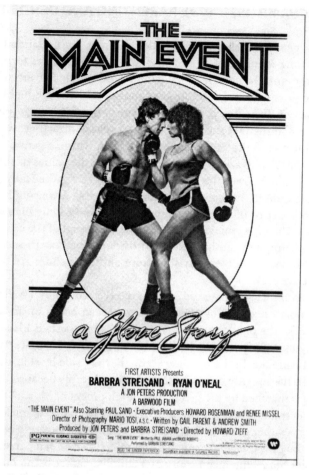

In the boxing film the masculine milieu of the prizefighter polarizes men and women. Courtesy of the Academy of Motion Picture Arts and Sciences.

in order to realize a fruitful union with a woman. During the comeback cycle of the 1970s, *Hard Times* (1975) responded to the rising woman's movement by posing an idealized masculinity that trumpets traditional male values. *Girlfight* (2000) counters with a tough woman ready to fight toe-to-toe with a man inside and outside the ring. Though characterized by an embattled masculinity, the boxing film chronicles a broad spectrum of response to gender portraying the evolving social roles of men and women with insight and sensitivity.

THE CHAMP (1931/1979): PARENTING AND GENDER

Many genre critics, including Rick Altman, have claimed that film genres promote ideological values that are inherent in the form (Altman 1987, 5). I argue, on the contrary, that genres pose widely felt social problems, but that the portrayal and resolution of those problems are highly variable. Two versions of *The Champ*, the first an enormous hit in 1931 and the second another commercial success in 1979, present contrasting treatments of gender that testify to the variability of expression within a genre. The gender conflict in *The Champ* arises from parenting. Will the values of the father or those of the mother train the boy? The 1931 film sympathetically portrays a failure of masculinity because the father is incapable of raising his son. The death of the boxer results in his surrender of the boy and finally redeems the boxer's flaws. The 1979 remake offers a hostile treatment of the career woman, featuring a delinquent mother reformed through the boxer's sacrifice. Both films address social problems arising from shifting gender roles typical of their respective eras.

In *The Champ* (1931), parenting roles are reversed. Andy (Wallace Beery), the ex-champion besotted by booze and gambling, hangs on to the illusion of a comeback. The only one who believes in his prospects is his ten-year-old son, Dink (Jackie Cooper), who idolizes his father. Andy is Dink's pal, his companion and bedmate. In the opening scene they jog side by side, their respective stages in life roughly equivalent in emotional terms because the Champ's immaturity is matched by the precocious development of his son. Dink supervises Andy in training and tries to keep him away from the saloon and the crap table. After his father goes on a binge, the boy guides the boxer to bed, undressing and chiding the lout, and generally assuming the role of a parent. The film's humor grows out of the incongruity of a childlike father being nurtured by a devoted, but long-suffering boy.

A crisis arises when, by chance, the Champ encounters Linda (Irene Rich), the boy's mother, who left Andy long ago and married the prosperous and elegant Tony (Hale Hamilton). Now Linda wants to rescue Dink from the Tijuana low life, send him to school, and embrace him as her son. At the track, where the meeting takes place, a race ensues between "Little Champ," Andy's and Dink's horse, and "Blue Boy," owned by Linda and Tony. The contest symbolizes the contending models the two parents set for Dink: "Little Champ" would have Dink follow his father, while "Blue Boy," a name alluding to the Gainsborough portrait, signifies a general association with art, culture, and wealth. In addition, "Blue Boy" serves as an allusion to Dink's sorrow, initially at losing the race and later at mourning the Champ.

In the race, "Blue Boy" initially moves out front, then "Little Champ" surges forward and leads the pack until he suddenly falls, leaving the field to "Blue Boy." The film plays out the analogy with the contest for Dink's future as Andy takes a series of falls that finally result in the boy joining his mother. Even as the horse is being helped to his feet, Andy sells out his affection for Dink. Tony approaches Andy, asking him to allow Linda to visit the boy. The father refuses, berating his former wife, but when Tony offers him cash in exchange for Dink's visit, Andy grabs the money. In spite of the Champ's affection, he is easily turned from what he believes to be best for his son.

The contest between father and mother refocuses on Andy and Tony as competing masculine models for Dink. Andy is impulsive, charming, and naughty. He throws on whatever shabby clothes are at hand, disregards business for play, and acts with no heed for the consequences. One day, luck shines on him at the gambling tables, the next day all is gloom. Andy moves from moment to moment, from instinct to feeling with hardly a thought. His pastimes—drinking, gambling and brawling—are little more than the play of boys corrupted by men. Tony stands in contrast. He is impeccably dressed with a trim mustache. He is polite and understands how to suggest a distasteful proposition to Andy without arousing his anger. He is solicitous of his wife, protective and patient with children, wealthy without being condescending or hypocritical. Though Tony is presented without a blemish, he is clearly removed from the sensibilities of the ten-year-old. He wants to raise the boy, but cannot befriend Dink because he embodies the distance between boy and man and the separation from the parent that is necessary for the boy to mature. The arrival of Tony signals a transition in Dink's life from the pleasures of boyhood to the responsibilities of the adult.

The relationship of the men to Linda is pivotal. Andy stands apart from his former wife, scowling at her from afar. Equally important, Andy has no relationships with other women. Tony, the more feminized man, serves as the negotiator who draws Dink from father to mother. The qualities he shares with women allow for marriage. Adulthood is Dink's destiny, but to realize it he must part from Andy, the overgrown child, the undeveloped man. Maturity, as represented by Tony, requires a mingling of genders and overcoming sexual differences, whereas boxing is a milieu exclusive to men. These contrasts extend to groups of subsidiary characters forming competing "families." Tim, the manager, and Sponge, the trainer, join Dink and Jonah, Dink's black friend, in surrounding Andy to make up a family—albeit one that is homeless, unstable, and devoid of women. In contrast, Tony, Linda, and Mary Lou, their little girl, are ensconced in a beautiful home. The mix of genders provides the balance necessary for the family to prosper.

In *The Champ* the boxer represents an underdeveloped man incapable of relationships with women, a man who fails to measure up to the standard of masculinity posed by the film, fatherhood. Andy embodies failure because in *The Champ* gender difference must be overcome in order to develop into a mature adult. In leaving his father, Dink manages to initiate that transition.

Because of its swings from joy to grief, *The Champ* poses questions about masculinity and emotion. In spite of Andy's failings, deep feelings bind father and son. By contrast, Tony is a pale model, as he lacks the passion, bravado, and humanity of the Champ. However, shifts from exultation to suffering inflict a terrible burden on the child, and Andy's lack of emotional control makes him an intolerable parent. The horse "Little Champ" illustrates the problem. In the film's initial episode, Andy loses financial backing for a fight because of his drunkenness, and Dink goes to sleep crestfallen at his father's weakness. Rising early, Andy sneaks off and wins a bundle at craps, rejuvenating the boy with a shower of gifts, including a horse that Dink dubs "Little Champ." Later his luck shifts again, and Andy hocks the horse to cover his gambling debts. When Linda supplies enough money to reclaim the animal, Andy takes the cash in order to return to the tables. Finally, moments before his death, the Champ uses his winnings from his boxing bout to reunite Dink with the horse. Andy is an unstable character who, in spite of his love for his son, regularly hurts him.

Suffering is the primary emotion portrayed. The Champ's agony reaches a climax in a prison scene. Andy has been thrown into jail for brawling. Coming to his senses the next day, he realizes that his behavior harms his child, and he decides to send Dink to Linda. But when the boy visits the prison he pleads to remain with his father. Andy responds with insults and anger, finally striking the boy to drive him away. In tears, Dink departs. Tormented at hitting the child and grieving at the loss of his son, the prisoner relentlessly pounds the cell wall with his fists until they are bloody and broken. His conflicts generate a wrenching pathos. The depth of this pain finally recommends Tony's more disciplined, if less intense, behavior. His sensitivity and constraint present a viable option to Andy's destructive emotions. Here the boxer embodies another masculine type: the man of intense feeling at the mercy of his moods who excites compassion and fear as we bear witness to his suffering.

The inadequacy marking the boxer is also associated with class differences apparent in the obvious social inequality between Andy and Tony. The setting in Tijuana amplifies this class issue, as "the other side of the tracks" comes to mean across the border. In Mexico, dusty streets, transient hotels, gambling halls, and saloons establish a netherworld that is poor, brutish, and full of pain— and distant from the elegant apartment and luxurious sleeping cars Linda and Tony inhabit. But as Dink observes in Linda's apartment, "The Champ and I

Andy (Wallace Beery) is ready for his comeback, with Dink (Jackie Cooper) at his side in *The Champ* (1931). Courtesy of the Academy of Motion Picture Arts and Sciences.

ain't fixed up as swell as this; but our joint's more lively." In the closing bout, the Mexican champion serves as Andy's double, embodying the forces contending within the Champ. The Mexican opponent signifies the flaws in Andy's character, while his championship points to Andy's nickname and to all that is superior within him. The bout itself literalizes the struggle within the Champ. Though his love for Dink emerges victorious, it comes at the cost of his life. The poverty associated with Mexico must be overcome for the boy to mature, but the father cannot escape from his limitations. More ominously, the film portrays a catalogue of fears haunting working class men during the Depression. Andy has already lost the championship and seems barely able to obtain work as a boxer. His wife abandons him for a more prosperous and respectable man. Drinking, gambling, and losing his temper only accelerate his demise. Finally, his most cherished companion, his son, is pried away. Heartbroken, he dies. *The Champ* expresses the masculine anxiety generated by joblessness and the economic threat of the Depression.

The boxing film regularly leads the protagonist to find a source of value apart from his physical prowess. For Andy, value lies in his son. The tragedy of the boxer arises from Andy's inability to sustain a union with the boy. Whereas Andy's emotions are volatile, Dink embodies constancy and selfless devotion. Dink's spiritual strength is given a tangible, natural quality. Its most physical manifestation is his spitting. He spits on the Champ's money, his dice, and his boxing gloves as a token of luck. Dink becomes an emblem of value that is contested by mother and father. Will Dink become impetuous and emotional like Andy, or disciplined and respectable like Linda? The power of the film arises from the affection the viewer feels for Andy, while simultaneously acknowledging that Linda's is the proper course for their son to follow. Dink's charm, exuberance, and devotion grow out of his love for the Champ, but finally the boy must be educated so he can become a responsible husband and father. The exclusively masculine ethos represented by Andy, unsocialized and without the balancing influence of the feminine, will result in the spirit wandering into the dark world of the boxer, a world which ultimately destroys the Champ.

◆ ◆ ◆

The Champ was among the top grossing films for the 1931–32 season. In addition to the Academy Award for best actor awarded to Wallace Beery, *The Champ* earned an Oscar for "Best Original Story" for Frances Marion, among the most celebrated woman screenwriters in early Hollywood. Indeed, her emphasis on parenting and the eventual triumph of the mother over an irresponsible, if lovable, father suggests a woman's perspective. *The Champ* exercised a lasting influence on the boxing film, and its long commercial life was noteworthy. *The Champ* was reissued in 1938, and Wallace Beery recreated his performance for the Lux Radio Theater program for NBC Radio twice, in 1939 and 1942. In 1979 the film was remade, and again it was a commercial success.

In the early 1930s, the boxing genre was influenced by a challenge to masculinity arising from the powerlessness experienced by men caught in the Depression. Forty-five years later, boxing films dramatized conflicts arising from social changes promoted by the woman's movement. The comeback motif typical of these films often indicates a desire to return to traditional values. As much as any production, the 1979 remake of *The Champ* is imbued with this sensibility.

The Champ (1979) was not directed by a Hollywood stalwart, but by Franco Zeffirelli, an esteemed Italian filmmaker. *The Champ* was his first American production. During the decade after World War II, he served an apprenticeship as an actor and assistant for Luchino Visconti, a founder of Italian neorealist cinema, as well as a leader of postwar Italian theater. Zeffirelli went on to establish an international reputation as a stage director, particularly in opera. After gaining recognition in the theater, Zeffirelli earned distinguished screen credits for the international hits *The Taming of the Shrew* (1967), starring Richard Burton and Elizabeth Taylor, and *Romeo and Juliet* (1968). He was invited to Hollywood in the wake of his success with the television drama *Jesus of Nazareth* (1977). For his first project, Zeffirelli remade an M.G.M. hit the filmmaker remembered vividly from his childhood. Shortly after the death of his mother at the age of eight, Zeffirelli saw *The Champ*, which he described in his autobiography as the "one film in particular [that] really upset me and stirred emotions that have lasted to this day" (Zeffirelli 1986, 15). One can imagine the enormous impact the film made on a boy the same age as the protagonist, who—his own mother only recently passed away—sees his film counterpart weeping over the death of a parent. Zeffirelli began filming in March 1978, and the picture was ready for release the following spring. The production went smoothly. As Zeffirelli remembers, "It was a lovely film to make" (Zeffirelli 1986, 308).

Critics found Zeffirelli's *The Champ* to be an old-fashioned tearjerker, but the public embraced the film. "Franco Zeffirelli makes an auspicious debut on these shores with his first American film bolstered by earnest performances...." *Variety* noted. "[A]n overabundance of sentimentality may turn off some segments of the audience, but it's doubtful there'll be a dry eye in the house at the closing credits" (Poll 1979, 20). Most other critics were harsh. David Denby accused the filmmaker of being "floridly emotional and glib.... [The film] embraces clichés that I thought had been laughed out of movies twenty-five years ago" (Denby 1979, 86). In spite of poor press, ticket sales were brisk. *Variety* reported revenues of over $12 million domestically, ranking the production twenty-fifth among the releases for 1979. The picture scored even greater returns overseas, where *Daily Variety* reported *The Champ* to be the biggest international hit for M.G.M. in fourteen years (Daily Variety 1979). Zeffirelli claims that the film grossed $146 million for the studio on a production budget of $9 million (Zeffirelli 1986, 308).

Many acknowledged Zeffirelli's close attention to the original film, but few noted significant changes that indicate a shift in values in the 1970s boxing film—including the addition of a beleaguered masculinity, a portrait of the boxer as an innocent, and the redemptive "comeback" of the career woman to motherhood.

Most conspicuous was the transformation of Annie (Faye Dunaway), the mother, into a villain. The 1931 production suggested that Andy, the Champ, was responsible for the estrangement from the boy's mother that precedes the film's narrative. Andy's drinking, gambling, and brawling, together with his brutish, immature behavior alienated his wife, who departed to marry a refined gentleman. However, in 1979 Annie is a career woman who leaves her husband and child to become successful in the fashion industry. She chooses ambition over her responsibilities as a wife and mother. When, after becoming a success, she encounters her son, her maternal feelings are reborn, and her love for TJ serves as a means for her redemption. Zeffirelli describes her as "the hard-bitten, self-centered bitch whose return sparks off all the trouble" (Zeffirelli 1986, 305). The 1931 King Vidor film portrays a kindly mother without a profession, and grants her a daughter by her second marriage, so childlessness does not serve as a motive. Furthermore, the earlier film makes it clear that the boy would be better off in the prosperous, comforting home of his mother. The emotional impact of the first film depends upon the conflict between the deep affection between father and son and the recognition that Dink needs to go with his mother if he is to mature properly. Zeffirelli undermines this conflict by moving the setting from the Tijuana netherworld to a Florida racetrack marked by a lyrical natural beauty. In addition, he provides the boy TJ with a female caregiver, Josie, to help the Champ, thus inserting another meaningful contrast to the impoverished, all-male world inhabited by Andy and Dink in the 1931 film. The result of these changes is to blame the liberated, professional woman for the trouble her selfishness has caused men and boys. This transformation also simplifies the story's dramatic conflicts and undermines the coming-of-age theme vital to the earlier production. Attention shifts from the fate of the child to the conflict between a beleaguered masculinity and the "new" woman.

Portrayal of the boxer as an innocent also simplifies the remake. Andy's childishness was central to the comic reversals of the 1931 film The interaction between Wallace Beery's Andy and Jackie Cooper's Dink, reminiscent of Charlie Chaplin and Jackie Coogan in *The Kid* (1920), begins with humor and develops into pathos. Jon Voight's Billy and Ricky Schroder's TJ act in a more restrained and realistic manner that contrasts with the clowning of the earlier film, so the move from laughter to tears is diminished along with an important dimension of the relationship between father and son. The 1931 film portrays Andy as both lovable and irresponsible. First, he demonstrates his affection for Dink, then in the next scene he seems heedless of the child's welfare. As a result, we see the love between father and son and understand that Andy is a poor father, whose parenting suffers in contrast to that offered by the boy's mother. Zeffirelli transforms the dad into an innocent saint in conflict

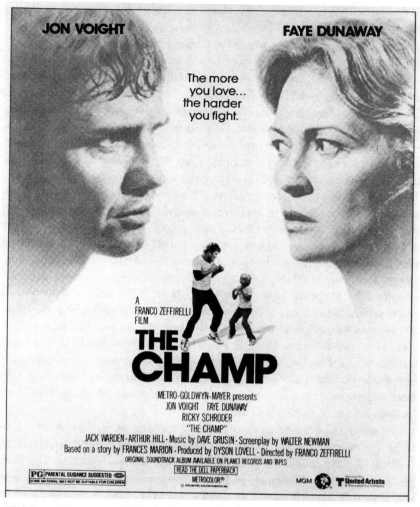

In *The Champ*, from 1979, the liberated, professional woman is to blame for the troubles of men and boys. Courtesy of the Academy of Motion Picture Arts and Sciences.

with a villainous mom. His drinking, gambling, and brawling are motivated by the heartless departure of his wife, or by his frustrated need to provide for his son. Billy is a victim who suffers. Melodrama is removed from the realistic performance style, but it is amplified by the simplistic moral opposition between husband and wife. In a reversal of conventional gender roles, Billy, a broken boxer, is the nurturing parent who speaks for the emotional intimacy of family, while Annie, the fashion queen, pursues career goals and acclaim in the public sphere.

Zeffirelli sets up a plot in which the Christ-like boxer sacrifices his life in a doomed comeback so the sinner can be redeemed. Spiritual themes, so typical of the boxing genre, find expression here. Billy feels pressed to try a comeback after a seven-year layoff from boxing because he needs to provide for his son. Annie's wealth exposes Billy's meager resources and makes him feel inadequate. Zeffirelli foreshadows Billy's death with numerous gestures and episodes absent from the original production, most explicitly with headaches and a warning not to return to the ring from Billy's faithful manager. In addition, Billy wears a conspicuous crucifix around his neck, signaling his sacrifice. The comeback bout becomes the arena of bodily suffering in which the Champ wills his death for the sake of his son and, inadvertently, for the boy's mother. In the 1931 production the boxing match represented an internal struggle between what was best in Andy—his love for Dink—and his low life habits, associated with Tijuana and embodied in his opponent, the Mexican champion. Andy's victory signified the triumph of love, but his death emphasized the flaws that crippled him. However, in the 1979 film Billy has little need to fight himself, and the Mexico motif has been eliminated. As a representative of materialism, Annie must be awakened to a redemptive love for her son. She learns of the Champ's comeback from TJ's letters and travels to attend the fight. In the 1931 version there are no cutaways during the boxing to the mother; by contrast, in 1979 numerous shots show Annie reacting to Billy's suffering in the ring. Even more expressive of the shifting significance of the second production is the closing reunion of mother and son.

The suffering of the boxer insures the "comeback" of mother to son. In the earlier production, the key transformation is in the boy Dink; however, in the Zeffirelli film the conclusion portrays the mother's transformation. The Vidor treatment has Dink moving around the dressing room after Andy's death, tearfully crying, "I want Champ." He moves around the room as different men try unsuccessfully to console the boy. Finally, the mother enters, appearing for the first time during the entire boxing episode. Dink sees her, stops crying, calls "Mother," and runs to her arms. She picks the boy up saying, "My baby." "The Champ is dead," Dink whispers to her. She turns and walks from the camera, carrying Dink in her arms from the dressing room. "The End." The film affirms the mother's ability to console and care for the boy. Dink acknowledges Andy's death, accepts his mother as his parent, and will be transformed by her love.

Zeffirelli handles the closing with subtle but meaningful differences. After Billy's death, TJ circles the dressing room in tears and the men fail to comfort him. The camera cuts away to Annie, moving to the dressing room after the fight. Her entrance is emphasized with a zoom toward her and swelling music. TJ looks toward Annie while standing by Billy's dead body. Annie says, "TJ". The boy walks toward his mother and away from the body, as Annie crouches to the boy's level. The two share a tearful, but speechless, embrace. They remain stationary as the camera rises to exclude them from the image and focus on the dressing room table that holds Billy's dead body. Fade out. Significantly, the 1979 film shows the mother bending down to the boy's level, rather than picking the child up and carrying him away. The film ends, not on the union of mother and son, but with the image of the dead father. The delinquent woman learns the value of parenting, the emotions of motherhood, from the man's self-sacrifice.

Like *Rocky*, *The Champ* (1979) portrays the boxer as an innocent victimized by social change. Rather than Apollo Creed, an African American supported by media hype, the chief emblem of social change in the 1979 remake of *The Champ* is "the new woman," who has given up her maternal duties to pursue professional success. Here the boxer's suffering in the ring is amplified by a broken marriage, and his sins are a manifestation of his sorrow. Most noteworthy is the shift in gender roles, whereby Billy assumes the traditional female role as the principle parent. Though Billy upholds fundamental emotional virtues, changing gender relations adapted by women provoke a doomed comeback that results in his Christ-like sacrifice. Rather than *Rocky*'s uplift, *The Champ* affirms the need for suffering and sacrifice to preserve traditional values. It is perhaps ironic that Frances Marion, credited again in 1979 for the "original story," was herself among the most honored professional women in the early years of the film industry. One can only imagine her discomfort at the treatment of a career woman in the revision of her Oscar winning screenplay.

Both versions of *The Champ* present the boxer as estranged from women and grappling with a beleaguered masculinity. Love between parent and child replaces the typical romance, and the son becomes the pivot in a competition between father and mother. The original film offers a compassionate treatment of the father's failings, along with recognition that maturity requires a combination of gender traits in order to establish a common ground for marriage. The 1979 remake testifies to warlike gender relations in which the career woman emerges as the villain. The contrast between the two films testifies to how apparently minor changes in a film can yield dramatically different ideological values. The vocabulary established by genre does not presuppose the significance of films. Rather, the productions can pursue divergent treatments of the social issues that lie at the foundation of film genres.

THE SET-UP (1949): THE VETERAN AND MARRIAGE

As in *The Champ*, boxing in *The Set-Up* is an extreme, aberrant masculine activity at odds with the feminine. As such it creates an obstacle for the couple to overcome. However, unlike the estranged parents of *The Champ*, in this film the romance succeeds. In the post–World War II era the scarred ring veteran frequently evokes the battle weary soldier. As in war, the brutality of boxing cripples the combatant, and it is necessary to rejuvenate him for romance to be realized.

Like many film noirs, *The Set-Up* found its source in literature, a narrative poem of the same name from 1928 by Joseph Moncure March. The poem features an African American, the middleweight boxer Pansy Jones, who is set-up, betrayed, and finally killed by racketeers in the fight game. Thomas Cripps claims that the project initially was to feature racial bigotry, highlighted in the poem, and star the black actor James Edwards (Cripps 1993, 213). On June 30, 1948, Dore Schary resigned as production chief at R.K.O., citing, among other causes, the decision of new studio owner Howard Hughes to cancel *The Set-Up*. However, within a month the project was again slated for production. The racial issue was abandoned, and R.K.O. turned to the rising actor Robert Ryan, who had been a boxing champion at Dartmouth and had recently made a mark in *The Woman on the Beach* (1947) and *Crossfire* (1947). Other changes also marked the adaptation. The R.K.O. production retained the basic plot of an aging boxer double-crossed by his manager and punished by racketeers for refusing to take a dive. In the poem, he is pushed in front of a subway train and killed; on screen he is brutally beaten by a gang of thugs who break his hand to end his boxing career. The film also introduces gender issues absent from the poem. For example, in the poem the raucous, vivid crowd is exclusively male, whereas the film features noteworthy women among the fans. The most conspicuous addition to the plot is the relationship between the boxer and his wife, completely original to the screenplay. In sum, the film turns from racial issues and makes gender central in its screen adaptation.

The Set-Up cultivates a self-conscious realism that brings greater complexity to gender types. The film draws our attention to a large clock on the boulevard of Paradise City reading 9:05 p.m.; at the close of the film the camera returns to the boulevard clock, which then reads 10:16 p.m. The running time of screen action matches the time in the fictive world. The news photographer celebrated for his urban realism, Weegee, is cast as the timekeeper at ringside. The sound track is limited to the ambient tones of the film's fictive world. The tawdry setting exchanges the glamour of prizefighting for bush league boxers in a backwater town. Blurring of gender types also contributes to the film's veracity. A double date, seen at ringside, matches an active male and passive female and then reverses the roles in the other couple, featuring an active woman and a passive man. The film's romance features a middle-aged couple experiencing the trials of marriage, rather than the courtship of young lovers. In contrast to the boxing film's promotion of masculine power, the wife asserts her power, threatening to leave unless her husband gives up boxing.

The Set-Up portrays a marriage in crisis. Stoker Thompson and his wife Julie are first shown in a hotel room just before Stoker appears as the closer at the bottom of a boxing program. Thompson is an over-the-hill fighter who at thirty-five has become a punching bag for rising talent. Julie urges her husband to leave the ring before he is maimed or killed. However, Stoker feels he is one punch away from becoming a headliner again and is confident that he can defeat the young Tiger Nelson (Hal Fieberling) that night. "You'll always be one punch away," Julie replies. "Maybe you can take the beatings. I can't." But Stoker concludes, "[I]f you're a fighter you gotta fight." The boxer leaves a ringside ticket for his wife and departs. Julie anxiously broods before heading out. Only at the last moment does she grab the pass Stoker has left. The conflict between husband and wife evokes those experienced by returning war veterans, or more precisely the experience of a soldier on leave who is about to return to the front.

After their estrangement, Stoker and Julie remain separated until the closing moment of the film. In fact, they seldom speak and—never to each other—until the conclusion. Nevertheless, the film develops their thoughts and feelings in response to their marital crisis. Both Stoker and Julie receive the conventional mirror shot visualizing their introspection. In the tradition of realism, the heightened interiority emphasizes the particularity of the man and the woman rather than gender types.

In the locker room, Stoker watches the other fighters on the evening's card depart and return, victorious or defeated. Each of the boxers preparing for their bouts speaks to Stoker's fears, hopes, and history. The first boxer returns victorious and brags about the "mouse" waiting for him. He argues with Gus (Wallace Ford), the locker room manager, over the value of women. Gus declares, "They're all for you as long as you're in the chips. I never seen a dame yet that's still around when you hit the skids." They provoke Thompson's anxiety over Julie, and he looks forlornly out the window toward the hotel. Next, the youth nervous about his first bout reminds Stoker of his past, his first fight twenty years before. Later, the battered "Gunboat" holds up Franky Manilla, the middleweight who lost twenty-one bouts before winning the title, as a model to sustain his hope. In him Stoker recognizes the pathos of his own career. Luther (James Edwards), the sharp headliner, infuses Thompson with the confidence that he can take his opponent. Finally there is Tony, who holds onto his Bible. When the locker room cynics mock Tony's faith, Stoker comes to his defense, reminding the fellows that everybody "makes book" on something. Collectively the boxers function as a projection of the protagonist's feelings, and his encounters with the other boxers foster reflection in the heavyweight. When Stoker enters the ring, he looks to Julie's seat but only sees an empty chair. His thoughts and feeling portrays a sensitive maturity that is unlike the boyish limitations of Andy in *The Champ*. That maturity only increases Stoker's desire to be reconciled with his wife.

Director Robert Wise complained about the casting of Audrey Totter as Julie. He wanted Joan Blondell to play the wife and fought with his boss, Howard Hughes, who preferred a younger, shapely R.K.O. prospect (Leeman 1995, 92). They compromised on Totter, who is adequate, but who fails to project the interiority with the eloquence that would have made the performance glow. Admittedly, Ryan receives more help because he has a colorful array of characters with whom to interact. Totter, however, must develop Julie almost completely alone. Her walk through the crowded summer night street expresses her ambivalence: She loves Stoker but can no longer tolerate boxing. Initially she goes to the arena to support her husband, but the bloodthirsty shouts from the audience terrify Julie, and she turns away to walk the street. The lonely woman passes a dance hall with silhouettes of couples projecting her desire. A dandy invites her to join him, but she hurries by. A radio report of a boxing match and the mechanical fighters at an arcade both arouse her fears. Couples nuzzling in doorways evoke her longing. Finally she walks to an urban bridge and watches the night trolleys pass underneath. The setting suggests that her conflicting feelings invite self-destruction. Instead, she tears up her ticket to the fights and drops the shreds into the traffic. One might assume that with this gesture Julie breaks with Stoker. But at decisive moments—when Julie looks from the bridge or when Stoker learns that he is supposed to take a dive—neither character speaks.

The Set-Up develops the individual, the crowd, and the couple as contrasting figures. The boxer is the individual as loner facing his rival in the ring with nothing but his body for protection. Bill "Stoker" Thompson intensifies this isolation. Tiny (George Tobias), his manager, and Red (Percy Helton), his trainer, have double-crossed him. They have taken a pay-off for Stoker to take a dive without telling their fighter. Then, when it appears that Stoker might win, they break the news and the fighter refuses to hit the canvas. His wife, distraught at the prospect of Stoker suffering another beating, fails to attend the bout. Gus abandons him in the face of the gangster's intimidation. Separated from Stoker, Julie personifies loneliness as well. Intimidated by the crowd's roar, she turns from the arena and walks the street. She dwells within her malaise, trying to

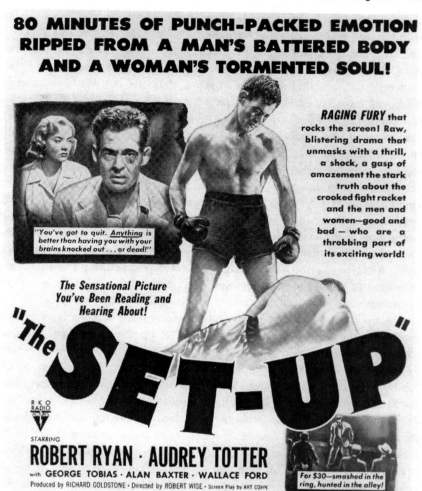

80 MINUTES OF PUNCH-PACKED EMOTION
RIPPED FROM A MAN'S BATTERED BODY
AND A WOMAN'S TORMENTED SOUL!

RAGING FURY that rocks the screen! Raw, blistering drama that unmasks with a thrill, a shock, a gasp of amazement the stark truth about the crooked fight racket and the men and women—good and bad — who are a throbbing part of its exciting world!

"You've got to quit. *Anything* is better than having you with your brains knocked out . . . or dead!"

The Sensational Picture You've Been Reading and Hearing About!

"The SET-UP"

RKO RADIO

STARRING
ROBERT RYAN · AUDREY TOTTER
with GEORGE TOBIAS · ALAN BAXTER · WALLACE FORD
Produced by RICHARD GOLDSTONE · Directed by ROBERT WISE · Screen Play by ART COHN

For $30—smashed in the ring, hunted in the alley!

Courtesy of the Academy of Motion Picture Arts and Sciences.

come to terms with the misery marking the fighter's demise. *The Set-Up* portrays the vulnerability and solitude of these individuals.

The Set-Up is noteworthy for its development of the fight crowd. The fans become another adversary for the boxer. Before Stoker goes into the locker room, he pauses to glimpse the opening bout and hears a patron cry, "Kill him! Kill him!" as a boxer slumps defenseless before a flurry of blows. *The Set-Up* delineates its crowd into people twisted by a handicap or by an obsession. There is the gangster and his moll, two gamblers, the blind man and his "eyes," the fan with baseball on his radio, the fatso with his food, the smoker and his cigar, and the punchy ex-pug selling programs. Robert Wise and the screenwriter Art Cohn found their models, not in the March poem, but by attending fights. "For instance, the blind man was an actual character he (Art Cohn) saw in weekly fights in San Francisco," Director Robert Wise explains. "Other characters I added myself out of my weeks of research (at the arenas around town). Like the man who has the radio tuned to the ballgame . . . and the man with the cigar" (Leeman 1995, 87). Once caught up in the bout, the mob's lurid craving for "action" demands punishment. "Cut him to pieces" they shout when a boxer breaks through his opponent's defense and pummels him around the ring. Only the ex-pug rallies behind the aging Stoker. The cruelty of the crowd, projecting its rage onto a surrogate, stands in contrast to the sensitivity and inwardness of the loner. Might the grotesque fans evoke the masses under the sway of totalitarianism, or the film industry's alarm at "patriotic" groups, such as the American Legion, threatening to boycott a production if its workers are suspected of Communist sympathies? Here entertainers, whether boxers or filmmakers, see their fans as tormentors whose pleasure they serve.

The opposition between lonely individuals and the threatening crowd is resolved in the unity of the couple. Here *The Set-Up* poses a balanced, humane alternative. Even the ugly fans are frequently paired with companions whose fellow feeling mitigates the hostility directed at the boxers. The problem of *The Set-Up* is the crisis of the couple, Stoker and Julie. Boxing separates them, and the fiction works toward resolving their conflict. The problems of masculinity are manifest in the tension between the violence of boxing and the sensitivity needed to sustain the couple. The meditative experiences of Stoker in the locker room and of Julie on the street allow for the ripening of sensitivity. Stoker's hardheaded integrity, his faith that he can take Tiger Nelson, and finally his refusal to pocket easy money and hit the canvas, all represent hope and fair play rather than the racket that boxing has become. Stoker's allegiance to his craft results in a back-alley beating by the gangster's thugs, who break his hand and end his boxing. The boxer's integrity works in a paradoxical way to save him from the ring and for Julie. The ironical closing lines suggest redemption. After Julie runs to nurse Thompson, fallen on the street, he declares, "I won tonight." "We both won," replies his beloved, knowing their reunion will result from his injury. Departure from the male world of the ring allows for the reaffirmation of marriage. Stoker finds victory in his humiliating beating. As in so many boxing films, the demise of the body releases the soul. But more than most works in the genre, *The Set-Up* resonates with an inadvertent grace that breaks through the confines of gender to reward the couple with a redeeming union.

As J.M. Welsh has argued in a similar religious interpretation, Stoker "is reborn into a new life—a higher existence" (Welsh 1978, 16). Many commentators have pointed to the bleak irony of calling the tank town at the end of the boxer's road Paradise City and the dance hall on the street Dreamland. I would suggest that the irony of these names finally resonates with a paradoxical affirmation. Paradise has touched the mundane when a divine hand can raise men and women to their dreams through suffering, integrity, and mutual caring. The uplift of the film's resolution arises from a seemingly unaccountable and mysterious force transcending the conspicuous limitations and nastiness of "realism." *The Set-Up* turns from taking the fall and redeems Stoker and Julie.

The press applauded *The Set-Up*, and Director Robert Wise won the Critic's Prize at the Cannes Film Festival for his work. Though a modest production without much commercial impact, this distinctive film is among the stellar boxing films dating from the studio era. Manny Farber described *The Set-Up* as "the grimmest, most brutal film in years" (Farber 1949, 539), and Gavin Lambert also noted the "extraordinary cruelty" of the final beating the boxer endures (Lambert 1949, 134). The suffering inflicted on the boxer reaches unprecedented intensity and contributes to the film's noir ambiance. However, in Stoker and Julie, suffering provokes reflection that refines their sensibilities and offers them a new direction. In contrast to the cruelty of the crowd, suffering can instill compassion, renew caring, and help to negotiate gender differences to create a deeper union between men and women.

HARD TIMES (1975): THE PHYSICAL IDEAL OF MASCULINITY

Masculinity arises from social values and codes of behavior distinctive to men and characteristic among them. This gender code finds its source in the social and physical differences between men and women. As a result, masculinity can be changed, but not eliminated. At any given time there are multiple codes of masculinity, depending upon, for example, class, race, or profession. These codes evolve over time as social conditions change, and they often compete with each other.

In and of itself, masculinity does not carry value. Rather, the traits associated with each particular masculinity model invite evaluation and social analysis. In American social practice the businessman entrepreneur who builds his empire with capital rather than arms has eclipsed the warrior ideal associated with the soldier. Few men in the United States direct their ambition toward the military; instead, most want to go where the money is, the market. A similar change might be found in the evolution from Thomas Jefferson's yeoman farmer to what Michael Kimmel calls "the heroic artisan," or what the chamber of commerce might identify as the independent small businessman (Kimmel 1996, 16–18). John Cawelti associates this model with the hard-boiled detective (Cawelti 1976, 144). One might see him as well in the screen trucker that Burt Reynolds and Clint Eastwood made so popular in the cinema of the late 1970s and early 1980s. Apart from either of these stands the urban dandy, Fred Astaire's dancer or Cary Grant's lover. A distinctive feature of James Bond is his blend of the warrior ethos with the sophistication and sexual prowess of the dandy. The study of stars and genres has helped delineate these various masculine types. Among the competing models, the screen boxer stands as a representative of a combative, physical ideal, occupying the border between warrior and athlete, promoted as a "man among men."

Many masculine types, such as the hard-boiled detective or the cowboy, embody a heroic ideal, but others, such as the gangster, are a more troubled mixture of positive and negative traits. Throughout the Hollywood studio period, the screen boxer typically functioned as a misguided protagonist who excites pathos in the audience, as in *The Champ* (1931) or *Golden Boy*. Sometimes he becomes an anti-hero, as in *Champion*, or a forsaken loser, as in *Requiem for a Heavyweight* (1956 and 1962). Rather than presenting an ideal of masculinity, the boxer typically portrays the limitations of male physicality. Even a positive portrayal of the pugilist usually concludes with him escaping the brutality of the ring, as he does in *The Set-Up* and *The Quiet Man*. Only by fleeing from this constricted male enclave can he be united with his beloved and find common ground with a woman.

In *Hard Times*, the idealization of the boxer as a physical hero was portrayed with unprecedented force at a time when the critique of the women's movement and self-consciousness about gender values assumed a new prominence in the culture. As the 1970s began, a renewed women's movement demanded equity in gender roles and legislation to promote the cause. In 1970 New York, Hawaii, and Alaska were the first states to pass liberal abortion laws, anticipating the Supreme Court's 1973 ruling in *Roe vs. Wade* that overturned many restrictions on abortion nationwide. In 1972 Congress passed the Equal Rights Amendment, sending it on to the states for ratification. In the same year Gloria Steinem began *Ms.* magazine. Under the banner "the personal is political," men and women across the nation began to reevaluate their relationships. Nineteen-seventy also saw the publication of "On Male Liberation," the Jack Sawyer essay that marked the initiation of a self-conscious gender movement among men. By the middle of the decade, gender politics had swept the culture. *Hard Times* responds to the challenge men faced with a celebration of traditional values.

On October 30, 1974, in one of the most stirring sports upsets of the era, Muhammad Ali knocked out George Foreman to regain the world heavyweight title. Shortly after Ali's comeback, the revival of the screen boxer in the mid-1970s followed with *Hard Times*, which, despite its modest success, anticipated the blockbuster impact of *Rocky*. This tough, unassuming, male action drama features Charles Bronson and marked screenwriter Walter Hill's debut as director. The movie was a solid hit, earning over $4 million and ranking fifty-sixth among the domestic box office leaders of 1975. Charles Bronson was among the top ten box office stars in the U.S. from 1973 to 1976, peaking at fourth place in 1975. The film rode the crest of his popularity. Reports claim that he was even more popular abroad, and Pauline Kael commented that Bronson was "the most popular movie star in the world" upon release of *Hard Times* (Kael 1975, 97). Jay Cocks at *Time* was among numerous film critics who praised Bronson for giving his finest performance to date in the film (Cocks 1975, 70). Kael described the production as a "triumph" of pulp filmmaking. Stephen Farber wrote that, "[I]n terms of style, it is one of the most exact approximations of Hemingway's prose ever captured on film—lean, tight, hard, spare" (Farber 1975, 52). The boxer was back.

The plot presents a tale of triumph. Nineteen-thirty-three finds Chaney (Charles Bronson) riding the rails in search of work, when he wanders into a "pick-up" boxing match in a warehouse after hours. Gamblers, who support their fighter by attracting bets from the crowd, sponsor the bare-fisted brawlers. After Chaney watches Speed's (James Coburn) "hitter" get knocked out, he follows the gambler into an oyster bar and proposes a partnership. The film portrays their relationship as Chaney wins a series of bouts making him the champ of New Orleans street fighters, while Speed relishes his winnings, only to lose all his cash shooting dice. Tension over money drives the boxer and the gambler apart, but eventually the reluctant Chaney rescues Speed from the punishment of loan sharks by agreeing to fight a "champion" brought from Chicago by Chick Gandil (Michael McGuire), the New Orleans "money belt" who insists on owning the town's toughest street fighter. Chaney overcomes his rival and departs in the night, hopping another train and leaving much of his cash with Speed and Poe (Strother Martin), his loyal sideman. Contrary to the downbeat realism typical of the boxing film, *Hard Times* portrays the prizefighter from a mythic perspective as a godlike embodiment of masculine virtue.

The valorization of physical manliness in this screen boxer is not a simple-minded elevation of the male protagonist. Rather, the film surrounds Chaney with characters whose inadequacies invite consideration of the masculine virtues embodied in the hero. As a result, Chaney becomes more than a superb warrior; his behavior embodies a code with liabilities as well as benefits.

Chaney—strong, courageous and invincible—is a variation on the warrior ideal. Though a master of combat, he uses violence reluctantly and exercises force with restraint. When Pettibon cheats him of his winnings, backed by a gun and a pack of friends, Chaney strikes back and secures his purse without killing or seriously harming his adversary. Upon agreeing to fight for Speed, Chaney declares, "When I get enough change in my pocket, I'm going." After three bouts he is ready to leave town and only fights the closing match to save Speed from his enemies. Unlike many screen boxers, Chaney takes little pleasure in his ring prowess. Though an idealized warrior, this hero does not relish violence; instead, he avoids fighting.

When Lucy Simpson (Jill Ireland) asks Chaney how he earns a living, he replies, "I knock people down." "Why?" she pursues. "There's no reason about it, just money." Money is his motivation, and yet disdain for cash and the comforts it buys is essential to his masculine ethos. He lives a simple life and dresses in functional workingman's clothes. A wanderer, he carries his few belongings in a plain bag. In New Orleans he rents a barren room without even a lock on the door. His ascetic habits express distain for material possessions. Money serves him chiefly as a foundation for his independence and a means of being generous to others: He freely offers cash to Lucy; he risks all his winnings to save his former partner in the climactic bout; at the close of the film, he leaves Speed and Poe a fistful of bills that constitutes much of his earnings, asking only that they take care of his cat. Though initially motivated by money, Chaney's independence from material needs underlines a paradoxical manliness, based on the physical yet exalting the spiritual.

Other traditional masculine values are in evidence. Chaney's quiet, understated presence serves to contrast his decisive actions with the deceptions of language. He carries with him little psychology and no history. As such he embodies morality rather than understanding. Chaney makes judgments and takes action. He is courteous to women, tender with his cat, loyal to his friends. For a boxer, he is surprisingly old (Charles Bronson was fifty-four when he made the film). "Aren't you a little bit past it?" chides Speed, upon being introduced to Chaney, with his weathered features and graying hair. But these signs of age testify to a wisdom that compliments the fighter's powerful body.

Freedom is the cornerstone of Chaney's values. He arrives tramping on the trains and departs into the night, his destination unknown. His appearance seems almost angelic. "I don't look past the next bend in the road," he tells Lucy. He turns down Gandil's lucrative sponsorship as an infringement on his freedom. Unconstrained by material desires or personal obligations, his integrity rests on independence from any attachment.

The boxer's godlike presence glows, but his idealized masculinity carries liabilities. Courtesy of the Academy of Motion Picture Arts and Sciences.

Hard Times places Chaney at the center of a circle of men. The boxer's godlike presence glows in contrast with the inadequacies of others. Pettibone is a bad loser who reneges on his wagers. Jim Henry, Gandil's hired fighter and bodyguard, is a clownish and brutal slugger who takes pleasure in inflicting pain. Gandil uses his wealth and power to make others do his bidding. Poetry, music, and learning distinguish Poe, but drugs and gambling disable him. The need to serve Gandil for money undermines the dignity of Street, the champion who arrives from out of town. However, the chief device for crystallizing masculine values arises from the contrast between Chaney, the fighter, and Speed, the con man who serves as his partner.

Overcompensation for inadequacy is the touchstone for Speed. Speed chatters incessantly; Chaney is a man of few words. Speed wears fancy clothes; Chaney is clothed in workmen's garb. Speed stands to arrogantly toast "the best man I know ... myself," while Chaney modestly rests in his chair. Speed orders women around, frequents prostitutes, and uses money to bolster his worth. Chaney is courteous, soft spoken, and respectful—and commands respect in return. Speed is in debt, whereas Chaney scrupulously avoids obligations. Speed, the speculator, puts up cash and organizes the bouts, but Chaney, the worker, does the fighting. As Chaney departs, Speed looks after him and whispers, "He sure was something." *Hard Times* expresses masculine values through the counterpoint between a group of inadequate men and the idealized male they surround.

Nonetheless, Chaney's masculinity carries liabilities. His independence is a source of melancholy. He is a loner who stands apart from the complexity and compromises of human relationships. The purity of his stance requires as much. His habits seem more appropriate to a member of a monastic order than to an underworld brawler. His code has no room for women, as his relationship with Lucy emphasizes.

Hard Times refuses to engineer a successful romance to complement the boxer's triumph. Rather, it underlines the division between women and the masculine ethos valorized in Chaney. Though courteous, generous and even tender, Chaney reveals little of himself to Lucy during their brief liaison. He comes and goes without indicating when he may return. Eventually Lucy declares, "I don't want to depend on you. You're not reliable." She asks him to leave, and Chaney goes to a bar where he forlornly drinks. He experiences an inchoate conflict between his desire for freedom and the demands of a woman.

The conclusion of the film presents the boxer with a crisis arising from his isolation. Poe goes to Chaney's room and asks him to save Speed, who has been captured by loan sharks demanding that Chaney fight Gandil's champion. "I don't owe that goddam Speed nothin," the boxer declares, and Poe departs, apprehensive. Afterwards Chaney goes to visit Lucy and discovers that she has another visitor who has made her a "better offer." In the following scene Chaney lies on his bed meditating in silence. He decides to fight on Speed's behalf and afterwards departs from town. The sequence implies that Chaney, after earning the cash he needed, only remained because of Lucy, but his unwillingness to make a commitment to her dooms their relationship. Only after failing with Lucy does the boxer decide to save his beleaguered, if fair-weather, friend. The closing bout becomes a substitute for a woman's affection. Furthermore, Chaney acknowledges that his mission in the male world is to save Speed and other men from their own foolish, self-destructive behavior. In this sense the masculine values he represents act as a means for men to protect themselves from their own excesses. His departure confirms his loneliness. In order to safeguard his independence and cultivate the masculine ethos he embodies, he must remain apart from relationships that for most of us constitute the basis of our humanity.

The masculine physical ideal found in the screen boxer ultimately chooses competition among men over intimacy with a woman. Physical expression becomes a contest for domination, rather than the means toward a cooperative, fertile union. As Joyce Carol Oates has written of machismo, it is the denial of the feminine in man (Oates 1987, 76). As a result, it is fundamentally solipsistic and barren. In its purest state, this ideal aspires toward a transcendent spirituality, because its tangible rewards dissolve with the decay of the body. The specter of thanatos hovers over idealized masculinity, even as eros cultivates the intermingling of male and female values. Most screen boxers act according to this underlying principle, so they must abandon the ring in order to realize a romantic union. *Hard Times* portrays a physical ideal of manliness, but in its pristine expression the film acknowledges the limitations of its model. Chaney fails to sustain human relationships, not because of a personal fault, but because of his complete realization of the values he represents.

Hard Times is a period film set in 1933, and it cultivates nostalgia in the simplicity of its ideals. The trials of the Great Depression and the backward glance suggest that these values have been lost and may even be irretrievable. The mythic perspective runs contrary to the naturalism that dominates the boxing genre from Jack London onwards. In this sense, the film embraces a lost ideal that was never valorized in the first place. But the tone of *Hard Times* coincides with a return to the simple, almost childlike, conventions of traditional genres that marked the rise of what came to be known as "New Hollywood," as the film industry crisis of the late sixties passed and a new stability took hold after 1975. *Hard Times* portrayed a physical ideal of masculinity that responded to the critique of feminism by endorsing an old-fashioned individualism. But the purity of the ideal exposed its liability, an isolating solipsism that turns away from union with a woman or cooperating in the community. The mythic acclaim of the boxer in *Hard Times* abandons the critique of masculinity typical of the boxing film and found an enthusiastic audience.

GIRLFIGHT (2000): A WOMAN STORMS INTO THE RING

The boxing film pits the masculine world of boxing against the feminine in a strongly gendered opposition. This conflict was softened occasionally in films like *Rocky*, but it was never abandoned. Female participation in the boxing world was reserved for comedies such as *The Main Event*, in which the woman manager becomes a source of humorous incongruity. Only recently, with *On the Ropes*, *Girlfight*, and *Million Dollar Baby* has the female boxer been treated seriously. *Girlfight* features a woman amateur fighter as the protagonist, and the production's female credentials are firmly established by the women who wrote, produced, and directed the film. The independent production proved a much-lauded debut for writer-director Karen Kusama and actress Michelle Rodriguez, winning the "Grand Jury Prize for Dramatic Film" and the "Best Director" awards at the 2000 Sundance Film Festival, among other awards. The filmmakers signed a lucrative distribution contract with Screen Gems, and their film opened to strong press.

Girlfight is a coming-of-age story about Diana Guzman (Michelle Rodriguez), a poor Afro-Hispanic teen living in the housing projects of Brooklyn's Red Hook. Rather than responding to racial or ethnic prejudice, Diana's anger is provoked by gender-based insults. The film opens with her attack on Veronica (Shannon Walker Williams), the campus flirt, for seducing another teen's boyfriend. Diana's assault is provoked by Veronica's alluring feminine behavior, which asserts power by attracting men. Rather than using men to shore up her self-esteem, Diana wants their power for herself. Diana's widowed father Sandro (Paul Calderon) is an underlying source of her rage. The troubled adolescent lost her mother to suicide years before, her father's abusive habits having contributed to his wife's torment. Now Sandro tries to enforce gender orthodoxy on his son and daughter. He sends Tiny (Ray Santiago) to boxing lessons and chides Diana to "wear a skirt once in a while." However, Tiny likes to draw and wants to go to art school, and Diana gets her gear from the army-navy store and walks with her fists clenched and ready. Neither child fits the models the culture has prepared for them. *Girlfight* presents gender as socialized behavior that often twists a child's emerging sensibility.

Sandro sends Diana to pay Tiny's trainer at the boxing gym, and the teen is hooked. When Tiny's sparring mate Ray takes a cheap shot at her brother, Diana immediately enters into the action. After Ray leaves the ring, Diana approaches and slugs the boxer. Hector (Jaime Tirelli), the trainer, resists taking on a woman. But soon Diana is secretly training, and Tiny even passes along his gym fees to her. When Sandro discovers his daughter is in the ring, a confrontation ensues. Diana overpowers her father and prepares to thrash him, when Tiny intervenes. The battle constitutes Diana's declaration of independence. Her dominance banishes fears that she might be abused like her mother, giving Diana the confidence to explore her desires and assert her freedom.

As a result, her romance with Adrian (Santiago Douglas), a talented feath-erweight preparing to turn pro, blossoms. As the only woman boxer at the gym, Diana draws Adrian's attention, but Karina (Belqui Ortiz), a neighbor-hood beauty, is already flirting with him. At first it appears that Diana must bow to her more feminine rival, but the fellowship of boxing fosters a bond. By moving into the masculine sphere of the ring, Diana establishes common ground with Adrian. The relationship, however, strains under the demands of competition as the lovers spar, and then, in a dramatic conceit that challenges the realistic premise of the film, Diana faces Adrian in a tournament bout and triumphs. Alone in her dressing room after the victory, she sobs, knowing that she has jeopardized her romance by winning. The film ends with the couple's reconciliation.

During the last quarter of the twentieth century, women increasingly challenged male prerogatives. Rather than simply spreading feminine values among men, the contemporary women's movement has succeeded largely by motivating women to take on masculine roles in order to assume positions of power once denied them. As a hyper masculine domain, boxing serves as one of the last bastions of male prerogative. *Girlfight*'s story of female conquest in the ring affirms a woman's freedom to explore the outposts of gender, even an outpost at the extreme limits of machismo. As Kusama explains, "We have so many rules about how to live in society, and in my mind this is a story about somebody who decides to break those rules and explore what works for her" (Baker 2000, 26).

The writer-director Karyn Kusama knows the boxing film genre. She points to *Fat City* and *The Set-Up* as fight films she admires, but apart from a gen-eral aspiration to social realism, few similarities with either are apparent in *Girlfight* (Baker 2000, 23). Nonetheless, *Girlfight* is awash with familiar genre conventions and types. The film features an ethnic-racial protagonist on the rise, whose social anger is redirected in the ring, a convention that goes back at least to *Kid Galahad*. The widowed parent who disapproves of boxing is promi-nent in *Golden Boy* and *Body and Soul*. *City for Conquest* presents the artistic brother in counterpoint with, but allied to the fighter. *Girlfight*'s plot focuses on the early part of the model story, with the "discovery" blow taking place during a chance errand to the gym, training montages, and a triumphant concluding bout. Maybe the film's closest connection is with *Somebody Up There Likes Me*, which shares with *Girlfight*: an abusive father; a delinquent protagonist; a poor New York City neighborhood; a hesitant, sweet romance; a fatherly manager who stands in for the inadequate parent; a psychological revival of the hero through boxing; and an upbeat ending. In spite of its gender reversals and its female perspective, *Girlfight* feels conventional and is firmly grounded in the boxing film genre.

So what's new here? The romance between the boxers is a fresh touch and has an authentic tone. Rather than forcing the boxer to leave the ring to commit to a heterosexual romantic relationship, here a woman becomes a boxer and at the same time finds companionship with a man. In *Girlfight*, boxing allows Diana to overcome her father's patronizing treatment as well as gain the confidence she needs to explore her sexuality. The power Diana experiences in the ring allows her to be vulnerable and sensitive to men, knowing that she can be a partner without becoming a victim. Diana's and Adrian's similar size, necessary for them to compete in the same weight class, gives them a physical equality to match their comparable, if unusual, gender status. Michelle Rodriguez and Santiago Douglas establish a sensitive rapport with a flirtation marked by uncertainties and ambivalence, trials and reconciliation. The strange gender roles throw both of them off balance but finally allow love to take hold. A sparring match finds the pair facing each other in the ring for the first time only days after Diana left a party after Adrian showed up with Karina. When she and Adrian are locked together in a clinch, Diana whispers, "I love you" to her opponent, only to land a punishing right hook to his jaw after the referee separates them. The contrast between the tough fighters and the awkward romance gives the film its freshest, most feminine quality. An authentic tenderness arises from the first kiss the couple exchanges while sitting on a street curb, from their sleeping together in an embrace without sex, and from their final faltering reconciliation. Though the press has touted Rodriguez for her tough pose, it is the counterpoint between hard-nosed aggression and tender vulnerability that makes her performance impressive. Finally, gender reversal forces Adrian to embrace the unexpected in himself. During their closing meeting, the sheepish man accepts his partnership with a woman, acknowledging her physical power, yet warming to her embrace. Confused and humiliated after his defeat, he assumes a conciliatory pose when approaching Diana days after the fight:

Adrian: So now I lose your respect.
Diana: No. . . . You boxed with me like I was any other guy. . . . You showed me respect. Don't you see what that means?
A: That life with you is war.
D: (smiles) Maybe . . . maybe life's just war period.
A: You said it. . . . Life's been a mess since I met you. So you gonna dump me now?
D: Probably

A: Promise. (Diana reaches out to touch Adrian. She kisses him and they embrace.

The tension between words and actions in the closing scene expresses the flipped gender roles the couple has assumed. Adrian accepts Diana's power and yields to her touch. In *Girlfight*, for the first time on screen, a couple comes together as boxers—and the woman throws the knockout punch.

◆ ◆ ◆

The transformation of gender relations in twentieth-century America is evident in the evolution of the boxing film genre. The boxer in *The Champ* (1931) evokes the powerlessness felt by an unemployed father during the Depression. In *The Set-Up*, the prizefighter suggests the scarred World War II veteran seeking rejuvenation through his union with a woman. The tension between men and women that emerged with the resurgence of feminism in the 1970s shapes the selfish mother in *The Champ* (1979) and the mythic masculinity in *Hard Times*. Finally, with *Girlfight*, a woman storms into the ring to prove that even the outer limits of masculinity are within her reach. These films bear witness to the major shift in gender roles in twentieth-century America, when masculinity was transformed by pressure from economic hardship, war, and the challenge to male prerogatives made by women. The vocabulary of genre does not determine the ideological message of films. Rather, genre allows for a variable response to the key issues that shape its conventions. Gender conflict is central to the boxing film, and the history of this genre testifies to shifting perspectives on gender relations in the twentieth century.

6

"HITTING BELOW THE BELT"
Violence, Suffering, and Male Emotion

Hollywood cinema has often been noted for its optimism, characterized by the proverbial happy ending. Though the boxing film has no shortage of happy endings, the marginal position of these movies within the entertainment industry arises from their disturbing subjects. Even Clint Eastwood had trouble finding a studio to back *Million Dollar Baby*, owing to fear of "serious pictures" (Bart 2005, 4). Anger and suffering are among the most troubling subjects portrayed in the boxing film. For the screen boxer, indignation at injustice is regularly blocked and his rage displaced onto his ring opponent. This disparity between the source of his troubles and the direction of his fury produces a perverse, often self-destructive violence. In tandem, the boxer's training instills discipline, undermining his sensitivity toward others, while preparing him to endure punishment in the ring. So the boxer's emotions are crippled, and a brooding violence marks his life. Suffering becomes his destiny. The screen boxer dramatizes two widespread conflicts for male emotion in our culture: first, anger at injustice conflicts with powerlessness to change the source of the affliction; second, the need for stoic discipline in the response to life's cruelty conflicts with cultivating sensitivity toward others. These conflicts arouse pathos in the audience and invite meditation on suffering.

Violence in the boxing film is deeply felt and central to its meaning. The boxing film addresses three myths about violence in American popular culture: the myth of equality through violence, the myth of the honorable code of violence, and the myth of regeneration through violence (Cawelti 1975, 521–44).

Though the rules of the ring promote the myth of equality through violence, the boxing film, with its emphasis on the set-up, exposes the equality of violence as a fraud. As violence spills outside the ring into the back alley beating, domestic abuse, or the gangster's vengeance the honorable code of violence associated with the Westerner or the hard-boiled detective dissolves. The myth of regeneration through violence is frequently at play in these films. Boxing often becomes analogous to captivity, with the pugilist under the thumb of the gangster, a victim of false consciousness like Samson, or literally enslaved by poverty or circumstance. Nearly naked, with only his body as a weapon, the prizefighter inflicts and endures violence at its most tangible. His departure from the ring is in a sense analogous to an escape from torment. As a result, the boxer's response to suffering and his prospective regeneration are issues. Though few viewers ever take a shot in the ring, the agony of the boxer touches upon easily understood conflicts.

Over the course of the boxing film's history, a range of perspectives on these issues has arisen. During the Popular Front era, *City for Conquest* (1940) valorized the boxer's suffering as an ennobling sacrifice for the benefit of others. After World War II, *From Here to Eternity* (1953) portrayed the former boxer as a principled, but tormented loner unable to come to terms with the military service he loves. *Somebody Up There Likes Me* (1956) portrays the optimism of the Eisenhower era, with goodwill saving an abused youth and boxing serving as a means of redemption. After the studio era pessimism became more conspicuous. The despair of *Fat City* (1972) offers no consolation to mitigate the existential loneliness of its boxers. The cynicism of the postmodern *Fight Club* (1999) fractures the unity of the human psyche. After the failure of bare-fisted brawling as a means of regeneration, the boxer's consciousness crumbles under pressure from its own inner turmoil.

CITY FOR CONQUEST (1940): BLINDNESS AND INSIGHT

Thwarted emotion and the suffering boxer drive the plot of *City for Conquest*. The influence of *Golden Boy* is readily apparent in the James Cagney-Warner Brothers hit that follows a group of ethnics from Manhattan's Lower East Side as they each strive for success. The Kenny brothers, Eddie (Arthur Kennedy) and Danny (James Cagney), divide Joe Bonaparte's talents between them. Eddie is a composer and pianist who evokes George Gershwin, while Danny reluctantly fights for an occasional purse to support his brother's musical education. More importantly, Danny loves his neighborhood sweetheart, Peggy Nash (Ann Sheridan), who grew up in the same tenement. Peggy is fond of Danny, but her desire to become a dancer diverts her affection, and she cannot understand why Danny would prefer his routine job as a truck driver to a career in the ring. But Danny has seen enough punch drunk bums to know that boxing is a fool's way to earn a living. Besides, his ambition is to marry Peg and settle down in the neighborhood. When Peg teams up with Murray Burns (Anthony Quinn), a dancing master, hoping to see her name in lights, Danny feels that only by pursuing fame in the ring can he hope to win her. Tour montages portray the parallel rise of Peg and Danny, using their professional names, the dancer Margalo and the prizefighter "Young Samson," to suggest the displacement of love by ambition. Each time Danny proposes to Peg, another career opportunity lures the woman back on the road. Simultaneously, another pal from the neighborhood, Googi (Elia Kazan), rises in the underworld as a gangster. Hoping to win Peg's hand, Danny pursues a title shot against the advice of Scotty (Donald Crisp), his fatherly manager, and is blinded in the ring by a dirty fighter. In revenge, Googi assaults the crooks and is killed in a shoot out. Peg, guilt-stricken by Danny's anguish, misses her chance at stardom and is kept from consoling her beloved by Scotty, who protects his stricken fighter from two-timing dames. Danny, Peg, and Googi all suffer for ambition. However, Eddie has been developing as a musician, and the film ends with him conducting his own symphony at Carnegie Hall. Afterwards Danny, working at a newsstand, and Peg, the down-and-out hoofer, encounter each other on the street and experience a tearful reunion. Suffering and compassion have sustained their feelings and allow them to see the worth of love's devotion.

In *City for Conquest* the boxer's anger is repeatedly displaced in order to sustain the romance. After Peg turns down Danny's first proposal, his loyal pal, Mutt, explains, "I wouldn't take it from the Queen of Sheba." But instead of turning from her, Danny neglects his job and broods. After Peg stands him up a second time, Kenny beats up his sparing partner at the gym. Eddie tells his brother that Danny's rival for Peg is not the dancer Murray Burns, but her ambition to become a star. So Danny replaces a normal courtship with his pursuit of success in the ring. Once he has become a contender, Danny visits Peg in her dressing room. She is pleased to see him until Murray appears and insults the boxer. Danny swings at Murray, but Peg steps between the men and takes the blow on her shoulder. The boxer's rage inadvertently finds its mark in spite of his intentions. Most film melodramas contrast the neighborhood sweetheart with the city vamp, thereby simplifying this conflict. By combining these features in Peg, *City for Conquest* intensifies problems associated with male emotion. The mixture of anger and desire produces the boxer's frustration, forces Danny to redirect his feelings, and results in his blindness. Suffering rather than success finally wins the beloved. When Danny takes a crippling beating in the title fight, Peg listens to it on the radio, tears running down her face. As a result of Danny's torment, she is unable to go on with her show and fails to become a star. Both Peg and Danny take their falls simultaneously. Ironically, the pain they endure finally leads to their reunion.

City for Conquest reverses typical gender roles in portraying the conflict between discipline and sensitivity. Ambition disciplines Peg's feelings for Danny as she represses her desire for marriage in order to succeed as a dancer. Furthermore, she prods her suitor to pursue a career in the ring. Danny accepts the discipline necessary for success, but he never loses sight of his love for Peg. However, her feeling overcomes her ambition only when Danny suffers on her behalf. In *City for Conquest* the death of Googi, the failure of Peg, and the blinding of Danny all serve as critiques of the success ethic. The film values emotions that foster sensitivity toward others over the drive for dominance.

The values of community, the arts, and self-sacrifice establish a contrast with ambition. Loyalty among the characters from the neighborhood of Forsyth and Delancy establishes lasting alliances between Danny, Eddie, Peggy, and Googi. A minor character, Mutt, most clearly expresses the bond. He follows Danny throughout the film, acting as Danny's pal in the gym, his sidekick in the truck, as his "second" in the ring, and finally his assistant at the newsstand. In an opening scene Mutt is harassed by a strutting boxer in the gym, who Danny—taking the insult to his friend personally—floors. The friendship between Mutt and Danny establishes a foundation for the values in *City for Conquest*. Returning to the old neighborhood, as Danny and Peg do for a dance after they have become headliners, represents the cooperation and community which hold genuine value compared to the heartless competition of the metropolis. A communitarian ideal, partly realized and partly nostalgia for the village-like neighborhood, serves as a counter value to the ambitions motivating the characters.

Eddie's music offers the other source of value. Eddie is the only one from the neighborhood who realizes his ambition without self-destructing. That ambition is not simply musical, becoming associated with classical music and high culture, in contrast to popular culture and the need to earn a living. On numerous occasions in the film Eddie's symphony is hampered by the need to exchange his musical skill for cash. Initially, he is introduced giving a piano lesson to an untalented boy who tries to withhold even the meager fee Eddie charges. When Danny arrives, the younger brother explains his ambition to compose concert music that will express the experience of the metropolis. Later Eddie is invited to play to swells at a lavish party. No one besides Danny cares to hear the classical composition, but when Eddie switches to a swinging jazz tune, they all gather around him at the piano. Finally after Danny has lost his sight, Eddie works with his collaborators on songs for a Broadway show, but Danny encourages his brother to evade the lure of commercial success, opting instead for the aspirations of high culture. After the symphony is finally played, Eddie turns to the audience and dedicates his composition to his selfless brother. Peg's failure as a dancer needs to be understood in relation to Eddie's success. *City for Conquest* implicitly faults Peg's popular style of dance as the cultural equivalent of boxing, a tawdry entertainment devoid of the elevating artistry of symphonic music. Underlying both the art and the communitarian ideals is Danny's self-sacrifice. Danny is willing to support his brother's music and to pursue the ambition necessary to satisfy Peg. This self-sacrifice expresses Danny's love for others, which serves as a basis for community and is presented as necessary for supporting the arts.

City for Conquest offers a turnabout in James Cagney's screen persona. No longer is he the childish brute of *Winner Take All*, a boxing film from 1932. The change was deliberately pursued by the Warner's star, who sought more humane roles rather than the studio assignments in which he would reappear as the brash, violent mug. In spite of his Golden Gloves title, Danny turns down invitations to pursue boxing. And devotion to his sweetheart is not marred by jealousy: Danny willingly allows Peg to partner with Murray Burns, the arrogant dance king, at the ballroom contest. In a reversal of gender roles, the heroine prods a man into the ring rather than coaxing him from it. Even after his injury Danny harbors no bitterness, but only yearns to someday meet Peg. Maybe *City for Conquest* derives its force from the serenity experienced by James Cagney's Danny at the close. Such serenity is especially affecting in a star usually associated with manic violence. Arising from the pathos of his suffering is the reward of the righteous, a benign spirit emanating from a broken body. *City for Conquest* rebukes ambition and praises the boxer's emotional vulnerability.

Thirties boxing films were invested with heightened feelings that played out the problem of male emotion. The sensitivity of Danny Kenny lacked the stoic reserve of the frontiersman or the hard-boiled detective. Instead, the contest between the discipline instilled by the success ethic versus the sensitivity fed by love's devotion informs *City for Conquest*. The softening of Cagney's boxer also underlines the social consciousness that influenced the genre. No longer are these films simply action fare appealing to adolescent bravado. Rather, the benchmark works portray the boxer as an urban hero who embodies emotional turmoil and the purpose of suffering.

FROM HERE TO ETERNITY (1953): SUFFERING'S DISCIPLINE

By focusing on the retired prizefighter, the films of the "after leaving the ring" cycle explore the consequences of boxing rather than the life in the ring. *From Here to Eternity* portrays suffering through the experience of the former Army boxer Private Robert E. Lee Prewitt (Montgomery Clift). The film develops a rich parallel narrative contrasting the sensitive Prewitt with the disciplined Sergeant Milt Warden (Burt Lancaster). Episodes shift from a focus on one soldier to the other, occasionally staging pivotal scenes between the two principals. Twin romances develop the counterpoint, with Warden carrying on an adulterous affair with Karen Holmes (Deborah Kerr), while Prewitt courts Alma/Lorene (Donna Reed), the hostess from the New Congress Club. The film qualifies its support for Prewitt's principled resistance by holding it in counterpoint to Warden's more pragmatic politics. Each man loves the army, but both suffer the army's injustice. Their struggle to deal with anger and powerlessness takes the measure of them both.

From Here to Eternity was a controversial best seller that won a National Book Award in 1951. The James Jones fiction is frequently grouped with *The Naked and the Dead*, *The Caine Mutiny*, and *Catch-22* as key novels expressing America's response to World War II. Like earlier literary influences on the boxer, *From Here to Eternity* shares Ernest Hemingway's concern with masculinity, warrior virtue, and postwar disillusionment, as well as Clifford Odets's engagement with social justice, egalitarian values, and the role of art. However, the story defied adaptation to the screen. Not only was it long, over eight hundred and fifty pages, but it was also filled with taboo behaviors (obscene language, adultery, prostitution, homosexuality, sadism) long prohibited in the movies, and it was critical of the United States Army during a period when any such criticism was open to suspicion. The popularity of the novel prompted Warner Brothers and Twentieth Century-Fox to negotiate for the screen rights, but these studios backed off when the U. S. Army would not cooperate with the production. Undaunted, Harry Cohn, head of Columbia Pictures, purchased the property. James Jones was hired and struggled unsuccessfully to write a screen treatment. However, Daniel Taradash produced what was to become a celebrated screenplay, and after tough negotiations, including some revisions in the script, the army agreed to cooperate. Then Fred Zinnemann was hired as director and the roles cast. Finally, in February 1953, shooting began. The film opened in August to rave reviews and big box office (Suid 1978, 117–29). The production earned over twelve million dollars and was second only to *The Robe*, the first Cinemascope production, in revenues for 1953. It was among the top twenty box office hits of the 1950s, generating far more income than any movie featuring a boxer until *Rocky* (1976). *From Here to Eternity* won numerous Academy Awards, including Best Picture, Best Director, and Best Screenplay. Other groups, such as the New York Film Critics, also honored the production. In an American Film Institute poll conducted at the close of the century, *From Here to Eternity* was among the one hundred movies ranked as classics.

From Here to Eternity opens in 1941, a few months before the bombing of Pearl Harbor, with Private Robert E. Lee Prewitt's arrival at a new company in the Schofield Barracks, Hawaii. Prewitt is already a U.S. Army veteran, with over five years in the service, who plans to make a career in the infantry. Protest motivates Prewitt's transfer. He was the top bugler in a corps when, out of favoritism, his superior promoted a less talented musician ahead of him. To lodge his protest, Prewitt took a demotion to private and transferred. However, another conflict between Prewitt and his new commanding officer, Captain Holmes, immediately arises. In a quest for promotion, the captain wants his company to win the regimental boxing title. Holmes requested Prewitt's transfer to his company because he knows about his skills as a middleweight fighter. But upon his introduction to Holmes, Prewitt declares that he has given up boxing, and declines the invitation to join the team. Angry after meeting resistance, Holmes orders the leaders of the company to give Prewitt the "treatment," a combination of demeaning chores, group pressure, and petty harassment, until the private agrees to box. Shortly thereafter, top sergeant Milt Warden tries to set Prewitt straight. The private affirms that, "A man don't go his own way, he's nothing." To which Warden replies, "Maybe back in the days of the pioneers a man could go his own way. But today you gotta play ball." The movie follows Prewitt as he endures weeks of abuse in order to maintain his principled decision.

Milt Warden serves as Captain Holmes's chief administrator, running the day-to-day business of the company. As such, he is ordered by Holmes to break Prewitt's resistance to box and supervise "the treatment." While Prewitt is portrayed as doggedly maintaining his virtue, Warden is divided and more complex, for the sergeant is assigned to carry out policies that he believes to be misguided. Even though his efficiency supports the officer's regime, Warden exercises a countervailing influence through the routine operations of the company and by slyly maneuvering Captain Holmes into mitigating his harshest orders. As *From Here to Eternity* unfolds, Prewitt's character begins on a high plane, but he deteriorates, almost mysteriously, in the end. By contrast, Warden begins as an ally of oppression, but gradually emerges as a humane and courageous soldier. In the course of the film, both men are described as model soldiers who love the army. Yet both of them experience the cruelty of the institution to which they are devoted. *From Here to Eternity* portrays an intermingling of good and evil that inevitably results in suffering.

Victimization, powerlessness, and agony lie at the center of *From Here to Eternity*. As Maggio (Frank Sinatra) explains upon seeing Prewitt's treatment, "I just hate to see a good guy get it in the gut." To which Corporal Buskley replies, "You better get used to it, Kid." Suffering draws the principle characters to each other. Though Holmes's bullies target Prewitt, Maggio befriends him. Later Prewitt tries to save Maggio from arrest and then avenges his death. Warden suffers, carrying out the directives of officers, and is attracted to Prewitt as he tries to shield the private from abuse. Karen and Warden endure the egregious Captain Holmes. Prewitt and Alma are both loners victimized by their superiors. The experience of *From Here to Eternity* invites one to ponder suffering. Prewitt is tormented over a sports competition that never takes place, and is finally shot under circumstances that render his death inconsequential. *From Here to Eternity* offers no explanation, justification, or purpose for the agony endured by its characters. All the principals end up dead or estranged. Suffering will continue, and the fiction affirms its inevitability with a poker-faced stare. However, the film dramatizes a range of human responses to suffering, and this becomes an important theme.

One response to suffering is to find consolation with a lover. Lorene and Prewitt exchange stories about their respective suffering, and intimacy develops. The two have contrasting attitudes which foster tension between discipline and sensitivity. First, Lorene recalls being jilted by an upper class lover for whom she was insufficiently respectable. Now she has become a "hostess," offering her favors to men at the New Congress Club and determined to return to her hometown "with a stocking full of money," to use her wealth to buy status. In response to suffering, Lorene's toughness leads her to commercialize her body. She becomes a prostitute, explicitly in the novel, but implicitly in the film. She even changes her name from Alma (spirit), alluding to her lost soul. When she is telling her story, Lorene's still body and monotonous voice establish a distance from the blows to her spirit. She has disciplined herself in the face of cruelty. Lorene's desire for money and power has become the basis of her strength. "I don't like weakness," she declares with assurance. The romance honors the longstanding alliance of the boxer and the prostitute, with Lorene's detachment serving as contrast to Prewitt's confession, highlighting his sensitivity.

Prewitt's story is cued by Maggio's reference to the "treatment." Prewitt explains to Lorene that the troopers harass him because he refuses to box for the company team, noting with pride that he was a pretty good middleweight. The soldier tells of his friendship with Dixie Wells, another sharp boxer preparing to turn professional after leaving the army. One afternoon the two were sparing "kind of friendly like" when Prewitt struck his buddy with "no more than an ordinary right cross," and Wells went down. In the hospital, Wells finally snapped out of a coma, but he was blind. Later Prewitt visited his buddy. Their talk turned to boxing, and Wells started to cry. After that Prewitt could never go back. For him, boxing was over. The confession ends with the former boxer silently holding back his tears.

Lorene's and Prewitt's stories express a fear of suffering, renewed now because they are about to embark on a new romance. The intermingling of discipline and sensitivity serves the integration of traits central to *From Here to Eternity*. Lorene has been victimized by her estranged partner's attitude, and her response is to strive for higher social position, even at the cost of prostituting herself. Her attraction to Prewitt upsets her plan for the future. Dixie Wells's blinding shows Prewitt the unintended consequences of his actions; one can inadvertently harm loved ones. Prewitt's suffering provokes a fresh sensitivity, and he turns from boxing to devote himself to the bugle. *From Here to Eternity* portrays ambivalence in both Lorene and Prewitt. Lorene sees her discarded vulnerability in the abused private, upon whom she can test her newfound detachment. Prewitt seeks to replace Dixie with Lorene, and his confession warns the woman of the inadvertent harm he inflicted on his former friend. The Samson model typical of boxing stories implicit in the story of Dixie's blinding also anticipates the lack of foresight that will lead to Prewitt's self-destruction. Lorene and Prewitt are fated to repeat the traumas revealed at the beginning of their romance. In spite of her pleas, her lover will once more abandon Lorene, and Prewitt will assume Dixie's position and be killed by friendly fire. *From Here to Eternity* places suffering at the center of human experience.

Other responses to suffering, closely related to romance, are illicit, excessive pleasures—principally drunkenness and demeaning sex—which bond people together in their agony. Drinking among troops appears to be matter-of-fact behavior, but the film links the habit with the deadening routine of infantry drill and institutionalized subservience. Drunkenness also sets the stage for camaraderie between Maggio and Prewitt and, later, for Warden's affectionate confession to Prewitt in the road as he shares his bottle with the private. But the dangerous pose of the two soldiers in the road expresses the danger of alcoholic escape from suffering. Even more vividly, Maggio's drunken fight with the MPs arresting him emphasizes the truism that his troubles are only compounded by booze. The doomed romances portrayed in *From Here to Eternity* carry similar implications. Lorene, in response to being jilted, rebuffs Prewitt's marriage offer because she is determined to return to her hometown and confront her enemies. Warden's desire for Karen appears motivated by hostility toward his commanding officer, and Karen's feelings are inflamed by the suffering inflicted by her faithless husband. But the furtive adultery finally withers, and Warden's loyalty to his men undermines any closer bond with a woman. Nonetheless, *From Here to Eternity* treats drunkenness and illicit sex with compassion and sympathy. The characters exchange intimacy and affection sharing these pleasures. However, the dominance and inevitability of suffering that characterize the film rob these sensations of any promise, condemning the relationships they foster to a painful end.

The most ubiquitous response to suffering in *From Here to Eternity* is violence. The film sets up a wide range of violent activity, which often has an accelerating and intensifying relationship to suffering. Boxing, a stoic discipline in the incorporation, management and release of pain, can channel aggression, serving as a healthy response to torment. But even sanctioned violence, like boxing, can also increase suffering, sometimes unintentionally. Prewitt blinds his ring buddy while sparring. Grief stricken, the soldier gives up boxing. As a result, he endures the "treatment." The cultivation of aggression easily spills over into brawling, exploitation, and sadistic cruelty. However, rather than simply condemning violence, *From Here to Eternity* suggests there is a range of violent acts—good, evil and ambiguous. The good arises near the conclusion, when the troops respond to the Japanese attack as a band of brothers finally realizing the task they have been trained to fulfill. The "treatment" Holmes institutes against Prewitt and Judson's sadistic beating of prisoners serves as an evil counterpart. The U.S. Army institutionalizes both these good and evil practices. But ambiguous violence provokes a thoughtful, less sensational, response. Maggio's comic battle against the MPs is an expression of his despair. Prewitt's vengeance upon Judson appears to be righteous, but is nevertheless misguided. The shooting of Prewitt, like the blinding of Dixie Wells, presents sanctioned violence that inadvertently harms an ally. These are acts with terrible, unintended consequences for which no one bears responsibility. In *From Here to Eternity* violence appears to be a common response to suffering. The initiation of a great war at the conclusion suggests that violence rules human affairs. However, the film cautions against violence because it can so easily rage out of control and intensify suffering.

The revival of Prewitt's aggressive temper ultimately leads to his doom. His fistfight with Sergeant Ike Galovitch initiates his return to violence. Throughout the "treatment," Galovitch torments the private with taunts and physical abuse. Finally Galovitch provokes a fistfight. The private fends off his bigger opponent with body blows, reluctant to strike the head because of his memory of Dixie Wells. But after taking a beating from Galovitch, Prewitt finally strikes back with his full arsenal of boxing skills and appears to gain an advantage before the fight is stopped. Bruised and exhausted, Prewitt accepts the support of his buddies, but insists that this acceptance does not mean he will return to the ring. Instead, the battle with Galovitch initiates a turn in Prewitt from passive resistance to active struggle against his adversaries, particularly after his buddy Maggio is murdered by Sergeant Judson in the stockade.

A pivotal act in *From Here to Eternity* is Prewitt's vengeance on Sergeant "Fatso" Judson (Ernest Borgnine). Judson, a brutal stockade guard, beats and kills Angelo Maggio, Prewitt's friend, while Maggio is serving a six-month sentence in the brig. Afterwards, Prewitt invites Judson into an alley, and a knife fight between the two leaves Prewitt seriously injured and the Sergeant dead. Following the fight, the wounded Prewitt flees to his girlfriend's apartment, the army searches for Judson's killer, and the unknown avenger is AWOL from his troop. By attacking Judson, Prewitt divorces himself from the army. While gradually recovering from his wounds, Prewitt descends into a drunken despair as a result of his alienation from the institution that gave meaning to his life. Upon learning of the attack on Pearl Harbor, Prewitt attempts to rejoin his unit, but he is mistakenly shot by an army patrol. After Prewitt has endured the abusive "treatment" without complaint, he takes justice into his own hands and consequently is killed. Though the film portrays Judson as an evil brute, Prewitt's vengeance proves to be self-destructive and, in retrospect, a serious misstep.

Warden's pivotal decision, one worth comparing to Prewitt's misguided vengeance, is his turn from promotion. Karen Holmes has urged her clandestine lover to become an officer to facilitate their marriage. Ironically, Captain Holmes also encourages his able subordinate to rise through the ranks. The important career move is easily within reach; Warden completes his application, but never submits it. All his life he has hated officers and devoted himself to the common soldier. For Warden, becoming a lieutenant would be like joining the enemy. When Karen asks why he withheld his request for promotion, another soldier walking nearby suddenly distracts Warden. The Sergeant rises and goes up to the man, who he thinks is Prewitt. Finding he is mistaken, Warden returns to Karen. "I'm no officer. I'm an enlisted man. I can't be anything else," Warden tries to explain. "If I tried to be an officer I'd be putting on an act. I just can't do it. Don't ask me why." But Warden's concern for the missing Prewitt has already supplied an explanation. His care for the common soldier prevents his promotion. Karen understands and replies, "I know why. . . . You just don't wanna marry me. You're already married . . . to the Army." Prewitt's pivotal decision alienates him from the soldier's life he cherishes, whereas Warden instinctively cultivates his attachment to his comrades in arms. He sacrifices the woman he loves and the opportunity for advancement in order to maintain his devotion.

Warden's response to suffering is compassion for the powerless, a selfless egalitarianism, which acts as qualified resistance to the injustices perpetuated by an authoritarian hierarchy.

From Here to Eternity concludes with the Japanese assault on Pearl Harbor. The final episodes elevate Warden and diminish Prewitt. Warden rallies the soldiers during the surprise attack and leads the resistance to the Japanese. His years of training as a soldier have made him a leader of men. The attack finds Prewitt hiding at Alma's apartment in a drunken stupor, completely cut off from the duties he was trained to perform. In his attempt to rejoin his unit, Prewitt fails to evade the fire from his own army. At the moment of crisis, Warden realizes the martial ideal and Prewitt flounders. In spite of the film's sympathy for the fallen soldier, it concludes with Prewitt's failure and Warden's triumph. *From Here to Eternity* addresses the problem of male emotion in offsetting the sensitive Prewitt with the disciplined Warden. In the end, the film leans towards Warden's communitarian pursuit of a limited justice and away from Prewitt's personal ethics and self-righteous anger. Warden realizes that outside a social framework like the army, the prospect for even limited justice will be lost.

The acclaimed response to suffering portrayed in *From Here to Eternity* is art. In a motif typical of the boxing film genre, the boxer finds an alternative to fighting in music. Prewitt is a master bugler, and after the death of his buddy Maggio he plays "Taps" in the most extended musical interlude in the film. The song "Reenlistment Blues" is also central to the fiction. The novel reprints the song's lyrics after the closing page, underlining its importance. In two film episodes, soldiers gather in moments of relaxation to sing the song. The tune returns on a few other occasions as a leitmotif for Prewitt, most prominently as Warden handles the bugler's mouthpiece while looking over his comrade's dead body. Typical of the blues, the song is about suffering, here that of a soldier who tries civilian life after a stint in the army, only to find it even more painful than life as a soldier. So he reenlists. Prewitt's closing action, his attempt to rejoin his company, is a gesture of reenlistment. So too with Warden, who turns away from the prospect of being an officer and marrying Karen, to resume his familiar post as top sergeant.

The art theme is highlighted in the closing scene of the film. Harry Cohn, head of Columbia Pictures, insisted that the movie not run a minute more than two hours. Daniel Taradash has been justly applauded for his economical screenplay taken from a long and unwieldy novel, but he could easily have ended the film with Warden's words over Prewitt's dead body. Instead, a final scene follows with Karen and Alma, strangers to each other, aboard ship leaving

Hawaii. As they stand on the deck looking back at Honolulu each remarks on the city's beauty, a puzzling response to the apparently sordid experiences they have had there. Rather than being ironic, the scene implies that their suffering has been ennobling. As they throw their leis into the ocean, Karen recalls a myth that claims one will return if the flowers float to shore. Alma explains that she departed because her fiancé, a bomber pilot, was killed going into action against the Japanese. His courage was awarded a Silver Star, she adds. Finally, she identifies him as being the son of a fine Southern family, Robert E. Lee Prewitt. Karen gives a startled look of recognition as she remembers the lowly rifleman she heard about from Warden. The camera closes in on the bugler's mouthpiece, Alma's memento of her dead lover, which is transformed in her story into the Silver Star. Alma's fable represents the impulse to use fiction as a consolation for sorrow, here an ennobling of Prewitt and of her experience—maybe even a just comparison between the private's death on the golf course and the deaths of others while fighting the Japanese. The invocation of beauty, the myth of return, the fabrication of heroism, and the musical token all underline the art theme and elevate it as a humane and gratifying response to suffering. Art transforms the energy so commonly perpetuated in violence into a creative act mixing self-deception with consolation, contemplation with an elevating compassion.

From Here to Eternity has often been cited as an exemplary screen adaptation. *Variety* claimed that it became "a much better motion picture than the novel was a book" (Borg 1953, 6). *Newsweek* agreed that the filmmakers took "a bawdy behemoth of a book . . . and have nursed it intelligently . . . without sacrificing anything of the novel's genuine value" (*Newsweek* 1953, 82). The skillful development of a large number of characters, along with a wide range of incident, in a two-hour film remains praiseworthy. However, the condensation and pacing of the film rob the viewer of a meditative repose during which to ponder. Though the conclusion of the film invites reflection, the alacrity with which the plot unfolds rushes one through the experience without cultivating the necessary thoughtfulness. Manny Farber recognized the problem when he described the cutting from one scene to the next as too abrupt. "The main trouble is that it is *too* entertaining," he wrote, "for a film in which love affairs flounder, one sweet guy is beaten to death and a man of high principles is mistaken for a saboteur and killed on a golf course" (Farber 1953, 178). Nonetheless, *From Here to Eternity* remains a remarkable Hollywood film, popular, profitable and showered with awards by the Motion Picture Academy, yet seriously portraying suffering as the bedrock of human experience. The conventions of the boxing film underlie *From Here to Eternity* and invite us to ponder the dimensions of violence and the meaning of suffering.

SOMEBODY UP THERE LIKES ME (1956): BOXING AS REDEMPTION

In 1949 *Champion* and *The Set-Up* were released within weeks of each other. Seven years later the directors of those films, Mark Robson and Robert Wise, each completed another significant boxing film: *The Harder They Fall* (Robson) and *Somebody Up There Likes Me* (Wise). Both films attracted a substantial audience. In its annual survey, *Variety* tallied the box office for Columbia's *The Harder They Fall* at $1.35 million, which M.G.M.'s *Somebody Up There Likes Me* surpassed with $2 million. *Somebody* also earned three Academy Award nominations and won the awards for Best Cinematography in Black and White and Best Art Direction in Black and White. The stars of these films set the tone. *The Harder They Fall* was Humphrey Bogart's last screen role. Cancer killed Bogart less than a year after the film's release. "If an actor ever looked like he was going through the motions," Robert Sklar writes, "it was Bogart in this film" (Sklar 1992, 250). By contrast, *Variety* trumpeted that Paul Newman "scores tremendously" in *Somebody*, sending the young actor on his way to stardom (Brog 1956, 6). *The Harder They Fall* marked an end, while *Somebody Up There Likes Me* signaled a new beginning.

Somebody Up There Likes Me comes up with an invigorating generic hybrid. The film integrates the boxing movie with juvenile delinquency pictures, such as *The Wild One* (1954) and *Rebel Without a Cause* (1955), and the biopic tradition that points back to the upbeat *Gentleman Jim* (1942). Newspaper ads tie the release to M.G.M.'s hit featuring urban delinquents from the previous year: "If you think 'The Blackboard Jungle' was great, wait til you see this one." The pitch aims at the teenage audience, then becoming a much more substantial portion of the ticket buying public. Promotions also declared, "From real life comes a powerful movie," touting the authenticity of the autobiography of popular middleweight boxing champion (1947–48) Rocky Graziano. The opening image before the credits even affirms, "'This is the way I remember it—*definitely.*' Rocky Graziano." Critics praised Paul Newman's performance as Graziano and compared it to Marlon Brando's Method style, thereby reinforcing the links to the delinquency movies, the appeal to the youth audience, and the claim to realism. In the *New York Times*, Bosley Crowther observes a conspicuous shift in attitude in the boxing film: "The other side of the coin from the recent 'The Harder They Fall,' which pictured professional prizefighting as sordid and corrupt, is being most touchingly presented by Metro-Goldwyn-Mayer's 'Somebody Up There Likes Me.'" The critic goes on to note that in this film, "[T]he prize ring is highly recommended as a fine place for a tough to vent his spleen and gain for himself not only money but also public applause and respect" (Crowther 1956, 16).

Somebody Up There Likes Me (1956) portrays boxing as a maladjusted youth's means of redemption. Courtesy of the Academy of Motion Picture Arts and Sciences.

Somebody Up There Likes Me reverses the traditional rise and fall pattern of the boxing plot. Instead, the film follows with Rocky's decline from abused child, to juvenile delinquent, reform school hooligan, and army deserter until he becomes a veteran convict moving between criminal gangs and the prison cell. However, fortune reverses Rocky's fall in spite of his belligerence. A visit to Stillman's Gym introduces him to boxing, his ring skills are sharpened in a prison boxing program, and Irving Cohen (Everett Sloan), his fatherly manager, guides his career upon Rocky's release from jail. While Rocky is on the rise as a fighter, his sister's girlfriend, Norma (Pier Angeli), courts the pug. Even though Rocky scoffs at tenderness, Norma persists and finally marries the middleweight, now a contender. In the final episodes, a crisis arises, and Rocky must take responsibility for himself rather than depend upon the support of others. The middleweight loses his first title shot to champion Tony Zale, and then the New York State Boxing Commission suspends him when he refuses to identify those who offered him a bribe to take a dive. Another title bout is arranged in Chicago, but Rocky's distress drives Norma to declare that her husband "has got a past and it's time he learned to live with it." Rocky travels back to Manhattan's Lower East Side to confront the origins of his troubled youth. Here he learns the sorry fate of his former street buddies (played by Sal Mineo and Steve McQueen, among others), and listens to the advice of Benny, the neighborhood candy store counselor (Joseph Buloff). Finally Rocky seeks out and reconciles with his abusive father (Harold J. Stone). The therapeutic journey invigorates the contender, and he knocks out Tony Zale in the sixth round of their rematch. The film ends with the new champ in a triumphant victory parade through his Lower East Side neighborhood. Like *Gentleman Jim*, Rocky's biography follows the fighter's quest for the championship and rises toward his moment of glory. *Somebody Up There Likes Me* portrays boxing not as a social problem, but as an opportunity for redemption.

In addition to a reversal of the typical boxing film plot, *Somebody Up There Likes Me* explores fresh treatments of the conflicts in the genre. Market competition is not a problem. The source of Rocky's maladjustment is psychological. In the opening scenes a drunken father strikes and taunts his young son. In anger the boy throws a stone through a store window advertising a father's day gift endorsed by boxing champion Gene Tunney. The cops chase the boy, but he disappears down a dark street. A cut finds Rocky, now a teenager, still running from the police. A belligerent father and an ineffectual mother cause the boy's delinquency. Psychological maladjustment, rather than poverty, accounts for the obstacles the protagonist must overcome. Late in the film when Rocky returns to his old neighborhood prior to the climatic bout, Benny at the candy store tells the young man, "[N]ever ask for a soda unless you are prepared to pay the check," affirming personal responsibility as a basis for a maturity. Before he can become champ Rocky must stop blaming others for his failures and become self-reliant. The traditional critique of the success ethic, epitomized by the struggle in the ring, is absent. In a similar fashion, prizefighting does not engender conflicts with women or divide loyalties in the ethnic neighborhood. Instead, boxing is a skill developed in street fighting. His prison trainer suggests that Rocky direct his temper into organized competition. His manager cultivates Rocky's skill further. Norma, his Jewish wife, wrangles Graziano into marriage in spite of his intransigence. The typical conflicts never develop. And tension between the physical and spiritual is not used to animate the film either. Rocky's pronounced physicality, his aggressive and energetic body, serves as the instrument that brings harmony to his soul. The film's title invokes a divine "Somebody" who uses boxing as a means to achieve Rocky's redemption. The film equates gaining the middleweight championship with the spiritual regeneration that usually requires the boxer to leave the ring. The major sources of conflict driving the boxing film genre appear to be working in harmony in *Somebody Up There Likes Me*.

The problem the film highlights is male emotion. Rocky's psyche, twisted in childhood as the result of poor parenting, must be healed in order for him to survive and mature. This process begins as the angry young man's rage drives him to crime. *Somebody Up There Likes Me* cultivates the conflict between anger and powerlessness when the fighter rages, not at the source of his oppression, but at surrogates such as a shop window, the army, or his opponents in the ring. However, the Graziano biopic portrays boxing as a therapy that eventually leads its subject to confront the cause of his torment. His psychic healing comes in stages: First he learns to redirect his anger into ring craft; then benevolent mentors, his manager and Benny at the candy store, compensate for an abusive father; and finally Norma, his nurturing wife, makes up for an ineffectual mother. The basis of his maladjustment is indicated by Rocky's mother's admonishing Norma to avoid the mistake that soured the older woman's marriage. She insisted that her husband give up boxing and, as a result, he turned his frustrated aggression into drinking and domestic abuse. Norma, by contrast, encourages Rocky's career, even though boxing repels her. More importantly, his mother's advice avoids gender conflict and suggests that harm arises from the feminization of the husband by marriage. Rather than a manifestation of masculine suffering, boxing represents a healthy arena for the expression of male aggression.

In the related conflict between discipline and sensitivity, *Somebody Up There Likes Me* portrays Rocky's acquisition first of discipline, and later sensitivity, as a sequential process. Both qualities are necessary to resolve conflicting male emotions. The early episodes of delinquency portray the young Rocky as utterly undisciplined. Reform school, the army, and prison all fail to restrain his rage, which remains unchecked until boxing finally offers a means of bringing direction to the man's life. Boxing discipline replaces powerlessness with might, and sets the stage for the courtship that cultivates sensitivity through Norma's influence. Though Rocky squirms at displays of tenderness, his reticence finally surrenders to the affection of his manager and Norma. Marriage and children mature the man, and when he is reprimanded by the boxing commission, his distress leads him to finally confront his father. When Rocky asks his bitter, wasted parent, "What can I do for you?" Pa replies, "Be a champ, like I never was." Rocky answers with his characteristic "Don't worry about a thing," then leaves for Chicago and his rematch with Tony Zale. Rocky reconciles with his past, and thereby gains the will to win the boxing title. Rather than conflicting, discipline and sensitivity function in tandem to turn the truculent youth into the neighborhood hero.

Rocky Graziano's three title bouts against Tony Zale were legendary fights, considered among the most exciting in middleweight history. In the first, on September 27, 1946, in Yankee Stadium, after being hurt early in the competition, Zale came back to knock out Graziano in the sixth round. *Somebody Up There Likes Me* stages the second bout, which took place in July 1947, in Chicago, where Zale was a local hero. With Graziano's victory by knockout in the sixth round the former delinquent and ex-con becomes champion and fulfills the redemption theme central to the film. The ringside announcer states the dramatic question at the beginning of the bout: "Can Rocky Graziano shake off every roof that has caved in on him in the past six months and bounce back to take the title?" The big fight sequence lasts for 10 minutes and 12 seconds, or about 9% of the total running time of the film. *Variety* praised the "authenticity" of the "potently staged championship match" that was "better than being ringside almost" (Brog 1956, 6). Bosley Crowther in the *New York Times* agreed that, "The representation of the big fight of Graziano with Tony Zale is one of the whoppingest slugfests we've ever seen on screen" (Crowther 1956, 16).

Somebody Up There Likes Me employs the traditional style of intensified realism for the boxing spectacle, with an emphasis on realism as opposed to the expressionist elements apparent in the climactic bouts in *Kid Galahad* and developed even further in *Body and Soul*. The accent on realism complements the biography film, in which the fiction is based on fact. Here the design of the screen bout arises from the record of the actual fight; Paul Newman copies Graziano's boxing pose and fighting style. The actor playing Tony Zale (Courtland Shepard) is a double for the champion. The ring announcer's commentary offers an oral record of the contest. Rather than a crooked set-up, the fight is a fair, clean, but brutal battle between two renowned boxers. Clarity, intensity, and objectivity are the visual hallmarks of the film's treatment of the fight. The soundtrack—the noise of the crowd, the ringside announcer, the chatter of the corner men with their fighter—is grounded in reality. There is no music during the sequence. Rather than a demonized antagonist, Zale is treated as a formidable obstacle to Rocky's need to take responsibility for his life by exercising his determination to win.

The exaggerated staging of the match presents an almost continuous exchange of blows, which arises from Graziano's boxing style. The middleweight was a celebrated brawler with little concern for defense or finesse. He came out swinging, and the fans loved his aggressive, constant attack. Robert Wise, the director, gets close to the boxers, shooting within the ring to intensify the action. Seventy-four of the ninety-nine shots of boxing are recorded inside the ring rather than from the standard ringside angle. Nonetheless, the camera position maintains an objective view, seeking the best perspective on the fight rather than portraying the interior feelings of the boxers. The cinematography freely follows the combat, but from a stable tripod, which keeps the battle at the center of the composition. In contrast to the expressionist, hand held, off center imagery found in *Body and Soul, Somebody Up There Likes Me* offers a balanced, more objective treatment. The black and white film has a glossy sheen with the clean graphic line thought to be characteristic of M.G.M. cinematography. The high contrast between the bodies of the boxers and the black background makes the shots glow, almost as if the boxer's physical prowess creates an aura of manliness. The editing pace is fast, with an average shot length [asl] of 3.75, which is a moderate asl compared to other famous boxing sequences (*Kid Galahad*'s asl registers 4.5, but *Body and Soul* comes in with an asl of 3.23).

Throughout the bout editing shapes the dramatic space by cutting to the distinct groups supporting each fighter. The fans within the Chicago arena are anonymous crowd members—some photographed at actual boxing matches—who all support the local favorite, Tony Zale. In counterpoint, the film cuts to Rocky's supporters, listening to the fight on the radio at four different locations in New York City. Each of the listeners is a character with a sentimental attachment to Rocky. These include: Norma, Rocky's wife, and his child; Rocky's parents, Mr. and Mrs. Barbella; neighborhood friends such as Benny, the store owner, and Romolo, Rocky's boyhood pal, gathered at the candy store; and finally Johnny Highland, the sergeant who trained Rocky in prison to be a fighter, listening in a New York bar. In similar fashion there are cutaways to Rocky's corner men (particularly his manager, Irving) as they react to the bout. All these characters have helped Rocky realize his redemption. These scenes of Rocky's supporters listening on the radio give special emphasis to the radio announcer's narration of the bout, which also informs the film viewer of the fight's development.

The six-round bout determines the dramatic time, and the ringside announcer explains the course of the action. Throughout the first five rounds, Zale the champion is on the attack, and Rocky fights off his assaults. At the close of round one, the announcer concludes, "A very rocky round for Mr. Graziano," while Norma anxiously paces near her radio. In round two, Zale opens up a cut above Rocky's left eye, and the announcer confirms that the challenger is bleeding badly as he goes to his corner. In round three, Zale scores a knockdown, and the radio voice confirms, "Rocky's in trouble. He's really in trouble now." In rounds four and five Rocky continues to fend off Zale's attack, but humor develops an upbeat counterpoint to the challenger's vulnerability that underlines Rocky's determination.

The corner drama between rounds finds Rocky and his manager Irving joking in spite of the blows the fighter has endured. When Rocky complains after round one that, "The guy hits hard," Irving prods, "Hit 'im back, it's legal." After the knockdown in round three, Rocky assures Irving, "I got 'im just where I want 'im." When the referee threatens to stop the fight and Rocky gets angry, Irving says, "Not him," then, pointing to Zale, "Him." The turning point comes in the corner after round five. Though Rocky has been unable to break the champion's assault, the fighter declares with confidence, "I got him ... I'm gonna bust his head open ... this round." Irving concedes, "I'm beginning to believe ya." The sixth round finds the champion fatigued, and Rocky attacks.

Somebody Up There Likes Me is the first and one of the few boxing films that photographs most of its "big fight" with a camera placed within the ring. Perspectives shift from full two-shots of both fighters from head to knees or waist exchanging blows and moving over the canvas. More intense shots single out each fighter's face as the two boxers fire punches, take blows, evade an attack, or look for an opening. Sometimes the close-up face of one of the boxers looks into the camera as he unleashes his punches. Round one gradually moves from a ringside camera, to within the ring, to closer and closer views of the battle. The remaining rounds start at a distance but quickly move in close to the exchange of blows. Most dynamically, the editing occasionally creates a match on action cut from a fighter in close up firing his punch to his opponent taking the blow. The most noteworthy example of this technique occurs in the sixth and final round, when Rocky throws a left that catches Zale in the face and throws the champion back on his heels. The cut reinforces the blow that breaks down the champ's defenses. In earlier rounds the rapid cutting on punches creates a rat-tat-tat effect something like Sergei Eisenstein's editing of a firing machine gun in *October* (1927). The editing pace of the rounds also increases with the asl in round one at 4.7 seconds, round two at 4.0, round three 3.15, and rounds four and five at 1.30 and 1.56, respectively. For Rocky's comeback triumph in round six, the asl increases to 3.31 to include fuller shots of Graziano's attack propelling Zale across the ring and finally into a corner, where the challenger pummels him into submission. Robert Wise's dynamic recreation of the Zale-Graziano title bout uses a series of cinematic elements to bring a new intensity to realistic staging of boxing.

Somebody Up There Likes Me brings to a positive conclusion the conflicts animating the boxing film in the studio era. Boxing noir promoted an irrational, self-destructive psychology; *Somebody Up There Likes Me* portrays positive psychic renewal. In the latter, even a brutish delinquent finds salvation. Initially one might see little in common with director Robert Wise's earlier boxing film, *The Set-Up*. A noir tone saturates *The Set-Up*, while *Somebody* radiates an upbeat M.G.M. sensibility in which every social problem has a solution. *The Set-Up* is deliberate and confined, whereas *Somebody* is energetic and expansive. But, as I have argued with regard to *The Set-Up*, the earlier film also ends with the boxer's salvation coming inadvertently through circumstances displaying affinities with a divine grace. Wise's coherent, self-effacing direction underlines the hopeful themes in both pictures. Here, in the most popular boxing film from the close of the studio era, conflicts the genre typically poses disappear or are satisfactorily resolved. The success of this movie suggests that the culture no longer found such problems compelling. The near disappearance of the boxing film, rather than the initiation of a new cycle supports such a suggestion. In 1961 Robert Rossen, the Academy Award winning director of *Body and Soul*, directed Paul Newman in the critically acclaimed *The Hustler*. Here Newman plays a young pool shark who challenges the champion, Minnesota Fats. In many respects *The Hustler* resembles the boxing film, a genre in which both Rossen and Newman had distinguished themselves. In an earlier decade, *The Hustler* may well have been a boxing drama. But the allure of boxing had passed, and pool offered a fresh setting in which to dramatize the rise and fall of a young sportsman making his way on the margins of the underworld. When the boxing film regained its attractiveness, it looked back toward *Somebody Up There Likes Me*. The middleweight Graziano was born Rocky Barbella, and the similarity between the names Rocky Barbella and Rocky Balboa hints at a connection between *Somebody Up There Likes Me* and *Rocky*. Indeed, twenty years later many of the characteristics of the hit film from 1956 emerge in the boxing film that animated the next major cycle in the genre.

FAT CITY (1972): CRIPPLED EMOTIONS AND PANGS OF LONELINESS

Fat City, a boxing film made by Hollywood stalwarts, exhibits a tension between genre conventions and the influence of the European art cinema. The movie was initiated when the influential producer Ray Stark sent the Academy Award winning director John Huston *Fat City*, described by Joyce Carol Oates as "everybody's favorite boxing novel" (Oates 1994, 55). Stark had already produced two Huston literary adaptations, *The Night of the Iguana* (1964) and *Reflections in a Golden Eye* (1967), and his hunch that the filmmaker would find *Fat City* appealing was on target.

Though John Huston had never made a boxing film, the director understood the sensibility of the genre. He was drawn to projects about outcasts and
losers, isolated tough guys living on the margins of society. Critics frequently
compared him to his friend, Ernest Hemingway. As a young man Huston had
briefly been a ranking lightweight boxer touring the small arenas of California.
He managed to win twenty-three bouts and got his nose broken before giving up the fight game. Later, Huston published two short stories about boxers,
"Fool" (1929) and "Figures of Fighting Men" (1931) in *American Mercury*. Furthermore, in the 1940s Huston directed two classic films noir, *The Maltese Falcon* (1940) and *The Asphalt Jungle* (1950), as well as working as an unaccredited
writer on *The Killers* (1946). The small town boxers in *Fat City* are ready made
for the filmmaker. Though an industry veteran, Huston cultivated an outsider
status in Hollywood. He had been living and working abroad for over a decade,
and *Fat City* was the first film he shot in the U.S. since making the *The Mis-
fits* (1961). Leonard Gardner was hired to adopt his novel for the screen, and
the Academy Award winning cinematographer Conrad Hall (*Butch Cassidy
and the Sundance Kid*) completed the distinguished production team. Though
the film lacked stars (Marlon Brandon was offered the lead, but no agreement
could be reached), the eventual mix of capable actors with non-professionals
and a few former boxers added an "art cinema" tone to a production managed
by Hollywood veterans. Though these filmmakers were familiar with the boxing genre, they incorporated art cinema qualities that resisted convention, particularly unusual plotting, realism in setting and performance, and ambiguity
in characterization and resolution. In fact, recent hits, such as *Bonnie and Clyde*
(1967) and *The Graduate* (1967), had demonstrated that art cinema traits could
be incorporated into mainstream genre movies and still have mass appeal.

Upon release, *Fat City* was widely hailed. The film premiered in 1972 at the
Cannes Film Festival, where the press greeted Huston with a standing ova-
tion after the screening. Generally the movie received excellent reviews, and
even garnered an Academy Award nomination for Susan Tyrell, but it found no
audience. The production was part of a series of box office failures that plagued
Huston during the late 1960s and early 1970s. Nonetheless, *Fat City* continues to receive serious attention, and most evaluators of Huston's career rank it
among his best work (Studlar 1993, 177–98; Brill 1997, 191–206).

Fat City cultivates the paradox suggested by its title. As Charles Thomas
Samuels points out, the title is "argot for 'out of condition' as well as a loser's
vain dreams" (Samuels 1972, 148). That is, "fat city" simultaneously refers to
one's aspirations and one's inability to achieve them. Arising from this paradox,
the plot turns from the linear rise and fall structure typical of the boxing genre,
to a pattern based on parallelism and circularity. The film opens with Billy Tully

(Stacey Keach), an aging ex-prizefighter, meeting the young Ernie Munger (Jeff Bridges) at the gym. After a little sparring, Tully assures the kid of his talent and encourages him to pursue a ring career. The film drifts back and forth between the two fighters, with Tully nursing an ambition to make a comeback and Ernie learning the ropes as a boxer. At the same time, they are each involved with a woman: Tully moves in with Oma (Susan Tyrell), a pugnacious drunk, while Ernie is maneuvered into marriage by his girlfriend, Faye (Candy Clark). Eventually Tully goes back into training and scores a victory against a fighter of some repute. Disillusioned in spite of his success, he drifts back into boozing. Ernie becomes a husband and father, but his prizefighting yields only a tepid mix of minor victories and defeats. The film ends with another chance encounter between Tully and Ernie. Sharing a cup of coffee in a late night gaming club, the two experience a strained comradeship fraught with lack of self-awareness and an aimless discontent. Aspiration to glory in the ring has come to nothing; in spite of a common experience, neither man can alleviate the loneliness of the other. The ambiguous ending conveys crippled emotions that leave both men isolated.

The characters in *Fat City* draw upon, but transform, the conventional oppositions of the boxing film. The boxer as loner finds expression in both Tully and Ernie. But the film never gives these fighters a villainous rival upon whom to project the wrongs they are combating; instead, a meaningful similarity between boxers emerges. The portrayal of Tully's valorized opponent in the closing big fight underlines similarity. Lucero, a renowned veteran, travels from Mexico City to Stockton to meet Tully in his comeback bout. The Mexican travels alone to a foreign country, just as Tully did on his way to an earlier defeat in Panama City, a defeat Tully blames for his decline. Before the bout we see Lucero pass blood into a toilet, revealing the internal injuries hidden behind his imposing physique. Like Tully, Lucero is a boxer whose wounds signal the close of his career. The bout itself is a clumsy, bruising affair in which Tully is knocked down before scoring a technical knockout. But at the final bell, Tully is so dazed that he asks his manager whether he got knocked out. Upon learning that he won, Tully crosses the ring to hug his rival. Lesley Brill points out that the paired close-ups present each boxer's exhausted face looking past the other as they embrace. The fighters "depict simultaneous intimacy and isolation, the unbridgeable gulfs that separate people even during their most ardent combative embraces" (Brill 1997, 204). Rather than distinguishing one fighter from the other, *Fat City* makes the big fight a shared experience in which both boxers suffer a defeat that is immediate for one and only slightly postponed for the other. Their closing embrace emphasizes a common fate as well as a troubling loneliness.

In similar fashion, the minor figures are characterized by the mixed motives typical of realism. Reuben (Nicolas Colasanto), the fight manager, cares about his boxers, but he cultivates his self-interest as well. He talks in racial terms about turning Ernie into a feature attraction because he is a white boxer, while his wife falls asleep next to him. His musings are part of his own dream of success rather than a nasty prejudice. Reuben and his trainer Babe (boxing veteran Art Aragon) are regularly matched in conversation, but frequently fail to listen to each other. When Reuben tells Babe about Ernie's physical, the trainer responds with an unrelated story about another boxer's clear urine sample. The exchanges mix humor with melancholy. Tully blames his decline on Reuben's failure to accompany him to a bout in Panama in which he is convinced that the corner men sabotaged his chances. However, Reuben's limited resources suggest that such a trip was beyond his means and that no malice towards the boxer compromised his good will. On other occasions, Reuben lends Tully money, takes him into his home, and expresses personal concern for his fighter. In spite of Tully's resentment of Reuben, he recommends the manager to Ernie, a paradoxical gesture typical of *Fat City*. The featured women, Oma and Faye, blend positive and negative traits rather than becoming vamps or sweethearts. Oma's drunkenness cannot disguise her sincere affection for Tully. Faye traps the reluctant Ernie into marriage, but becoming a husband and father may alleviate the threat of replicating Tully's dereliction, and offer the young man a comforting hedge against loneliness.

A surprising and moving reversal of convention occurs in the closing meeting between Tully and Earl. In order to return to training, Tully leaves Oma, but after his disappointing victory purse, the fighter knocks on the woman's door. The door opens and Earl, Oma's former companion, appears. The African American has returned from jail to take Tully's place. However, instead of a confrontation between romantic rivals, the scene concludes with two men stepping into the hall and exchanging conciliatory gestures, finally sharing their similar experience with Oma. Rather than emphasizing dramatic conflict, *Fat City* develops similarity between characters, points in common that portray repetition, the cyclical nature of experience.

The settings in *Fat City* evoke the conventional trappings of boxing, while giving them an unusual, realistic edge. Boxing fiction, usually set among the lower classes and socially conscious, was already associated with screen realism. However, by working against expectations, *Fat City* makes the typical unfamiliar. For example, rather than being set in the metropolis, the film is shot on location in Stockton, a small agrarian city in California's San Joaquin Valley. Huston exchanges the dark, shadowy ring world, so familiar in film noir, for sunshine, often reflecting off of whitewashed exteriors. As Lesley Brill notes,

Huston "replaced the dreariness of Gardner's setting with sunlight and a chipper, colorful palette" (Brill 1997, 193). For example, the gym where Tully and Ernie meet is bright, open and airy, as is Reuben's training center. The streets of Stockton are generally bright. Even though the film remains centered in Stockton, the sense of transience, the homelessness of the boxer, is conveyed by the flophouses, bars, buses and automobiles that frame the action. These downbeat locales are never exotic; rather, a mundane texture prevails.

Settings and objects also evoke important themes throughout the movie. At the beginning of the film, Billy rises from sleep, looking for a match to light his cigarette. Later that morning he finds his match when he encounters Ernie in the gym. The match device returns at the end when Tully bumps into Ernie for the last time. In a similar vein, Tully returns to Oma's hotel room after an unsuccessful morning looking for work, and helps her play out a hand of solitaire, thus evoking their mutual striving for intimacy amidst loneliness. The eye scarring and blindness motif common in boxing fiction also operates in *Fat City*. The allusion to blindness arises because Tully carries boxing scars above his eyes that are opened and bleed during his bout with Lucero. The boxer claims that these scars originated when his corner men in Panama secretly cut him with a razor. At two key moments in the film, the camera presents a close-up of Tully staring. These intense looks, apart from point of view editing, indicate a moment of self-realization. The first takes place in the boxer's corner between rounds of the Lucero bout; the second in the closing episode while Tully shares a coffee with Ernie. However, the film allows the look to be ambiguous, no dialogue or gesture clarifies the meaning of the stare. As Charles Thomas Samuels complains, "[T]his moment implies a portentous realization, but we cannot imagine what Tully is thinking" (Samuels 1972, 150). The ambiguity invites interpretation. Robin Wood surmises that in staring at the crowd of men in the gaming room the boxer recognizes the "universal nature of his predicament" (Wood 1980, 517), which is, to Wood's understanding, a ubiquitous loneliness. Blankness, or lack of understanding, may itself be the point. For Tully there is no coming to consciousness in the tradition of *Golden Boy* or *On the Waterfront*. His blindness cannot penetrate to an interior understanding. Furthermore, both boxers display an inability to make genuine contact. This paradox of similarity without insight ends the film on a note of despair.

Critics such as William S. Pechter have faulted Huston's detached tone in *Fat City*. The director invites sympathy for his characters without arousing identification. Their bleak condition, and by implication the human limitations with which we all must cope, fail to engender pathos. However, this distance arises from the paradoxical qualities that lie at the center of the film's design. Paradox accounts for the comic tone that Lesley Brill ascribes to the film, as the

Tully (Stacy Keach), the veteran boxer, and Ernie (Jeff Bridges), the novice, meet at the close. The paradox of similarity without insight ends *Fat City* (1972) on a note of despair. Courtesy of the Academy of Motion Picture Arts and Sciences.

incongruity of humor colors so many episodes even though the drama as a whole is far from funny. This tone, especially peculiar in the context of realism, leaves the audience off balance, uncertain as what to feel. Though unsatisfying, the detached treatment invests the film with complexity. Pechter describes the result as an "art house version" of a classic Huston Hollywood film (Pechter 1972, 82). This distinctive approach transforms the dramatic conflicts that I have argued constitute the foundation of a genre.

The conflicts in *Fat City* are elusive rather than clearly articulated. The dramatic rhythm of the film is diffuse; the plot circles around its themes rather than driving forward toward a resolution. Lesley Brill claims that boxing is the central metaphor in the film, but not boxing as a contest producing a winner. Rather, as noted above, the big bout between Tully and Lucero becomes a failure of the fighters to recognize that they share a common fate; even their concluding embrace suggests an impasse. The film presents a quest for fellowship that paradoxically pits prospective comrades against one another as rivals. In a similar fashion, Tully blames Reuben for his defeat in Panama, but Reuben's treatment of Tully in the film is consistently helpful. The manager rescues the declining boxer from his own self-destructive behavior, but gets no thanks in return. The viewer comes to doubt whether there is any truth to Tully's tale, but the issue is never resolved. In *Fat City* the inadequacies of men and women undermine a longing for fellowship that can only be realized in brief occasional experiences.

Fat City resists the typical conflicts of the boxing film genre. Conditions in the film are impoverished, but the economic system is not blamed for this state of affairs. There are no gangsters exploiting the boxer. The film shows its protagonist's problems as human rather than social. Racial and ethnic differences abound, with African Americans, Hispanics, Mexicans, and Asians populating the film, which even prominently features an interracial couple, Oma and Earl. But rather than emphasizing differences, the film portrays a common humanity. In *Fat City*, race is only a minor manifestation of deeper traits separating people. The gender divide between Tully and Oma, Ernie and Faye, even Reuben and his sleeping wife, vividly marks the film, but the alienation of couples is no deeper than that between the men themselves. A pervasive loneliness replaces the conventional gender conflict with an underlying gravity. The problem of male emotion is expressed in the discipline of boxing, and the sensitivity between men and women and of men for each other. However, a sharp contrast between discipline and sensitivity never emerges. Tully must leave Oma in order to return to training, and Reuben complains that he lost a boxing prospect to marriage when Ernie weds Faye. However, Ernie returns to the ring and scores victories after becoming a husband. No tension emerges between the need to maintain discipline and the struggle for sensitivity. The vulnerability and inevitable deterioration of the body finds expression in *Fat City*. Huston accents Tully's disheveled appearance and scarred body. The film lingers on Ernie's bleeding face after his first bout. Sharing breakfast, Reuben and Babe exchange stories about their broken noses. After having sex with Faye in a car on the roadside, Ernie flounders in the mud when a rainstorm traps his vehicle. *Fat City* emphasizes a gross physicality rather than elevating the body. Nonetheless, no sheltering truth lies in the spirit. The family, religion, art, learning are all banished from the film. Tully speaks longingly of the wife who left him, and there is a suggestion that Ernie's marriage, however reluctantly he wed, will ameliorate his loneliness, but such hedges against despair barely improve the existential isolation manifest in *Fat City*.

John Huston fashioned an artful film in *Fat City*, but its bleak vision, as much as its unusual design, made for a limited audience. Nonetheless, the film's portrait of suffering and the inadequacy of human emotion positions it squarely in the tradition of the Hollywood boxing film, even as it resists many of the genre's conventions.

FIGHT CLUB (1999): "NO PAIN, NO GAIN"

Upon the release of *Fight Club* in the fall of 1999, critical reaction was intense and polarized. "*Fight Club* is the most incendiary movie to come out of Hollywood in a long time," reported David Ansen in *Newsweek* (Ansen 1999, 77). Roger Ebert accused the film of being "fascist ... macho porn" (Ebert 1999, 1). Kenneth Turan complained of a "witless mishmash of whiny, infantile philosophizing and bone-crunching violence" (Turan 1999, 1). But others described a screen triumph. David Rooney in *Variety* raved, "[R]arely has a film been so keyed into its time ... this bold, inventive, sustained adrenaline rush of a movie ... should excite and exhilarate young audiences everywhere" (Rooney 1999, 1). Susan Faludi praised the production as a male *Thelma and Louise*, a "consciousness-raising buddy movie ... incisive gender drama ... a quasi-feminist tale, seen through masculine eyes" (Faludi 1999, 89). Charles Whitehouse in *Sight and Sound* described the film's heterogeneous, postmodern sensibility, "So *Fight Club* is all of the following: a conspiracy thriller that never leaves the splashy imagination of a paranoid narrator; a value-free vessel that offers conflicting views on Nietzschean ideas about men and destruction; a dazzling entertainment that wants us to luxuriate in violence as we condemn it; a brilliant solution to depicting the divided self as a protagonist" (Whitehouse 1999, 4). Whether critics loved the movie or hated it, the controversy surrounding its release confirmed that *Fight Club* had touched a nerve in the culture.

The $63 million production, starring Brad Pitt and directed by David Fincher (*Se7en*, *The Game*), had a disappointing domestic box office of only $37 million, but the film did well abroad, taking in another $71 million. In home DVD format, *Fight Club* became a cult favorite. The DVD won the Online Film Critics Society's 2001 awards for "Best DVD," "Best DVD Commentary" and "Best DVD Special Features." The Internet Movie Data Base web site reports 92,885 votes from viewers, scoring the film a stellar 8.5 on a scale of 10 and placing *Fight Club* at #41 among all films ever polled by the site. The film's complex design rewards close study from fans, and the DVD fosters their enthusiasm (http://www.imdb.com/title/tt0137523).

The well-crafted but elusive film invites, maybe even requires, repeated screenings. As Janet Maslin admits, "[T]his film twists and turns in ways that only add up fully on the way out of the theater and might just require another viewing" (Maslin 1999, 2). Even after close scrutiny, uncertainties remain because nearly the entire fiction takes place in the confused mind of the protagonist-narrator, sometimes known as Jack (Edward Norton). The opening credit sequence features a digital image zipping through a cavernous abstract landscape standing in for the interior of the narrator's brain. The boundary between his subjectivity and the credible social world in *Fight Club* remains shifting and ill defined, especially after the film's puzzling climax. As a result, the film gives the viewer a sensational ride, but it also raises questions and invites interpretation. Repeated viewing reveals that the filmmakers have deftly set up their subjective perspectives, so that the entire plot skirts paranoid fantasy. Some might simply want to throw up their hands and walk away from a film too clever for its own credibility. As Roger Ebert complained, *Fight Club* is like "a lot of recent films [that] seem unsatisfied unless they can add final scenes that redefine the reality of everything that has gone before" (Ebert 1999, 2). In addition, the film's tone switches between grotesque humor, sensational violence, and philosophical conjecture ("things you own, end up owning you"). These shifts leave the audience off balance, perplexed, and disturbed or exhilarated.

But is it a boxing film? *Fight Club* is distinct from the conventional, classical Hollywood boxing film. Nevertheless, key elements link this film to the genre. Bare-fisted boxing, as in *Hard Times* and *Every Which Way But Loose*, is central to the action and the film's title. The gloomy neo-noir stylistics and the critique of contemporary metropolitan culture also establish connections between the David Fincher film and the boxing genre. Midway through the picture, the narrator asks Tyler to name the celebrity he would most like to fight at the club. "Hemingway," Tyler replies, and the reference points to the common heritage of the boxing drama. Most importantly, the cultural conflicts at the heart of the boxing genre are on vivid display. Anger conflicts with powerlessness, discipline opposes sensitivity, and pain plays a central role. Few movies are as explicit as *Fight Club* in portraying a beleaguered masculinity seeking regeneration through violence. However, self-conscious play with incompatible forms, typical of postmodernism, is at work in *Fight Club*, where elements of a realistic social drama are combined with psychological fantasy. *Fight Club* dramatizes many of the cultural concerns of the boxing film genre with a fresh intensity.

The masculinity crisis common to the boxing film develops in *Fight Club* out of the conflict between the discipline of the job versus emotional sensitivity. The narrator-protagonist has a sleep problem. His life as a drone in a corporate hierarchy has left him with insomnia. His senses are dead, his instincts numb. His only source of self-worth is to buy things. Though his apartment is a showcase for the Ikea catalogue, it offers no comfort. The conflict between the discipline of the job and sensitivity to others sends him to crisis encounter groups, where he poses as disabled so he can confess and cry with victims of testicular cancer, tuberculosis, or alcoholism. The satirical turn on New Age therapy places sensitivity at a comic distance that expands when Jack spies Marla (Helena Bonham Carter), another tourist faking sickness to get cheap emotional comfort. Marla mirrors the narrator's deception and mocks Jack's attempt to "explore his inner cave." Suddenly, the sensitivity groups no longer soothe his troubles. *Fight Club* presents a contemporary emotional wasteland and laughs at our fledgling attempts to cope. Then Jack wakes up on a business flight, where he meets Tyler Durden (Brad Pitt), who offers him another solution. Blow-up your apartment, learn to strike out, take a hard punch to the eye, and relish the pain.

In *Fight Club* boxing means pain, which is the key to liberation. Only through the willing embrace of suffering can one overcome fear, exercise power, and resurrect one's masculinity. At the club, members engage in knock down, but "feel good" fist fights. Soon the regenerative effect of friendly brawling attracts a mob of disciples who look to Tyler as their leader. Durden takes on a mission urging his followers to reclaim their masculinity by renouncing possessions, comforts, and stale routines, and expressing their rage through bloody, bare-knuckled fistfights. The triumph of *Fight Club* is paradoxical: One overcomes powerlessness by channeling anger into bare-knuckled boxing that regenerates the psyche, but batters the body. Power arises from willing self-immolation. At club night the desire to hit and be hit, to find the pleasure in pain is the goal of the bouts. There are only winners in the bloody fisticuffs, as confederates cheer on the fighters, each ready to enter the ring and enjoy a slugfest. Soon Jack is showing up late to work with bloody gums and blackened eyes, and he begins talking back to his boss.

The quest for freedom turns into a perverse embrace of pain. The narrator moves in with Tyler, a squatter in an abandoned building. Durden's special lessons include pouring lye on Jack's hand, so Jack can revel in his burning flesh: "[W]ithout pain, without sacrifice we would have nothing . . . you have to know, not fear, that someday you're gonna die. After we've lost everything, we're free to do anything." High-speed highway driving against the traffic and off an embankment provides more thrills: "[S]top trying to control everything and just let go." These exercises soon instill a swaggering bravado in place of the narrator's white collar whimpering. When the bar owner tries to throw the fight club out of his basement, Tyler cheerfully invites a beating that shocks the man into relenting. Jack's boss thinks the narrator is crazy, but after the "recall coordinator" beats himself up in his manager's office, the supervisor surrenders to Jack's demands for pay without work. The conquest of pain provokes such awe that it grants power over others.

The Fight Club works out of a shadowy basement, and its underground existence signals its perversity. With the promotion of pain, sensitivity wanes. Like everyone else, Marla is attracted to Tyler's daring, frankness, and sensuality. But Durden treats his lover heartlessly the morning after their sexual bouts. Jack becomes envious of attention Tyler gives to Marla and Angel Face, a Fight Club disciple. In a jealous fit, the narrator nearly beats Angel Face to death at the club, continuing to pummel him after he has signaled his surrender. When Marla inquires about Jack's wounded hand, he rebukes her with "[T]his conversation is over." The shadow of repression hovers over the ethos of *Fight Club* ("The first rule of Fight Club is not to talk about Fight Club."). Tyler's narcissism suggests an unbridled id asserting its domination over others. Soon the lessons of Fight Club are turned against an emasculating social order provoking another crisis.

Fight Club escalates into pathology. Tyler's homework assignments for club members include picking fights with strangers and losing, and terrorizing clerks into pursuing their dreams. Project Mayhem completes the cycle of bringing the lessons of Fight Club into society. Tyler recruits Fight Club loyalists to carry out guerilla attacks on computer firms, banks, and franchise businesses. The narrator is shocked by a casualty of the fighting and questions Tyler's plan. But the first rule of Project Mayhem is that you don't ask questions. Jack attempts to stop the movement, and a confrontation ensues after Marla calls the narrator "Tyler." "Why does everyone think I'm you?" he asks. "All the ways you wish you could be, that's me," Tyler replies. "Little by little, you are just letting yourself become Tyler Durden." Panicked into recognizing that Jack and Tyler are warring alter egos within his consciousness, the narrator scrambles to check his doppelganger before the violence spreads. *Fight Club* makes Tyler a charismatic hero only to disown him. The narrator's madness becomes an escape hatch through which the film abandons coherence. The postmodern multiplication of perspectives evaporates until the viewer is left empty handed. "It's called a change over," the narrator quips. "The movie goes on but nobody in the audience has any idea." At its conclusion, the film becomes a conjurer's trick. *Fight Club* portrays regeneration through violence, but the film rejects the invitation to social action it suggests. The film's anarcho-nihilism limps toward an ambiguous conclusion.

Determined to stop his doppelganger before a metropolitan bombing, the narrator places a gun barrel in his mouth in order to bring a halt to the violence. The film returns to the moment of the flashback, however no "objective" frame stands apart from the consciousness of the protagonist. Even after he smokes Tyler with a bullet to the head and is reunited with Marla, the corporate skyline explodes as the film ends. The ambiguity of the closing leaves one to wonder whether this, too, is simply one of Jack's visions, or maybe an actual event, Tyler's legacy. The uncertainty lingers as the credits roll.

The postmodern sensibility that imbues *Fight Club* leaves one with multiple perspectives, but no coherent understanding. Susan Faludi applauds the ending's optimism, finding Jack liberated to pursue a healthy romance with Marla now that the false consciousness of consumer culture has been exploded. From this perspective, the entire fiction is merely a psychodrama fought out in Jack's head, an ideological purging necessary for maturity. The playful, sensationalist uncertainties allow one plenty of latitude in digesting *Fight Club*. The options concerned some viewers, like Roger Ebert, who writes "[S]ophisticates will be able to rationalize the movie as an argument against the behavior it shows, my guess is that the audience will like the behavior but not the argument" (Ebert 1999, 2). *Fight Club*'s cleverness may leave one feeling as powerless and insensitive as the narrator seems at the beginning. The movie plays with serious problems in our culture, but it opts out of any resolution.

All in all, *Fight Club* presents a discipline of violence as a cure for masculine powerlessness. Such a discipline prepares a man for the pain necessary to contest social power at his job, in personal relationships, and conceivably in the larger socio-political arena. In the last case, *Fight Club* finesses its claims, backing away from the madness of its protagonist. The film never convincingly resolves the battle within the self, or the insensitivity that arises from an ethos promoting aggression and pain. The division within the self mirrors the divisions of irony, and one is left with a sly, but dead-end aestheticism.

This postmodern indeterminacy addresses traditional concerns of the boxing film and gives them a novel treatment. At its best, the boxing film presents suffering as a means of achieving insight and compassion, rather than endorsing pain as an avenue to power. *Fight Club* appropriates conflicts, iconography, and action from the boxing film and brings the genre into a foreign territory. The play of form and the provocation of the viewer finally become more important than working through the dramatic conflicts the film presents. Nonetheless, *Fight Club*'s lineage can be traced back to the boxing film, and viewed through the lens of genre criticism its perversity becomes more understandable.

◆ ◆ ◆

Though an entertainment, the boxing film portrays suffering as central to experience. Furthermore, the genre highlights conflicts between righteous anger and powerlessness, as well as the dilemmas posed by the tension between emotional discipline and sensitivity. Over the course of the twentieth century these films present shifting attitudes toward suffering, but no clear progression as to how our culture understands this problem. During the Popular Front era, *City for Conquest* found wisdom in suffering and portrayed the elevating qualities of self-sacrifice. In the wake of World War II, *From Here To Eternity* testified to the ubiquity of suffering and pondered the range of human response, finally endorsing a pragmatic discipline as a means of moderating agony. *Somebody Up There Likes Me* countered with an irrepressible optimism that benign social institutions, loving comrades, and a measure of good fortune could triumph over hardship. *Fat City* despaired at our existential loneliness and could only recommend compassion as a means of endurance. *Fight Club* rages sardonically at our comfort culture and portrays an aggressive male discipline as an antidote. However, when faced with the consequences of its own vision, the film's postmodern aestheticism retreats into a coy ambivalence. The boxing film presents a vocabulary for portraying suffering, which will continue to be useful, as these fundamental conflicts remain central to the human condition.

7

BODY AND SOUL
The Conflict between the Flesh and the Spirit

The boxer is his body. Physical prowess defines his worth. Stripped of clothing, without tools, this warrior must conquer or be vanquished using nothing more than his flesh and bones. The physical sensibility that is the prizefighter extends outside the ring to the sensual rewards that come with victory and the primal urges that fuel his drive for success. The boxer's rise highlights our animal nature, grounded in the body, and prepares the drama for the champion's physical decline and the inevitability of death. As Charlie Davis acknowledges in the closing line of *Body and Soul* (1947), "Everybody dies." The crisis of consciousness that plagues the boxer arises from a recognition of his physical limitations. As a result, the dramatic conflict between body and soul, the material and the spiritual, is central to the genre. More than simply a sport's drama, the boxing film addresses fundamental issues of human experience embedded in primal conflicts.

From the death of Andy in *The Champ* (1931) to the assisted suicide of Maggie in *Million Dollar Baby* (2004), the pathos of the boxer's passing is widespread in the genre. Also central is a regeneration that counters physical decay. Regeneration may simply be the succession of the coming generation, implied in Marie's marriage to Kid Galahad, or the reunion of husband and wife in *The Set-Up*. Common is the boxer's departure from the ring as a result of an awakening to the limitations of his body. Joe Bonaparte's epiphany after he kills Chocolate Drop in *Golden Boy* is a milestone in developing this theme. The death of his rival provokes the boxer to face his own vulnerability even at

189

the moment of his triumph. Another central contribution of *Golden Boy* is the clear articulation of the body and soul conflict in Bonaparte's choice between boxing and the violin. The art motif foregrounds the spirit as an alternative to the physical. The development of the boxing film highlights the quest in our culture for a spiritual alternative to the sensual. In the genre art, education, romance, the family, and religion all serve as manifestations of the spiritual.

The history of the boxing film charts our culture's search for values that transcend the body. *Here Comes Mr. Jordan* (1941), a comic fantasy, portrays a conflict between body and soul in which a heavenly agent helps the boxer find a new body after his accidental death upsets the divine plan. The traditional conflict between body and soul turns into a harmonious union reflecting the values accompanying our entry into World War II. After the war, *Body and Soul* returned Americans to the issues posed in *Golden Boy* and developed them with renewed eloquence in the noir style. *On the Waterfront* (1954) featured a retired boxer, haunted by his fall. In this film Christian values point the way toward redemption. *Rocky* (1976) begins with an image of Christ painted on the ceiling of the Resurrection Athletic Club, and the film raises its innocent fighter to glory from the tawdry streets of the ethnic ghetto. Butch the boxer and Julius the hit man in *Pulp Fiction* (1994) strive to escape from death in the underworld, but the ironic play of pop culture toys with the earnestness of their quest. These films engage with the body and soul conflict, offering up fresh perspectives that bear witness to the fertility of the genre in addressing the deepest concerns of its audience.

HERE COMES MR. JORDAN (1941): THE FANTASTIC AND THE PHYSICAL

Boxing films in the 1930s were generally cautionary tales, like *Golden Boy*, that urged men to trade their glorification of physical strength for the spiritual benefits of the family, education, and the arts. However, with the approach of World War II, a pronounced change occurred. The critique of the physical was abandoned for a celebration of warrior virtues and a reassuring optimism. The Oscar-winning *Here Comes Mr. Jordan*, with its Capraesque fantasy, contributed to the trend. Melodrama and pathos were replaced by whimsical comedy. The film is noteworthy because of its clear presentation of the body and soul theme, and its turn from antagonism between these elements to treating them as a harmonious union.

The film opens with Joe Pendelton (Robert Montgomery) training for a title fight, only to be killed in a plane crash just before the bout. The boxer finds himself in line with other souls at the heavenly gates, when the divine administrator Mr. Jordan (Claude Rains) finds that Joe has been called to his death fifty years too soon. With Joe's body cremated after the crash, Mr. Jordan guides his spirit on a search for another body in which he can resume his life. Joe, having been a boxer "in the pink," demands a body with which he can pursue his championship quest. The two invisible spirits come upon Bruce Farnsworth, an unscrupulous financier, who is about to be murdered by his wife and his business manager. Joe dismisses Farnsworth, but then the plight of Bette Logan (Evelyn Keyes) arouses the boxer's compassion. Bette's father has been swindled by Farnsworth, and she arrives at his mansion to plead with the millionaire on her father's behalf. Joe's spirit enters the speculator's body in time to grant Miss Logan's request and to confound Farnsworth's business cronies. Affection blooms between the couple, but Mr. Farnsworth must contend with his murderous wife, who succeeds in ending his life on the second try. Mr. Jordan intervenes once more: on this occasion he places Joe in the body of another boxer, shot by the mob for refusing to take a dive. Joe rises from the canvas in his now appropriate body and wins the championship. On departing from the arena, he runs into Bette and, though Mr. Jordan has erased the memory of his transformation, a spark of intuition draws the couple together. The film ends with them destined for marriage. (In 1978 Warren Beatty remade *Here Comes Mr. Jordan*, using football instead of boxing as a setting. As *Heaven Can Wait* the film was again an Oscar-winning, commercial success.)

Here Comes Mr. Jordan highlights the division between the body and the soul. The boxing genre regularly emphasizes the flesh, with the spirit only rising within the prizefighter after his ordeal in the ring accelerates the body's decline. This film portrays a reversal. The boxer is separated from his body at the outset, and he spends the balance of the film striving to regain his physical self. From the beginning, *Here Comes Mr. Jordan* affirms the ascendancy and permanence of the soul.

Mr. Jordan, the heavenly administrator, embodies the omnipotence and prescience of the divine. He acts like a government bureaucrat, an angelic New Dealer. He and his underlings wear uniforms like airline pilots, a blend of business suit and military issue. Supervising the boarding of a large airplane nestled in clouds, they assign each soul an anonymous number, execute the policy of their unnamed superiors, and know exactly what should—and what will—happen. Claude Rains, formerly the "invisible man," plays Jordan as a benign guide for the boyish Joe. Rather than the grim reaper, he is a guardian angel refurbished for the twentieth century. One expects to find his like at the local draft board, the Social Security office, and at the Air Force chapel, ministering to a congregation. His cousin runs the government campground in John Ford's film version of *The Grapes of Wrath* (1940). Through Mr. Jordan, heaven controls destiny; even matters of life and death can be reversed. When life runs its course, death promises the soul a gentle comfort. What better role for government to assume as it prepares to send millions of men into combat?

Mr. Jordan is a transformed version of the evil gangster promoter of the boxing genre. Whereas Eddie Fuseli in *Golden Boy* or Turkey Morgan in *Kid Galahad* controlled the fight game with pay-offs, threats, and murder, Mr. Jordan functions as an officer to carry out God's will. No longer is the deck stacked against the fighter, instead a blessed helper shields him. The grim underworld is turned on its head to become the heavens above. The government appears as a divine protector, sheltering the individual even as it maps out his destiny. The web of the rackets that trapped the boxer becomes the hands of God in which, though man may be unaware of his future, he can be confident that his fate is guided by a sacred power. As the United States government marshaled its resources for the coming war, Mr. Jordan prepared the audience for the ordeal.

Though Mr. Jordan may be associated with the soul, Joe Pendelton wants a body. Joe is the common man closely related to Frank Capra's Mr. Deeds, Mr. Smith, and John Doe, simple, decent, and a fiercely loyal idealist. He is a man of the flesh, and he wants to win the boxing championship because his training and skill have earned him a title shot. Furthermore, Joe is confident of his righteous triumph. He expresses the determination of the model soldier. Social conscience drives him, like a good soldier, to aid a virtuous woman in her battle against scheming businessmen. Rather than having to choose between boxing and the violin, like Joe Bonaparte, Joe Pendelton plays his lucky saxophone as he trains for the ring. His soul serves as the foundation for his excellent body, a body ready to be directed in the national service. So, even when Joe assumes Farnsworth's wealth, he immediately begins his training anew, knowing that he has the will to become a champion.

Class differences elaborate the contrast between Pendelton and Farnsworth. The common man is decent and helpful, whereas the rich, even when they have all they need, scheme for greater wealth. After Joe helps Miss Logan, he is "extricated" from his upper class position by a murdering spouse. The class divisions typical of screwball comedies, such as *It Happened One Night* (1934) or *The Philadelphia Story* (1940), set the stage for humorous incongruities. But the understanding that crosses class lines in these earlier comedies is abandoned in *Mr. Jordan*. Here greed turns the wealthy into villainous caricatures that contrast with virtuous ordinary folk. Class tensions rather than social understanding mark the film—the same tensions that beset Frank Capra's heroes, who find themselves alienated and uncomfortable with the wealth and power of the ruling elite. Mr. Jordan, like President Roosevelt, stands above the wealthy elite and allies himself to the virtues of the common Joe.

Romance promotes the union of body and soul. The boxer, as usual, lives in a world without women. When Bette Logan appears before Joe, she seems to be the first woman he ever desired. Significantly, she pleads not for herself, but for her father. Her petition conveys a selfless family spirit, which contrasts with the greedy Bruce Farnsworth, who has a miserable home, devoid of children and inhabited by an adulterous wife determined to murder him. Fighting itself, when clean and fair, embodies virtue for Joe. The film unabashedly endorses these warrior values, which the boxing genre typically questions. However, the romance between Joe and Bette moves the boxer toward a union with the selfless daughter.

Joe Pendelton's emotions display none of the displaced rage ordinarily manifested in the boxing film. Rather, Joe is annoyed at his accidental death, intrigued by his surprising quest, and thoroughly determined to realize his ambition. The feelings expressed by this film are the humor and detachment of comedy, rather than the pathos and compassion of the boxing melodrama. Audience response arises from the incongruities of the fantasy, rather than identification with the emotional turmoil of the characters. The gift that Mr. Jordan leaves with the soul of Joe, now planted in the body of Ralph Murdock, is a sensitive intuition. Having lost any memory of his fantastic escapade, Ralph encounters a stranger, Bette Logan. The couple exchange pleasantries, and each party feels a heavenly attraction to the other that the audience knows has been implanted by a divine agent. Rather than a misunderstood rage, *Here Comes Mr. Jordan* evokes a faith in the union of body and soul, which recognizes the beloved in a stranger. The comedy postpones the bout, the acknowledged destiny of the fighter, in order to instill in Joe Pendelton's body the intuition of divine power. Distinct from earlier comic boxers, Joe is neither the childish brute of *Winner Take All* (1932), nor the carefree philanderer from *The Prizefighter and the Lady* (1933). He is, rather, a saintly innocent, a comic cousin to James Cagney's Danny Kenny and a forerunner of Rocky Balboa.

The division between body and soul in the boxing film typically animates a conflict between a degrading physical life and spiritual values. However, in *Here Comes Mr. Jordan* these elements are presented as complementary. Mr. Jordan upholds the ascendancy of the soul, but Joe proclaims the glory of the body. The film allies itself to the war effort. Unlike Joe, the American public between 1939 and 1941 resisted being drawn into international conflict, but like this screen boxer, the powers that orchestrated destiny prepared the public for impending combat. *Here Comes Mr. Jordan* transformed the conventions of the boxing film genre into a comic tale, thereby helping to prepare its audience for the approaching war. The public's warm response indicated it was ready.

BODY AND SOUL (1947): GOLDEN BOY TEMPTED BY SIXTY GRAND

Body and Soul opened in New York City on November 8, 1947, and was an immediate hit. The film was produced for $1.8 million dollars and earned $4.7 million (Neve 1992, 126). In the decade after World War II, *Body and Soul* was the boxing genre's box office leader, only surpassed by *From Here to Eternity*, which portrayed the boxer apart from the ring. Furthermore, *Body and Soul* was greeted with enthusiastic reviews and three Academy Award nominations: best actor for John Garfield, best original screenplay for Abraham Polonsky, and best editing for Francis Lyon and Robert Parrish, who won the award. *Body and Soul* set the trend for the post–World War II genre cycle and became the key boxing film for the Hollywood studio era.

The Enterprise Studio production distributed by United Artists combines the principal conventions of the late thirties cycle of boxing films, with vital innovations—particularly Ernest Hemingway's story "Fifty Grand" and noir values. In addition, *Body and Soul* reanimates the Popular Front social consciousness circulating around Joe Louis and *Golden Boy* by drawing upon scandals rocking professional boxing and the post–World War II trend towards social problem films. As the title indicates, the film highlights the body and soul conflict already well established in the boxing film genre.

John Garfield was a moving force behind the production. In 1946 Garfield, an established star who worked largely for Warner Brothers, became independent of the major studios, joining with his business partner Bob Roberts to form Roberts Productions. The experience of *Golden Boy* attracted Garfield to the boxer. The actor came to prominence in New York's Group Theater, and Clifford Odets wrote the part of Joe Bonaparte with Garfield in mind. But Harold Clurman, the director of the Group, passed over Garfield and cast Luther Adler as Joe in the original production. Instead, Garfield played a secondary role as Siggie, Joe's brother-in-law, but the young actor never got over the longing to play Odets's boxer. Garfield, a Jewish kid who grew up on the Lower East Side and in the Bronx, had been a street tough until he found his vocation in the theater. The hungry ethnic fighter on the rise mirrored his experience. Finally, near the end of his life, Garfield played Joe Bonaparte in a 1952 Broadway revival of *Golden Boy*. The figure of the boxer also marked the beginning of Garfield's screen career. In his first starring role, Warner's cast him as the cynical prizefighter in the 1939 remake of *The Life of Jimmy Dolan*: *They Made Me a Criminal*.

When Garfield found himself free of studio obligations, he turned again to the boxer. For his first project, he planned a film based upon the life of the champion Jewish boxer and World War II combat hero Barney Ross. (Garfield had successfully negotiated for the screen rights to Ross's life story in 1945.) However, while the Barney Ross biography film was in preproduction in 1946, a scandal surrounding the former champion hit the press and the project had to be revised. On July 11, 1946, the first draft of the screenplay based on the life of Barney Ross, *The Burning Journey*, was submitted to the Production Code Authority (PCA), the Hollywood censorship office, for approval (*Body and Soul* file). In the middle of September, Barney Ross held a press conference announcing that he was a drug addict and enrolling himself in a hospital rehabilitation program (*Time* 1946, 47). The news threw the production team for *The Burning Journey* into a panic. The model sportsman and decorated veteran was a junkie! Barney Ross was out as the subject for a heroic screen biography. Robert Parrish, the Academy Award winning editor of *Body and Soul*, describes the scene in his memoir, with Robert Rossen, the director, arguing against canceling the production:

> "I say we go ahead. It doesn't have to be about Barney Ross. Polonsky's script can be about any bum who comes up the hard way. We'll just change the title and change the ending. We'll use the ending from Hemingway's 'Fifty Grand.'"
> "We don't own the motion-picture rights to 'Fifty Grand.'"
> "OK, so in our picture the payoff will be sixty grand. The thing is, we have a good story, a good cast, and crew, and we're ready to go" (Parrish 1976, 168–69).

Announcements followed, stating that the Enterprise Pictures production had nothing to do with Barney Ross, and correspondence with the PCA regarding script revisions continues in October 1946. The first mention of the new title, *Body and Soul*, in correspondence with the PCA appears on January 9, 1947, the day shooting began (*Body and Soul* file). The final shooting script is dated January 13, 1947 (Robert Rossen collection). So throughout the fall of 1946 and into the winter of 1947, changes were made in the screenplay. The Ross biography is dropped, but elements of his experience are still apparent, now meshed with the elements from *Golden Boy* and the substance of "Fifty Grand."

The residue of the Ross story is apparent in *Body and Soul*, though most of these incidents were already common to boxing fiction. In 1923, Ross's father was murdered during a holdup of his grocery store in Chicago's West Side ghetto, leaving the family destitute. After his father's death, the teenage Barney turned to boxing, in spite of his mother's objections. By 1929 Ross had won the national Golden Gloves featherweight crown and became a professional. During his stellar career in the 1930s, he held the lightweight, junior welterweight, and welterweight boxing titles. He became a hero in the Jewish community, demonstrating the courage and strength of his people just as the Nazi threat took hold in Germany. In May 1938, he lost his welterweight title to Henry Armstrong, taking a fierce beating. In order to maintain his record of having never been knocked out, he refuses to give up in spite of the advice of his handlers. Afterwards, Ross retired from the ring, but as a result of reckless living he lost most of the $500,000 he had earned boxing. *Body and Soul* kills the boxer's father in a gangland bombing and retains the disapproving mother, the debauchery, and the political underpinnings circulating around the Jewish champion. The filmmakers reluctantly acknowledged these similarities. After Ross threatened to sue, he was paid the agreed $50,000, in spite of the declaration that *Body and Soul* had nothing to do with Barney Ross (Riess 2000).

"Fifty Grand" provided a model upon which to frame the tale of the rising fighter and invest the fiction with a noir mood. Robert Rossen's former colleague at Warner Brothers, Mark Hellinger, had turned Hemingway's "The Killers" into a box office bonanza in the late summer and fall of 1946. The success of this adaptation may have suggested to Rossen a key for transforming *The Burning Journey* into *Body and Soul*. The revised screenplay, like "Fifty Grand," uses a fix as the crisis that organizes the plot. The film pivots around a noir flashback that begins in training camp just before the big fight, reviews the course of the boxer's career for the bulk of the film, and ends with the title bout originally anticipated in the film's opening scenes. The two episodes in "Fifty Grand", the training camp where the fix is set and the bout where the plan goes awry, serve as bookends for *Body and Soul*. The pay-off for the fix, as reported by Parrish, is no longer Hemingway's $50,000, but the $60,000 proposed by Rossen. The insomnia motif is also borrowed from the short story. In Hemingway, Jack Brennan can't sleep in training camp, soured because of his declining skills and then compromised by his willingness to take a dive. On screen, Charlie Davis opens the film waking from a troubled sleep and, tormented, wanders the city at night. Eventually, his nap before the bout cues the flashback. The closing bout also offers a reversal on the fix, but it lacks the complexity of Jack Brennan's victory in defeat. Most importantly, the switch from the Barney Ross story to Hemingway's hard-boiled fiction incorporates the noir mood. The plot develops the internal crisis facing the boxer, and the conflict between body and soul becomes a choice between money and integrity.

Body and Soul was shot between January 9 and late March 1947, with additional filming in late April. The independent production worked under the auspices of a new, but short-lived studio, Enterprise. The talented cast and crew blended the New York Jewish sensibility of John Garfield, Abraham Polonsky, and Robert Rossen with the Warner Brothers social melodramas of the 1930s that had been the training ground for Garfield, Rossen, and the cinematographer, James Wong Howe. Robert Parrish describes their aspiration to make "a straightforward, gutsy melodrama, right off the streets. The kind of stuff that Zanuck did at Warner Brothers only better" (Parrish 1976, 168). Weeks before the completion of the final shooting script and the beginning of production, investigations into the corruption in professional boxing hit the press, highlighting the film's relevance. (See chapter 2, "Boxing Noir Cycle," pp. 47–52 for more details.) As a result, *Body and Soul* incorporated the tone of the Warner studio in the thirties.

Variety observed that *Body and Soul* has a "familiar narrative," adding, "It's the telling, however, that's different, and that's what will sell the film" (Kahn 1947, 15). Abraham Polonsky's celebrated script revised the boxer's tale. The writer has acknowledged that his screenplay deliberately "kidded" "*Golden Boy* and that dear old violin" (Sarris 1967, 391). Thomas Cripps notes that Polonsky drew upon the original sense of *Golden Boy*, while dispensing with its literary cachet (Cripps 1993, 211). In the *New York Times*, Bosley Crowther observed the similarities to the Odets play, as well as noting that the twist in the climatic bout was "reminiscent of Ernest Hemingway's 'Fifty Grand'" (Crowther 1947, 21). Polonsky avoided the grandiloquent speeches of *Golden Boy* to fashion a more colloquial, rhythmic dialogue that carries the ring of street talk while cultivating thematic echoes. At the same time, he was able to develop the social issues circulating around the boxer with a dexterity that penetrated deeper than the Warner Brothers urban boxing dramas, such as *Kid Galahad* or *City for Conquest*. When Charlie departs from boxing at the conclusion and tosses "Everybody dies" at the threatening gangster, the remark refers back to the opening of the film. Polonsky's dialogue gives *Body and Soul* a lyric resonance, along with a social consciousness that surpasses the earlier generic model.

A tension between Rossen's harsh cynicism and Polonsky's social optimism developed the body versus soul conflict. Polonsky explains: "Rossen was hired after the script was done," but "there was a struggle during the shooting to prevent Rossen from rewriting the script and changing the ending" (Sarris 1967, 390). The editor Robert Parrish confirms Polonsky's report that Rossen, dissatisfied, rewrote the ending and shot an additional scene in which the boxer is murdered by the mob for backing out of the fix. However, Polonsky's upbeat climax prevailed. I suspect that during the months that followed the transformation of the Barney Ross story and throughout the shooting, the contending attitudes of Polonsky and Rossen were at war. Polonsky has described *Body and Soul* as a "folk tale," and his affirmative vision contrasts with darker values found in "Fifty Grand," promoted, I suspect, by Rossen. In the end, the film benefits from the tension. Rossen's spare, sharply paced mise-en-scène brings force to Polonsky's lyrical dialogue. Polonsky maintains in his hero the "animal faith that survives moral weakness and defeat" (Sarris 1967, 391). Dramatic conviction arises from the genuine conflict between the two.

Cinematographer James Wong Howe (*They Made Me a Criminal, City for Conquest*) contributed to the body and soul conflict by developing the noir tension between realism and expressionism. He enhanced the haunted tone of *Body and Soul* with the gloomy training camp opening and the neon in darkness flight to the city. Howe also crafted off-balance depth of field compositions expressing an emotional tension between the characters. Take, for example, Charlie's obstructed encounter with Peg during the prologue, while Ma stares away in the foreground. Once into the flashback, a studio-bound, gloomy urban milieu takes shape, but eventually Howe pushes that to stylish extremes with his flattened, over lit, jittery newsreel style for the famous boxing finale. Here Howe used multiple cameras, including one operated by a cameraman moving on roller skates within the ring. Raymond Borde and Étienne Chaumeton have noted that noir blends expressionist and documentary techniques to achieve a dreamlike mix of the bizarre and the realistic (Borde and Chaumeton 1996, 24). The tense noir imagery Howe brings to the film enhances the body and soul conflict around the play between realistic and expressive visual styles.

In the tradition of film noir, the plot is organized around a flashback, motivated by the boxer's guilt, which only gradually reveals its source. The film opens the night before the boxer's final title defense, with Charlie Davis (John Garfield) waking from a troubled sleep, crying "Ben." He abruptly departs from his training camp for the city where, at his boyhood home, he seeks out his mother (Anne Revere) and encounters his former fiancée, Peg Born (Lilli Palmer). "Ben died," Charlie tells Ma, but an unexplained estrangement drives the boxer away, and he leaves to find consolation with Alice (Hazel Brooks), a nightclub singer. The next day, as Charlie tapes his hands in the dressing room before the fight, Roberts (Lloyd Goff), the promoter, visits to remind the boxer of their agreement. The bets are placed for Charlie to lose. After Roberts departs, the Champ lies down to rest, mumbling, "All gone down the drain," and the next scene is a flashback to the innocent young Davis during an alderman's celebration touting his amateur boxing talents. From here the typical rise and fall pattern of the boxing genre's master story follows. However, the opening sequence emphasizes the self-conscious feelings of guilt, loss, and melancholy. This plot foregrounds Charlie's fall and in the noir manner intensifies the psychological. The boxer has already sold out; the flashback explains why. In the thirties screen boxers, such as Kid Galahad, Joe Bonaparte, and Danny Kenny, were frequently threatened by gangsters or compromised by their managers, but the protagonist boxer had never taken a dive. His attraction to the gangster was motivated by impulse or indiscretion, but he resisted dirty deals. His hands were clean. In most cases, the villainous gangster was allied to the protagonist's ring rivals. From the beginning, Charlie Davie is morally compromised and, like Hemingway's Ole Anderson in "The Killers," the consequences of his wrongs haunt the entire story. The screen boxers who defined the post–World War II pugilist are no longer misguided innocents, but fallen souls whose awareness of their sins invests them with the doomed self-consciousness typical of film noir.

Self-awareness illuminates the battered soul of the boxer. Charlie Davis is smart as well as hungry. He is neither a pure hearted naïf like Joe Pendleton, nor an angry, confused youth like Joe Bonaparte. The flashback presents the internalized reflections of the boxer as he reviews the circumstances that have brought him face to face with his own fall. Charlie conjures up the moral dilemmas that gradually eroded his soul. He resisted boxing until poverty brought on by the untimely death of his father prodded him into the ring. He fought clean and straight until he could rise no further without selling a piece of himself to the rackets. He won the title by a knockout and only later learned that Roberts had set-up Ben Chaplin (Canada Lee), the injured Champ, to take a fall. He was engaged to Peg until she insisted that he break with the racketeers. But how could he start all over after winning the championship? He had defended his title against all comers, until Roberts insisted that he pay his debts and take a dive for the big money. He had befriended Ben until the confrontation between the ex-champ and his promoter struck down the old fighter for the last time. Every aspiration to righteousness has been countered by circumstances engineering his demise; all his striving for success twisted his ambitions until he was left empty-handed. The noir boxer is savvy, but cornered by vicious dilemmas; his sensitivity has turned to cynicism. Moral clarity disappears. His anger at injustice has been taken over by resignation to the compromises demanded by circumstance.

The conflict between the material and the spiritual in *Body and Soul* is organized around the commodification of the boxer. The film portrays the fighter's pursuit of cash, and then, his growing realization that he must establish his personal worth apart from money. In *The Hollywood Social Problem Film*, Peter Roffman and Jim Purdy feature *Body and Soul* as an exemplar of the post–World War II trend, explaining that, "Polonsky's script plays up the economic imagery to emphasize Charlie's function as a 'money machine,' ever greedy for more money at the expense of his personal integrity, family and friends" (Roffman and Purdy 1981, 247). "I want money … money … money," Charlie shouts at his mother, after throwing a welfare worker from their flat. "Better to buy a gun and shoot yourself," she chides. "You need money to buy a gun," Charlie replies. "He's not just a kid who can fight," Shorty tells Peg after Charlie returns to New York a contender, "[H]e's money." For Alice, the vamp, money is the distinguishing mark of manliness, and Charlie's wealth prompts her desire. The influence of "Fifty Grand" echoes in the equation of money and the boxer. Robert Sklar has noted that, "Polonsky, for one, hoped that the film would be understood not as an expose of prizefight corruption ... but as an allegory of the actual and spiritual corruption of human values in the American capitalist system" (Sklar 1992, 185). The conflict between materialism and the human spirit was given a broader treatment to suggest that the corrupt business of boxing was representative of capitalism in general.

The transformation of the gangster promoter is indicative. Roberts is characterized as a businessman rather than as a criminal. His finely tailored suits, fedora, and carnation present him as a respectable member of the established order. Roberts disdains the vulgarity of Turkey Morgan and the tasteless ostentation of the ethnic Eddie Fuseli. Addressed only by his last name, restrained in speech, polite in manner, emphasizing calculation rather than violence ("It's all addition and subtraction. The rest is conversation."), Roberts appears to be the chairman of the board rather than a street thug. Roberts's visit to Charlie's dressing room during the prologue, emphasizing money and business in his threats, sets the tone. Roberts talks fluently, if by implication ("Everybody dies ... Ben, Shorty, even you Charlie.") He stares directly at his fighter and gets a full-face treatment in shot/counter shot. Finally he underlines his instructions by rising above the seated boxer, and forcefully twisting his hand:

> Charlie: I still think I can knock that Marlowe on his ear in two rounds.
> Roberts: Maybe you could, Charlie, but the smart money is against it.
>   And you're smart.
> C: It's a deal. It's a deal.
> R: You gotta be businesslike, Charlie. And businessmen have to keep
>   their agreements.

Taking cues from the revelations of District Attorney Hogan's grand jury investigation, *Body and Soul* displays an institutional understanding of how the gangster promoter recruits and controls boxers. By programming the principal urban arenas, and demanding a dominant financial interest in boxers before they can compete in premiere matches, the gangster promoter controls the fighter. These circumstances portray why the otherwise upstanding athlete has little choice, but to strike an alliance with criminals. Otherwise, his career in the ring would be permanently blocked. So the competitive system, rather than simply the immoral behavior of individuals, is criticized. Boxing becomes equated with business, and Charlie represents the upwardly mobile man on the make, ready to

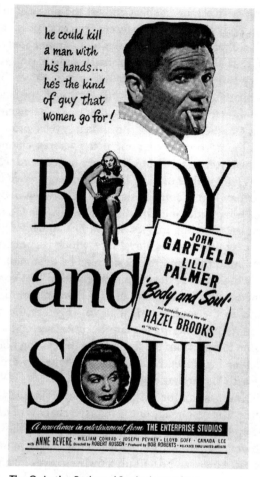

The Os in the *Body and Soul* ad copy frame competing images. The vamp's alluring figure stares from the O in "Body," in contrast to Peg's oval face contained by the O in "Soul." Courtesy of the Academy of Motion Picture Arts and Sciences.

sacrifice human values for financial success. As Michael Rogin observes, "Made at the apogee of Communist influence in the motion picture business, *Body and Soul* was a creature of the Popular Front, the Communist/liberal alliance that joined reform politics to popular culture" (Rogin 1996, 211–12). *Body and Soul* intensifies the elements of social criticism latent in the boxing film to produce one of the most politicized films in the Hollywood genre tradition.

Forces fighting for the human spirit contest the physical being's subservience to money. In *Body and Soul*, these forces are portrayed through romance, the art motif, and compassion for the oppressed. *Body and Soul* replaces *Golden Boy*'s violin with the beloved. Peg Born is an art student, who sketches Charlie and recites poetry to him ("Tyger, Tyger burning bright . . ."). She gives the fighter her self-portrait, which hangs on his luxurious turnstile opposite the bar. The picture comes to haunt Davis long after their estrangement. One night during a party in Charlie's apartment, a drunken reveler propels the turnstile around to reveal the portrait staring out at the veteran champion. This surprise motivates the boxer to seek out his former fiancée and woo her with the news that his next fight will be his last. The romance amplified by the art motif functions as an expression of spirit in the conflict between body and soul. The newspaper advertising underlines the theme visually. The O's in the *Body and Soul* ad copy frame competing images. The vamp's alluring figure stares from the O in "Body" in contrast to Peg's oval face, which is contained by the O in "Soul". The violation of the temptress is signaled by the angular image and by her crossing over the framing device, a configuration that contrasts with the smooth, contained, and rounded look of Lilli Palmer, in which her face and eyes, the windows to the soul, are highlighted. Together the mother and the beloved condemn money, offering the family, education, and art as alternative values. In choosing to turn from the fix and win the closing bout, Charlie loses his payoff as well as his wager. He must reject money in order to claim the beloved, reunite with his mother, and affirm his spirit.

Furthermore, compassion for the oppressed stirs Charlie's conscience and rekindles his spirit. The first image of the film, the shadow of a body bag swaying in the night over an empty boxing ring, provokes Charlie's nightmare cry: "Ben." The outburst establishes the former champion's haunting influence. Though the African American boxer only slowly emerges during the flashback, such suggestive images and persistent foreshadowing magnify his presence. As Bosley Crowther wrote in the *New York Times*, "It is Canada Lee who brings to focus the horrible pathos of the cruelly exploited prize fighter" (Crowther 1947, 21). In a climactic confrontation with Roberts, Ben vents his righteous fury on the gangster, but consumed by his frenzy, Ben collapses, dead. Ben's death brings the flashback to its climax and sets the stage for Charlie's defiance of the racketeer. Ben serves as Charlie's tormented conscience.

Charlie's resistance to the racketeer's blandishment and coercion has also been prompted by an earlier episode. When Charlie visits his mother and Peg to announce that he will retire after his next fight, Shimin the grocer punctures the joy Charlie's news provokes. Stopping at the apartment on a delivery, Shimin exhibits his pride in Charlie's boxing prowess, declaring him a beacon for the

Jewish community. The fighter's success challenges the abuses endured by people persecuted by the Nazis, and his heritage makes the Champ a leader of an oppressed people. Shimin bets on Charlie in the upcoming fight not because he is a boxing fan or hopes to score gambling, but out of ethnic fellowship. With Shimin's departure, Charlie cringes in shame because his scheme to take a dive has made him an ally of kingmakers, who, like the fascists, exploit the vulnerable. Charlie has betrayed his ethnic community for money, but compassion for the common man prods the boxer's conscience. "Standing with the immigrant Jewish working class, *Body and Soul* attacks the parvenu who rises, like the jazz singer, by leaving his community behind," Rogin explains (Rogin 1996, 214). Together the romance, the art motif, and compassion for the oppressed allow Charlie to overcome the powerful alliance between the body and money to embrace the intangible values of the spirit.

The veteran Charlie Davis faces his final test in his championship defense against the young challenger Jack Marlowe, the "Big Fight #2." The setup engineered by Roberts promises to earn Charlie $60,000 if he allows Marlowe to win by decision. Roberts agrees to spare Davis the knockout; Charlie can go the distance without going down. The big fight scene takes ten minutes and forty seconds of the 104-minute film, about 10 percent of the total running time. The technical quality of the boxing sequence was widely celebrated. John Houseman praised James Wong Howe's "creative photography," claiming "The fight is, as far as I know, the best ever filmed" (Houseman 1947, 64). Bosley Crowther in the *New York Times* agreed that the film features "a climactic knockout that hits the all-time high in throat-catching fight films" (Crowther 1947, 21). Howe is reported to have used eight cameras, three placed on cranes around the ring, three mounted on dollies, and two handheld cameras to provide a newsreel effect (American Film Institute 1971, 269). Howe describes how he filmed handheld shots using cameramen on roller skates, pushed by assistants, to follow the movement of the boxers (Higham 1970, 89). As a result, the cinematography brings the audience forcefully into the ring, where the struggle between body and soul reaches its climax.

Body and Soul establishes the signature noir variation on the classic design of a boxing sequence. A cluster of visual devices portrays Charlie Davis's entrapment. Close shots and tight framing of the boxers, the spectators, and even the bell at ringside convey a menacing confinement. The lighting is darker, and a harsh contrast between shadows and glaring illumination contributes to the threatening atmosphere. In the closing three rounds a strobe-like popping from ringside flash bulbs imparts a pulsating intensity to the scene. In contrast with the big fight in *Kid Galahad*, here the number of cutaways to spectators or corner men is reduced, replaced with a sharper, more continuous focus on the isolated boxer battling his opponent. The editing is faster as well, with the average shot length down to 3.23 seconds, compared to 4.5 in *Kid Galahad*. Unbalanced compositions, especially during the frenzied closing rounds, frequently frame the fighters off center. The shots within the ring are well integrated with the ringside perspectives, while the movement of the handheld shots conveys the tension and dynamism of the struggle. The uneven lighting and the mobile, unstable shots contribute to a newsreel-like effect, investing the fight with the mix of realism and expressionism distinctive to noir.

The championship fight is divided into four sections: the prefight ceremonies (52 seconds); the fake fight condensing the opening twelve rounds (2 min. 27 sec.); the battle during the closing three rounds (5 min. 41 sec.) and the postfight departure (1 min. 40 sec.). The closing three rounds convey the intensity of the bout. Here innovative qualities—particularly the mobile, handheld shots and the off-balance compositions—as well as the more extreme close ups and the pulsating flash lighting, are concentrated. This climax of the fight contains 69 shots of boxing; twenty-nine, or 42 percent, were filmed by a camera within the ring, while the balance were shot from the orthodox ringside perspective. Charlie begins the bout as a prisoner to Roberts, having agreed to take a dive, but Roberts and Marlowe betray the deal by trying for a knockout. With the double-cross, Charlie's spirit revives, and he fights to win and thereby to regain his soul.

The prefight ceremonies emphasize realism, with the ring announcer's introduction of the boxers and the meeting of opponents and referee in the middle of the ring. The fourteen- shot episode (asl 3.71) receives its expressive undercurrent in the exchange of looks signaling the set-up. As Charlie walks from the dressing room to the ring, he passes Roberts and looks up at the gangster promoter. During the announcement, three cutaways to the spectators show Alice, the vamp who knows the fix is on, the boxing commissioner looking uneasy, and another look from Charlie in the ring, prompting a cut to Roberts receiving a light for his cigarette from the thug at his side. Through an exchange of glances, the cutaways anticipate the conspiracy. An extreme close-up of the bell signals the opening of the fight.

The fake fight begins with the boxers jabbing and clinching, then fades to shots of a progression of round numbers and of the crowd's growing impatience. The orthodox ringside camera records the bout with an uneventful regularity, and the soft fades underline the mock competition. At the end of round twelve, the eye motif signals the transition with a series of point of view shots. Roberts nods and glances to Quinn, Charlie's manager, who passes the glance along to Marlowe's manager, who signals his fighter to move in for the knockout. Charlie is shut out of this conspiracy and is left alone in the ring to take the fall.

Marlowe's powerful blow to the head knocks Charlie down and initiates the serious ring battle that takes place during the final three rounds. With this blow the camera moves inside the ring for the first time, following Charlie's fall to the canvas in close-up. The immediate perspective and the moving camera bring a fresh intensity to the action. Throughout the closing sequence, cuts replace fades, and the pace of the editing increases to an asl of 2.88 seconds from the first knockdown to the end of the bout. Now the boxing imagery alternates the orthodox ringside perspective with a mobile, close-up camera filming within the ring. Even the ringside perspective now favors lower angles, harsher contrast lighting and skewed compositions to heighten the tension. Marlowe continues his attack throughout round 13, and Charlie falls twice more. He is saved by the bell on his third knockdown. Dragged to his stool by his two corner men, Charlie bleeds from his nose and mouth and just above his left eye. The blood signifies the boxer's suffering, his penance for having agreed to take the dive. Now Charlie sees that he was the victim in this conspiracy. He has reached his turning point.

Once in his corner Charlie understands the double cross and scowls at Quinn, declaring, "You sold me out, you rat ... sold out just like Ben." The camera returns to the eye motif with an extreme close-up of Charlie's eyes. Though bloodied, the eyes now register an inward look: Charlie has decided that he must win to regain his soul. With the second close-up of Charlie's eyes, the boxer mutters, "I'm gonna kill 'im," as the bell sounds for the fourteenth round.

The fighting resumes with Marlowe on the offensive, and he scores another knockdown. But this time Charlie rises for good and begins to counterpunch, starting to advance on his opponent. The crowd cheers his revival. Peg is among those shouting, appearing among the spectators for the first time. The emblem of Charlie's soul, she rises like the spirit within the boxer.

Back in his corner before the final round, Quinn asks his fighter, "You know what you're doin', Charlie?" Davis now knows he must win, and the fifteenth round begins in silence as the Champ maneuvers to cut off the ring and corner Marlowe for the knockout. The announcer declares, "Davis is following Marlowe around the ring now like a tiger stalking his prey," recalling the imagery Peg once used to describe her young suitor. Charlie has regained the fierce determination that made him a champ. The eye motif culminates with a series of point-of-view close-up face shots of each boxer: Marlowe from Charlie's perspective and then Charlie looking for his opening, ready to strike. The sense of mobility in the handheld images places the spectator right in the ring with the boxers as Charlie fires his blows for the knockdown. Marlowe falls and rises twice before Davis corners him and unleashes a flurry of blows to score a victory.

This virtuoso sequence of the closing three rounds of the bout contains 120 shots: sixty-nine of boxing, with the balance images of the crowd or the corner drama between rounds. The variety of shots of the boxers in action, as well as the mastery of tempo, movement, and continuity, make this film a landmark in the genre. Francis Lyon and Robert Parrish, who won the Oscar for best editing, displayed the high point of their expertise during these five minutes and forty-one seconds.

The postfight departure brings the film to a close and the opposition between the spiritual and the material to its resolution. As Charlie walks from the ring, cross cutting begins between the boxer and Peg making her way through the crowd to join him. Just outside the ring, the boxing commissioner, the representative of fair play, congratulates Davis. Opposite the champ stands Alice, the sensual predator, whom Charlie snubs. The two figures underline the counterpoint between righteousness and hedonism. Roberts waits at the exit from the arena. Instead of looking up at the fixer, as Charlie did during his entry, now he and the fixer face each other eye to eye. "Get yourself a new boy, I retire," Charlie declares. "What are you gonna do, kill me? Everybody dies." At this moment Peg rushes to the champ's side, asking, "Are you all right?" "I never felt better in my life," he declares, ending the film. Finally, Charlie demonstrates that he has resolved the conflict between spiritual and material, embodied by Peg and Roberts, by placing his arm around his beloved and walking away from the ring.

Between October 20 and 30, 1947, only weeks before *Body and Soul* opened in New York City, The House Un-American Activities Committee (HUAC) of the United States Congress held highly publicized hearings investigating communist influence in the motion picture industry. These hearings prompted the initiation of a political blacklist. The "Cold War" in Hollywood had begun. In the coming decade, hundreds of employees of the film industry were dismissed or denied job opportunities because of their political affiliations or suspected communist sympathies. Among them were many of the principal contributors to *Body and Soul*, including John Garfield, Abraham Polonsky, Robert Rossen, Bob Roberts, Canada Lee, Ann Revere, Lloyd Goff, and Art Smith. As Robert Sklar observes, "*Body and Soul* did come as close to a work of the left as any produced to that time in Hollywood" (Sklar 1992, 183). The crusade against subversives brought to a close the flowering of the social problem film, which dominated Hollywood between 1945 and 1947. Criticism of established institutions now excited suspicion that communists and their sympathizers were at work in the film industry. *Body and Soul* had pushed the boxing film into the forefront of social criticism in popular culture. Though it remained a model for the postwar boxing film cycle, later productions exercised caution in tapping the political implications highlighted in *Body and Soul*. Nonetheless, the boxing genre remained a vehicle for social criticism. Its veneer as an apolitical sports melodrama often helped to shield a boxing film from threatening accusations, while still delivering an implicit social message.

ON THE WATERFRONT (1954): GOLDEN BOY AFTER THE FALL

Of all the works portraying the boxer after leaving the ring, *On the Waterfront* is the most influential and celebrated. The film proved to be a substantial commercial hit, grossing over $4 million in its initial release on a cost of less than $900,000. Critically, it was even more successful. Like *From Here to Eternity*, the film swept Hollywood's Academy Awards, winning nine Oscars, including Best Picture, Best Director (Elia Kazan), Best Screenplay (Budd Schulberg), and Best Actor (Marlon Brando). The New York Film Critics also cited *On the Waterfront* for Best Picture, Director, and Actor. The film represented a high water mark in the careers of Kazan, Schulberg, and Brando. Fifty years later, *On the Waterfront* remains a landmark in American cinema. At the end of the century, the American Film Institute's poll of the one hundred most outstanding Hollywood productions, *On the Waterfront* placed eighth. Furthermore, *On the Waterfront* has exercised a powerful influence on later boxing films, particularly *Rocky* and *Raging Bull*.

On the Waterfront affirms the vital intersection between the social problem film and the boxing genre. Its lineage can be clearly traced back to the Group Theater and its most popular production, Clifford Odets's *Golden Boy*. In the original stage production, Elia Kazan played the gangster Eddie Fuseli. Two other principle actors in the film, Lee J. Cobb and Karl Malden, also appeared in the Group Theater's famous boxing drama. Cobb even went on to play Papa Bonaparte in the Columbia Pictures screen production. Kazan's Fuseli garnered him his first film role as the gangster Googi in the Warner Brothers boxing drama *City for Conquest*. Like Joe Bonaparte, Terry Malloy, protagonist and ex-pug of *On the Waterfront*, experiences an awakening of social consciousness in the course of the drama. In both works the boxer represents the political struggles of the ethnic working man.

On the Waterfront portrays the labor racketeering widespread on the New York docks. In 1949, Arthur Miller dramatized the tale of Peter Panto, a dissident Brooklyn longshoreman, killed in the 1930s by mobsters controlling the waterfront. During the research and writing of his screenplay, *The Hook*, Miller had consulted with Elia Kazan, his collaborator on the widely praised stage productions of Miller's *All My Sons* (1947) and *The Death of a Salesman* (1949). Together, Miller and Kazan sought financing for their new project at

Of all films portraying a boxer who has left the ring, *On the Waterfront* is the most influential and celebrated. Courtesy of the Academy of Motion Picture Arts and Sciences.

Twentieth Century Fox and Columbia Pictures, but they met with no success. In 1952, Kazan's cooperation with HUAC resulted in a falling out with Miller, who opposed the political tactics of the Committee. About the same time, Budd Schulberg was also working on a screenplay about waterfront corruption. Inspired by Malcolm Johnson's Pulitzer Prize winning articles in the *New York Sun* on labor corruption at the docks, Schulberg had completed *Crime on the Waterfront* in the spring of 1951. But when his original production agreement derailed, Schulberg joined with Kazan to pursue an investigation of the docks in preparation for a film.

Budd Schulberg was well versed in boxing lore. He had a distinguished career as a sports journalist reporting on prizefighting, and he wrote the boxing novel *The Harder They Fall* (1947), which was adapted for the screen in 1956. *On the Waterfront*'s ring ambiance was increased by a group of retired prizefighters familiar to Schulberg including Tony Galento, Abe Simon and Tami Mauriella, who were recruited to play thugs for the racketeers. Terry Malloy earned his credentials as an ex-boxer from filmmakers thoroughly familiar with prizefighting and the conventions of the boxing film genre. With the script completed in the spring of 1953, Kazan and Schulberg sought financial backing, but they were turned down by the major studios. Sam Spiegel's independent Horizon Pictures eventually financed the project, which was distributed by Columbia Pictures.

In *On the Waterfront* Terry Malloy (Marlon Brando) experiences a conflict between personal loyalties, linked to the body, and ethical imperatives, associated with the soul. Terry works with Johnny Friendly (Lee J. Cobb) and his mob, which controls labor at the New York docks. Terry's cooperation with the mob grows from a family bond, as his brother Charlie (Rod Steiger) is Johnny's chief financial officer and faithful lieutenant. Johnny's sponsorship has bestowed wealth and power on Charlie, who guides his younger brother. The murder of Joey Doyle initiates Terry's crisis. At Johnny's request, Terry lures his friend Joey onto a tenement roof, from which Joey is thrown as punishment for cooperating in an investigation of the rackets. Terry is disturbed by the death of his innocent buddy, by the accusations of Joey's sister Edie (Eva Marie Saint), and by pressure from a local priest, Father Barry (Karl Malden). In the ensuing investigation, Malloy is divided between his loyalties to Charlie and Johnny and the moral claims of Edie and Barry, who want to bring Joey's killers to justice. A budding romance between Terry and Edie intensifies the conflict between personal loyalties and justice. Finally, Terry's history as a boxer comes into play, serving a pivotal role in helping Terry decide between his material interests and his spiritual welfare. My analysis will focus on three scenes that link Terry's struggle to his career as a boxer: the rooftop conversation with investigator Glover, the taxicab ride with his brother Charlie, and his fight at the docks with Johnny.

After confessing to Edie and Father Barry about his role in Joey's murder, Terry remains reluctant to cooperate with the commission investigating waterfront crime. However, the memory of his boxing career leads Terry to question his own loyalties. One day, Glover, an investigator on the case, meets Terry when Malloy goes up on the roof to tend his flock of pigeons. The policeman appears to be resting between errands when he encounters Terry and casually follows the dockworker over to his coop. "Didn't I see you fight in the Garden three or four years ago with a fella named Wilson?" the policeman asks. The officer's next comment—"He really dumped you"—provokes Terry to turn

In the taxi, the affection between Charlie (Rod Steiger) and Terry (Marlon Brando) over-powers the social forces turning brother against brother. Courtesy of the Academy of Motion Picture Arts and Sciences.

from his birds and reply, "I held the bum up." The ex-boxer explains his defeat by declaring, "I was doing a favor for a couple of pals of mine." Drifting toward an accusation, Terry blurts out, "My own . . ." and stops, returning his attention to his pigeons. Glover begins to walk away, then turns to ask, "Was that a hook or an upper cut you caught him with the first time?" Now Terry's memory of the fight vividly returns, and he replays his ring battle raising his arms and throwing punches until his opponent has collapsed in his arms " . . . and from there on in we was just dancin'. And that's a fact." Glover listens, encouraging Malloy's reminiscence, until Terry murmurs, "When those guys wanna win a bet there's nothing they won't stop at." Here an abrupt cut ends the scene and switches to one of Johnny's spies reporting on Terry's meeting with the investigator.

Glover cleverly entices Terry with a feigned interest in his boxing career. He plays his mark, reminding Terry that his "friends" betrayed him. Brando's "Method" performance reconstructs the past in a manner analogous to a psy-chotherapy session. The dockworker remembers that Johnny set him up to take a fall that was not like the fatal dive of Joey Doyle, but nonetheless crushed his self-esteem. This fresh confrontation with a suppressed memory allows the man to resurrect his soul. In *On the Waterfront* boxing functions as the memory of betrayal, an experience in which Charlie betrays Terry's trust and Terry betrays himself. Both pay their debt to Johnny by corrupting themselves and the spiritual bond between brothers. Joey's fall from the rooftop reminds Terry of his own fall, and the intersection of the two crimes becomes a catalyst for what Glover puts into action. The stage is set for the transfer of Terry's loyalty. Like *Golden Boy*, *On the Waterfront* portrays the coming to consciousness of its boxer protagonist in his growing awareness of the conflict between body and soul. The rooftop scene ends without the conversation reaching a conclusion, creating uncertainty as to how much Terry has revealed to the investigator. But the ex-boxer has already given up his secret and made an accusation that anticipates his later testimony to the crime commission.

  On the Waterfront invests its realistic location with a density of associations. Throughout the scene, the connection between Terry and Joey is underlined. Terry is on the rooftop from which Doyle was pushed; he feeds Joey's birds and wears Joey's jacket. Throughout the conversation with the investigator, the coop, a semi-enclosed ring-like structure, imprisons the former boxer in his misplaced loyalties. Just as in the Garden years before, Terry punches against his nemesis while Glover watches. Terry's position also plays upon his resemblance to the pigeons. At the beginning, Joey is compared to birds by Johnny's scoffing henchmen ("The canary could sing but he couldn't fly."). After Terry's testimony, his young buddies in the Golden Warriors massacre his flock, leaving behind a message, "A pigeon for a pigeon." The bird metaphor expresses Terry's softer, more feminine side, and links him to Joey. The bird imagery evokes the spirit striving to fly above the sordid streets that have corrupted Terry and Charlie.

  The meeting of Glover and Malloy is a prelude to the famous taxicab scene, in which the Wilson bout becomes the primal memory toward which the confrontation between Terry and Charlie moves. Charlie has been delegated to secure his brother's silence or have him executed. Their mutual greetings suggest the Wilson bout, as they are going to the Garden after a stop for Charlie to cover a bet. Terry welcomes his brother because Terry wants to talk, but that is just the problem. Charlie silences Terry's voice in the first part of the conversation, inquiring about the subpoena Terry has received from the Crime Commission and offering the docker a big money "boss-loader slot" in exchange for his silence. During the second phase of their conversation, Terry equivocates, confesses his uncertainty, and asks his brother to listen. Charlie responds with commands, insults, threats, and finally draws a gun. Amazed when he realizes that he is "being taken for a ride," Terry disarms his brother with the gentle touch of his fingers against the revolver. Terry's understanding of his brother's fundamental devotion allows him to overcome Charlie's bullying. An expression of love punctures the confrontation and elicits a pause introducing the next movement. Charlie breaks the silence, "Look, kid. . . . How much you weigh, son. When you weighed one hundred sixty-eight pounds you were beautiful." The memory of Terry's boxing glory recalls his fall from grace. Charlie blames the fighter's manager for his defeat, and Terry replies with the famous, "It was you, Charlie" speech. Charlie has turned his brother into a bum by "making him take the dives for the short end money." After the Wilson set-up, the boxer took a "one way ticket to Palookaville." Terry's pleas for the opportunity to bear witness against those responsible for his fall. By standing up to Johnny's threats Terry can regain his self-esteem. The prospect emerges of regaining his self-esteem by standing courageous against Johnny's threats. Guilt stricken by Terry's denouncement, Charlie lets his brother go, knowing that Terry's release means his own death. The taxicab scene conveys a sense of brotherly devotion once betrayed, but now reaffirmed. The ride to "the Garden" is the return bout, only this time Terry resists the temptation to failure Charlie offers.

The enclosed space of the taxicab serves as a counterpoint to the openness of the rooftop pigeon coop. Though the taxi is intended as a death trap for Terry, the confined space turns the victimizer into the victim by fostering a liberating intimacy. Here the affection between Charlie and Terry overpowers the social forces that are trying to turn brother against brother. The domineering Charlie is silenced, and the younger man gains his voice through a physical closeness that evokes the "beautiful" boxer, the idealized Terry. In the taxicab, Terry makes his decision to testify. At the moment Charlie pulls his gun, his brother sees vividly the enemies who have corrupted the boxer. Terry now knows that he must work with the crime commission. "Wow," he murmurs, both at his brother's attempted treachery and at his own insight, now clearly felt and about to be articulated. The illumination gained through a retrieved memory, the process begun on the rooftop with Glover, now crystallizes into coherent, self-understanding: "It was you, Charlie." The pauses, hesitation, groping for words, the physical gestures that constitute the psychic search that is part of "The Method" have finally come together with the memory of the Wilson bout and its repetition in Joey's murder. The enclosed cab allows the brothers to examine with fresh intensity the lives they have shared. When Terry gently pushes aside the pistol, reversing the balance of power between the brothers, he assumes a new strength.

The relationship between Charlie and Terry animates the family theme common to the boxing film genre. In films such as *Golden Boy* or *City for Conquest*, the father or older brother guides his younger charge with wisdom and self-sacrifice. But in other films, such as *The Champ*, *The Crowd Roars*, or *Champion*, it is the younger man whose innocence and devotion prove superior. For Terry, his victory over Charlie marks a movement away from the insular bonds of the ethnic ghetto characterized by the "deaf and dumb" code of the dockworkers and towards Edie, Father Barry, and the spiritual values represented by the crime commission's search for truth. Terry exchanges his bad surrogate father, Johnny Friendly, for the priest. He seals his union with Edie with the blood of their brothers as the racketeers murder both Joey and Charlie. In the process, Terry makes the crucial transition from his loyalty to the ethnic neighborhood to new values. In this regard, *On the Waterfront* marks a reversal from the plot of *Golden Boy*. Here the corruption of Charlie and Terry arises from their loyalty to the ethnic ghetto, tied to the longshoreman's racket, rather than from the ruthless competition in the outside world. Boxing offers an opportunity for Terry to separate from the neighborhood, but he loses that chance. Joey's death gives Terry a second chance to be somebody, to regain his soul.

Most of the films in the "after the ring" boxing cycle show the ex-boxer returning to the ring near their conclusions. In an important sense, these battles revive the protagonist's boxing career and allow him to resolve troubles that linger in the wake of his retirement. Terry Malloy fits this pattern. After his testimony to the crime commission, he returns to the neighborhood as an outcast. In spite of Edie's plea to leave the city, Terry goes to the waterfront to "claim his rights." At Johnny Friendly's dockside office, he shouts his defiance. The mob boss storms out, and a fistfight ensues at water's edge. Work teams line the wharfs, along with the thugs enforcing Friendly's regime as the two battle. Dockers remark that Terry is fighting like he did in his ring days, but once Malloy dominates his adversary, Johnny calls to his roughnecks, who descend on Terry and beat him senseless. After the fight, Father Barry and Edie arrive. Together with other workers, they attend to the crippled man. The workers announce that they will not unload the ships without Terry, and the priest tells Malloy that he can break Friendly's hold on the docks if he can lead his fellows back to the wharf. Barely able to walk, Terry struggles forward and succeeds in defying the racketeers by leading the men in solidarity back to work.

The boxer's rise removes the stain left by the Wilson dive. In spite of suffering the mob's reprisal, Terry triumphs. The closing fight patterns itself on the climatic bout in many boxing films. That is, the boxer endures horrific punishment in works such as *Kid Galahad, City for Conquest, Body and Soul, Champion,* and *The Set-Up,* but prevails to win the bout, or to achieve a moral victory as a result of his suffering. *On the Waterfront* finds in Terry's ordeal a necessary purging, a means to personal growth, and a way of asserting political leadership. Malloy's suffering serves as recompense for immoral acts—the Wilson dive, Joey's set-up,—thus allowing Terry to purge his guilt. The violence on the waterfront, from Joey's murder, to Charlie's, to Terry's beating, is brutal and underhanded. By contrast, Terry's call for Johnny to face him man to man to settle their score in a public fight earns the dockworkers' respect. Earlier in the film, Johnny displays a wound received years before in battles to control the docks; this stigmata confirms his right to leadership. In comparable fashion, Terry has wrestled control from Johnny by demonstrating his endurance and will. Nonetheless, Terry transcends the limitations of the physical by fighting in multiple ways: in formal testimony and finally in a public display of defiance. His heroism confirms his right to leadership and invests his comrades with new strength.

In addition to the explicit social problems addressed by *On the Waterfront*, the film is famous for its implicit meaning. Elia Kazan and Budd Schulberg played conspicuous roles in the Cold War politics engulfing Hollywood. *On the Waterfront* serves as their testimonial. Both had briefly been members of the Communist Party in the 1930s, though their affiliations with the party had been severed for years before they came to the attention of HUAC. After World War II, they were prominent liberals in Hollywood and the arts community. Under pressure from HUAC, Schulberg and Kazan gave cooperative testimony in 1951 and 1952, respectively, naming those they knew to be communists, and publicly urging others to follow their example by cooperating with the committee. Many liberals and leftists, Arthur Miller and Abraham Polonsky among them, viewed Schulberg's and Kazan's testimony as a betrayal that reinforced the power of McCarthyism and political blacklisting. Kazan and Schulberg declared themselves to be liberals who hated communist authoritarianism and who cooperated, however reluctantly, with HUAC as a means of combating the totalitarian menace. For the remainder of their lives, Kazan and Schulberg endured enmity as a result of the cooperation with HUAC.

The political experience of Elia Kazan and Budd Schulberg has been closely linked to Terry's struggles in *On the Waterfront*. The film, made less than two years after their testimony, dramatized themes of loyalty and betrayal surrounding testimony before a government investigating agency. Among the issues which Kazan and Schulberg highlighted in their screenplay was the problem of testifying against former friends and associates. Schulberg and Kazan suggest their own behavior in the acts of their protagonist. Kazan has acknowledged as much: "When critics say that I put my story and my feelings on the screen, to justify my informing, they are right. That transference of emotions from my experience to the screen is the merit of those scenes ... in the mysterious way of art, I was preparing a film about myself" (Kazan 1988, 500).

In *On the Waterfront*, the political associations surrounding the boxer, originally animated by the Group Theater's *Golden Boy*, are evident once more.

Whereas *Golden Boy* expresses the leftist ethos of the Popular Front of the 1930s, *On the Waterfront* transforms the boxer's politics into the Cold War rhetoric of the fifties. In both cases boxing represents a primal, but misguided physical experience upon which the consciousness of the protagonist pivots. Seeing the ugly consequences of prizefighting allows the hero to be transformed and redirects his spirit toward higher goals. The tradition of the screen boxer gains a deeper significance by carrying important political implications into popular culture.

ROCKY (1976): COMEBACK TO INNOCENCE

Rocky opens at the Resurrection Athletic Club on a ceiling painting of Christ holding the host and chalice representing the ritual transformation of common materials into instruments of grace. The camera slowly descends from this elevated image to the extended shot of a crowd watching two boxers exchange blows in a dingy arena. Spider Rico appears to be beating Rocky Balboa (Sylvester Stallone) until Spider fouls his opponent with a head butt and Rocky becomes enraged. The southpaw, in a flurry of punches, avenges the violation by knocking Rico to the canvas. Rocky's spirit is released by moral indignation, linking him to the divine image overseeing the ring. The film highlights the initial bout with a contrast between the divine and the human, soul and body, and suggests a principle theme of the genre: the boxer's transformation. In *Rocky* the conflict between body and soul is renegotiated as the common man realizes his spiritual destiny through a renewed faith in his physical ability.

Though Rocky wins the bout, there is no one to share his victory. The crowd grumbles in response to the awkward fight, and the victor, without even a cigarette to his name, defines his condition by bumming a smoke from a spectator. Rocky Balboa is a fallen boxer. This is not the grand fall of Charlie Davis from *Body and Soul*; this is about a bum, like Terry Malloy of *On the Waterfront*, a disgruntled laborer who has already lost whatever chance at success may have passed his way. *Rocky* revises the conventional plot by portraying the boxer's fall at the outset in preparation for a comeback reminiscent of *Somebody Up There Likes Me*. *Rocky* has a four act structure—the fall, the lucky break, the training, and the bout—and each act integrates the boxer's ring career with the progress of a romance.

The first act portrays Rocky's spiritual crisis. He is a poor inhabitant of a decaying urban neighborhood. In his one room apartment, Rocky has only his pet fish and turtles to hear the news of his victory. In succeeding episodes, he fails to charm Adrian (Talia Shire), the pet store clerk; he suffers a reprimand from Gazzo, his gangster employer; and he endures the contempt of Marie, an adolescent he counsels. Rocky is turned out of his locker at the boxing club, and Mickey (Burgess Meredith), the club owner, berates him for wasting his talent as a strong arm for the mob. However, in the opening episodes the boxer also expresses the beliefs that will propel his rise.

At the Lucky Seven tavern, Rocky watches the heavyweight champion Apollo Creed (Carl Weathers) on TV. When the barkeep calls the champ "a clown," Balboa takes offense: "This man is the champion of the world. He took his best shot and became Champ. What kinda shot d'you ever take?" "Rocky, you're not happy with your life," the bartender responds, "but me, I got a business goin'. I don't have to take no shots." Rocky looks at him in disgust, throws his bills on the counter and walks off mumbling, "Take that up your business." What does Rocky mean when he says "take a shot"? The colloquialism suggests pursuit of an ideal goal in spite of the evident risks, striving for excellence for its own sake. The conversation defines the concept in contrast with an expedient business ethos. "To take a shot" runs contrary to the practical advice Apollo Creed offers the television audience, "Stay in school and use your brain." The champ expresses the values of the dominant culture. In these conventional terms Rocky is an irredeemable failure, a loser without prospects. But the boxer's belief in "taking a shot" is central to the film, which was promoted with the slogan, "His whole life was a million-to-one shot." In *Rocky* the "shot" becomes the high stakes gamble, the spiritual quest through which the soul finds its destiny. "Taking a shot" is the only means available to Rocky Balboa, social underdog. In his fallen state all other avenues have been cut off.

Rocky's spirit is firmly anchored to his body, as he explains on his date with Adrian when she asks, "Why do you fight?" Rocky admits, "Ya gotta be a moron to wanna be a fighter. It's a racket where you're almost guaranteed to end up a bum." The boxer concedes that he has no other skills; he is bereft of promise and defined by his physical being: "My father he says to me you weren't born with much of a brain so you better start using your body." His ambition is to gain self-esteem through craftsmanship: "All I wanted to do outta fightin' was prove I weren't no bum—that I had the stuff to make a good pro." Rocky's spirit, though tied to a body, needs self-esteem and longs to excel. Rocky speaks for working people who believe in the promise of American life, but who feel relegated to an inferior status.

Rocky's transformation begins with an unlikely stroke of fortune. When the challenger has to withdraw from a bicentennial bout because of an injury, Apollo Creed uses a marketing gimmick to prevent the contest from being cancelled. He selects "the Italian Stallion" as the "snow-white underdog" for the championship fight. *Rocky* was inspired by an actual fight, the March 24, 1975, heavyweight championship bout between Muhammad Ali and Chuck Wepner, an unheralded "white hope" selected by Ali. Stallone explains how the fight became a catalyst for his screenplay,

> I thought why not do a story about people who can't fulfill their desires? . . . Then, as fate would have it, I saw the fight between Ali and Chuck Wepner. And the fight was really undistinguished until the man who was considered an absolute pushover knocked the unbeatable champion down. I saw how the crowd reacted, and I said to myself, "This is what it's all about." Everybody wants a slice of immortality, whether it's for fifteen rounds in a fight or two minutes in their own life. They want that sensation that they have a shot at the impossible dream, and that solidified the whole thing for me (Hauser 1991, 300–301).

Nonetheless, many critics were troubled by the lucky break that allows a clumsy club fighter a shot at the heavyweight title. Neither the conventions of the boxing genre nor the proverbial suspension of disbelief could shield from criticism the device which Vincent Canby dismissed as "too foolish" to describe and Richard Schickel dubbed "preposterous . . . a howler" (Canby 1976, 19; Schickel 1976, 97). The lucky break appears to violate the realistic tone of *Rocky*'s opening as well as key values of the boxing film.

In *Rocky* chance replaces rigorous training and victorious bouts as the chief cause of the boxer's rise. The conventional drama incorporates the myth of the self-made man associated with Horatio Alger. Rocky Balboa, in contrast, has already been in over sixty fights and gotten nowhere. The gambler's ethos of striking it rich ("His whole life was a million to one shot") runs contrary to a fundamental tenet of the Alger myth: that people get what they deserve, that those who work hard will be rewarded according to the effort they invest.

Daniel Leab among others describes *Rocky* as "a celebration of the American Dream" (Leab 1988, 259). This claim, however, warrants reexamination. The American dream is a slogan evoking a success ethic, the Alger myth. Most boxing films criticize the myth, illustrating that hard work and talent alone cannot win the boxer a shot at the title. Instead, a deal with established authority, embodied in the gangster promoter, has to be struck. Success requires moral compromise; the proverbial dive literally expresses the necessary fall. *Rocky* neither replicates the cynicism of this model, nor, as explained above, the myth of the self-made man. Nevertheless, *Rocky* does endorse a modified success ethic.

Magical intervention, being chosen by Creed, is key. Though frequently good fortune facilitates the boxer's rise, the improbable selection of Balboa is remarkable. *Rocky* implies that one has to get a break, and only then can one heroically exploit the opportunity. As a result, the film provides an excuse for all those who lack success ("I never got a break") and allows the illusion of equality to be sustained ("It's not that he worked harder or is more talented. He just got the breaks."). *Variety* described *Rocky* as portraying a "Cinderella notion that the least of us still stands a chance of making it big" (Murf 1976, 20). However, the film offers a lottery concept of equality ("His whole life was a million to one shot"), whereby luck replaces the level playing field. More implicitly, the intervention of a powerful agent becomes the basis for opportunity. *Rocky* displays the filmmaker's ambivalence toward these social conditions by making the agents of intervention, Jergens and Creed, its antagonists. They are not divine emissaries like the angels in *Here Comes Mr. Jordan*; rather, the film suggests these manipulators are the powerbrokers who keep decent folks like Rocky down. Furthermore, the plot implies that without such an intervention, the common man cannot escape his social position. A discomforting undercurrent lingers in Rocky's luck. The film conspicuously longs for a culture of opportunity, while bearing witness to its demise. The despair so evident in the opening of *Rocky* seeps into the uplift that follows. Here, in residual form, is the social critique common to the genre. Pauline Kael, with typical insight, explained, "What holds it together is innocence" (Kael 1976, 154). This innocence points to the way in which Rocky's luck evokes a Christian idea of grace, a divine and mysterious gift that allows fallen creatures to become sanctified.

At the outset the innocence of Rocky's soul is muted by his physical awkwardness. During the training phase, Rocky builds his spirit along with his body. Now Balboa, surrounded by his helpers Adrian, Mickey, and Paulie (Burt Young), undergoes a transformation. His first lonely jog is followed by a generic standard, the training montage, which culminates with a triumphant run up the steps of the Philadelphia Art Museum. Humiliated in his first television appearance, Rocky answers during the meat locker interview by ferociously pounding sides of beef, and draws the respect of Creed's trainer. The film moves toward a conjunction, just before the bout, in which the perfection of the boxer's body matches his pure spirit.

In spite of his new confidence, Rocky withdraws from the competitive winner-take-all standard of the success ethic. His training reaches its conclusion when Rocky declares his goal to Adrian: "It really don't matter if I lose this fight. . . . All I wanna do is go the distance . . . if I can go the distance I'll know for the first time in my life that I weren't just another bum from the neighborhood." The fighter fixes upon this personal objective as the means to self-esteem. His declaration to the beloved is crucial, because his goal focuses on his desire— not to defeat Creed—but to marry Adrian, for without sufficient self-regard

Rocky's luck evokes a Christian concept of grace
allowing fallen creatures to become sanctified.
Courtesy of the Academy of Motion Picture Arts
and Sciences.

one cannot love others. *Rocky* is concerned with the traditional endorsement of
spiritual enlightenment over physical triumph.

Following a pattern common in the boxing film, *Rocky* constructs a compos-
ite protagonist, the fighter flanked by his manager and sideman: here the trio
of Rocky, Mickey, and Paulie. Adrian's brother Paulie develops a grim character
in contrast to the boxer. Paulie represents all those left behind by the success of
the million-to-one shot. Like the protagonist in the earlier John Avildsen film

Joe (1970), Paulie portrays the frustration of the white ethnic working class. Daily he leaves the deadening routine of his job in the meat packing plant to fall into a drunken stupor before his television. Paulie's rage simmers, threatening to erupt. What at first appears to be generous matchmaking turns violent when he orders his sister from the house on Thanksgiving. As Rocky's luck rises in the face of Paulie's despair, Paulie lashes out, threatening Balboa and Adrian with a baseball bat. He is the angry man with meager resources who vents his bitterness on anyone within reach. His desperation excites sympathy, but his violence darkens the bleak circumstances of the lower classes. Paulie assumes the rage that the boxer usually directs against his ring opponent, thereby exempting the fighter and granting Rocky an unusual innocence.

Mickey, the manager, offers the contender his "pain and experience." A hardnosed ex-pug who runs the gym, Mickey has faced life's assault directly, in the ring, and returned blow for blow without excuses or compromise. A gruff self-sufficiency gives Mickey the dignity Paulie lacks, but it fails to raise him. The stroke of luck that blesses Rocky eludes Mickey. The old man promises to develop in Rocky the craft Balboa has yearned to attain and the self-respect that it will garner. Suffering, rather than intellect, is the measure of Mickey's worth. His moral stature overshadows his technical expertise. He draws Rocky away from the gangster and reanimates the boxer's faith in himself.

From Paulie, Rocky gains his beloved; from Mickey, his craft. The faults usually found in the boxer are shifted to Paulie and Mickey, allowing Balboa to rise unsullied. As Pauline Kael notes, Rocky is "the embodiment of the out-of-fashion pure-at-heart" (Kael 1976, 154). The boxer becomes sanctified like a holy fool or a child untutored in social calculation. Rocky tosses a ball as he walks and places a poster of his idol, Marciano, on the wall of his room. A photo of Rocky taken when he was ten years old is stuck in the corner of his mirror, as if the boxer's spirit remains that of a boy. He won't muscle the trembling longshoreman out of the money he is assigned to collect; indeed, he carries sleeping drunks in from the gutter. Rocky stands apart from the aggressive confidence of Garfield's Charlie Davis, or the silent assurance of Charles Bronson's Chaney. Stallone's primitive evokes the child-like pathos of Wallace Beery in *The Champ*, the Capraesque Joe Pendleton in *Here Comes Mr. Jordan*, and Mountain in the teleplay "Requiem for a Heavyweight."

The animal motif, widespread in the "comeback" cycle, amplifies Rocky's innocence when the fighter falls in love with the clerk at the pet store. The animal motif cultivates in Rocky a Franciscan sanctity. Balboa talks like a child to his turtles and fish; in a similar fashion he brings jokes to his girlfriend. Mickey and Paulie see animals only as food: The manager suggests using the turtles for soup, and Paulie works in meatpacking. Pets, on the other hand, suggest loyalty and caring. Adrian affirms her love for the boxer by giving Rocky Butkus, the dog. Pets serve as substitute children. Rocky's and Adrian's affection for animals characterize the couple as prospective parents.

Rocky exemplifies the ethos of the bodybuilder rather than that of the fighter. Whereas the fighter attacks his rival, the bodybuilder cultivates his physique. Throughout his training Rocky exercises, but never once do we see him sparring with an opponent. His physical power is not animated by anger, but instead radiates an optimism that flies above conflict. In Rocky's triumphant ascent of the museum steps, his renewal is compared with art, his body glorified as an expression of spirit unhampered by social turmoil.

Rocky abandons the common genre division between the neighborhood sweetheart and the vamp. The vamp's absence is indicative of a transformation of the body and soul conflict into a union based upon a shifting treatment of the erotic. Producers are wary of boxing films because they do not appeal to women. The advertising images for *Rocky* overcame this problem by picturing Adrian in an embrace or hand in hand with the bare chested Rocky, clad in trunks. Rather than featuring a beautiful woman, the romance highlights the boxer as bodybuilder. Rocky becomes a beefcake pinup whose attraction for the female audience may be enhanced by pairing him with a woman of negligible sexuality. For example, in the seduction scene "the Italian Stallion" strips to his undershirt, thrusts out his chest, and exposes his flesh while the demure Adrian cowers at the door until Rocky embraces her. By contrast, in a similar episode in *On the Waterfront*, Edie is half dressed when Terry, fully clothed, kisses her, and they slide to the floor. The deeroticization of the female continues when Adrian meekly retreats from embracing Rocky after his warning against "playing around" during training. When she sleeps with the fighter her nightgown covers her body from neck to ankles. The spirit of the boxer's beloved is frequently embellished with learning or the arts, like Edie in *On the Waterfront* or Peg in *Body and Soul*. By contrast, Paulie's sister is associated with the loyal animals from the pet shop. Adrian, substituting the childlike Balboa for her brother Paulie, embodies the spirit of the family rather than sexuality, the maternal rather than the erotic. Their union personifies the compatibility, rather than the conflict of body and soul.

Rocky Balboa's innocence is connected to the consensus of the Eisenhower era, a period before the contending forces of the 1960s arose to challenge dominant values. Rocky Marciano, the champ who retired undefeated in 1956, becomes boxing's analogue for the fabled purity of that era. Balboa's fall is not one of morality, but of faith. Shaken by the experience of the Vietnam War and the Watergate scandal, the boxer, like the nation, has lost confidence in simplistic ideals. Rocky Balboa's rise, in conjunction with the nation's bicentennial celebration, marks a longing for the lost unity of the Eisenhower era.

In the bout, the trickster Apollo Creed challenges Rocky's purity of heart, and the contender's physical suffering elevates his spirit. The bout is presented in three stages: the dressing, the entry, and the fight.

The dressing presents a parallel montage of the two fighter's body parts in close ups as they suit up for the contest. The sequence emphasizes the physical and suggests a collision and fragmentation of eyes, fist, nose, and so on in anticipation of the exchange of blows. The absence of dialogue and the careful composition give the sequence a solemnity appropriate to ritual combat. Rocky's prayer when kneeling at the washbasin anticipates the spiritual contest. The dressing sequence balances the concluding montage that will culminate in Rocky's spiritual union with Adrian.

The entry contrasts the sensibility of the two fighters. Rocky walks to the ring in an unassuming fashion, greeted by cheers. A child offers the challenger a small American flag that he accepts, then returns in a quiet, restrained gesture. The challenger is a commoner, simple, sincere and innocent. Creed enters on a stage float, masquerading as George Washington crossing the Delaware. "The father of his country" throws pennies to the crowd, which scrambles for money. Once in the ring, the champ assumes the guise of Uncle Sam, pointing playfully at his opponent and taunting, "I want you." The gesture, however, is not an invitation to a righteous crusade, but a threat. The trickster Creed mocks the bicentennial by denigrating the spirit of the founder with a parody of the market, a wild rush for coin. The challenger's sincerity evokes a longing for national unity, while in contrast the champ's cynicism conveys the disillusionment wrought by the turmoil of the previous decade.

In "The Black Intellectual and the Sport of Prizefighting," Gerald Early analyses the yokel and the trickster as traditional opponents in the ring. He traces their genesis back to the 1915 title bout between Jess Willard and Jack Johnson and to the 1936 publication of *Kid Galahad*. The yokel is the unschooled slugger, powerful, pure of heart—and white. In the ring, the yokel takes punishment from the more talented black trickster, a master of ring skills, but the yokel finally lands the ultimate blow. "Against black opponents the white yokels were not even really fighters: they were more like preservers of the white public's need to see Tricksters pay a price for their disorder . . . the ring itself becomes the place where ideas of order are contested" (Early 1994, 12). Rocky continues the tradition of the yokel, just as his nemesis, Apollo Creed, is a classic trickster.

Rocky's antagonist is more than a Muhammad Ali surrogate, he is a figure whose origins go back to Brer Rabbit from the African American oral tradition.

The trickster is the wily slave, the uppity freedman who through role-playing and deception gains the upper hand on his oppressors and schemes to upset the social order. As his name implies, Apollo has become God-like, a pagan incarnation who serves as contrast to Jesus at the Resurrection Athletic Club. Creed personifies a false belief, with his misrepresentation of George Washington and Uncle Sam. The trickster denigrates honorable traditions while using them to elevate himself. Apollo enjoys a joke in which his white audience laughs uneasily at a parody directed against itself. Creed's cleverness expresses the political disillusionment of the post-Vietnam era.

Rocky uses racial antagonism to mask fears of class division, contrasting the challenger's mental simplicity with the champ's wit. In the champion's first appearance on television, Apollo is elegantly dressed with a beautiful woman at his side. Articulate and self-confident, he urges viewers to give up sports and get an education, suggesting the disproportionate rewards for mental and physical labor. Creed embodies what Rocky lacks. Typical of the genre, the black opponent personifies anxieties inherent in the boxer himself. Later the champ appears in suit and tie, concocting deals. Apollo displays the negotiating skills of a businessman, a representative of a professional class closed to Balboa. Economic and class differences associated with the education meritocracy are presented in the division between African American and Italian American.

Anxieties over class division, camouflaged in a conflation of race and education, propels the film. In response to these social fears, Rocky's innocence confounds his opponents' trickery. In the film, professionalism appears as the sophistry of Jergens (Thayer David), Creed, or TV interviewers, as opposed to the wisdom of Mickey and Adrian, who exhibit an unschooled response to experience. *Rocky* expresses the distress of common people who can no longer secure a livelihood based on physical labor in the absence of professional skills. Even the knowledge gained from experience is in jeopardy in a meritocracy that links upward mobility to education. The film projects this legitimate fear onto African Americans—a population equally, if not more, vulnerable to these conditions—and this displacement reveals what Vincent Canby describes as "latent racism that may not be all that latent" (Canby 1976, 19). The black fighter represents more than Muhammad Ali or African Americans, embodying an underlying racial antagonism, class division, and the breakdown of a culture of opportunity.

The bout emphasizes Rocky's suffering; pain transforms the boxer. The fight is condensed into the opening and closing rounds, but the boxing tactics are identical. Rocky absorbs numerous punches from the elusive champ to gain an opening for his powerful blows. The challenger's white trunks indicate his virtue, while their red stripes evoke the bloody toll necessary to achieve transformation. The suffering is amplified at the end of the bout when Rocky hits the canvas, apparently down for the count. Even Mickey, voicing the viewer's anxiety, urges him to "stay down," but the challenger struggles to his feet. At this point, Adrian, the spiritual helper, appears on the walkway from the dressing room and starts her slow movement toward the ring. In his corner after the fourteenth round, Balboa orders his trainers to cut the wounds swelling his eyes, echoing the experience of Chuck Wepner. The blood that results consecrates Rocky's blindness as insight. Vision no longer can focus on the physical, but instead looks inward to the soul. The battle continues with Creed's assault and Rocky's response until the closing bell.

After affirming his self esteem through suffering, Rocky rises above the physical trappings of the ring. By the close of the fight his body has proven vulnerable to assault, but Rocky, blinded by blows, looks inward and calls out to his spiritual mate Adrian. Rocky's triumph sidesteps any epiphany; instead, it features others' recognition of Rocky's virtue. The film shrugs off the decision in favor of the champ, instead focusing on the parallel cutting in which Adrian moves through the mob toward Rocky. The liberation of the boxer from the ring, the victory that comes with his defeat, is affirmed in the mutual declaration, "I love you." The beloved replaces Rocky's opponent as Adrian's and Rocky's bodies entwine. In conclusion, the image becomes still, implying a spiritual liberation from time and movement in the embrace.

Rocky ends in a battle between sophistication and innocence. Sophistication replaces simplicity with complexity, clarity with ambiguity, political consensus with disillusionment that undermines faith in the simple maxims promoted by the culture. But the longing for unity based upon innocence also illuminates its underlying anxiety: the suspicion of learning and a related fear of division among the peoples comprising the nation. The vamp and the gangster tempt the conventional boxer, but Rocky evades these personifications of lust and greed. Instead, the film poses an opposition between tricksters like Creed, who disingenuously trumpet their patriotism and announce that "American history proves that everybody's got a chance to win," and the child-like Rocky, who holds such proverbs to be sacred truths. The traditional conflict between ideals associated with the soul and material wealth associated with the body finds a substitute in the conflict between innocence and sophistication.

In the standard plot the boxer's rise is based on a false premise, since basing his success on his physical skill carries with it the inevitable decline of the body. The boxer must finally turn from the commercial values embodied in the business of sport toward a spiritual ethos associated with the family and the beloved. Likewise, Rocky qualifies his embrace of a competitive success ethic by refocusing his goal on winning respect for his craft—going the distance, rather than defeating Creed. His destiny is to transcend the suffering of the ring and win, not the title, but Adrian. The bout concludes with the decision for Creed, Rocky's blindness, and the union with Adrian. The conflict between the body and the soul, usually sharply drawn at the conclusion of a boxing film, is muted in *Rocky*. Here the boxer remains dependent on his body for self-esteem and his consciousness, rather than being enlightened, remains fundamentally naive. A feeling lingers that the film longs to endorse the American Dream, while at the same time portraying the social conditions that undermine its aspirations. Rather than the wisdom of a seer, Rocky's blindness appears as the desire to maintain comforting, but simplistic ideals in the face of a disturbing racial and class antagonism. In this regard, *Rocky*'s success realizes a widely noted function of genre film: expressing deep-seated cultural conflicts, even if its symbolic solutions prove to be illusory.

PULP FICTION (1994): REDEMPTION FROM THE POP CULTURE UNDERWORLD

Few viewers associate *Pulp Fiction* with the boxing film. However, upon reflection key elements of the prizefight genre link the multiple stories that make up the film's convoluted plot. Butch (Bruce Willis), the hero of "The Gold Watch," is a boxer. The fix arranged by the gangster Marcellus (Ving Rhames) ties the hit men, Vincent (John Travolta) and Jules (Samuel L. Jackson), to the fighter who double crosses the mob boss, wins the bout, and kills Vincent. "I like mixing things up," Tarantino explains. "For example that golden watch story begins in the spirit of *Body and Soul* and then unexpectedly ends up in the climate of *Deliverance*" (Tarantino 1998, 87–88). Indeed, after the flashback of Captain Koons (Christopher Walken) delivering the gold watch to Butch as a boy, the veteran boxer wakes before the big fight, just like Charlie Davis in *Body and Soul*. "The three stories in *Pulp Fiction* are more or less the oldest stories you've ever seen," Tarantino continues. "The boxer who's supposed to throw the fight and doesn't—that's about the oldest chestnut there is. . . . The whole idea is to have these old chestnuts and go to the moon with them" (Tarantino/Smith 1994, 41). In addition to the plot devices the filmmaker borrows from the genre, conflicts central to the boxing film—in particular the pervasive body and soul conflict—, are evident.

Pulp Fiction "goes to the moon" building the conflicting body and soul elements. Humor and exaggeration pump up the physical. Butch is introduced receiving his payoff from Marcellus, who explains, "Ability don't last and your days are just about over." The evocation of decline develops further when Butch kills his opponent in the ring. Of course, the various assassinations, accidental killings, and near fatal coincidences in *Pulp Fiction* are constant reminders of death. Explicit attention to various body parts—the foot massage, the hypodermic needle through the heart, the blood and brains splattered over a car—give the flesh a tangible presence in *Pulp Fiction* that exceeds the mayhem of your typical action film. But nothing emphasizes our anchor to the physical in *Pulp Fiction* like the anal motif. The constant scatological profanity highlights bodily taboos. The anus becomes the body part that represents the person. For example, Butch confirms his deal with Marcellus by repeating, "In the fifth, my ass goes down." The taboo and repellent quality of defecation allows Tarantino to highlight our bodies by associating death with the bathroom. A gunman who springs from his hiding place in the bathroom ambushes Jules and Vincent. Vincent excuses himself to go to Mia's bathroom to ponder the consequences of making a move on his boss's wife. While Vincent goes to the coffee shop men's room, Ringo gets the jump on Jules. Butch shoots Vincent, who falls back onto the toilet. Since Marion Crane flushed incriminating evidence in *Psycho* (1960), few movies have made such a staging ground of the bathroom. Even more explicit are the male rape in the basement of the Mason-Dixie Pawnshop, and Captain Koons's report on the years the gold watch spent hidden up the anus of the prisoner of war. Tarantino takes the body motif "to the moon" with comic exaggeration in *Pulp Fiction*.

The spiritual elements are closely tied to the countervailing theme of redemption. David Ansen observes, "Each of the main characters is granted a shot at redemption. How they cope with that opportunity is what the movie is about" (Ansen 1994, 71). Resurrection analogies are prominent. Vincent injects Mia's heart with adrenaline, bringing her back to life after a drug overdose. Butch rescues Marcellus from his basement captivity at the Mason-Dixie Pawnshop, and the gangster rewards Butch for his heroics by dropping his vengeance quest. Liberated, Butch departs on the chopper, "Grace." When a shower of bullets misses Jules, he experiences a "moment of clarity" and decides to leave the criminal underworld. Costumes, props, and dialogue all establish spiritual associations, both true and false, reinforcing the redemption theme. Lance, the drug dealer, is made up with a beard and haircut to look like a holy card Jesus. Jules embellishes a passage from Ezekiel that he pronounces with wrathful solemnity before shooting his victims. The prophetic posturing anticipates his spiritual renewal. Body and soul, death and resurrection, establish the thematic foundation for the complex of stories in *Pulp Fiction*.

"The Gold Watch," the boxer's tale, occupies the center of the film. The watch represents the spirit of warrior virtue. Captain Koons reports to the boy Butch that it has been passed down to him through four generations of courageous soldiers. Throughout the episode, temptations of the flesh contest the spirit of the watch. Butch is introduced facing the mob boss and receiving instructions on taking the fall, along with a fat wad of bills. Marcellus is associated with the devil through the satanic number 666, the combination to his brief case, and through the warm red lighting at his headquarters. Later, when Butch escapes from the boxing arena, we learn that he has literally left death behind as the radio reports that his opponent, Wilson—an allusion to *On the Waterfront*— has died in the ring. When Butch arrives at the rendezvous with his girlfriend Fabienne (Maria de Medeiros), the body motif returns as Fabienne, leading up to lovemaking, muses over her desire for a potbelly. The next morning, Butch discovers that Fabienne has left the gold watch at his apartment. Butch risks death to retrieve the watch, but while fleeing with the token he ends up captive at the Mason-Dixie Pawnshop with Marcellus. Butch escapes, but the spirit of the watch calls on him to return and save the gangster. Being true to warrior virtue allows the boxer to free Marcellus, who then grants him liberation from his vengeance. Free at last, Butch rides off with Fabienne on "Grace" to the musical theme from the *Twilight Zone*. The boxer's redemption has been assured owing to his loyalty to the spirit of warrior virtue, represented by the gold watch. But doesn't the playful exaggeration of the story turn the celebration of manliness into a joke? Besides, having been buried up the anuses of prisoners of war for years, the watch seems more than a little tarnished by the body.

The controversy over *Pulp Fiction* highlights the problem of tone. The plot appears to endorse loyalty, honor, and courage as a means to redemption. However, parody, irony, and hyperbole suggest that these virtues are being mocked. This confusing, postmodern play with meaning and humor has generated controversy. In the *New York Times* Janet Maslin writes, "*Pulp Fiction* leaves its viewers with a stunning vision of destiny, choice and spiritual possibility" (Maslin 1994, C1). She continues, "When he (Tarantino) offsets violent events with unexpected laughter, the contrast of moods becomes liberating, calling attention to the real choices the characters make. Far from amoral or cavalier, these tactics force the viewer to abandon all preconceptions while under the film's spell" (Maslin 1994, C34). Peter Travers agrees: "Tarantino never loses his film's moral center" (Travers 1994, 80). But Anthony Lane, writing in the *New Yorker*, argues to the contrary: "Tarantino functions in a moral vacuum.... [H]e has cooked up a world where hamburgers matter, and nothing else" (Lane 1994, 96). Amanda Lipman of *Sight and Sound* agrees: "If Tarantino has anything to say, it seems to be that there is no morality or justice in the patterns of life and death. Instead, the nihilist argument continues, there is trivia" (Lipman 1994, 51). Beyond the immediate reactions of film journalists, the division continues in more extended essays such as those written by Todd F. Davis and Kenneth

Womack, who use ethical criticism to argue earnestly for the redemption theme in *Pulp Fiction* (Davis and Womack 1998). But as John Fried explains, "Parody, as we know, is a double edged sword. It also protects and reinforces the very 'norm' it seeks to disclose" (Fried 1995, 6). He finds that *Pulp Fiction* endorses the retrograde behaviors it appears to criticize. The controversy continues among African American critics, with Stanley Crouch applauding Tarantino for revealing "how evil works in our time of arrested moral comprehension" (Crouch 1994, 36), while bell hooks finds only nihilism and cynicism in the film (hooks, 1996). Gary Indiana faults Tarantino for "have-it-both-ways determination to be the coolest of all filmmakers" (Indiana 1995, 65). *Pulp Fiction's* smashing box office success, enthusiastic fans, and many awards—including the Palm d'Or at the Cannes Film Festival, Oscars for "Best Original Screenplay," "Best Film," and "Best Director," and awards from the National Society of Film Critics—appear to offer a cumulative endorsement of the film's achievement. Few would question its influence, or its insight into the temper of the times.

The necessity of grappling with the critical problem posed by *Pulp Fiction* is one of its claims to artistry. The controversy testifies to the complexity of the film, solicits our serious attention, and leads viewers back to repeat the experience of the movie. My initial response to the film was an exhilarating confusion that attracted me to see it again. Only after repeated viewings did I gain a more coherent sense of its form and meaning. The redemption theme gains validity by being treated with increasing seriousness. In the initial episode, "Vincent Vega and Marsellus Wallace's Wife," this theme is treated as farce when the hit man manages to revive Mia from a drug overdose. In the second episode, "The Gold Watch," there is more balance between the send-up and the serious in the boxer's struggles to escape. Finally, the "Bonnie Situation" returns to humorous hyperbole, but the debate between Jules and Vincent in the coffee shop earnestly addresses the redemption theme. Jules declares without irony that he intends to "leave the life." The audience realizes that Vincent's arguments against such a course result in his death. The mixed chronology of the film has already portrayed Vega's death, and as a result the elaborate time scheme of the film supports Jules. *Pulp Fiction* concludes with a serious debate about the redemption theme, thereby endorsing the film's earnest intent.

How are we to understand redemption? What is the underworld from which Butch and Jules struggle to escape? Tarantino engages his low life characters in serious conversation over trivia, such as the labeling and value of junk food. There does not appear to be any escape from pulp fictions, the trivial popular culture that consumes the souls of its inhabitants. For these criminals, and for the audience, popular culture becomes the underworld from which they must escape. But as bell hooks notes, Jules has nowhere to go. The film exists wholly within the belly of the beast, its vocabulary is constructed from popular culture itself. *Pulp Fiction* even affectionately embraces the landscape of the underworld from which its characters strive to escape. However, it is the self-conscious distance that *Pulp Fiction* establishes between the film and the viewer that allows us to see the banality that surrounds us. Ultimately, it is the film's serious intent and elegant design that allows *Pulp Fiction* to rise above the debris of popular culture from which it is constructed.

Quentin Tarantino confesses that his films are about himself: "When I sit down to write, everything that's going on in my personal life finds a place in the film. When I've finished a scenario, I'm always astonished by what it reveals about me" (Tarantino 1998, 88). So what might we suppose redemption in *Pulp Fiction* reveals about its maker? How can that knowledge help us to know the film's significance? Tarantino was making *Pulp Fiction* during his transition from video store clerk, struggling actor, and wannabe director into a leading American filmmaker. The production was being prepared even as *Reservoir Dogs*, Tarantino's first film, was winning recognition. The resurrection portrayed in *Pulp Fiction* may refer to the filmmaker's own ascent from the routine of lower middle-class life to artistic celebrity. The experience of being a gadfly film enthusiast provided Tarantino with the tools to engineer his ascent. After his rise, new possibilities for power and creativity are only just being explored. The filmmaker's personal ascent from movie consumer enmeshed in trivia to influential film artist may underlie the redemption theme in *Pulp Fiction*.

◆ ◆ ◆

The body and soul conflict is a pervasive element of the boxing film genre, but treatment and resolution of this theme is highly variable. The social circumstances of production and the imaginations of filmmakers influence the search for a proper relationship between the material and the spiritual. In 1941, the nation's impending entry into World War II undermined the traditional conflict with the light-hearted comedy, *Here Comes Mr. Jordan*, promoting harmony between a strong body and a righteous cause. After the war, *Body and Soul* returned once more to exploring the tension between financial gain and personal integrity. It uses this conflict to criticize capitalism and presents the market system as a threat to our culture's spiritual values. *On the Waterfront* also challenged the boxer to choose between collusion with racketeers and fighting for justice. But now the mobsters were designed to be surrogates for communism and served the film's Cold War sensibility. *Rocky* expressed a longing for innocence and a desire for return to an earlier age, when both body and spirit were untarnished by the conflicts that tore our culture apart in the 1960s. For *Pulp Fiction*, a pervasive popular culture clouds the reality of the body and the spirit. Trivia replaces traditional values with a world so saturated by media confections that one needs a sense of detachment in order to regain one's soul. The sensual temptations of our consumer society continue to challenge traditional spiritual values. The boxing film engages with this conflict, which arises from problems central to the experience of its audience.

8

ART AND GENRE IN
RAGING BULL (1980)

Genre films are often understood to be inimical to the originality, complexity, and intensity that characterize high art. Indeed, European art cinema has often been distinguished from Hollywood productions because it rejects genre conventions in favor of films with a greater emphasis on social realism, the psychological development of characters, self-conscious style, and a cultivated ambiguity.

But many of the most celebrated cinematic achievements of Hollywood filmmaking are vividly realized genre films. Many classics of the studio era, such as *Trouble in Paradise* (1932), *The Big Sleep* (1946), and *Vertigo* (1958) were regarded as little more than generic entertainments at the time of their release. Even films from the "Hollywood Renaissance" (1967–77) influenced by the European art cinema, such as *2001: A Space Odyssey* (1968), *The Godfather* (1972), and *Chinatown* (1974), were based on conventions typical of genre films. Noël Carroll has written of the two-tiered address of such classics: The obvious level of incident, character, and sensation engages a mass audience, while the more subtle development of implicit themes and stylistic patterns is understood by the attentive film enthusiast (Carroll 1998, 240–64).

Raging Bull arises from this Hollywood tradition of using genre to construct a work that realizes ambitious aesthetic goals. By contrast with *Raging Bull*, *Fat City* is a Hollywood boxing film that avoids genre conventions, building its artistic sensibility upon its literary source. For many, aesthetic aspiration rather

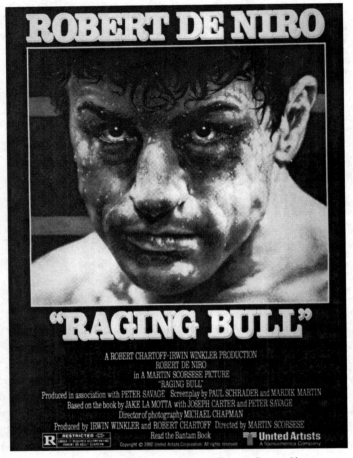

Raging Bull is the most stellar achievement of the Hollywood boxing film genre. Courtesy of the Academy of Motion Picture Arts and
Sciences.

than genre borrowing is the most conspicuous aspect of *Raging Bull*. Black and
white cinematography, a repellent protagonist, and the ambiguous conclusion
all prevent the film from becoming a routine entertainment. Qualities contributing to the popularity of boxing films dating from around 1980—*Rocky*'s
upbeat ethos, *The Champ*'s sentimentality, and the light-hearted humor of *The
Main Event*—are conspicuously absent. But Pauline Kael was among those who
noted the filmmaker's debt to conventions of the boxing film genre: "*Raging
Bull* isn't a biographical film about a fighter's rise and fall; it's a biography of the

genre of prizefight films. Martin Scorsese loves the visual effects and the powerful melodramatic moments of movies such as *Body and Soul, The Set-Up* and *Golden Boy*" (Kael 1980, 217). The working methods of the filmmaker testify to the influence of the boxing film genre on *Raging Bull*.

"I love movies—it's my whole life and that's it," explains Martin Scorsese (Christie/Thompson 1989, 1). In discussing his films, Scorsese regularly cites the motion pictures that have influenced him, and he frequently watches movies that have some bearing on the project he is working on at the time. Scorsese refers to, among other films, *Body and Soul, The Quiet Man,* and *On the Waterfront* as points of reference in developing *Raging Bull*.

This chapter will review *Raging Bull*'s production history and reception, and then analyze the genre conventions governing plot, character, setting/iconography, mise-en-scène, and its dramatic conflicts to understand how *Raging Bull* adopts and transforms these practices to achieve its artistry. An awareness of the interaction of genre conventions with cinematic art offers an illuminating perspective on *Raging Bull*—for many, including me, the most stellar achievement of the Hollywood boxing film.

PRODUCTION AND RECEPTION

Raging Bull had a long production history, beginning with the publication of Jake La Motta's autobiography in 1970 and ending with the film's opening on November 14, 1980. Even the period of intense filmmaking initiated in the late summer of 1978 lasted over two years. The high quality of the film arises from the thoughtful and intense commitment of numerous filmmakers, particularly Roberto De Niro and Martin Scorsese. "The idea had been to make this film as openly honest as possible, with no concessions at all for box office or audience," Scorsese affirms (Kelly 1991, 150).

In 1973 while in Sicily filming *Godfather II* (1974), Robert De Niro read La Motta's autobiography, *Raging Bull*, written by the boxer with his friends Peter Savage and Joseph Carter. The middleweight's story inspired the actor, and De Niro began his campaign to recreate La Motta on the screen. As in many noteworthy boxing movies, including *Body and Soul* and *Rocky*, the actor playing the boxer initiated the production and was central to the success of the film.

In 1974, De Niro gave La Motta's autobiography to Martin Scorsese while the director was finishing *Alice Doesn't Live Here Anymore* (1974). Though Scorsese had no interest in boxing, he was drawn to the book's portrait of New York City's Italian American culture in the 1940s and 50s, a period when he was growing up in Manhattan's Little Italy. Later in the year, Scorsese visited De

Niro in Parma, Italy, on the set of *1900* (1976) to confirm the actor's participation in *New York, New York* (1977). For the first time, they seriously discussed *Raging Bull*, including their favorite scenes from the book. De Niro decided to move forward with the project.

Mardik Martin, the screenwriter on Scorsese's *Mean Streets* (1973), was engaged to develop a scenario from the La Motta autobiography. "*Raging Bull* was Robert De Niro's idea," Martin recalls (Kelly 1991, 123). After two and a half years of research, interviews, and writing, Martin produced an expansive screenplay that included Jake's childhood, his prison term, and his testimony before Senator Estes Kefauver's commission investigating boxing. The screenplay attempted to explain Jake by drawing on the recollections of various people. Scorsese compared it to *Rashomon* (1950), but the screenplay's sprawling perspective was unsatisfying. In 1977, De Niro read the script, only to declare, "This is not the picture we agreed upon" (Kelly 1991, 123). Scorsese and De Niro turned next to Paul Schrader, the screenwriter of *Taxi Driver* (1976).

Schrader reviewed the existing screenplay and all of Martin's materials. In six weeks, he rewrote the script, giving the film greater structure by focusing on Jake's sexuality. Schrader cut the first part about Jake's early life, but he included La Motta's first marriage, his gambling, his session before the Senate committee, and other episodes later discarded. Schrader introduced the idea of connecting Jake's stage act to his first defeat in Cleveland, thereby generating immediate sympathy for the boxer. However, De Niro and Scorsese wanted to simplify further. Schrader responded to Scorsese: "You pulled *Mean Streets* from your guts. Do the same thing now, but this time just use two or three characters" (Henry 1999, 88).

During the summer of 1978, Martin Scorsese went through a personal crisis in the aftermath of the commercial failure of *New York, New York*. He lost interest in Jake La Motta and considered giving up his Hollywood career. He was depressed and eventually hospitalized. On Labor Day weekend, De Niro visited the ailing director and convinced him to make *Raging Bull*. As a result of his crisis, Scorsese suddenly felt he understood Jake La Motta, and he believed that both his and the boxer's struggles for self-awareness were similar. "I said yes to Bobby . . . because I unconsciously found myself in Jake" (Henry 1999, 90). After Scorsese's decision, Irwin Winkler, the producer, held a meeting with the financial backers, De Niro, and the director. They had the Schrader screenplay and Scorsese spoke of his plans, among other things, to film in black and white. After the meeting, the project received approval to move into production. With the film in mind, Scorsese attended a boxing match at Madison Square Garden, where a corner man's bloody sponge made a vivid impression on the director.

In September 1978, Scorsese and De Niro departed for St. Martin in the Caribbean to devote themselves to revising the script. In addition to Martin's and Schrader's drafts, they consulted newspaper and magazine stories about La Motta. They reworked the screenplay scene by scene, condensing and simplifying the story. La Motta's first marriage was nearly eliminated; Pete Savage and Jake's brother were combined in the character Joey. "We spent two-and-a-half weeks there rewriting everything. We combined characters and in fact rewrote the entire picture," Scorsese recalls (Christie/Thompson 1989, 77). He and De Niro came back to New York with the screenplay that served as the basis for the production. After his return, Scorsese went back to Madison Square Garden to see more boxing. This time he sat in the third row and saw blood dripping from the ropes, another image that he would later use in the film.

The producer Irwin Winkler read the script and was enthusiastic. About $14 million had been raised based on De Niro's commercial appeal and Winkler's success as the producer of *Rocky*. De Niro began his boxing training at a gym on 14th Street, guided by Jake La Motta and others. During the fall and winter, production meetings and casting progressed. Scorsese worked on the nine boxing sequences. Jimmy Nickerson and Jake La Motta designed the bouts in the gym with De Niro. Scorsese made videotapes at ringside and then drew storyboards developed from the tapes. Michael Chapman, who had already worked with Scorsese on *Taxi Driver* and *The Last Waltz*, became the director of photography. Aside from De Niro, Scorsese wanted unknown actors to enhance the film's documentary feel. De Niro remembered Joe Pesci from a minor film, *Death Collector*, but the actor had given up on Hollywood and was running a restaurant in the Bronx. However, Scorsese and De Niro talked with Pesci and liked him. Pesci thought acting with them would be different from his earlier Hollywood assignments and signed on. Later Pesci saw a picture of Vickie La Motta and steered the production team to a novice actress from his neighborhood who looked remarkably like the boxer's young wife. As a result, Cathy Moriarty joined the cast.

In April 1979, shooting began in Los Angeles with the fight scenes staged at the Olympic Auditorium. Using elaborate storyboards, Scorsese designed the fights in a distinctive and detailed manner, much like dance choreography. Each bout had a particular aura based on Jake's feelings during the fight. The blocking of the characters, the landing of each blow, and the movement of the camera were all carefully coordinated, using one camera on a shot-by-shot basis. As a result of the complex design and repeated takes, sometimes only two or three shots would be completed in a day. De Niro had a boxing bag installed so the fighters could punch themselves into a sweat while they waited between shots. The fighters could then move into each take as if they were in the throes of the bout. La Motta served as a consultant during the boxing episodes, but as soon as the fight scenes were filmed, he was told to go home. The shooting was originally scheduled to take five weeks, but the painstaking work took ten.

The production moved to New York City in the summer for ten weeks of filming the dramatic scenes on location. Here Scorsese simplified his camera approach, in contrast to the boxing sequences using fuller, longer takes and traditional editing to give the actors greater opportunity for gesture and move-ment. "With the amount of camera movement and editing pyrotechnics in the fight scenes, I felt that in the dramatic scenes I had to hold back. So the camera moves were simpler," the director explains (Kelly 1991, 136). Pesci remembers that in rehearsal the actors improvised, often reducing the dialogue to sharp one or two line exchanges. The director gave the actors latitude until the dia-logue was set and movement determined. Only then would the camera roll. In August the New York shooting was completed.

Then De Niro took off for France and Italy to go on an eating tour to gain weight in order to portray Jake in retirement. At the same time, Scorsese worked on the editing with Thelma Schoonmaker, who was cutting her first feature film. "Don't worry," Scorsese assured her, "we'll do it together" (Kelly 1991, 146). In the fall, De Niro returned to shoot scenes, such as the Florida swimming pool episode, at an intermediate weight. Then the actor returned to eating three rich meals a day until the end of December, when the Miami scenes were shot in San Pedro, California. Though De Niro's excessive weight tired him, the actor felt that the labor of breathing and moving his bloated body enhanced his por-trayal of La Motta. Scorsese remembers that De Niro's weight was so disabling that the actor lacked the stamina to do many takes. After ten days shooting in San Pedro, the filming was complete.

The producer Irwin Winkler remembers that *Raging Bull* "took a long time to film and even longer to edit" (Kelly 1991, 148). Scorsese worked at his New York City apartment with Schoonmaker, putting the pieces together through the fall of 1979 and into 1980. Important adjustments were made during the editing. Scorsese claims that the cut from "That's entertainment" to the young Jake getting punched in the ring happened as the result of a chance juxtapo-sition in the sound mix that caught his attention. Twenty-three weeks were spent mixing the sound, since none of it was preplanned. "The sound of *Rag-ing Bull* was particularly difficult because each punch, each camera click and each flashbulb was different. . . . Each scene is set at a certain date and there's not a song in the background of the film that wouldn't have been played on the radio at that time."(Christie/Thompson 1989, 83) With the film almost completed, Winkler and Scorsese were still unhappy with its continuity until

Scorsese broke the ending into a framing device linking the opening and the close, tying the picture together. "I put everything I knew and felt into that film and I thought it would be the end of my career," Scorsese declared. "It was what I call a kamikaze way of making movies: pour everything in, then forget all about it and go find another way of life" (Christie/Thompson 1989, 77). A final cut was screened for United Artists executives on November 9. After the show, Andy Albeck, the CEO of United Artists, walked over to the director and said, "Mr. Scorsese, you are a genius" (Kelly 1991, 149). The film opened in New York City on November 14, 1980.

Upon release, *Raging Bull* provoked a wide range of reactions from film critics. There was lavish praise for the performances, the intensity of the boxing sequences, and the realistic depiction of Italian American New York in the 1940s and 1950s. In the *New Republic*, Stanley Kauffmann called *Raging Bull* "electrifying and rich." Jack Kroll wrote in *Newsweek* that it was "the best film about prizefighting ever made." Charles Champlin, writing in the *Los Angeles Times*, found the film to be "a paradox, it is both passionate and bleak, intimate and clinically removed . . . Scorsese's most perfectly shaped film" (Kauffmann 1980, 27; Kroll 1980, 128; Champlin 1980, 5). In the *New York Times*, Vincent Canby described the movie as "violent," "humane," and "lyrical." He enthusiastically praised its ambition, emotional power, and aesthetic achievement (Canby 1980, C11). But putting aside those who objected to the film's profanity and violence, many critics offered thoughtful reservations. Though Andrew Sarris acknowledged that Scorsese might be the most talented contemporary American filmmaker, he faulted *Raging Bull*'s weak storytelling and "remorseless pessimism" (Sarris 1980, 55). Joseph MacBride, writing in *Variety*, praised the film's craft, but found the exploration of "Catholic sadomasochism" to be "morbid," "grotesque," and alienating. He predicted that the film might flounder in the mass market because of its repugnant protagonist (Mac 1980, 26). Others criticized the film's weak moral stance and lack of any psychological explanation or character development. Probably the strongest and most articulate attack on *Raging Bull* came from Pauline Kael. Though Kael had praised Scorsese's *Mean Streets* and *Taxi Driver*, she turned on *Raging Bull*. She attacked its "highbrow flash reeking of religious symbolism" and regretted the film's lack of the "particulars of observation and narrative." Kael was cool towards the self-conscious style that "aestheticizes pulp and kills it." The result, she argued, is "overripe," a "new sentimentality" (Kael 1980, 217–25). In spite of the film's apparent distancing of La Motta, the critic found that Scorsese loved his protagonist's suffering too much. Many viewers were shaken by the film's emotional intensity and left wondering at its ambiguity. In the years that followed, the reputation of *Raging Bull* grew as a result of repeated viewing, thoughtful discussion, and the appreciation articulated by filmmakers, scholars, and fans. The production did not, upon its initial release, garner the esteem it enjoys today.

Stuart Byron described the box office performance of *Raging Bull* as a "disappointment in relation to costs" (Byron 1981, 54). The production budget was $18,000,000, and the domestic theatrical gross yielded $30,000,000. Weighing the expenses of advertising, prints, and the split with exhibitors against the foreign income and its continuing non-theatrical revenues, the film most likely produced a modest profit.

The critical awards *Raging Bull* earned boosted profits. The film received nine Academy Award nominations, including "Best Picture" and "Best Director." It won Oscars for Robert De Niro's performance as "Best Actor" and for Thelma Schoonmaker for "Best Film Editing." The National Board of Review and the New York Film Critics honored Robert De Niro and Joe Pesci, respectively, as "Best Actor" and "Best Supporting Actor." The National Society of Film Critics named Martin Scorsese as the year's "Best Director," as well as Michael Chapman as "Best Cinematography" and Pesci as "Best Supporting Actor." As the years passed, praise for *Raging Bull* grew. In 1990, numerous critics, when polled, named the production best film of the 1980s by a wide margin. At the end of the century the American Film Institute's poll of the one hundred outstanding Hollywood films placed *Raging Bull* twenty-fourth, and once again, it was judged the top film from the 1980s. In *Sight and Sound* magazine's 2002 international poll of film directors, *Raging Bull* tied for sixth place among the greatest films ever made (Christie 2002, 24). At this point, *Raging Bull* is firmly established as one of the masterpieces of the cinema.

PLOT

Raging Bull presents the rise and fall of a boxing champion, a narrative pattern typical of the boxing film genre going back at least as far as *Iron Man* (1931). The pattern appears in key works such as *Golden Boy* and *Body and Soul*. By contrast, hit boxing films from the 1970s, such as *Hard Times*, *Rocky*, and *The Champ*, moved away from this classic plot, even though these films exhibited other familiar genre traits. In addition, *Raging Bull* incorporates a flashback framework that links the film to the boxing noir movies of the 1940s, particularly *Body and Soul* and *Champion*. The flashback initiates a nostalgic tone, setting the stage for the self-conscious reflection that marks the conclusion of a film employing this technique. *Raging Bull* shares this sensibility with its film noir antecedents.

Numerous events characteristic of the rise and fall plot appear in *Raging Bull*, including: the fighter's rise as portrayed by a montage chronicling victorious bouts; negotiations with a gangster promoter who controls access to a title fight; and the dive required by the mob boss controlling the prizefighter. Among the noteworthy revisions in the rise and fall plot offered in *Raging Bull* is the elimination of the discovery of the boxer's talent and his early training. Instead, Scorsese jumps into La Motta's career with the middleweight already an established fighter. Rather than discovery and training episodes, the film expands the postboxing epilogue into an elaborate "after leaving the ring" segment.

As with Hollywood films generally, *Raging Bull* develops a romance that parallels the quest characteristic of the film's particular genre. In the boxing film, the romantic couple typically serves as counterpoint to the male world of boxing and the predatory sensuality of the vamp character. At the conclusion of the plot, the prizefighter usually leaves the ring to marry his sweetheart, as in *Kid Galahad* (1937) and *Golden Boy*. Though there are numerous variations on this ending, the beloved usually promotes a gendered opposition between the masculine values of fighting and feminine nurturing. In *Raging Bull*, the relationship between romance and the parallel quest is central to the significance of the work.

An awareness of the generic plot of the boxing film allows similarities and differences in *Raging Bull* to deepen our understanding of the film. The plot of *Raging Bull* divides into four parts: the prelude and postscript frame that portrays Jake in his dressing room preparing his stage act; act one, which follows Jake's early boxing career and his courtship of Vickie, ending with the still image home movie montage of ring victories and domestic bliss; act two, which presents, his quest for the middleweight title and his growing jealousy of Vickie, and which ends with his championship victory; and act three, which includes Jake's estrangement from his brother, his loss of the title, and the end of his marriage. The key distinctions between the generic plot and that of *Raging Bull* are the function of boxing, the treatment of romance, the "after leaving the ring" episodes, *and Raging Bull*'s ambiguous conclusion. Each of these variations transforms a generic convention into an arresting aesthetic device.

In discussing the plans for *Raging Bull*, Martin Scorsese declared, "One sure thing was that it wouldn't be a film about boxing! We (Scorsese and De Niro) didn't know a thing about it and it didn't interest us at all" (Henry 1999, 85)! Though the film adapts the autobiography of Jake La Motta, the sport serves as a means for exploring more fundamental human experience. Nevertheless, boxing in *Raging Bull* is more widely distributed and integral to the plot than is common in the Hollywood boxing genre. The boxing film generally uses boxing sequences as important spectacles of physical action that punctuate the plot at key intervals, like the song and dance numbers in the musical. Most Hollywood boxing films display a well-established pattern of three or four boxing episodes, culminating in an extended bout at the film's climax. Earlier episodes may include sparring in a gym, action that results in the discovery of the boxer's talent, as in *Golden Boy*, or a montage of ring action, newspaper headlines, and speeding trains as a means of representing the rise of a fighter on tour, as in *Champion*. Occasionally the protagonist will exhibit his talent in an important bout mid-way through the film in anticipation of the concluding confrontation, as in *Hard Times*. The typical Hollywood boxing film moves steadily toward an extended bout that brings the film to its climax. As a result, we anticipate that the final boxing match will be the culmination of the fiction.

Raging Bull changes this plotting significantly by adding more bouts. There are nine boxing sequences (counting the montage condensation as one episode), stretching from the beginning of the flashback in 1941, to Jake's loss of the middleweight title, about three-quarters of the way through the film. Together, these episodes run approximately nineteen and a half minutes, and constitute about 15 percent of the movie. Though the number and range of bouts are increased, Scorsese removes boxing from the film's conclusion. Instead, after Jake's retirement, two standup comic stage routines and his struggle in a prison cell suggest a series of ring analogies that are related to the motifs and themes of the earlier bouts.

These boxing sequences portray the inner feelings of the boxer, rather than a spectacle concept of exhibition designed to replicate the experience of an audience at a boxing match, typical of the classical Hollywood cinema. I will discuss the boxing sequences in a later section, but at this point, note that Scorsese's plotting of the bouts intensifies the physical action through a wider distribution, and intensifies the emotional content by basing his design, not on the experience of the spectator, but on that of the boxer. Scorsese explains, "I wanted to do the ring scenes as if the viewers were the fighter and their impressions were the fighter's—of what he would think or feel, what he would hear" (Kelly 1996, 132). This expressive approach facilitates the continuation of this emotional motif in similar episodes after the boxer retires from the ring.

The relationship of the boxing sequences in *Raging Bull* to the film as a whole is closer to the practice of the European art cinema than to the typical Hollywood boxing film. The subjective style of these sequences is distinct from the more objective qualities shaping the body of the film. Take for comparison, Fellini's *8 1/2* (1963) (a Scorsese favorite), in which Guido's dreams, memories and fantasies are presented in a much more lyrical, exaggerated and symbolic manner than the social reality Guido experiences in common with the other characters. In a similar fashion, the heroine's memory in *Hiroshima, Mon Amour* (1959), is given special treatment. That is, the subjective experience of characters in the art cinema frequently is conveyed in an exceptional form that both intensifies that experience and sets it apart. Such a pattern offers a precedent for the boxing sequences in *Raging Bull*, but Scorsese's picture presents the experience of intense physical interaction, the exchange of blows, instead of the reverie or self-conscious reflection characteristic of art films. *Raging Bull* cultivates subjectivity in the boxing episodes, but it is a subjectivity characterized by sensation rather than reflection. Instead of developing a film based on dream imagery and association, the boxing sequences strive to convey a more physiological reaction to stimuli—similar to Sergei Eisenstein's behaviorialist concepts of montage that aims to "plow the psyche" of the spectator.

Romance in *Raging Bull* parallels the rise and fall of La Motta's ring career. The relationship between Jake and Vickie avoids the simple counterpoint between fighting and loving, common to the boxing film. Instead the film shows a complex interaction between La Motta's relationship to his wife and his ring exploits. Scorsese ends act one with the couple marrying, rather than featuring the romantic union at the film's conclusion to usher the boxer from the ring. The champion's fall extends beyond the loss of his title to include separation from his beloved. Most important is the displacement this plot device develops between boxing and romance. The first lovemaking encounters between Jake and Vickie appear between La Motta's bouts with Sugar Ray Robinson. In the first, a photo of Jake and Joey in playful fisticuffs holds the screen as Jake and Vickie move off toward the bed, then the film cuts to the Robinson bout. The next episode finds Jake dousing his genitals with ice water to interrupt foreplay with Vickie because he doesn't want sex to weaken his fighting power. The second Robinson bout immediately follows. After the decision for Robinson, Jake soaks his bruised hand in ice water, a scene echoing the earlier gesture and suggesting a parallel between his physical embrace of Vickie and his assault on his ring opponent (Wood 1986, 245–69).

The most important displacement occurs in the parallel between Jake's jealousy of Vickie and his quest for the title. Jake's quest is thwarted because the gangster promoter, Tommy Como, who oversees boxing, blocks the contender from getting a title shot unless he takes a dive on instructions from the mob. In spite of his determination to win the title on his own merits, Jake relents and takes the fall against Billy Fox. Jake's powerlessness to control his destiny, in spite of his domination in the ring, results in impotence and jealousy. Weaving together domestic scenes and prizefighting, the movie portrays the boxer projecting his guilt at having to compromise his skills onto his innocent wife. His marriage is infected with the corruption of prizefighting. This association is underlined in the scene where Joey reports to Jake on his meeting with Como. The brothers meet at the neighborhood swimming pool where Jake was introduced to Vickie. A summer rainstorm falls as Joey breaks the news that the boxer must take the dive. The pool is associated with romance, but the storm casts a shadow over this association. Before hearing Joey's report, Jake begins to rant against Vickie's infidelity. Controlling his anger at the mob, La Motta redirects his rage at his wife. Jake's jealousy of other boxers, and even of the aged Como, amplifies the relationship between romance and boxing in Jake's tormented consciousness. Rather than idealizing courtship like other films in the boxing genre, *Raging Bull* presents self-destructive, neurotic conjugal sexuality as central to the couple's relationship. As a result of interweaving romance and boxing, the plot of *Raging Bull* suggests a complex psychological relationship that builds upon a generic convention, elaborating it in a fresh and penetrating manner.

Most boxing films conclude with the prizefighter ending his ring career after the climactic bout. Usually a brief postboxing episode—such as the death of the boxer in *Champion* or the victory parade in *Somebody Up There Likes Me*— ties up loose ends and concludes the film. However, I have argued that there are a series of important films dating from the early 1950s that take the generic boxing plot as a back-story, and develop the film around the boxer's experience after leaving the ring. These films include *The Quiet Man, From Here to Eternity*, and *On the Waterfront. Raging Bull* displays the influence of these films. Martin Scorsese has explicitly cited *The Quiet Man* and *On the Waterfront* as among his points of reference, and he develops La Motta's story after the boxer's retirement, from 1956 to 1964, in a series of episodes that constitute the conclusion of the film.

Four actions during these episodes evoke the inner feelings that characterize the boxing sequences. Two are stand-up stage routines, the first seen in La Motta's Miami club and the second in a sleazy Manhattan lounge. A third finds Jake incarcerated in the Dade County Stockade, where he pounds the wall and mutters to himself. The final episode shows the performer alone in his dressing room reciting his lines to a mirror. By placing Jake on a stage or other enclosed, isolated space, all four scenes suggest a similarity with the earlier boxing episodes by alluding to boxing, and by portraying Jake's interior struggles.

"After leaving the ring" films send their protagonist on a quest for value. The experience of boxing is primarily physical, and the close of the ring career brings with it a crisis. The boxer, who achieves his self-esteem through his fighting prowess, must find value apart from the physical. In *The Quiet Man*, Sean Thornton seeks his ethnic roots in Ireland, strives to overcome his guilt at killing a man in the ring, and weds Mary Kate to begin a new life. Prewitt in *From*

Here to Eternity seeks fellowship in the army and love from Alma. Terry Malloy in *On the Waterfront* wants to clear his conscience and gain self-respect.

Scorsese never completely accounts for Jake La Motta's rage; neither does he absolve La Motta's brutality. But as he moves toward reflection and self-examination in the postboxing episodes, the protagonist is calmed. Jake's retirement is introduced with an interview. The former boxer appears with his wife and children at the poolside of his Florida home. Family, home, and prosperity serve as the standard culmination of the boxing film, with successful romance bringing domestic contentment. However, Jake's grotesque, fat body belies his declared satisfaction. The following scenes, set at his club, serve to set up his next fall.

The stand-up comic routine Jake offers his club patrons explicitly evokes his boxing. Introductory music consists of the "Gillette Blue Blades" theme, evoking the name of the traditional the sponsor of television boxing. La Motta's closing verse compares his comic performance with boxing Sugar Ray, concluding: "So gimme a stage/ where this bull here can rage/ and though I can fight/ I'd much rather hear myself recite . . . that's entertainment." The performance also mixes boxing with Jake's marriage. He announces to his audience that he is about to celebrate his eleventh wedding anniversary, and then tells a joke that mocks the concept of marriage with the suggestion that a husband offers his wife to a friend for sex. Indeed, before the Miami club sequence ends, Jake is presented in sexually compromising behavior, and Vickie appears to announce that she is divorcing him. The image of retirement bliss is shattered. Jake's club is another ring in which he plays out emotions without understanding or contrition.

Jake's fall reaches its nadir when he is thrown into the Dade County Stockade. Once again, emotion is mixed with boxing—but this time with an added note of reflection. Locked into a shadowy, confining cell, Jake begins pounding first his head, then his fists and arms, against the concrete wall shouting, "Why, why, why?" and repeatedly weeping, "You're so stupid . . . I'm not an animal." Here the brute finally chides himself, inflicting the same kind of punishment previously administered by his boxing opponents. While he is still in the cell, voice-over sound bridges to another La Motta stand-up routine at the sleazy Hotel Markwell in Manhattan the following year. Responding to hecklers in the small audience, the comic threatens to make a "come-back." His contentious repartee again links his ring battles with his stage performances. However, rather than brawling, Jake tries to make peace. Upon leaving the club after his show, he bumps into his brother Joey on the street and makes an awkward attempt at reconciliation. The self-realization La Motta gained in prison has softened the former boxer, even though his brother greets Jake's gesture with wary reserve. La Motta has moved beyond his raging sensations to reflection and toward self-awareness.

The closing scene returns to the framing episode where the film began. The flashback suggests memory without explicitly having Jake recall his past. The audience observes the boxer's history, but remains uncertain as to whether Jake is pondering it himself. The boxing noir films *Body and Soul* and *Champion* also employed a flashback frame to demonstrate reflection in the boxer, but then returned to the present before the big fight brought these films to a close. But for *Raging Bull*, the move from sensation to reflection is the conclusion.

The closing dressing room scene suggests self-awareness through setting and allusion, without allowing the protagonist to acknowledge his thoughts or express any understanding. The scene finds La Motta alone facing a mirror. However, the pose of self-examination is qualified, because Jake is practicing his stage routine. Scorsese uses a reference to the boxing film genre to bring his film to a close. La Motta recites Terry Malloy's famous speech to his brother Charlie in a taxicab from *On the Waterfront*. Here Terry blames his brother for sabotaging his boxing career by making him take a dive for racketeers. The allusion uses the genre as a source for a penetrating complexity. The director reports that Robert De Niro performed nineteen takes and that take thirteen was used. Here De Niro gives a performance in which the borrowed speech is delivered with little inflection or dramatic color. Scorsese claims that the only way to deliver it was "so cold that you concentrate on the words" (Christie/Thompson 1989, 77). It opens with "Charlie, it was you," and closes with Jake repeating twice, "It was you, Charlie." La Motta's speech gives rise to an ambiguity: That is, does "Charlie" refer to Jake's brother, Joey, who seems to be in an analogous situation with Terry's brother Charlie, or does Jake's pose before the mirror imply that he himself is culpable? Does Jake blame his brother for his compromises, his rings failures, Vickie's ostensible infidelities? Or has he finally faced up to his own responsibility? "When he says in the mirror, 'It was you, Charlie,' is he blaming his brother, or putting the blame on himself? It's certainly very disturbing for me," Scorsese acknowledges (Christie/Thompson 1989, 77). Scorsese's incorporation of the film reference allows the ambiguity to simmer. De Niro's cool, detached delivery and his blank expression give no clue.

After La Motta's rehearsal, a voice calls from off screen, telling the "Champ" he is on in five minutes. Before facing his audience, Jake rises, says to the mirror, "Go get 'em, Champ," assumes a boxer's pose, and lets loose with a flurry of warm-up punches while repeatedly muttering, "I'm the boss." The analogy between the dressing room and boxing is underscored as the film ends. Both have served as arenas for Jake's inner struggle. In the prison cell Jake expresses introspection, regret, and appeals to his humanity. But in the dressing room, the boxer's understanding of his fall remains ambiguous, or qualified at best.

La Motta has been moving from sensation to reflection as he has gone from being a fighter to becoming a stage performer. Before the camera enters the dressing room, a sign invites the public to see Jake La Motta performing the words of Shakespeare and Tennessee Williams, among others. The "after leaving the ring" episodes call up the art motif in the boxing film genre. From Joe Bonaparte's violin in *Golden Boy*, to Prewitt's trumpet in *From Here to Eternity*, to Rocky running up the steps of the Philadelphia Art Museum, art plays an important role in the genre, generally as an alternative to boxing. In *Raging Bull* the move towards art serves as a move towards reflection, and as a meaningful turning away from the blinding sensation of the boxing ring. Jake's recitation from *On the Waterfront* prepares for the literary passage that closes the film. Scorsese presents with deliberation a quotation from John's Gospel as part of a dedication to his recently deceased film teacher, Haig P. Manoogian. In the passage, the Pharisees identify a "fellow" (Jesus) known to be a "sinner" to a man whose sight was restored by Christ. The man replies, "Whether or not he was a sinner, I do not know. . . . All I know is this: once I was blind and now I can see." The Biblical text points in two directions. Most obviously, the student is saluting his mentor for shaping his vision as a filmmaker. On the other hand, "the sinner" evokes Jake La Motta, the wild brute who arose out of New York's Italian American ghetto when Scorsese was growing up. In interviews the director claims that his engagement with the work resulted from his similarities with La Motta. Furthermore, the filmmaker acknowledges that the production was initiated when he was coming out of a deep personal crisis. As a result, the passage from John suggests that the boxer's anguish has given Scorsese perspective on his own raging spirit. The filmmaker has found in the cinema a means of reflecting upon the Italian American culture from which he came. He has used his art as a means of gaining insight he hopes to pass along to his audience.

CHARACTERS

Character types that usually populate the boxing film are recognizable in *Raging Bull*, but they have been given a fresh, more complex humanity. Tommy Como is the gangster promoter controlling the boxing racket. This stock figure is recognizable in the genre as early as Humphrey Bogart's Turkey Morgan in *Kid Galahad*, fully developed in *Golden Boy*'s Eddie Fuseli, and realized most memorably in Roberts from *Body and Soul*. However, Tommy Como acts more like a wise grandfather than a criminal operator, using intimidation and violence to impose his authority. He is older and softer than the gangster over-lord in La Motta's autobiography. Tommy courts the boxer with drinks and flattery, serves as a peacemaker between Joey and Salvy, and negotiates with Joey by offering rewards in return for cooperation. Compared to Jake, with his swaggering belligerence, Tommy Como acts like a neighborhood elder. Because La Motta's chief antagonist is patient and affable, the boxer seems even more stubborn in his refusal to come to terms. *Raging Bull* jettisons a simplistic opposition between the integrity of an athlete and a racketeer's greed, instead the film alludes to generic figures to help the audience understand the characters from a new perspective.

Joey La Motta is another illuminating case. The boxer's brother is a character type usually employed to express qualities that contrast with the boxer's. In *City for Conquest*, the brother is a talented musician, whose education the boxer finances with prizefighting. In *Champion*, the brother is a crippled saint scolding Midge Kelly's demonic roughneck. In *Rocky*, Paulie, Balboa's brother-in-law to be, underscores the boxer's innocence with his bitterness. *Raging Bull* combines two characters from the autobiography, Joey La Motta and Pete Savage, the boxer's close friend, into the more generic screen brother. Rather than illuminating the protagonist through opposition, Joey shares a perverse Italian American machismo with Jake. Similar in personality, but less extreme than his brother, Joey La Motta emphasizes that their behavior is a product of a pervasive ethos, rather than particular to a crazy boxer. When Joey finds Vickie at the Copacabana sharing drinks with Salvy, his furious attack on Salvy mirrors what Jake might have done. Later, when Jake storms over to Joey's home to assault his brother, the camera anticipates Jake's attack, showing Joey threatening to stab his child at the dinner table if the boy puts his hand on his plate one more time. The violence which constantly spills out of the boxing ring and into daily life gains credibility from Joey, who stands apart from the exceptional physicality embodied by the boxer. *Raging Bull* appeals to realism by resisting a melodramatic polarity between stock figures. Instead, the film gains conviction by going against generic expectations.

The most striking aspect of characterization in *Raging Bull* is its repellent protagonist. As Cis Corman, the casting director, observed after reading the script, "Jake La Motta is a terrible, evil man. Why would you want to do a movie about this?" (Kelly 1991, 128). Most mainstream films engage the audience through their sympathy for its characters. The boxing film genre underlines this sympathy with the habits of spectator sports, the fan's loyalty to an attractive competitor. La Motta's thuggish self-indulgence, accented by his abusive treatment of women, his racism, and his semi-literate, obscene language, must make him one of the most repellent protagonists in motion picture history. Initial

Rather than illuminating his brother through opposition, Joey (Joe Pesci) shares a perverse Italian American machismo with Jake (Robert De Niro). Courtesy of the Academy of
Motion Picture Arts and Sciences.

press response to the film indicated respect for its craft, but disquiet because of
the film's brutal subject. David Bordwell and Kristin Thompson have noted "the
film's uneasy balance of sympathy and revulsion toward its central character"
(Bordwell/Thompson 1997, 426). *Raging Bull* allies the audience forcefully with
Jake: he appears in nearly every scene, and his behavior is the foundation for
the dramatic action. How is the viewer to cope with what becomes an assault
on humane sensibilities?

Jake La Motta is not the first anti-hero to appear in a boxing film. Midge
Kelly, *Champion*'s protagonist, was also a rogue, as was his literary model in
Ring Lardner's short story. But *Champion* spends most of its resources explaining how Midge became a heartless bully, and our sympathy is enlisted as he
fights back against exploitation, only to become an exploiter himself. Furthermore, he is punished with estrangement, suffering, and death, in addition to the
condemnation of the righteous. The constraints of studio era censorship softened Kelly's sins. The psychological explanation for Kelly's motivation, comple-
mented by the moral condemnation of his mistreatment of others, tempered
the impact of his roguishness. *Raging Bull* refuses both of these options.

In numerous interviews, Martin Scorsese has dismissed the simplistic psychology found in Jake La Motta's autobiography: "Jake is constantly analyzing himself in the book. He very pedantically explains why he did this or that. But I didn't think that Jake was really able to analyze himself like that" (Henry 1999, 85). *Raging Bull* avoids presenting a psychological explanation for its protagonist's behavior. In this regard it stands in sharp contrast to *Champion* or *Somebody Up There Likes Me*. *Somebody* is another film adaptation of an autobiography written by a middleweight champion, Rocky Graziano. Graziano shares some striking similarities with La Motta. In fact, as young toughs they terrorized New York's Lower East Side together. Both went to prison, where they developed their roughneck skills to become successful prizefighters after their release. Each of them became the middleweight champion for a brief time. After leaving the ring, Graziano had a successful TV career, and he helped Jake La Motta get his start in show business. In the film Rocky's juvenile delinquency results from his father's abuse, urban poverty, and a lack of nurturing. However, with the help of a prison chaplain, a paternal manager, and a loving wife, Rocky pulls his life together. He uses boxing to purge his anger at childhood mistreatment and becomes a lovable everyman. Before the title bout, Graziano has a confrontation with his father that lays his psychic anxieties to rest, allowing him to realize his dream of winning a championship. Scorsese criticizes La Motta's book because, "the book's psychology is close to that of the 50s" (Henry 1999, 86). *Somebody Up There Likes Me* illustrates what the director sought to avoid. Even though the autobiography relates La Motta's early years in detail, Scorsese refuses to indulge psychology as a means of explaining the boxer's behavior.

Talking about *Raging Bull*, Martin Scorsese explains, "The motive became to achieve an understanding of a self-destructive lifestyle" (Kelly 1991, 122). However, it is important to note that self-understanding eludes Jake, though he learns to quiet his rage. Scorsese and Robert De Niro built La Motta's character in *Raging Bull* on a combination of perverse realism and a disturbing subjectivity through a mix of detachment and immersion.

Realism in the arts has long featured the common and the ugly as a means of undermining the idealization of form allied to aesthetic value. Realism makes truth trump beauty and precise attention to social detail more important than classical harmony. The realism of *Raging Bull* strives for authentic detail that cultivates the repellent. For example, the movie's fights were carefully modeled on films and written records of actual contests, and Jake La Motta coached De Niro's ring craft, but their exaggerated brutality makes the audience wince in horror. A highly publicized aspect of realism in *Raging Bull* is Robert De Niro's enormous weight gain in order to play La Motta in the film's late episodes. The public was amazed that the actor had disfigured his body to such an extent. As De Niro explained, "As far as my gaining the weight, the external speaks for itself. But the internal changes, how you feel and how it makes you behave—for me to play the character it was the best thing I could have done. Just by having the weight on, it really made me feel a certain way, and behave a certain way" (Kelly 1991, 143).

In addition, common period details set the stage for the dramatic action and often contrast the mundane with the outrageous. For example, the faulty reception of a 1950 television set prompts the quarrel that tears the brothers apart. "We came up with the scene right on the set," De Niro recalls, "We said, 'How about fixing a TV?' Some stupid, little, domestic sort of thing, where there's an incident waiting to happen. It can erupt from the most mundane kind of thing that just triggers something off and then that's it. . . . [A]ll of a sudden it creates a drama" (Kelly 1991, 140). The prop serves as an analogue for the breakdown in communication between Jake and Joey. These details anchor the incident in a specific time and place, even as Jake's outlandish accusation of adultery gives the episode a perverse, almost unbelievable, sense of human folly.

Film noir of the 1940s, preeminently *Double Indemnity* (1944), brought a fresh perspective to the psychology of the crime film by presenting the drama from the perspective of the criminal. This technique brings the audience closer to the crime itself, allowing viewers to share in the lure of the forbidden. Indulgence in outlaw behavior carries with it a fascination, even as the emotional alliance with the perpetrator leads the audience, along with the characters, to doom. *Raging Bull* borrows from this noir perspective by allying the viewer intimately with Jake's twisted subjectivity. As De Niro notes, "Jake himself is primitive, he can't hide certain feelings" (Kelly 1991, 126). Jake's unrestrained aggression carries a forceful, but disturbing attraction. Being with Jake in the boxing ring as he punches, bobs, and endures blows imparts an exhilarating sensation. But gradually Jake's loutish impositions, his demented jealousy, and his assaults on his family—and eventually himself—leave one repelled and shaken. Finally, a detached sense of fear and awe—maybe the purging Aristotle refers to as catharsis—arises in response to Robert De Niro's boxer.

Raging Bull's Jake La Motta developed in the wake of Rocky Balboa, the "Italian Stallion." The enormous commercial and critical success of *Rocky*, and then *Rocky II* (1979), created a benchmark for the boxing film. *Rocky* portrays the boxer as an innocent whose simple but earnest sensibility fosters his personal triumph. *Rocky*'s pure-hearted underdog invites an embrace. Scorsese's boxer shares Balboa's animal nature, but turns its associations upside down. As with so many other genre conventions, Scorsese takes the dominant trend and transforms its meaning. *Raging Bull* portrays La Motta as a beast whose underdeveloped humanity scars everyone he touches, even himself. Further-more, the film binds us to the boxer in spite of his repellent behavior. For Scorsese, Jake's cruelty, ignorance, and rage cannot be accounted for by his childhood, poverty, or the common explanations sought to understand human suffering. Finally, ambiguity overtakes the desire to explain, and an unsatisfying recognition of limitations takes hold. Experiencing compassion for this man gives the viewer a strange and complicated feeling. The push and pull of immersion and detachment, sensation and reflection leaves one exhausted, but the experience asks one to face the mysterious complexity of human behavior that fulfills a goal of art striving to realize its highest aspirations.

SETTING AND ICONOGRAPHY

The relationship between boxing and life independent of the ring is central to the iconography of the boxing film. *Raging Bull* addresses this relationship with complexity and insight. The film weaves together a realistic treatment of a historical era and the subjectivity of the boxer Jake La Motta. A stylistic distinction divides the scenes of social interaction from the subjectivity of the boxing episodes. For scenes of personal exchange, Scorsese employs a simple camera style favoring classic shot-counter-shot or long takes that encourage improvisation in performance. The boxing sequences, on the other hand, were meticulously designed, using storyboards, greater camera movement, closer perspectives, and faster cutting for a much more precise treatment of gesture and movement. The sound design is also distinctive, with the dramatic scenes using standard recording while the boxing scenes are fortified with Dolby stereo. So the distinction between social life and boxing is sharply drawn, only to have the division evolve into a fundamental connection during the "after leaving the ring" episodes, when the evocation of boxing merges subjectivity with the style portraying everyday life. As a result, setting and iconography develops the relationship between Italian American culture and the false consciousness it cultivates. The rule-bound violence of prizefighting spills with unfettered brutality into daily life, just as the conventions of the boxing genre intermingle with the self-conscious style of an art film.

In trying to make a case to his backers for a black-and-white *Raging Bull*, Scorsese described a period look based on documentary style: "'I want it to be something very special. On top of that, though, it would also help us with the period look of the film.' We had an idea of making the film look like a tabloid, like the *Daily News*, like Weegee photographs" (Kelly 1991, 125). As a result, Scorsese often designed shots based on newspaper or magazine photos reporting on events that appear in the film—such as Jake kissing the canvas with his gloves after his victory over Dauthuille, and Vickie crying with her face in her hands during the third Robinson bout. The iconography of the popular press calls up ethnic New York in the 1940s and 50s and adds to the historical tone of the biography film. Martin Scorsese's experience as a documentary filmmaker helped him to fashion a realistic treatment. Indeed, many boxing films in the past, such as *Golden Boy* or, most conspicuously, *The Joe Louis Story* (1953), incorporate newsreel footage along with staged scenes. *Raging Bull* employs a variety of documentary elements to underscore its authenticity, including titles announcing the year, city, and opponents during the bouts; the actual radio announcer's ringside description of the Dautuille fight; and footage from the television broadcast of the Robinson championship bout. *Raging Bull* develops the tradition of urban realism in the boxing film often associated with ethnic New York. In doing so, the film recreates the Italian American culture that produced La Motta and shaped the young Scorsese. The film's iconography cultivates the intersection between the boxer and the filmmaker as products of ethnic New York.

The director enhances the intersection between realism and subjectivity by using objects, settings, and episodes taken from his own experience as an Italian American growing up in New York City in the 1940s and 1950s. Scorsese's father plays a member of Tommy Como's entourage. The crucifix over Jake's and Vickie's marriage bed was taken from Scorsese's parents' bedroom. And the Italian landscape picture hanging over the kitchen table where Jake and Vickie flirt on their first date came from Scorsese's grandmother's apartment on Elizabeth Street. The church dance was filmed in the hall where Scorsese's parish held dances when he was growing up. The quarrel between Jake and his first wife is modeled on Scorsese's childhood memories of fights between his parents (Scorsese/Schoonmaker 1990). The improvisation encouraged by the director frequently intertwines the experience of La Motta and Scorsese. For example, Joey's wedding party on the roof was modeled after the wedding party of Scorsese's parents. When Scorsese got sick during production, Papa Scorsese was told by his son to "Go up there and direct it." So the buffet was changed, candelabras were taken away, and the players were encouraged to behave the way the filmmaker's father remembered the guests at his own party behaved (Kelly 1991, 137–38). The scene itself was shot like a home movie, further embellishing the film's documentary tone. As a result, the realistic treatment of ethnic New York intertwines the memories and associations of the filmmaker's Italian American experience with those of Jake La Motta. Of course, the career of the champion itself played a part in the culture of Martin Scorsese's youth. Careful reconstruction of historical detail develops through the filter of the filmmaker's own emotionally charged associations.

Boxing is central to the fight film, and *Raging Bull* portrays its ring battles with a distinctive iconography based upon subjectivity and sensation. The boxing matches in Hollywood feature films typically replicate the experience of the fan at ringside. *Raging Bull* turns from the spectator's view to the experience of the boxer in the ring. *Raging Bull* employs an array of image and sound devices to portray Jake La Motta's emotions in the course of the fight. The camera almost always stays in the ring with Jake, rather than shooting from the side or above the ring. The film develops the sense that the inside of the ring is equivalent to the inside of Jake's psyche. Earlier boxing films, such as *Kid Galahad* and *Body and Soul*, include shots within the ring which, intercut with more distant perspectives, highlight decisive moments in their respective bouts. With the exception of *Somebody Up There Likes Me*, no boxing film has filmed its fighting sequences almost exclusively within the ring. Nor has any boxing film used the boxer's subjectivity as a basis for its distinctive view. In order to realize this design, Scorsese employed storyboarding, a production technique used only for these sequences. Tight shots amplify the impact of swift camera movements, and quick action cuts convey the intensity of the fight. The camera presents hitting and being hit with sensational immediacy.

One influential model for the design of his boxing sequences that Scorsese has acknowledged is a brief episode (67 seconds) in John Ford's *The Quiet Man*. Here the protagonist Sean Thornton remembers, in a highly subjective fashion distinct in style from the balance of the film, an experience in the ring. Thornton's vision follows a blow he receives at a wedding party, and his grief stricken stare frames the memory. There is no boxing: Instead, from within the ring, the camera shoots reactions to the death of a fighter after a fatal knockout. *The Quiet Man* presents the episode in the manner of a silent film; only music accented with a little background noise breaks the quiet. The characters, presented in a montage, pose, strongly foregrounded and almost still, except for a telling gesture, such as the trainer chewing his tobacco, the doctor placing a towel over the face of the dead man, and the photographers clicking their flash cameras. An intensification of Thornton's subjectivity portrays his feelings of guilt and impotence. These feelings link Ford's dream-like treatment with *Raging Bull*, but the episode from *The Quiet Man* constitutes an isolated instance, rather than serving as the basis for a pattern of events throughout a film, as is the case with the boxing in *Raging Bull*. This intensified, expanded treatment of subjectivity moves the Scorsese production from the classic conventions of the boxing film genre toward the art film.

This subjective perspective in the Scorsese film establishes a pattern, whereby a variety of visual devices distort and exaggerate the contest in order to express La Motta's emotions. For example, when Robinson or Janiero is knocked down, the scene is filmed in slow motion, amplifying Jake's feeling of domination over his opponent. The second Robinson fight is shot with a flame before the lens to give a rippling, hazy mirage-like quality to the image that expresses Jake's illusion of dominance before he finds the judges' decision going against him. The exaggeration of sound effects is even more emphatically subjective than the images. Each blow in the fight is given a kinetic aural texture by sound effects specialist Frank Warner, who has never revealed the actual sounds he manipulated. As punches land, one hears a mix of amplified and distorted noises that sound like melons cracking. Rifle shots stand in for snapping flash cameras. Gushing water roars as blood bursts from cuts. Drumbeats mimic the sound of body blows. All these sounds are mixed with the same technique that goes into creating the rhythm and tempo of a musical score. These noises are integrated with selected ambient sounds, such as shouts from the crowd, ringing bells, or an announcer's commentary. In two instances in the musical score, excerpts from operas of Pietro Mascagni (*Cavalleria Rusticana*, *Guglielmo Ratcliff*, and *Silvano*) add a lyric note to the flow of noise and speech. A number of key moments, such as the knockout punch on Janiero or the preface to Robinson's final attack on La Motta, are accented by completely eliminating this barrage of sound to produce an ominous silence. The result is an aural assault that is very different from what one encounters attending a boxing match. Instead, the film produces an aesthetic experience based on distortion and exaggeration to convey the subjectivity and sensations of the fighter himself, rather than those of the sports fan.

The association of subjectivity with ring battles sets the context for violence in daily life. After losing the first bout against Jimmy Reeves, Jake's protest against the decision provokes the crowd to riot. His anger reaches outside the ring to the spectators. This outburst anticipates Joey's attack on Salvy, and Jake's assault on Joey and Vickie. The distinction between the ring and the outside world breaks down as violence erupts in daily life. The emotional intensification of boxing links sensation and attack, so when Jake becomes unhinged outside the ring, he resorts to a physical rampage. In the closing "after leaving the ring" episodes, Jake's psyche calms as he moves from the sensations of ring battles to stage performances that engender self-examination.

In revising the screenplay drafts of Mardik Martin and Paul Schrader, Robert De Niro and Martin Scorsese decided to have Jake recite Terry Malloy's monologue at the close because "*On the Waterfront* was our iconography," explains the director (Christie/Thompson 1989, 77). On the one hand, the quotation from a benchmark 1954 film about an ex-boxer in ethnic New York combines period, genre and realism that establish the context for *Raging Bull*. On the other hand, the words of Terry Malloy show Jake's consciousness to be the product of popular culture. His effort to understand himself is filtered through that culture to the point that his reflections slide into ambiguity. The boundary between that culture and the boxer's personality become murky. Popular culture is part of the ideology that produced Jake La Motta and Martin Scorsese; it may also become a means toward their salvation. For the audience as well as the filmmaker, genre serves as a foundation for art that guides our understanding—and also bears witness to the conditions that produced it. The conventions of the boxing film genre provide *Raging Bull* with the elements for a penetrating artistic vision.

BOXING AS SUBJECTIVITY AND SENSATION

Martin Scorsese rejects the intensified realism characteristic of Hollywood boxing films for an expressionist model based upon the boxer's subjectivity. The nine boxing episodes are organized according to Jake's perceptions, and each expresses the particular sensations and emotions he experienced at the time. The episodes cluster into an early group, which unites Jake with Vickie and Joey, the title pursuit overseen by Tommy Como, and the title defenses that present Jake's fall. The early group includes the Reeves fight expressing La Motta's rage, the first two Robinson bouts matched with Jake's passion for Vickie, and finally the montage of bouts between 1944 and 1947 which presents rage quieted by affection. The second group highlights jealousy with the Janeiro victory, humiliation in the Fox dive, and joy in winning the title from Cerdan. The title defenses against Dauthuille and Robinson portray a division within La Motta between penitence and pride. Jake's desire, first for Vickie and then for the title, shapes the boxing sequences through the first two clusters. The title quest results in a fall, in the submission to Tommy Como and, indirectly, the estrangement from Joey and Vickie, which establishes the emotional tone of the closing bouts. The conflict between penitence and pride in Jake is never resolved, and so the protagonist remains unredeemed and Jake's struggle persists. However, the film offers its vision of Jake's suffering as a means of providing insight and prospective redemption for the viewer. A more detailed review of the nine bouts follows.

Rage characterizes the first fight, Jake's 1941 loss to Jimmy Reeves. A sound bridge covers the cut from Jake's introspective, backstage remark in 1964, "[T]hat's entertainment," to a close-up of the young La Motta being hit in the face. This transition suggests the boxer is reminiscing. The shocking cut emphasizes the violence of the ring through use of a grotesque irony. The split message, pleasure in pain, anticipates the pattern that characterizes Jake's subjective perception of the Reeves fight: victory in defeat. Victory is realized, first by directing his rage toward downing his rival, and then by projecting his rage onto the crowd, which responds by embracing the feeling, and through the shared feeling, Jake himself.

The film's rehearsal of La Motta's boxing career begins with his fury at his first defeat. Jake absorbs his opponent's blows, seemingly unmoved, but he then is taunted by his corner men to score a knockout because he is behind on points. Anger at the prospect of losing by decision sparks Jake's assault, which brings Reeves down three times in the final round before he is saved by the bell. Encouraged by his brother Joey, Jake raises his arms in victory, throws his robe to the fans and refuses to leave the ring, contesting the judgment against him with defiant gestures. The crowd shares Jake's rage, erupting into a brawl. The subjective perspective highlights Jake's striving for dominance, not simply over his opponent, but also over the judges and the crowd. Jake perceives himself to be robbed of his rightful triumph, and his opponent's shame at being declared the victor is apparent (when the referee raises Reeves' arm in victory, the dazed boxer remains on his stool). The riot among the fans, whose behavior reflects La Motta's rage, continues as the camera cuts away, testifying to the ongoing tumult of Jake's emotions. The violence among the audience, where even women are assaulted, appears to foreshadow the domestic violence that marks Jake's return home in the following episode.

The two early Robinson bouts and the montage condensing the years from 1944 to 1947 relate to Jake's passion as he woos and wins Vickie, as Jake equates romance and marriage with conquest and dominance. Nevertheless, his union with Vickie marks an emotional triumph that quiets the rage, first seen in the Reeves bout, with a tranquility that is unusual for La Motta.

The initial Robinson contest follows Jake's first sexual experience with Vickie, and an interrupted lovemaking scene between Jake and Vickie separates the first Robinson bout from the second. Both Robinson fights show Sugar Ray hitting the canvas, knocked down by Jake. The film presents both Vickie and Sugar Ray as worthy conquests for Jake, whose dominance is clear in the slow motion knockdowns. Though the film shows La Motta on the attack in both fights, Jake wins the first and loses the second. Scorsese uses a hazy, mirage-like image for the second bout to convey Jake's illusion of triumph, despite the judges having scored the bout decisively in Robinson's favor. In Vickie's case Jake never understands that love based upon dominance is an illusion or that yielding to the beloved may establish a more permanent union.

The lovemaking episodes that precede each Robinson bout invest the latter with latent associations. The first lovemaking is alluded to off screen, its successful consummation replaced by and equated with the physical exchange between La Motta and Robinson. The second is interrupted by Jake's teasing equivocation because he cannot decide between satisfying his desire by having sex with Vickie or by exchanging blows with Sugar Ray. In the second instance, Jake is frustrated, initially by interrupting his embrace of Vickie and later by the decision against him. The film links the lovemaking with the fight through the ice water motif: First Jake doses his genitals and later, after the bout, he soaks his bruised hands in freezing water.

A montage condensation of the boxer's rise, a typical Hollywood motif, serves as a means to portray another type of ascendancy: the triumph of romance over the fighter's fury. *Raging Bull* develops this convention with a double perspective: On the one hand, six bouts identified with title cards are evoked with still, freeze frame, and stop action, black and white images of La Motta in the ring; on the other, color "home movie" images of Jake's courtship and marriage to Vickie, his brother Joey's wedding, and other domestic celebrations are intercut with the boxing images. The water motif elaborates the equation of boxing with courtship when, in the home movies, Jake and Vickie take turns assuming boxing poses and playfully knock each other into a swimming pool. Both the black and white stills and the grainy, rough compositions of the home movies appeal to the emotional associations of family albums and portray the common rituals of the period. However, the limited time and the freezing of the ring action contrast with the awkward but affectionate home life of Jake, Vickie, and Joey to imply that Jake's rage has been tamed, if not banished. Furthermore, this montage marks one of the rare occasions in the film when Mascagni's operatic score is the only sound. Lyrical music and smiling faces evoke a personal scrapbook of memories of events that occurred between 1944 and 1947, complete with the feeling of idyllic reminiscence. The juxtaposition of the two devices underlines the fragile artifice and subjectivity of each. The parallel emphasizes the interdependence between boxing and domestic life, but the spirit of familial affection rises in temporary ascendancy over the physical sensations of the ring. The condensation that results expresses a fleeting joy marking both endeavors; Jake's rise through the ranks of middleweights and the brothers' embrace of marriage and family.

The Janiero fight, connected with Jake's jealousy after Vickie comments on the boxer's good looks, introduces the next cluster of three related bouts that are part of the quest for the middleweight title. The prize is guarded by Tommy Como, the mob godfather, who exercises control over each of these three bouts. In order to realize his quest for the championship, Jake must submit to Tommy's authority. Initially La Motta resists, but his thwarted drive for the title tangles his desire for Vickie into a web of impotence and jealousy. The rival he imagines to be vying for Vickie's attention appears to be a projection of his own infidelity. The boxing title has mesmerized Jake and alienated his affection for his wife.

The Janiero fight evokes the Reeves bout with a similar transition. The bout begins with a shocking cut from a quiet full shot of a troubled Jake at Vickie's bedside, to an amplified close up blow. However, in the Reeves fight Jake takes the blow and snatches victory from defeat; in the Janiero fight Jakes fires the blow, and his subjectivity is contested in order to imply a defeat in victory. The film presents only the final round. La Motta pummels Janiero across the ring and against the ropes until finally Jake unloads a devastating blow, breaking his opponent's nose with a crunch and sending him to the canvas in a slow motion collapse. The fight ended in a decision, rather than a knockout, but Scorsese never shows Janiero's recovery, thus expressing Jake's sense of dominance over his imagined rival for Vickie. As La Motta tours the ring with arms raised in triumph, the film cuts away to a reaction shot of Vickie, stunned by Jake's mauling of his helpless opponent. Her unspoken distress is amplified because she understands the disfigurement of Janiero to be motivated by an obsessive and unfounded jealousy. In another reaction shot, as Jake looks out from the ring, Tommy Como quips, "He ain't pretty no more."

In the earlier fights Jake's subjectivity was dominant. Here, the reaction shots convey alternate perceptions. Como's remark resonates over the fight because his words apply not merely to Janiero; they also express Vickie's growing discomfort with her husband. Jake has become ugly. Though he has physically disfigured Janiero, his jealousy has twisted his own sensibility. Rage has become madness. Furthermore, the corruption of Jake's affection serves as a transition to the next fight, where Jake takes a dive and compromises his power as a boxer. However, that compromise is based upon Jake's submission to the authority of Como, a peacemaker who represents the ascendancy of tradition and community over Jake's domineering emotional excess. As a result, the dive appears to be a curse and a blessing; a curse because it violates the rules of competition and Jake's craft, but a blessing because it disciplines Jake's swaggering self-indulgence and gives him the title shot he covets.

The set up with Billy Fox ends in La Motta's humiliation. The film features the opening, rather than the climax, of the bout. The announcer introduces the feature attraction, while Jake anxiously paces the ring. The boxing commissioner, whom Jake has assured of his honor, enters after La Motta's introduction, emphasizing his oversight. By contrast, after Fox is introduced, he is associated with Tommy Como by a cut to the mob boss being seated, and then switching chairs. The first round exchange of blows presents La Motta's perspective on the fix, with the camera in the ring right behind him. Jake, after initially walloping his opponent against the ropes, clearly pulls his

258 Art and Genre in *Raging Bull* (1980)

punches. The cries from the crowd, "Whata doin' Jake," "Come on Jake, I got some money on ya," reflect La Motta's discomfort. Jake's trainer scolds his fighter after the first round, again drawing attention to the boxer's guilt. The only cutaway to the time clock suggests Jake's impatience at his prolonged humiliation, as well as his detachment from the contest. A shot of Jake, arms down and impervious to Fox's final assault, underlines his emotional distance. A cutaway to the suspicious commissioner, departing in disgust, anticipates Jake's own feelings upon exiting from the ring. In the early fights Jake's body conveys eloquence and passion, which neither his speech nor his thoughts can articulate. The Janiero bout ends with the body disfigured by the irrational, and the Fox dive presents the body as a deceiver controlled by another. Nonetheless, these corruptions of Jake's body serve as a necessary price for his most celebrated triumph.

Before the championship bout with Marcel Cerdan, Tommy Como visits Jake's hotel room to offer his support to the challenger. Here the film introduces a marriage trope in which the imagery suggests that Jake is wed to his ring opponents. During the visit, Tommy and Vickie exchange a kiss and the gesture, which sparks Jake's anger, draws attention to the ceremonial quality of the title fight. Indeed, the godfather has appeared to formally give away the bride. The extended minute and a half take devoted to following Jake and his entourage as they walk to the ring becomes the groom's wedding march to the altar. A comprehensive survey of the contest is offered, with La Motta on the attack in rounds one, three, seven, and nine, until Cerdan is unable to answer the bell for the tenth round. The parade of round numbers and these assaults appear as a ritual prelude to the closing embrace when, in response to the referee-priest's declaration of victory, Jake crosses the ring to hug Cerdan. The sound track sets the tone: By replacing the crunch of blows with the Mascagni opera score, the sound track turns the fight into a joyful culmination of a worthy quest. The music links the title bout to the montage condensation that portrayed earlier marriages and blissful celebrations. As he dons the championship belt, Jake's body has finally been consecrated by the ring to become an emblem of physical grace lifted by the low camera angle to the summit of achievement while the flashing cameras crown a halo on his joy.

A rivalry emerges between the two marriages, the first to Vickie and Joey, and the second with boxing itself. The ring now isolates Jake. The boxer finds in his wife and brother the reasons for the compromises he has had to endure in order to win the title, and he attacks them for their supposed betrayal. The triumph of sensation leaves the boxer blind. The championship brings the physical to its peak, to be followed by its decline into suffering. The final two boxing matches convey that suffering motivated by penitence and pride. Here Dauthuille and

Robinson become phantom figures of the beloved ring, demonic brides who arise to punish Jake for his misplaced affections. Sensation turns to torment.

A startling cut on a close up blow introduces the Dauthuille title defense in a manner linking it to the Reeves and Janiero fights. Just as those bouts deal with a reversal, victory in defeat or defeat in victory, this bout presents a penance/pride reversal whose meaning arises from the preceding episode. After Jake has assaulted his wife and brother in a jealous rage, he contritely asks the battered Vickie to stay with him. She responds with a hesitant embrace, which is followed by a cut to Dauthuille punching La Motta against the ropes. After the initial shot, the camera moves outside the boxing ring to look over the shoulder of the radio announcer, who explains, "La Motta is taking terrible punishment on the ropes." Jake endures a barrage of blows, seemingly helpless until suddenly he catches the Frenchman by surprise with a startling counterattack. As Jake resumes the offensive after "playing possum," the camera cuts between both fighters in distorted point of view close-ups as La Motta drives his opponent across the canvas with punches. Finally a close up of Jake's gloved fist in motion and an ominous silence precedes the thwhoop! of the knockout blow which ends the fight with only thirteen seconds remaining.

When the contest begins, it is as if Jake is being punished for his crazed assault on his wife and brother. At this point, the announcer distances the audience from Jake's perspective, but then the commentator is shown to have been taken in, like Dauthuille, by Jake's ruse. Jake's seeming surrender also suggests he is doing penance for his sins, enduring the punishment as contrition for the attack on his family. In this case, the reversal from penance to pride constitutes a second thought, possibly triggered by a reminder of the dive he took to Fox. Jake harbors pride, which energizes his skill as a boxer, but also distorts his humanity as a brother and a husband. And pride prevents Jake from submitting to anyone, even when justice calls for penitence. Pride unleashes the rage that, at the last moment, brings Dauthuille down. Defeat colors Jake's victory. As in the Janiero bout, the exaggerated brutality of Jake's knockout appears ugly and demented. Amplification of the blows turns this boxing into a horror that contrasts with the lyricism of the Cerdan bout. As a surrogate for Cerdan, who died in a plane crash returning from the title bout, Dauthuille is the phantom beloved, the bride of the ring, who inflicts and then receives the punishment arising from a marriage to sensation. The themes of the Dauthuille fight are developed in the final boxing event in the film, when Sugar Ray Robinson takes the title from La Motta.

Between the Dauthuille and Robinson fight, Jake appears walking arm in arm with Vickie, who gently prods her husband to the telephone to initiate reconciliation with his brother Joey. However, after Vickie dials and Jake hears

Joey on the line, he fails to respond. Instead, he listens as Joey curses at a silent caller he takes to be Salvy. The ambivalent play between penitence and pride marks the episode, linking it to the Dauthuille fight and anticipating the final encounter with Robinson.

Two themes mark the final bout, the growing distance from Jake's subjectivity and the corruption of penitence by pride. In the final bout the camera withdraws, assuming a more critical distance from Jake's perspective. The audience's bond with the boxer's subjectivity is moderated. A commercial for Pabst Blue Ribbon beer during the television broadcast asks, "What'll you have?" The image cuts to Joey, absent since Jake's attack, watching the match at home on television. The editing results in addressing the question to Joey, as he watches his brother take a beating. Rather than feeling vengeful, Joey observes with sympathetic resignation that Jake's flurry of punches in the twelfth round was "his last shot." As Jake is pulverized in the final round, four shots register Vickie at ringside, grief-stricken at her husband's suffering. After the referee stops the fight, Joey sinks into his chair with a sigh, a sigh he repeats when Jake stalks to Robinson's corner to boast after the bout. Joey sees Jake's unyielding pride, which motivates his reluctance to seek reconciliation. These shots expand the growing distance from Jake's subjectivity, first initiated in the Janiero fight and increased in the Dauthuille bout. But now the reactions come from victims of Jake's domestic rage. Nevertheless, Joey and Vickie express wonder, compassion, and pain witnessing Jake's trial in the ring. The audience is invited to share their feelings. Joey's and Vickie's response opposes the experience of Jake's sensation as the film develops the contrast between blindness and insight.

The fight is framed in blood. The opening finds Jake in his corner before the twelfth round. A sponge bath results in a mix of blood and water pouring over his body. Boxing resumes in the twelfth round with La Motta punching Robinson fiercely, but unable to "score the big one." The thirteenth round shows Robinson assaulting the now defenseless champ in three increasingly fierce attacks, punctuated by pauses that underscore Jake's feelings. At the first pause, Jake cries "C'mon, Ray, C'mon," prodding his opponent to resume his fire. Here Scorsese introduces an ominous silence, using a low angle and strong back lighting on Robinson, combined with a distorting mix of camera movement and zoom to underline Jake's anticipation of the harrowing assault. The director has explained that he used the shower murder in *Psycho* as the basis for the visual design of the conclusion of the bout. Rapid cutting accents Robinson's punching, which cuts open Jake's face. La Motta grabs the ropes to prevent a knockdown, but finally the referee stops the fight and declares Robinson the winner by technical knock out. His face swollen and bleeding, Jake approaches the victorious Robinson and taunts him with, "You never got me down, Ray."

The camera swings around the ring to end in a close up of blood dripping from the ropes. Jake endures, even prompts, a beating, and his suffering mixes punishment with pride. When the camera moves away from Jake, its close-up of the blood makes the viewer wonder what purpose was served by Jake's anguish.

The blood and suffering, especially in conjunction with the film's concluding citation from the Gospel of John, may suggest the passion of Jesus. John reports on the Roman soldier drawing blood by piercing the side of the crucified Christ. The sanctifying blood of the sacrificial lamb is a common image in the New Testament. Furthermore, the film vividly amplifies the sensation of Jake's suffering and his compliance in the ordeal. In the two previous bouts with Robinson, Sugar Ray has been closely linked to Vickie, even serving as a surrogate for the beloved. Even here Robinson seems allied to Joey and Vickie in their mutual amazement at La Motta's willingness to endure pain even after the contest is lost. Robinson becomes, like the other champion, Cerdan, the beloved of the ring, and as such, a phantom of Jake's willingness to punish himself for his inadequacies. Nevertheless, the redemptive qualities of Jake's bloodshed are qualified by his pride, his bewildering claim of superiority to Robinson because "you never got me down." Pride blinds Jake and compromises the redemptive potential of suffering.

The ring becomes in *Raging Bull* a symbol of Jake's psyche, which is dominated by subjectivity and sensation. Scorsese designs his nine boxing sequences as battles within the consciousness of his protagonist, rather than sporting events experienced by spectators. Each episode is designed to express a distinct sensation closely tied to the dramatic development of the plot. After La Motta's retirement, the image of the ring as the enclosure of the self is restated, particularly in the prison cell and finally in the dressing room. In both places, Jake struggles for insight, through self-inflicted suffering in jail and through art, as reflected by his dressing room mirror. The film leaves the boxer unredeemed, but with the passage from John's Gospel, *Raging Bull* invites viewers to alleviate their blindness through the vision offered by the filmmaker.

CONFLICTS

Raging Bull presents the conflicts central to the boxing film genre. The filmmaker's approach hinges upon an attraction/repulsion dynamic: First the audience identifies with Jake's behavior, and then this behavior's ugly consequences disturb the viewer. The formal tension between sympathy and detachment, subjectivity and objectivity, sharp montage and longer takes elaborates on the attraction-repulsion dynamic. As a result, an emotional tension develops the thematic conflicts with exceptional force. Furthermore, the film weaves the traditional thematic conflicts into a relationship to the more obvious conflicts driving the plot, particularly Jake's fight against his ring opponents, Jake's resistance to mob control, Jake's turn against Vickie and Joey, and finally Jake's battle against himself.

The critique of the success ethic is introduced in Jake's first bout on screen, when he goes up against Jimmy Reeves in Cleveland. The viewer's sympathy is established with the cut to Jake taking a blow in close-up. Then La Motta proceeds to knock out his opponent, who is saved by the bell even though he has to be carried from the canvas. The film positions us to favor the boxer as an exemplar of competitive individualism, now robbed of his victory. However, Jake's demonstration against the decision leads to unsavory consequences. When he refuses to leave the ring, his protest sparks a riot in the crowd. Commotion spreads through the audience, fights break out, and women are trampled in the melee. The scene closes with the violence in progress punctuating the episode with a disquieting note.

From a broader perspective, the film follows Jake's quest for the middleweight title, and the viewer, like a sports fan, roots for the boxer to triumph. Finally, his efforts are rewarded with the victory over Marcel Cerdan. The celebration that ensues lifts the boxer into the air wearing the championship belt, supported by the lyrical Mascagni music, which expresses the joy of the competitor realizing his dream. But soon Jake's belligerent narcissism leads to attacks on his wife and brother, and the benefits of the success ethic are thrown into doubt. No lasting satisfaction arises from the ring victories. La Motta's extreme behavior makes him intolerable. At the conclusion he is isolated, imprisoned by his flesh, and confused by his torment. The portrait of the boxer as a repellant anti-hero condemns competitive individualism as an indulgence leading to suffering.

As explained above, *Raging Bull* presents a variation on gender conflict by having Jake and Vickie marry early in the film. Their happiness, presented in a home movie sequence, runs parallel with La Motta's success in the ring. The conventional conflict between the masculine ethos of boxing and the sweetheart from the neighborhood dissolves. However, soon Jake projects his conflict with the mob onto his wife. Obsessive jealousy and impotence poisons the marriage. Jake's powerlessness to gain a title bout generates a crisis of masculinity that is twisted into suspicions of adultery. Following the genre convention, the audience first rejoices with Jake at his pleasure in Vickie, only to have a crisis arise from an unexpected, even more disturbing source.

A homoerotic undercurrent also elaborates on the gender conflict. Robin Wood and David Friedkin have explained that *Raging Bull* portrays a repressed homosexuality in Jake's relationships with his brother and with his opponents

Initially one sympathizes with Jake, because Irma, his first wife, is a scold. Only later, when the film suggests the boxer's troubled sexuality, does our understanding of the conflict change. Courtesy of the Academy of Motion Picture Arts and Sciences.

in the ring (Wood 1986, Friedkin 1994). The ice water link between Jake's genitals and his fist, as well as the displacement of sex with Vickie by fighting with Robinson, constitute one instance among many. Friedkin has carefully explored the erotic attraction between Jake and Joey, which informs the quarrel between Jake and his first wife after the boxer returns from Cleveland. Jake denies "foolin' around," but he can't allay Irma's suspicions. Only in retrospect does the tension between the couple make sense. Vickie later complains to Joey about Jake's sexual neglect, and Irma's accusations probably resulted from the same problem. She assumes that Jake must be getting satisfaction elsewhere. This erotic undercurrent takes a perverse turn as the scene closes, and Jake provokes Joey into punching him while Irma peeks from her room at the strange antics of the two brothers. Initially, one sympathizes with Jake because his first wife is a scold; only later does the film take an ominous turn as the boxer's troubled sexuality informs the gender conflict.

Martin Scorsese's evocation of the New York Italian American culture of the 1940s and '50s grows out of affection and misgivings. Life in the tenements, summers at the public swimming pool, and dances in the parish hall are reconstructed from the director's memories in impressive detail. Attention to clothing, colloquial speech, and popular music builds nostalgia for the ethnic ghetto. However, the brutal conditions, whether connected with fights at the dance hall, mobsters' control of the neighborhood, or the domestic violence at home, convey the sense of a culture torn by its crippling values. The ethnic world becomes a prison that traps people within its false consciousness. "I think I really captured the strangeness of that way of life," Scorsese explains (Henry 1999, 92). The ideology of Italian American machismo promotes the crisis of masculinity at the heart of the film.

In the boxing film success in the ring usually offers the prospect of assimilation, but in *Raging Bull* Jake finally gets his title shot by complying with the gangster ethos of his community. Pam Cook notes that Jake's "do it alone" stance expresses his unsuccessful resistance to the mobsters who dominate ghetto life (Cook 1982, 45). But more generally, boxing stands for the primitive practices of the ghetto and is intended to serve as a contrast to art. Unlike many boxing films from the "comeback" cycle of the 1970s, *Raging Bull* criticizes the native community, whose ideology cripples the protagonist. Though the ethnic culture is portrayed in vivid detail, it is rejected in favor of a more cosmopolitan sensibility. For Scorsese, art—particularly music and the movies—is a means of escaping the confines of the parochial ghetto. The art motif is bolstered by the self-conscious style of the film. Whereas boxing confirms the limitations of the ghetto, art presents the prospect of understanding and release. Jake moves toward a restless reflection after he leaves the boxing arena for his stage act. At the same time, he moves from New York City to Miami, but even when he returns to Manhattan, he maintains a distance from the ethnic neighborhood and its constraints. *Raging Bull* endorses assimilation into the broader community, despite its affectionate portrayal of Italian American culture. The film develops this conflict through a nostalgic evocation of time and place, which is set against the grim consequences the ethnic ideology inflicts upon those under its spell.

The conflicts between anger and powerlessness, stoicism and sensitivity are central to the crisis of masculinity in *Raging Bull*. Behind them lurk the specter of violence and the necessity of suffering. Jake's rage drives his bold attack in the ring and his resistance to the mob's control. At first the boxer earns our sympathy. But Jake cannot control his passion, and soon his brutality moves outside the ring. His jealous delusions direct his fury first at Vickie and then Joey, exploding in shocking domestic violence. Eventually his rage invites his self-destruction as a means of assuaging his guilt by encouraging Robinson's assault and pounding his own body against his cell walls. Jake's emotional rampages do not overcome the gangster's power, restore the affection of his wife and brother, or satisfy his need for reconciliation. After the boxer's rage spends its force, Jake's suffering confirms its powerlessness. In the Dade County Stockade Jake berates himself for his stupidity, and in response to his agony he affirms his humanity with the cry, "I'm not an animal." Suffering quiets his rage, but the muted peace brings little self-understanding.

Jake's stoicism feeds his hardheaded ferocity, his ability to take a punch in order to strike a blow. But enduring pain only undermines his sensitivity and fuels the violence governing his life. At first, the boxer's stoicism supports his courage and determination, but finally the distortion of his feelings blinds him, and allows the attack that destroys his family. Later Jake is silent when Vickie beckons him to speak to Joey on the telephone. After enduring Robinson's assault in the ring, La Motta's unyielding pride leads him to gloat, "Ray, ya never got me down." His embrace of Joey at the garage fails to renew their intimacy. The film leaves its anti-hero muttering, "I'm the boss," as he prepares to face the crowd as if they were another in an endless series of opponents. Sensitivity eludes the boxer even after he abandons the ring and tries to speak through the arts.

Jake La Motta's instinctual animal energy, the boxer as a raging bull, underlines the burden of his flesh. His primitive feelings and physical power muffle his soul and brings him to the edge of self-destruction. The animal motif indicates the boxer's distance from the spirit and sets the terms for the body and soul conflict. Martin Scorsese claims that his film is a tale of redemption. In the Dade County Stockade La Motta "has fallen so low that he can only come up to be reborn. When we find him in the strip-tease joint, he has changed," Scorsese explains. "He has found a kind of peace with himself. He is no longer the same man" (Henry 1999, 97). The director claims that Jake's change is a product of grace, a mysterious divine intervention. Though Jake may have attained a measure of peace, his attempt to reconcile with Joey fails. Jake appears almost crippled by his bulging weight, in sorry contrast to the trim fighter he was in his prime. The rehearsal for his stage act verges on pathos, but it offers no evidence of the ex-champion's spiritual awakening. The affirmation of spirit marking the conclusion of many boxing films eludes Jake La Motta.

After the ambiguity of the closing scene, the quotation from the Gospel of John brings the body and soul theme to its conclusion. However, the implication of "Once I was blind, and now I can see" in the postscript is altered by Scorsese's personal dedication of the motion picture to his teacher, Haig Manoogian. The Gospel passage now appears to apply to the filmmaker rather than to the screen boxer. I agree with David Friedkin, David Bordwell, and Kristin Thompson, who argue that the postscript refers to the insight Scorsese gained into the dark side of his character and into the Italian American culture from which both he and Jake La Motta emerged (Friedkin 1994, 130; Bordwell and Thompson 1997, 431). Hope rises through the artwork and the artist. With the experience of *Raging Bull,* the filmmaker offers the understanding that he has gained to his audience. Here lies the affirmation of the spirit.

Raging Bull's distinctive attraction/repulsion dynamic conveys the traditional conflicts of the boxing film genre with remarkable force. The film presents a cautionary tale of an anti-hero. Its intensity comes from the potential for narcissism in the success ethic; the submerged sexual confusion that ignites gender antagonism; the self-destructive habits arising from the ideology of an immigrant community; the violence and suffering fed by a perverse play between restraint and rage; and a quest to satisfy the aspirations of the spirit while weighed down by the cravings of the flesh. *Raging Bull* is hardly limited to these traditional conflicts, but its eloquent engagement with these themes ties it closely to the heritage of the boxing film genre.

EPILOGUE
Into the Twenty-First Century

The tradition of genre criticism goes back to Aristotle's *Poetics*. Though respected for its honorable lineage, genre analysis deemphasizes accepted Romantic aesthetic values, such as originality, imagination, and personal expression. Rather, genre criticism seeks out the patterns which reveal shared aesthetic conventions, embedded social practices which foster fluent communication between the artist and his or her audience. Film genre criticism seeks to articulate the common models of narrative, characterization, and setting, as well as the viewer's typical emotional response, all of which unify a body of films over time. Such an analysis strives to describe patterns (that filmmakers and the film audience may only vaguely sense) in order to uncover their social significance. Dramatic conflicts arising from widespread social problems experienced by the audience are the foundation upon which film genre conventions are built. The dynamic picture of genre presented in this book has emphasized the substantial range of response to these conflicts. More than anonymous products of the culture industry, film genres are also aesthetic vocabularies that carry the potential for complex achievement.

Contemporary genre study emphasizes historical evolution in presenting a dynamic picture of repetition and innovation over time. Film genres change in response to new developments in films themselves, as well as changes in the film industry and society at large. Viewing genre history as a series of distinct cycles allows for a more precise understanding of shifting trends and social influence. Furthermore, such a history highlights gaps in production, periods of decline that call for explanation as much as times when the genre flourished. Genre criticism exceeds the confines of individual films and extends the boundaries of analysis around a wide and expanding field of practice. It can group fiction with nonfiction, bring new appreciation to works generally dismissed as trivial, and enrich the context for comprehending masterworks. Film genre criticism is more than a formal investigation of evolving conventions; at its best, the method illuminates the social significance of entertainment.

This study brings the boxing film, a neglected genre, into sharp focus so we can see its influence on the history of American filmmaking. Contrary to what one might expect, the investigation reveals a critique of the manly ethos of the ring. Films that celebrate the prowess of boxers, like *Hard Times*, prove to be exceptional. Instead, the genre features the limitations of the body and a quest for spiritual alternatives to the physical. Though few members of the audience ever take up boxing, the conflicts central to these films (individualism versus cooperation, dominant versus indigenous communities, gender wars, rage at powerlessness, stoicism versus sensitivity, and material versus spiritual values) portray viewers' own problems. These entertainments seriously ask about the reason for, and purpose of, suffering. Analysis of films from different historical cycles that address similar conflicts demonstrates an enormous range of treatments, as well as the continuing influence of social experience. My historical perspective has expanded the boundary of the boxing film to include feature-length documentaries, as well as the "after leaving the ring" cycle, which brings a fresh perspective to classic films such as *From Here to Eternity* and *On the Waterfront*. Neglected movies like *Kid Galahad* gain new importance, and masterworks like *Raging Bull* are placed in a context that deepens our understanding.

◆ ◆ ◆

The boxing film was conspicuous on screen and television in 2005 with *Million Dollar Baby*, *Unforgivable Blackness: The Rise and Fall of Jack Johnson*, and *Cinderella Man* attracting both critical acclaim and commercial success. At the beginning of the twenty-first century the boxing film genre maintained its status as a stellar Hollywood entertainment.

Million Dollar Baby was among the most highly praised films of its year. Following its opening in December 2004, Clint Eastwood's film won Academy Awards for "Best Picture," "Best Director," "Best Actress," and "Best Supporting Actor," a significant accomplishment for any film. Numerous associations of films critics, including the National Board of Review, the National Society of Film Critics, and the New York Film Critics Circle also honored the film with multiple awards. In addition, the film attracted a large, enthusiastic audience. Though produced on a modest budget of $30 million, *Million Dollar Baby* generated over $200 million theatrically at home and abroad (*Variety* 2005, 8).

Ken Burns, the producer-director of PBS blockbuster documentaries including *The Civil War* (1990), *Baseball* (1994), and *Jazz* (2001), drew special attention to his boxing documentary, *Unforgivable Blackness: The Rise and Fall of Jack Johnson*. Produced for television and scheduled for a PBS broadcast in January 2005 on the Martin Luther King holiday, Burns's film was honored with screenings at the Telluride, Toronto, and New York Film festivals in advance of its premiere broadcast. This engaging, well-crafted documentary brought the legendary prizefighter's story and the legacy of American racism to wide public attention, garnering an audience of 13.6 million people with its premiere broadcast. The show won three Emmy awards, including "Outstanding Nonfiction Special" and "Outstanding Writing for Nonfiction Programming." Furthermore, it added to the distinguished cluster of documentaries devoted to boxing and the African American community discussed in chapter two, including *The Fallen Champ: The Untold Story of Mike Tyson* (1993), *When We Were Kings* (1996), and *On the Ropes* (1999).

Cinderella Man was a highly publicized summer "tentpole" from Universal Pictures, with a substantial budget estimated at $88 million. The uplifting biography of Depression heavyweight champion Jim Braddock features Russell Crowe as a sympathetic underdog. The Ron Howard film combines a sentimental comeback plot reminiscent of *Rocky* with dynamic boxing sequences patterned on the subjectivity devices so effective in *Raging Bull*. Though critical response was positive, the movie was a disappointment at the box office, earning only slightly over $60 million in domestic theatrical revenue, $108 million worldwide. Nonetheless, that winter Universal Pictures expressed its confidence in the film's achievement by initiating a widespread awards campaign in trade publications like *Variety*. The Academy of Motion Pictures responded with nominations for "Best Supporting Actor" for Paul Giamatti, "Best Film Editing," and "Best Makeup." *Cinderella Man* satisfied a substantial audience in the summer of 2005 and affirmed the staying power of the boxing film.

The conflicts and conventions of the genre were on display in each film. *Million Dollar Baby* emphasizes spirit in the face of the body's vulnerability in its tale of the rise and fall of a woman boxer. At the same time, the film features manager Frankie Dunn's struggle to overcome his masculine reserve and compensate for his failure as a husband and parent through his alliance with Maggie Fitzgerald. *Unforgivable Blackness* portrays Jack Johnson, the legendary heavyweight champion, contesting the oppression of Jim Crow America by leading the life of a free man in spite of the threats, intimidation, and legal sanctions imposed by the white establishment. The traditional contest between assimilation and loyalty to the native community is given an unusual treatment, however, in Johnson's insistence on his independence from African American society as well as the dominant culture. *Cinderella Man* is distinctive for turning the boxer into a saint. While the film fluently engages the conventions of the boxing genre, its peculiar treatment of its protagonist diminishes the tension necessary for creating a compelling dramatic conflict. Each of these films rewards further analysis.

MILLION DOLLAR BABY

A modest genre movie with an emphasis on plot and characters, *Million Dollar Baby* was widely recognized for its traditional qualities. The Clint Eastwood film follows the master plot of the boxing genre, adding some provocative revisions. Act one weaves together the "discovery" and the "crisis" by reversing the roles played by the boxer and the manager. Maggie Fitzgerald (Hilary Swank) struggles to convince the aging boxing trainer Frankie Dunn (Clint Eastwood) to manage her career. Frankie reluctantly acknowledges Maggie's talent, finally prodded into recognition as a result of a startling disappointment. At first Frankie shrugs off the phenomenon of women boxers as a grotesque fad, but when his own heavyweight prospect, Big Willie, leaves him because Frankie won't press for a title fight, a crisis ensues. Subsequently Frankie, alone at home watching TV, sees Willie, now under a new manager, win the championship. Forlorn, Frankie wanders back to the gym that night seeking consolation from his old friend Scrap (Morgan Freeman). There he finds Maggie still punching the speed bag and grudgingly agrees to train her until she can find another manager.

The second act affirms Maggie and Frankie's loyalty to each other. Here Maggie's promise becomes clear, and her rise begins. But "the deal" receives a fresh treatment. The manager and his buddy push the fighter to sign with others, but the boxer is steadfast. First, Frankie passes Maggie off, only to reclaim her when her new manager victimizes her. After Maggie proves her talent in a series of ring victories, Scrap introduces her to a rival manager because he fears that Frankie lacks the confidence to push her to the title, as he demonstrated in his treatment of Big Willie. However, Maggie turns down the deal, declaring, "I ain't ever leaving Mr. Dunn."

The third act continues Maggie's rise as a boxer and her growing bond with Frankie. "Big Fight 1" portrays Maggie's London victory and leads Frankie to set up the title bout, overcoming the hesitation that led to his break with Big Willie. The "debauchery" move finds moral failure projected onto Maggie's family members, who are portrayed as ungrateful welfare bums who deny their daughter affection. When Dunn learns that his boxer is estranged from her family, just as he is from his daughter, his bond with his boxer grows. Frankie strives to maintain his masculine reserve while expressing his fatherly affection for Maggie as a means of reconciling his own parenting failure. Nonetheless, the third act ends in catastrophe when, on the verge of victory in "Big Fight 2," Maggie is paralyzed in the ring as a result of foul play and circumstance. The champ cheats Maggie out of victory with a blow after the bell, recalling "the dive" as a plot convention of the boxing film.

The film concludes with an extended "after leaving the ring" resolution. Frankie witnesses the medical failure of Maggie's recovery; instead, he faces her complete physical breakdown. Tormented, Dunn accedes to Maggie's request to aid in her suicide and then disappears. The epilogue consists of Scrap's voice-over narration of a letter to Dunn's daughter, striving to explain Frankie and gain him a posthumous reconciliation.

Million Dollar Baby is the story of Frankie's struggle for reconciliation. He fails Big Willie, haunted by his memory of Scrap's last fight, in which his friend was blinded in one eye. Dunn blames himself for pressing on with the bout, and rather than protecting his buddy. As a result, Frankie is psychologically crippled and prevented from capturing the title shot he craves. His own pigheaded gender attitudes prevent him from recognizing Maggie's talent, but Scrap, in spite of his injury, leads his friend to the prospective champion. The growing emotional bond between Maggie and Frankie, a bond that exceeds any professional contract, ultimately develops into a blood kinship that allows Frankie to break out of the solitude wrought by his estrangement from his wife and daughter. But his attempt to rectify his past mistakes brings calamity. In spite of all the training Frankie has lavished on Maggie, her skills falter in the face of the unexpected. Instead of being vindicated, Dunn faces Maggie's agonizing demise. Even though she is paralyzed, Frankie wants her companionship. Tormented at being unable to protect those he cherishes, and witnessing the suffering of his surrogate daughter, Dunn is torn between his wish to keep Maggie near him and her request to end her life. "Boxing is an unnatural act," Scrap declares, "because everything in boxing is backwards." So too, Frankie's attempts to reconcile himself with his past lead him into the unnatural paradox of killing the person he loves. The complexity that distinguishes *Million Dollar Baby* arises from its elegant, fresh treatment of a traditional narrative design.

Million Dollar Baby eliminates the common romance and fails to develop any overarching antagonist, cultivating instead the relationship between the multiple protagonists, Maggie, Frankie, and Frankie's former fighter, gym mate, and confidant Scrap. Maggie represents heart, and her drive to rise above her

Million Dollar Baby revolves around the relationship between Maggie (Hillary Swank), Frankie (Clint Eastwood), and Scrap (Morgan Freeman). Merie W. Wallace/Warner Brothers.

white trash origins and achieve self-esteem propels her into the ring. "Boxing is about respect," Scrap confides, and Maggie's quest illustrates the truth of his observation. Unlike Dunn, Maggie achieves her goal through her physical prowess, the cheering crowd, and the affection she wins from Frankie. "I got what I needed, boss. Got it all," she affirms from her deathbed. Maggie is much like Rocky Balboa in *Rocky*: She loses her title fight, but gains personal dignity. However, for her, at the end of the bout the cheering stops, and her paralysis threatens to rob her of her newly won feelings of self-worth. Rather than a romantic partner like Rocky's Adrian, her beloved is a surrogate father to whom she appeals to free her spirit from her body before she loses the memory of her triumph. Like so many boxing films, *Million Dollar Baby* elevates physical prowess, only to undermine its force and remind us of the body's inevitable decay. Maggie's optimism contrasts with Frankie's bitter dilemmas, his experience of remorse without redemption. Scrap plays the contemplative, half-blind seer, a figure harking back to classical mythology. His voice-over begins the film, and his continuing reflections often aim to alter the audience's perspective on the action, or draw a connection between images. Throughout the picture, Scrap's coaching of the inept Danger ("I only ever met one fighter who was all heart") parallels Frankie's training of Maggie. His closing words tell us in retrospect that his commentary is a plea for understanding. The voice-over narration and the understated comradeship between the two old men shift our attention from Maggie; it is Frankie's story that Scrap tells. Scrap keeps *Million Dollar Baby* on a meditative plane that balances the wham-bang boxing, establishes a melancholy tone, and prepares us for the introspective ending. Maggie embodies hope, but Scrap expresses compassion. Both serve as counterpoints to Frankie's suffering, while the intersection of the three is what gives *Million Dollar Baby* its emotional depth.

Million Dollar Baby portrays life's trials, disappointments, and calamities. As Scrap advises, "Don't run from the pain, step into it." Defeat rather than victory establishes the measure for their fortitude, loyalty, and endurance. However, Frankie, Maggie, and Scrap never resign themselves to despair. Their fellowship allows them to endure and contest the vicissitudes of fate. For a successful Hollywood film, *Million Dollar Baby* portrays remarkable pessimism. The misfortunes that cripple Maggie suggest the mysterious and unaccountable conditions that influence us all. The unrelenting determination of the hillbilly woman to box is matched by Frankie's constant questions to his priest. Scrap explains that once a fighter loses the drive to challenge authority, he is no longer a fighter. That determination is then aimed at the unfairness and chance governing the world. To fight back and struggle to shape our destiny rather than surrender to fate— this sentiment lends Eastwood's characters nobility.

The bond between Frankie and Maggie is a response to the ruptured parent-child relationships that haunt both characters, one that marks the boxing film from *The Champ* to *Girlfight*. Maggie's success in the ring and Frankie's devotion temporarily mend the boxer's breach with her mother. Frankie has greater difficulty compensating for the estrangement from his wife and daughter. The masculine conflict between a disciplined reserve, on the one hand, and sensitivity toward others, on the other, traditional in the boxing film, holds Dunn back. His job as a cut man is to stop bleeding. His motto is, "Protect yourself at all times." In the face of life's cruelty, the trainer has learned to shield his feelings and keep up an impenetrable guard. But as he tells Maggie, "Tough ain't enough." However, Frankie uses his secret language to slowly arise from the solitude of his pain. Throughout the film Frankie studies Gaelic and reads the poems of W.B. Yeats, activities contrary to the manly ethos of the ring. At a key moment during Maggie's rise, when she moves from her corner after having her nose broken to score a knockout, Frankie whispers his admiration in the Gaelic, "Mo cuishle." Later, he buys Maggie a silk boxing robe embroidered with "Mo cuishle" in gold. The fighter asks her manager what the words mean, but Frankie won't tell. When Irish fans support Maggie with shouts of "Mo cuishle," one senses that they are speaking for Frankie. Finally, at her death Frankie reveals that the inscription means "My darling, my blood," thereby declaring his claim to fatherhood even as he kills his child. Maggie's boxer is a figure of the heart, much like the boxer's beloved in more traditional films. She provokes feelings even from a man hardened by life's cruelty. *Million Dollar Baby* affirms the idea that the greater the obstacles to emotion, the stronger the feeling once those obstacles are overcome.

The broken family theme is developed in a home motif. Dunn advises his fighter to save her money and buy a house. But Frankie's own Los Angeles bungalow is only seen at night, dimly lit, and empty except for him. Visits to the house underline Dunn's loneliness. The first visit occurs when Big Willie comes to tell his manager that he is leaving him. Later, we see Frankie receiving unopened letters back from his daughter, marked "return to sender." When Maggie does save enough, she buys a house for her mother, rather than for herself. But Ma only complains that once the government finds out about her house they will cut off her welfare. For both Frankie and Maggie lodging speaks of lost family. In the boxing film the home and family ties are frequently placed in contrast to the hotel or rented room, transient urban locales for alienated people. Frankie's longing for home is expressed by his desire for home-cooked lemon pie, not a pastry with "that canned filling crap." After Maggie's mother advises her daughter to quit boxing and get married, the boxer tells Frankie, "I got nobody but you." They stop at a diner nestled in the woods where Maggie used to go with her father before he died. There Frankie has his wish fulfilled, eating delicious home cooked lemon pie. Frankie has replaced Maggie's father, and the boxer and her manager share the diner as if it were a home of their own. After her injury, Frankie reads Yeats to Maggie: "I will arise and go now, and go to Innisfree,/ and a small cabin built there, of clay and wattles made:/ . . . And I shall have some peace there. . . ." Maggie suggests that he retire to Yeats's cabin with his books and lemon pie; Frankie invites her to join him. At the film's close, Scrap hopes that Frankie has found peace. As he speaks, the viewer peers through the window of the diner, making out through the haze a man who may be eating home cooked lemon pie.

Frankie's disappearance after Maggie's death strikes a sorrowful, ambiguous note. One doesn't know whether Dunn is lost, as his priest predicted, or if his departure is closer to the transcendent passion of a romantic double suicide. Eastwood cultivates the uncertainty. "You provoke certain emotions," the director explains, "and you let the imagination take over" (Taubin 2005, 29). Like so much in *Million Dollar Baby*, the closing develops a subtle emotional balance. In the gym alone, Scrap looks up as his voice-over declares, "A ghost came through the door." However, the ghost is not Frankie, but Danger returning to the boxing club in spite of a humiliating beating. The backward man's return counters Dunn's disappearance. "Anybody can lose one fight," Danger declares. Scrap smiles and reassuringly tells him, "Go put on your gloves, you missed a

The misfortune that cripples Maggie speaks of mysterious and unaccountable conditions that affect us all. Merie W. Wallace/Warner Brothers.

lot of training." Maggie's death is answered with the determination of her comic "ghost" to resume his hopeless quest to become the welterweight champion of the world. In a similar fashion, Scrap's letter to Frankie's estranged daughter ends the picture with a heartfelt attempt to mend an emotional schism even after death seems to have extinguished any hope. *Million Dollar Baby* omits the daughter's reply: The film's subject is not triumph, but struggle.

UNFORGIVABLE BLACKNESS: THE RISE AND FALL OF JACK JOHNSON

The life of Jack Johnson, the first African American heavyweight boxing champion (from 1908 to 1915), is a compelling story, especially in the context of the virulent racism of Jim Crow America at the turn of the twentieth century. The first part of *Unforgivable Blackness* portrays Johnson's rise through the underworld of saloons, brothels, and prizefighting until his undisputed triumph as world heavyweight champion in 1910 with his defeat of the former champ Jim Jefferies in the "Battle of the Century." The second half portrays his fall, as white authorities scheme to bring him down by investigating his flamboyant sex life. The result was a dubious conviction in 1913 for violating the Mann Act outlawing transportation of women across state lines for illicit purposes. After Johnson's flight abroad, the country is scoured for boxing prospects, and Jess Willard arises as the "great white hope". In a 1915 title bout in Havana, Willard defeats Johnson in the twenty-sixth round. Finally, in 1920 Johnson returns to the U.S. and serves a one-year prison term. Johnson's memorable life story, already the subject of Harold Sackler's Pulitzer Prize winning play from 1968 and the subsequent film, *The Great White Hope*, numerous biographies, and often repeated stories, receives vivid new life in the Florentine Films production. The flow of images, commentary, and music carries the audience along at a brisk pace, so one is hardly aware of the film's extended running time, nearly four hours. The documentary unfolds with the engaging appeal of a fiction film, while its wealth of authentic detail and social observation surpasses previous films about Johnson. The conflict between mainstream America and the African American community is central to *Unforgivable Blackness*, but the documentary makes an unusual choice in emphasizing Johnson's disregard for both.

Unforgivable Blackness portrays more than the highlights of a champion's career. The film recreates the social circumstances and the public ethos at the turn of the twentieth century. "Johnson in many ways is an embodiment of the African American struggle to be truly free in this country—economically, socially and politically," says Ken Burns. "He absolutely refused to play by the rules set by the white establishment, or even those of the black community. In that sense, he fought for freedom not just as a black man, but as an individual" (Dan Klores Communications 2004, 1). To evoke broader issues, the film features Johnson's notorious womanizing (including three marriages to white women), his love for fast cars and glamorous attire, his vaudeville tours, and his activities in the sporting world that flourished on the margins of respectable society. By contrast, the documentary underlines the oppression of African Americans by showing the demeaning caricatures promulgated in the press and popular culture, legal segregation, and the physical intimidation, assaults, and lynching, all of which were commonplace. Burns features the special White House screening of *The Birth of a Nation* in 1915, along with its inflammatory commercial success, to illustrate the country's endemic racism. In Johnson's famous bouts he fought as a lone black man surrounded by thousands of white men, some of whom were ready to kill him if the opportunity arose. As the first black celebrity of American mass culture, Johnson thrived on applause. He provoked the outrage of the white public as well as reservations in the black community. The film is a detailed, vibrant, and often disturbing picture of America in the early twentieth century.

Ken Burns organizes his material around the theme of individual freedom, particularly Jack Johnson's determination to be his own man versus the power of a racist society to enforce its standards. "Johnson's story is more than the story of a tremendous athlete, or even one who broke a color line," Burns explains. "It is the story of a man who forced America to confront its definition of freedom, and that is an issue with which we continue to struggle" (Dan Klores Communications 2004, 3). Though an extraordinary boxer, Jack Johnson is even more important as an individual African American who largely succeeded in realizing his grand aspirations in the face of an oppressive culture. James Earl Jones notes that Johnson's story is also one of hubris, of the boxer's often arrogant reveling in social opposition and of the price he paid in harassment, exile, and imprisonment. The self-discipline of other legendary black athletes, such as Joe Louis, Jackie Robinson, and Arthur Ashe, contrasts with Johnson, because in addition to their own achievements, these champions served the African American community and American culture at large. But Johnson's attitude, as Randy Roberts observes, was "I'm gettin' mine," even as Booker T. Washington and W. E. B. Du Bois were struggling to promote social consciousness and collective responsibility among beleaguered African Americans. Indeed, the emphasis on individual freedom in *Unforgivable Blackness* leads to excessive valorization of Johnson, whose extraordinary qualities are beyond question, but whose colossal self-indulgence defied prudence, ethics, and social responsibility. Joyce Carol Oates's observation that "Johnson would seem to have been the very essence of male narcissism" seems closer to the mark than Burns' portrait (Oates 2004, 28). The superman bravado of Johnson testifies to a quest for personal freedom, but it hardly speaks to the more common struggle to exercise one's rights against a powerful antagonist. Faced with the conflict between mainstream America and his native community, Johnson strives to rise above the division, only to increase the pathos of his fall.

For Burns, race is an obstacle to be overcome, and Johnson wins his admiration because he lived as if being black didn't matter—even though, to everyone else, it did. Burns' historical films testify to the importance of race—the distinct heritage, values and achievements of, most conspicuously, the African American community—and reveal the equality of individuals as a central value in American culture. But there is a tension here arising from the larger conflict between the individual and the community that remains unarticulated and unresolved. Of course, this is a problem in American culture itself, and central to the boxing film genre. How are we to cherish and even cultivate the distinct contributions of diverse communities within our culture without exciting rivalries and prejudice that undermine fair treatment? *Unforgivable Blackness* concludes with a claim that Jack Johnson is distinctly American. Stanley Crouch has the last word: "He's the kinda person who could have only come about in the United States. Because America, whatever its problems, still has a certain kind of elasticity, a certain latitude that allows the person to dream a big enough dream that can be achieved if the person is as big as the dream." Thus, Burns ends his film on a typically optimistic note, affirming the positive achievements of American culture even while acknowledging the grim reality of racial injustice. Upon reflection though, this conclusion is disquieting, because celebration of the extraordinary individual as an embodiment of freedom overlooks the experience of ordinary individuals, and the sense of social responsibility that comes with extraordinary talents. The greater challenge for our culture is to protect the freedom of our weakest—the poor, the aged, the young—and to respect and nurture subordinate communities within the larger nation. One is left with a suspicion that Jack Johnson would have little time for these matters as he zoomed past in his sports car with one woman beside him and another in the back seat.

CINDERELLA MAN

Cinderella Man was a disappointment compared to the popular success of *Million Dollar Baby* and *Unforgivable Blackness*. Nonetheless, the film illustrates the continuing appeal of the boxing film as a staple of Hollywood entertainment, and its limitations suggest principles central to the genre.

On screen the boxer Jim Braddock is patient in the face of injury, the censure of the boxing commissioner, and the financial disaster brought on by the Depression. Even with his family facing starvation, the pug maintains his good nature until fortune turns his way. Roger Ebert notes, "Jim Braddock is almost transparent in the simple goodness of his character" (Ebert 2005, 2). In a manner reminiscent of Paulie in *Rocky*, *Cinderella Man* uses the boxer's friend and brother-in-law, Mike Wilson (Paddy Considine), to articulate the common man's rage at life's unfairness, while leaving Braddock untainted. However, Jim

Braddock's unflappable goodness in *Cinderella Man* robs the film of sufficient conflict to sustain its drama. To make up for the blandness of featuring its protagonist as an untroubled nice guy, Max Baer (Craig Bierko), the reigning heavyweight champion, is exaggerated into a villain whose swaggering promiscuity and aggressive ring style (he has killed multiple opponents with his blows) contrasts with Braddock's humility and devotion to family. Baer even baits his challenger by insulting Mrs. Braddock. Beyond the limitations of these characters, the film lacks persuasive power because it is hard to believe that Braddock's gentle Irishman would ever take up boxing in the first place. Instead of cultivating the complex conflicts typical of the boxing film genre, *Cinderella Man* features a simple contest between good and evil, spirit and body, Braddock versus Baer, all laid bare in its climactic bout. The film's lavish production values and the fine performances by Russell Crowe and Paul Giamatti, as Braddock's manager, are compromised by the absence of compelling dramatic conflict.

Cinderella Man shows compassion for the poor in representing the hardships of the Braddock family during the Depression. Nevertheless, its clichés and platitudes produce ambivalence. For example, Braddock scolds his son for stealing from the local butcher shop and makes him return the goods. But later, Mae Braddock (Renee Zellweger) joins other women in vandalizing an Esso billboard to get wood to heat the home, an act presented without any moral opprobrium. The anger of the common man is presented in Mike Wilson, a former stockbroker turned radical agitator who is killed in the Central Park Hooverville. On the other hand, James Braddock repays his welfare money at the government office, implying that decent citizens should not look to the state for assistance in time of need. Having it both ways undermines the film, as its conflicts dissolve in Ron Howard's feel-good sensibility.

Cinderella Man diffuses the traditional genre conflicts that creep into the film. Though the promiscuous villain Baer is indulgently physical, Jim Braddock uses his disciplined body to serve the needs of his family, harmonizing the tension between body and soul that is so central to the genre. While Mike Wilson expresses criticism of the success ethic, Jim Braddock's triumphant comeback to win the heavyweight title confirms the hope that with sufficient pluck one can overcome adversity. The gender conflict arising from the boxer's romance is absent, too, as Braddock is already happily married. When Mae Braddock refuses to attend her husband's bouts and later urges him not to fight Baer, her fears are dismissed as women's worries. Besides, anyone who knows boxing history realizes that Jim will win the title and bring home his prize money to save the family. There is no tension between female nurturing and the boxer's violence. Furthermore, Jim never cries out against injustice and responds only with sensitivity to the hardships endured by his family. Braddock embodies an ideal from the film's opening moments. The hero only needs to await his justified and inevitable recognition. Such a saintly protagonist leaves aside the problems that generate and sustain film genres.

An understanding of the boxing genre brings the film's shortcomings to the fore. The filmmakers of *Cinderella Man* are aware of the generic tradition, and they draw upon the comeback theme of *Rocky*, the bio-pic heritage of *Somebody Up There Likes Me*, and the editing expertise from the ring action in *Raging Bull*. They want to evoke the gritty Warner Brothers Depression ethos that gave *Body and Soul* its spark. As *Variety*'s Robert Koehler explains, *Cinderella Man* "exhibits a loving understanding of Warners' raw 1930s films of desperate working-class lives and hardscrabble heroes, and of the boxing genre from *Champion* to *Raging Bull*" (Koehler 2005, 30). But genre allusions cannot pump life into a film without the human conflicts that speak to a viewer's experience. Jim Braddock's screen tale rings false because all his adversity provokes is a saintly response whose eventual reward strains credibility. Worse, the lack of a dramatic conflict undermines the foundation of a genre's significance. It makes sense that the audience for the film faded.

The boxing films of 2005 participate in the trends characterizing the genre from the 1990s to the present, as outlined at the close of chapter two and in appendix I. Clearly *Unforgivable Blackness* contributes to the African American documentary cluster. On the other hand, *Million Dollar Baby* and *Cinderella Man* address the masculinity crisis by reacting against the postmodern sensibilities of *Pulp Fiction* and *Fight Club* in choosing a more traditional treatment. The contemporary setting and the women boxers of *Million Dollar Baby* set the stage for grappling with male troubles. The film presents a moving masculinity crisis that offers no ready answer to the problems it portrays. On the other hand, *Cinderella Man* whole-heartedly embraces a fairy-tale vision of traditional manliness to match its conventional form. Like *Unforgivable Blackness*, it returns to the past, but the film portrays a reassuring, if unpersuasive, perspective on a beleaguered man overcoming adversity. Certainly the principle conflicts featured in the boxing film genre are adaptable and enduring. They continue to resonate in our culture today.

✦ ✦ ✦

Two thousand and five was a noteworthy year for the boxing film. A well-established and longstanding entertainment formula, the boxing film continues to offer a viable model for Hollywood production. Movie cameras may be stimulated by the rise of another great champion, like Joe Louis or Muhammad Ali, whose athletic prowess makes an impact beyond the boundaries of the ring and captures the attention of the general public. Or a boxer may gain fame on the stage or in a novel; even more likely, he or she will come off the pages of a comic book or from a video game. Just as Kirk Douglas, Paul Newman, and Sylvester Stallone played boxers to breakthrough to stardom, another aspiring actor may be drawn to the physical drama of the ring as an avenue to celebrity. Boxing history leaves an important legacy, especially in the African American community, and that history offers a wealth of stories about oppression endured and resisted that are readily adaptable to the screen. Worldwide enthusiasm for sports provides an attractive intersection with the movies, and boxing is the sport that has proven to be best suited for films. No doubt the fighter's quest for the title will continue to shape screen drama. Furthermore, as this study has shown, the boxing film genre portrays vital social conflicts immediate to the experience of the public. These conflicts remain troubling, and so they will provoke new dramas that address the dilemmas of the human condition, and these films will attract an audience eager to be engaged by the struggle for the resolution of recognizable and deeply felt problems.

APPENDIX I
Cycles/Clusters of the Boxing Film Genre

1931–33, DEPRESSION CYCLE

Benchmark Hits	*The Champ* (1931) *Iron Man* (1931)
Significant Films	*Winner Take All* (1932) *Life of Jimmy Dolan* (1933) *Prizefighter and the Lady* (1933)
Internal Influences	Buddy films, Dramas of male pathos, *The Kid* (1921), W. Beery star persona
External Influences	Masculinity crisis sparked by Depression, W. R. Burnett novel, *Iron Man*, decline and corruption of boxing after Gene Tunney's retirement, ban on nonfiction boxing films.
Dominant Features	Trouble w/women ruins male friendship
Semantic/ Syntactic Conjunction	Boxing as marker of primitive maleness. Confrontation w/women threatens male bonding; men separate and protagonist broken.

1937–42, POPULAR FRONT CYCLE

Benchmark Hits	*Kid Galahad* (1937) *City for Conquest* (1940)
Significant Films	*Spirit of Youth* (1937) *The Crowd Roars* (1938) *Golden Boy* (1939) *They Made Me a Criminal* (1939) *Keep Punching* (1939) *Here Comes Mr. Jordan* (1941) *Gentleman Jim* (1942)
Internal Influences	Warner Bros. style, hybrids w/crime films, gangster films, social problem films, and later w/comedy and bio-pic. Stars [Robinson, Cagney, Flynn].
External Influences	Rise of Joe Louis, anti-Fascist Popular Front/New Deal politics, Leftist Theater/Odets play: *Golden Boy* (1937), racism, ethnic prejudice, Production Code, World War II.
Dominant Features	Ethnic difference prevents successful white immigrant from leaving the underworld and gaining respectability. Transition passed to next generation.
Semantic/Syntactic Conjunction	Boxing as lawless underworld that tempts characters w/wealth, pleasure and power, but hero must ascend to respectable society or fall.

1946–51, NOIR CYCLE

Benchmark Hits	*Body and Soul* (1947) *Champion* (1949)
Significant Films	*The Killers* (1946) *Whiplash* (1948) *The Set-Up* (1949) *Iron Man* (1951)

Internal Influences	Warner Bros. crime films, film noir, social problem films, J. Garfield
External Influences	Rise of independent production, Group Theater and *Golden Boy*, racketeering and crime investigations into boxing, Hemingway, problems of war veterans
Dominant Features	Anxiety and regret—struggle for success transforms ambitious, talented young man into corrupt cynic. It may be too late to escape from the materialist jungle and recover values one knows to be true.
Semantic/ Syntactic Conjunction	The past grips the present, boxing is a racket where money talks, duplicity reigns and human values are degraded. Wealth and celebrity are meaningless without self-worth built on mutual human respect. Is it too late to make the right choice and escape from the ring?

1950–54, RACIAL/ETHNIC PREJUDICE CYCLE

Benchmark Hit	*Right Cross* (1950)
Significant Films	*The Fighter* (1952) *The Ring* (1952) *The Joe Louis Story* (1953)
Internal Influences	Noir realism, Hollywood psychology, documentary, social problem film.
External Influences	Jack London's "The Mexican," racial-ethnic prejudice. Independent production.
Dominant Features	Suffering from prejudice, boxer expresses his anger in ring battles, but displacement prevents him from coming to terms with his oppression and sparks neurosis.

Semantic/
Syntactic Conjunction   In spite of success in the ring, racial prejudice plagues the boxer. He must find a better way to fight back and realize social justice.

1950–56, AFTER THE RING CYCLE

Benchmark Hits   *The Quiet Man* [1952]
On the Waterfront (1954)

Significant Films   *From Here to Eternity* (1953)
99 River Street (1953)
teleplays "The Battler" (1955), "Requiem for a Heavyweight" (1956)

Internal Influences   Method acting. Boxing plot as back story. Hybrids—romantic comedy, war films, social problem film. *The Killers* (1946).

External Influences   HUAC Hollywood mass hearings, criminal investigation into waterfront racketeering, novel: *From Here to Eternity*, war vets.

Dominant Features   Boxer tormented by ring experience that undermines his success after leaving the fight game. He must be reconciled through a symbolic return to ring competition in order to regain his self-respect and realize a good life.

Semantic/
Syntactic Conjunction   Apparently successful after leaving boxing, the ex-prizefighter faces a crisis in which his ring failure haunts him. He must be reconciled with his past if he is to prosper.

1955–57 FAILED HYBRIDS CLUSTER

Distinctive Hits	*Somebody Up There Likes Me* (1956) *The Harder They Fall* (1956)
Significant Films	*It's Always Fair Weather* (1955) *Killer's Kiss* (1955)
Internal Influences	Hybrids—musical, documentary, bio-pic, etc. Upbeat resolutions.
External Influences	Relaxation of the Production Code, TV, autobiographies, and novels.
Dominant Features	Misfire, none emerge.
Semantic/ Syntactic Conjunction	No stable conjunction takes hold.

1975–80 MUHAMMAD ALI ERA, COMEBACK CYCLE

Benchmark Hits	*Hard Times* (1975) *Rocky* (1976) *Every Which Way But Loose* (1979)
Significant Films	*The Great White Hope* (1970) *Hammer* (1972) *Fat City* (1972) *Mandingo* (1975) *Movie, Movie* (1978) *Rocky II* (1979) *The Champ* (1979) *The Main Event* (1979) *Raging Bull* (1980) *Any Which Way You Can* (1980) *Rocky III, IV, V* (1982, '85, '90)

Internal Influences   Blaxploitation films, "New Hollywood" return to classic genres, parody and pathos, Stars—Eastwood, Bronson, animal motif, "Beat the odds" comeback.

External Influences   Muhammad Ali, new ratings system, Black power, struggles between white ethnics and African Americans, sports culture, women's movement.

Dominant Features   Revived African American culture places black protagonist in contest with dominant white culture, or downtrodden white protagonist in "beat the odds" contest with racial rivals. Nostalgic turn to revisionist historical perspective or traditional values. Comeback story. Boxer as innocent.

Semantic/   Boxing associated with struggles of racial-ethnic-
Syntactic Conjunction   class community. Veteran fighter finds his identity at stake in decisive ring battle vs. outsider. Comeback tale. Gender troubles.

1993–2005 AFRICAN AMERICAN DOCUMENTARY CLUSTER

Benchmark Hits   *The Fallen Champ: The Untold Story of Mike Tyson* (1993)
When We Were Kings (1996)
Significant Films   *Joe Louis, For All Time* (1985)
The Hurricane (1999)
On the Ropes (1999)
Ali (2001)
Undisputed (2002)
Unforgivable Blackness: The Rise and Fall of Jack Johnson (2005)

Internal Influences   Sports documentary, generic tradition.

External Influences	Mike Tyson vs. Ali legacy, legendary African American boxing champions, African American culture.
Dominant Features	African American history.
Semantic/ Syntactic Conjunction	No stable syntax, fiction/nonfiction intersection.

1993–2005 MASCULINITY CRISIS/POSTMODERN CLUSTER

Distinctive Hits	*Pulp Fiction* (1994)
	Fight Club (1999)
Subsidiary Films	*Play It To the Bone* (2000)
	Girlfight (2000)
	Million Dollar Baby (2004)
	Cinderella Man (2005)
Internal Influences	Comedy, postmodernism, noir tradition, biopic.
External Influences	Gender struggles.
Dominant Features	Masculine inadequacy and uncertainty.
Semantic/ Syntactic Conjunction	Narrative complexity, unstable voice, weak conjunction.

APPENDIX II
Boxing Films Cited

TITLE	YEAR	DIRECTOR
Battling Butler	1926	Buster Keaton
The Champ *	1931	King Vidor
Iron Man	1931	Tod Browning
Winner Take All	1932	Roy Del Ruth
The Life of Jimmy Dolan *	1933	Archie Mayo
The Prizefighter and the Lady	1933	Willard Van Dyke
Kid Galahad *	1937	Michael Curtiz
The Spirit of Youth	1937	Harry Fraser
The Crowd Roars	1938	Richard Thorpe
Golden Boy *	1939	Rouben Mamoulian
They Made Me a Criminal	1939	Busby Berkley
Keep Punching	1939	John Clein
City for Conquest *	1940	Anatole Litvak
Here Comes Mr. Jordan *	1941	Alexander Hall
Gentleman Jim	1942	Raoul Walsh
The Killers	1946	Robert Siodmak
Body and Soul *	1947	Robert Rossen
Whiplash	1948	Lew Seiler
Champion *	1949	Mark Robson
The Set-Up *	1949	Robert Wise

TITLE	YEAR	DIRECTOR
Right Cross *	1950	John Sturges
Iron Man	1951	Joseph Pevney
The Fighter	1952	Herbert Kline
The Ring *	1952	Kurt Neumann
The Quiet Man	1952	John Ford
99 River Street	1953	Phil Karlson
The Joe Louis Story	1953	Robert Gordon
From Here To Eternity *	1953	Fred Zinnemann
On the Waterfront *	1954	Elia Kazan
Killer's Kiss	1955	Stanley Kubrick
It's Always Fair Weather	1955	Gene Kelly- Stanley Donen
"The Battler"	1955	Arthur Penn
"Requiem for a Heavyweight"	1956	Ralph Nelson
The Harder They Fall	1956	Mark Robson
Somebody Up There Likes Me *	1956	Robert Wise
Monkey on My Back	1957	Andre de Toth
Kid Galahad	1962	Phil Karlson
Requiem for a Heavyweight	1962	Ralph Nelson
The Great White Hope	1970	Martin Ritt
Hammer	1972	Bruce Clark
Fat City *	1972	John Huston
Mandingo *	1975	Richard Fleischer
Hard Times *	1975	Walter Hill
Rocky *	1976	John Avildsen
Every Which Way But Loose *	1978	James Fargo
Movie, Movie	1978	Stanley Donen
Rocky II	1979	Sylvester Stallone
The Champ *	1979	Franco Zeffirelli
The Main Event	1979	Howard Zieff
Raging Bull *	1980	Martin Scorcese
Any Which Way You Can	1980	Buddy Van Horn
Rocky III	1982	Sylvester Stallone
Joe Louis, For All Time	1985	Peter Tatum
Rocky IV	1985	Sylvester Stallone
Rocky V	1990	John Avildsen
The Fallen Champ: The Untold Story of Mike Tyson *	1993	Barbara Kopple
Pulp Fiction *	1994	Quentin Tarantino

TITLE	YEAR	DIRECTOR
When We Were Kings *	1996	Leon Gast
Fight Club *	1999	David Fincher
The Hurricane	1999	Norman Jewison
On the Ropes	1999	Nanette Burstein/ Brett Morgen
Play It To the Bone	2000	Ron Shelton
Girlfight *	2000	Karyn Kusama
Ali	2001	Michael Mann
Undisputed	2002	Walter Hill
Million Dollar Baby *	2004	Clint Eastwood
Unforgivable Blackness: The Rise And Fall of Jack Johnson *	2005	Ken Burns
*Cinderella Man**	2005	Ron Howard

* discussed in detail

WORKS CITED

Agee, James. "Films," *Nation* (November 8, 1947) 511.

Altman, Rick. *American Film Musical*. Bloomington: Indiana University Press, 1987.

———. *Film/Genre*. London: B.F.I., 1999.

———. "A Semantic/Syntactic Approach to Film Genre," in *Film Genre Reader II*. Austin: University of Texas Press, 1995. 26–40. (originally published in 1984.)

American Film Institute Catalog of Motion Pictures Produced in the United States, vol. F4, feature films 1941–50. Kenneth W. Munden, executive editor. New York: R. R. Bowker/ University of California Press, 1971.

Andy Warhol's Interview. "*Mandingo*." (August 1975) no page notation.

Ansen, David. "The Redemption of Pulp," *Newsweek* (October 10, 1994) 71.

———. "A Fistful of Darkness," *Newsweek* (October 18, 1999) 77.

Baker, Aaron. "A Left/Right Combination: Class and American Boxing Films," *Contesting Identities: Sports in American Film*. Urbana: University of Illinois Press, 2003. 100–40.

———. "A New Combination: Women and the Boxing Film, an Interview with Karyn Kusama," *Cineaste* 25:4 (2000) 22–26.

Bart, Peter. "Birth Pangs for Clint's $30 Mil Baby." *Variety* (January 3–9, 2005) 4.

Berg, Charles Ramírez. "*Bordertown*, the Assimilation Narrative, and the Chicano Social Problem Film," in *Chicanos and Film*. Minneapolis: University of Minnesota Press, 1992. 29–46.

Body and Soul file. MPAA/PCA Collection, Academy of Motion Picture Arts and Sciences Library, Beverly Hills, California.

Bookbinder, Robert. *Classics of the Gangster Film*. Secaucus, N.J.: Citadel, 1985.

Borde, Raymond, and Étienne Chaumeton. "Towards a Definition of Film Noir," in *Film Noir Reader*. New York: Limelight, 1996. 17–25.

Bordwell, David. "Classical Hollywood Cinema: Narrational Principles and Procedures," in *Narrative, Apparatus, Ideology*. New York: Columbia University Press, 1986. 17–34.

Bordwell, David, and Kristin Thompson. "*Raging Bull*," in *Film Art: An Introduction*, fifth edition. New York: McGraw-Hill, 1997. 426–31.

Boyum, Joy Gould. "The Sexy Side of Slavery," *Wall Street Journal* (May 12, 1975) 12.

Brill, Lesley. *John Huston's Filmmaking*. New York: Cambridge University Press, 1997.

Britton, Andrew. "*Mandingo*," *Movie* 22 (Spring 1976) 1–22.

Brog. "*From Here to Eternity*," *Variety* (July 29, 1953) 6.

———. "*Somebody Up There Likes Me*," *Variety* (July 4, 1956) 6.

Brooks, Peter. *The Melodramatic Imagination*. New Haven: Yale University Press, 1976.

Byron, Stuart. "Rules of the Game," *Village Voice* (May 27–June 2, 1981) 54–55.

Canby, Vincent. "Movie: Robert De Niro in 'Raging Bull,'" *New York Times* (November 14, 1980) C11.

———. "'Rocky,' Pure 30s Make Believe," *New York Times* (November 22, 1976) 19.

———. "What Makes a Movie Immoral?," *New York Times* (May 18, 1975) section 2, 19.

Carroll, Noël. *Interpreting the Moving Image*. New York: Cambridge University Press, 1998.

———. *The Philosophy of Horror*. New York: Routledge, 1990.

Cart. "*Any Which Way You Can*," *Variety* (December 17, 1980) 16.

Cawelti, John G. *Adventure, Mystery, and Romance*. Chicago: University of Chicago Press, 1976.

———. "Myths of Violence in American Popular Culture," *Critical Inquiry* 1:3 (March 1975) 521–44.

Champlin, Charles. "Portraits of the American Experience," *Los Angeles Times Calendar*, (November 9, 1980) 5.

Char., "*Life of Jimmy Dolan*," *Variety* (June 20, 1933), 11.

Christie, Ian. "The Rules of the Game," *Sight and Sound* 12:9 (September 2002) 24–50.

Christie, Ian, and David Thompson, ed. *Scorsese on Scorsese*. London: Faber and Faber, 1989.

Cocks, Jay. "Down and Out," *Time* (November 3, 1975) 70.

Cogley, John. "The Mass Hearings," in *The American Film Industry*. Madison: University of Wisconsin Press, 1976. 410–31.

Cook, David A. *Lost Illusions: American Cinema in the Shadow of Watergate and Vietnam, 1970–1979*. Berkeley: University of California Press, 2000.

Cook, Pam. "Masculinity in Crisis?," *Screen* 23:3–4. (September–October 1982) 39–46.

Cripps, Thomas. *Making Movies Black*. New York: Oxford University Press, 1993.

Crouch, Stanley. "Pulp Friction," *Los Angeles Times Calendar*" (October 16, 1994) 5, 34–37.

Crowther, Bosley. "The Screen in Review," *New York Times* (November 26, 1942) 40.

———. "The Screen in Review," *New York Times*. (November 10, 1947) 21.

———. "The Screen: Hate Worked for Him," *New York Times* (July 6, 1956) 16.

Daily Variety. "RKO Brands 'Champion' as Pirate" (March 23, 1949) 1, 10.

———, "'Champ' Nearing $48 Mill in World B.O., Looms Biggest MGM Int'l Film in 14 Yrs.," (September 19, 1979) page unknown.

Dan Klores Communications. "New PBS Ken Burns Documentary, '*Unforgivable Blackness: The Rise and Fall of Jack Johnson*,' to Air on PBS Stations on January 17, 2005—Martin Luther King Day," press release, PBS.Org/Pressroom, 2004, 1–4.

Davis, Todd F., and Kenneth Womack. "Shepherding the Weak: The Ethics of Redemption in Quentin Tarantino's *Pulp Fiction*," *Literature Film Quarterly* 26:1 (1998) 60–66.

Denby, David. "Put Away Your Handkerchiefs," *New York* (April 16, 1979) 86–87.

Dexter, Charles E. "With Odets' Latest Play," *Daily Worker* (November 12, 1937) page unknown.

Dooley, Roger Burke. *From Scarface to Scarlett: American Films in the 1930s*. New York: Harcourt, Brace, Jovanovich, 1981.

Early, Gerald. "Ali's Rumble," *Sight and Sound* 7:5 (May 1997) 10–12.

———. "The Black Intellectual and the Sport of Prizefighting," in *The Culture of Bruising*. Hopewell, N.J.: Ecco Press 1994. 5–45.

———. "'I Only Like It Better When the Pain Comes': More Notes Toward a Cultural Definition of Prizefighting," in *Reading the Fights*. New York: Henry Holt, 1988. 39–60.

Ebert, Roger. "*Cinderella Man*: Good Guy Packs Strong Punch," June 2, 2005 www .rogerebert.com 1–2.

———. "*Fight Club*," *Chicago Sun-Times* http://www.suntimes.com/ebert/ebert_ reviews/1999/10/101502.html 1–3.

Eder, Bruce. Audio commentary on laser disc of *Champion* (Republic Pictures Home Vide, 1992).

Ellison, Ralph. *Invisible Man*. New York: Random House, 1952.

Faludi, Susan. "It's 'Thelma and Louise' for Guys," *Newsweek* (October 25, 1999) 89.

Farber, Manny. "Films," *Nation* (May 7, 1949) 538–39.

———. "Films: *From Here to Eternity*," *Nation* (August 29, 1953) 178.

Farber, Stephen. "Dog Days and Hard Times for Sex Roles," *Coast* (November 1975) 52–53.

Feaster, Felicia. "*Fallen Champ: The Untold Story of Mike Tyson*," *Film Quarterly* 47:2 (Winter 1992–93) 45–47.

Ferguson, Otis. *The Film Criticism of Otis Ferguson*, edited by Robert Wilson. Philadelphia: Temple University Press, 1971.

Fight Club. http://www.imdb.com/title/tt0137523.

Finler, Joel. *The Hollywood Story*. New York: Crown Publishers, 1988.

Fried, John, and Pat Dowell. "Two Shots at Quentin Tarantino's *Pulp Fiction*," *Cineaste* 21:3 (Summer 1995) 4–7.

Friedkin, David. "Blind Rage and 'Brotherly Love': The Male Psyche at War with Itself in *Raging Bull*," in *Perspectives on Raging Bull*. New York: G. K. Hall, 1994. 122–30.

Gevinson, Alan, ed. *Within Our Gates: Ethnicity in American Feature Films, 1911–1960*. Berkeley: University of California Press, 1997.

Gorn, Elliott J. *The Manly Art: Bare-Knuckle Prize Fighting in America*. Ithaca, N.Y.: Cornell University Press, 1986.

Grindon, Leger. "*The Quiet Man* and the Boxing Film: Allusions and Influence," in *John Ford in Focus*. Jefferson, N.C.: McFarland, 2008. 169–75.

———. "Tod Browning's Thematic Continuity and Stylistic Development in *Iron Man*," in *The Films of Tod Browning*. London: Black Dog Publishing, 2006.

Guerrero, Ed. *Framing Blackness*. Philadelphia: Temple University Press, 1993.

Hall, Mordaunt. "The Screen," *New York Times* (June 14, 1933) 22.

Hanson, Patricia King. "*The Set-Up*," *The American Film Institute Catalog of Motion Pictures Produced in the United States, Feature Films, 1941–50 M-Z*. Berkeley: University of California Press, 1999. 2126.

Hauser, Thomas. *Muhammad Ali: His Life and Times*. New York: Simon and Schuster, 1991.

Hege. "*Every Which Way But Loose*," *Variety* (December 20, 1978) 30.

Hemingway, Ernest. *The Short Stories of Ernest Hemingway*. New York: Charles Scribner's Sons, 1953.

Henry, Michael. "*Raging Bull*," from *Martin Scorsese: Interviews*, edited by Peter Brunette. Jackson: University of Mississippi Press, 1999. 84–99.

Higham, Charles. *Hollywood Cameraman*. Bloomington: Indiana University Press, 1970.

Hollywood Reporter. (October 30, 1942), page unknown.

hooks, bell. "Cool Cynicism: *Pulp Fiction*," in *Reel to Real*. New York: Routledge, 1996. 47–51.

Houseman, John. "Violence, 1947: Three Specimens," *Hollywood Quarterly* 3 (Fall 1947) 63–65.

Indiana, Gary. "Pulp the Hype on the Q.T.: Geek Chic," *Art Forum* 33:7 (March 1995) 62–66, 104, 108.

Jones, Dorothy B. "Communism and the Movies: A Study of Film Content," in *Report on Blacklisting: Part I, the Movies*. New York: Arno Press, 1972.

Judges 8:14–16.

Kael, Pauline. "The Current Cinema: Stallone and Stahr," *New Yorker* (November 29, 1976) 154, 157.

———. "The Current Cinema: The Visceral Poetry of Pulp," *New Yorker* (October 6, 1975) 97–98.

———. "Religious Pulp, or The Incredible Hulk," *New Yorker* (December 8, 1980) 217–25.

Kahn. "*Body and Soul*," *Variety* (August 13, 1947) 15.

Kapsis, Robert E., and Kathie Coblentz, ed. *Clint Eastwood: Interviews*. Jackson: University Press of Mississippi, 1999.

Kauffmann, Stanley. "Look Back in Anger," *New Republic* (December 6, 1980) 26–27.

Kazan, Elia. *Elia Kazan: A Life*. New York: Doubleday, 1988.

Kelly, Mary Pat. *Martin Scorsese: A Journey*. New York: Thunder Mouth Press, 1991.

Kimmel, Michael. *Manhood in America: A Cultural History*. New York: Free Press, 1996.

Koehler, Robert. "Lord of the Ring," *Variety* (May 23–29, 2005) 30, 40.

Kroll, Jack. "De Niro's "Bronx Bull," *Newsweek* (November 24, 1980) 128–29.

Lambert, Gavin. "*The Set-Up* and *Champion*," *Sequence* 9 (Autumn 1949) 132–34.

La Motta, Jake, with Joseph Carter and Peter Savage. *Raging Bull: My Story*. New York: Da Capo Press, 1997. (originally published in 1970).

Land. "*Kid Galahad*," *Variety* (June 2, 1937), no page number.

Lane, Anthony. "Degrees of Cool," *New Yorker* (October 10, 1994) 95–97.

Lardner, Ring. "Champion," in *The Collected Short Stories of Ring Lardner*. New York: Random House, 1941. 109–27.

Leab, Daniel J. "The Blue Collar Ethnic in Bicentennial America: *Rocky*," in *American History/American Film*. New York: Ungar, 1988. 257–72.

Leeman, Sergio. *Robert Wise on His Films*. Los Angeles: Silman-James Press, 1995.

Lipman, Amanda. "Pulp Fiction," *Sight and Sound* 4:11 (November 1994) 50–51.

London, Jack. "The Mexican," in *The Short Stories of Jack London*. New York: Macmillan, 1990. 502–22.

Los Angeles Times. "Picture Copied by Rival Studio, RKO Suit Charges," (March 23, 1949) page unknown.

Mac (Joseph McBride). "*Raging Bull*," *Variety* (November 12, 1980) 12.

Mailer, Norman. "All the Pirates and People," *Parade* (October 23, 1983) 4–7.

Maltby, Richard. "The Politics of a Maladjusted Text," in *The Book of Film Noir*. New York: Continuum, 1993. 39–48.

Maltby, Richard. "The Production Code and the Hays Office," in *Grand Design: Hollywood as a Modern Business Enterprise, 1930–1939*. New York: Charles Scribner's Sons, 1993. 37–72.

March, Joseph Moncure. *The Wild Party/ The Set-Up/A Certain Wildness*. Freeport, Maine: Bond Wheelwright, 1968.

Maslin, Janet. "'Fight Club': Such a Very Long Way from Duvets to Danger," *New York Times* (October 15, 1999) http://www.nytimes.com/library/film/101599fight-film-review.html 1–4.

———. "Quentin Tarantino's Wild Ride on Life's Dangerous Road," *New York Times* (September 23, 1994) C1, C34.

Mead, Chris. *Champion: Joe Louis, Black Hero in White America*. New York: Penguin, 1986.

Medvedev, P. N./Bakhtin, Mikhail. *The Formal Method in Literary Scholarship*. Trans. A. J. Wehrle. Baltimore: Johns Hopkins University Press, 1978.

Murf. "*Mandingo*," *Variety* (May 7, 1975) 48.

———. "*Rocky*," *Variety* (November 10, 1976) 20.

Neale, Steve. *Genre and Hollywood*. New York: Routledge, 2000.

———. "Questions of Genre," in *Film Genre Reader II*. Austin: University of Texas Press, 1995. 159–83.

Neve, Brian. *Film and Politics in America, a Social Tradition*. New York: Routledge, 1992.

Newsweek. "*From Here to Eternity*," (August 10, 1953) 82.

Nugent, Frank. "The Screen," *New York Times* (May 27, 1937) page unknown.

Oates, Joyce Carol. *On Boxing*. London: Bloomsbury, 1987; Hopewell, N.J.: Ecco Press, 1994.

———. "The Man with the Golden Smile," *New York Review of Books* (November 18, 2004) 25–29.

Odets, Clifford. "Democratic Vistas in Drama," *New York Times* (November 21, 1937) section 11, 1–2.

O'Neill, William L. *American High: The Years of Confidence, 1945–1960*. New York: Free Press, 1986.

Parrish, Robert. *Growing Up in Hollywood*. Boston: Little, Brown, 1976.

Pechter, William S. "Holding the Horses," *Commentary* 54 (November 1972) 82–83.

Poll. "*The Champ*," *Variety* (March 28, 1979) 20.

Propp, Vladimir. *Morphology of a Folk Tale*. Bloomington: University of Indiana Press, 1958.

Ray, Robert B. *A Certain Tendency of the Hollywood Cinema, 1930–1980*. Princeton: Princeton University Press, 1985.

Riess, Steven A. "Barney Ross," *American National Biography Online*. (February 2000), http://www.anb.org/articles/19/19-00477.html.

Robert Rossen Collection. University of California at Los Angeles, Theater Arts Library, see Box 6 for the final shooting script of *Body and Soul*.

Roffman, Peter, and Jim Purdy. *The Hollywood Social Problem Film*. Bloomington: Indiana University Press, 1981.

Rogin, Michael. *Blackface, Whitenoise: Jewish Immigrants in the Hollywood Melting Pot*. Berkeley: University of California Press, 1996.

Rooney, David. "*Fight Club*," *Variety* (September 13, 1999) http://www.variety.com/index.asp?layout=print_review&reviewid=VE111775211 6&categoryid=-1.

Ross, Barney, and Martin Abramson. *No Man Stands Alone: The True Story of Barney Ross*. New York: J. P. Lippincott, 1957. 241.

Sammons, Jeffrey T. *Beyond the Ring: The Role of Boxing in American Society*. Urbana: University of Illinois Press, 1988.

Samuels, Charles Thomas. "How Not to Film a Novel," *American Scholar* 42 (Winter 1972) 148–50.

Sarris, Andrew. "The Greatest," *Village Voice* (June 6, 1977) 41.

——, ed. *Interviews with Film Directors*. New York: Avon, 1967.

——. "Mean Fighter from Mean Streets," *Village Voice* (November 19–26, 1980) 55.

——. "Why Sports Movies Don't Work," *Film Comment* 16:6 (November–December 1980) 49–53.

Sayre, Nora. "Winning the Weepstakes: The Problems of American Sports Movies," *Film Genre: Theory and Criticism*. Metuchen, N.J.: Scarecrow Press, 1977. 182–94.

Schatz, Thomas. *Hollywood Genres: Formulas, Filmmaking, and the Studio System*. New York: Random House, 1981.

Schickel, Richard. *Clint Eastwood: A Biography*. New York: Alfred A. Knopf, 1996.

——. "The Contender," *Time* (December 13, 1976) 97.

Scho. "*Gentleman Jim*," *Variety* (November 4, 1942) 8.

Scorsese, Martin, and Thelma Schoonmaker. *Raging Bull* laser disc audio commentary. Santa Monica: Criterion, 1990.

Sklar, Robert. *City Boys: Cagney, Bogart, Garfield*. Princeton: Princeton University Press, 1992.

——. *Movie-Made America: A Cultural History of American Movies*. New York: Random House, 1994.

Smith, Paul. *Clint Eastwood: A Cultural Production*. Minneapolis: University of Minnesota Press, 1993.

Sontag, Susan. "The Imagination of Disaster," *Against Interpretation*. New York: Dell, 1969. 212–28.

Streible, Dan. *Fight Pictures: A History of Boxing and Early Cinema*. Berkeley: University of California Press, 2008.

——. "A History of the Boxing Film, 1894–1915," *Film History* 3:3 (1989) 235–57.

Studlar, Gaylyn. "Shadowboxing: *Fat City* and the Malaise of Masculinity," in *Reflections in a Male Eye: John Huston and the American Experience*. Washington: Smithsonian Institution Press, 1993. 177–98.

Suid, Lawrence H. *Guts and Glory: Great American War Movies*. Reading, MA: Addison-Wesley, 1978.

Sussman, Warren. *Culture as History: The Transformation of American Society in the Twentieth Century*. New York: Pantheon, 1984.

Tarantino, Quentin. "Interview with Quentin Tarantino," by Michel Ciment and Hubert Niogret, in *Quentin Tarantino: Interviews* edited by Gerald Peary. Jackson: University Press of Mississippi, 1998, 80–88.

——. "Quentin Tarantino on *Pulp Fiction* As Told to Manohla Dargis," *Sight and Sound* 4:11 (November 1994) 16–19.

——. "When You Know You're in Good Hands: Quentin Tarantino Interviewed by Gavin Smith," *Film Comment* 30:4 (July–August 1994) 32–38, 40–43.

Taubin, Amy. "Staying Power," *Film Comment* 41:1 (January–February 2005) 26–29.

Time. "New Pictures," (October 20, 1947) 101.

————. "*On the Ropes*," (September 23, 1946) 47.

————. "*Right Cross*." (October 30, 1950) 100.

T.M.P. "A Fight Film from Metro Studios," *New York Times* (November 16, 1950) 39.

Travers, Peter. "Movies: Tarantino's Twist," *Rolling Stone* (October 6, 1994) 79–81.

Turan, Kenneth. "Movie Review: *Fight Club*, The Roundhouse Miss," *Los Angeles Times* (October 15, 1999) http://www.calendarlive.com/top/1,1419,L-LATimes-Print-X!ArticleDetail-5276,00.html?search 1.

Variety. "Box Office Report." (June 6–12, 2005) 8.

————. "*Right Cross*." (August 16, 1950) 11.

Warshow, Robert. "The Gangster as Tragic Hero," *The Immediate Experience*. New York: Atheneum, 1975. 127–33.

Welsh, J. M. "Knockout in Paradise," *American Classic Screen* 2:6 (1978) 14–16.

Whitehouse, Charles. "*Fight Club*," *Sight and Sound* (December 1999) http://www.bfi.org.uk/sight and sound/1999_12/fight_club.html 1–4.

When We Were Kings. "Production Notes" (press kit). 1996. 1–29. No author noted.

Wood, Robin. "John Huston," in *Cinema: A Critical Dictionary*, vol. 1. New York: Viking, 1980. 513–17.

————. "*Mandingo*: The Vindication of an Abused Masterpiece," in *Sexual Politics and Narrative Film*. New York: Columbia University Press, 1998. 265–82.

————. "Two Films by Martin Scorsese," in *Hollywood from Vietnam to Reagan*. New York: Columbia University Press, 1986. 245–59.

Zeffirelli, Franco. *Zeffirelli: The Autobiography of Franco Zeffirelli*. New York: Weidenfeld and Nicolson, 1986.

Zmijewsky, Boris, and Lee Pfeiffer. *The Films of Clint Eastwood*. New York: Citadel Press, 1988.

INDEX

Lightning Source UK Ltd.
Milton Keynes UK
UKOW03f1914091013

218792UK00006B/521/P